June 1982.

To Dear Trickers,

all my love.

Veronica xxxx

Enoch Powell

By the same author:

The English Middle Classes (with Angus Maude)
Professional People (with Angus Maude)
The Boss: The Life and Times of the British Businessman
    (with Rosemary Stewart)
A Force for the Future: The British Police in the Next Decade

Sierra Leone: A Modern Portrait
The British in Africa (with Yvonne Foy)
The British Empire (jointly)
The Colonial Problem (jointly)
Colonial Problems and Peace (jointly)
Shall I Emigrate?

The Visitors' Book (with Harry Ballam)
The Evolution Man

Roy Lewis

Enoch Powell
Principle in Politics

Cassell

London

CASSELL LTD.
35 Red Lion Square, London WC1R 4SG
and at Sydney, Auckland, Toronto, Johannesburg,
an affiliate of
Macmillan Publishing Co. Inc.,
New York

First published 1979

ISBN 0 304 30072 1

Printed and bound in Great Britain at
The Camelot Press Ltd, Southampton

Contents

Damn your principles, stick to your party.
Disraeli

He changed his front, but he never changed his ground.
Morley on Burke

The secret of the greatest fruitfulness and the greatest enjoyment of
existence is: to *live dangerously*. Build your cities under Vesuvius! Send
your ships into uncharted seas! Be robbers and conquerors – you
lovers of knowledge!
Nietzsche

There is a sense in which, unless one is alone, one is unimportant. I live
the life of the Party in the House of Commons. I feel myself to belong
to it. And yet the fact is that the things which are worth saying are
things which have to be said alone. I wish as a human being to
be very much a member of a team. But my mind climbs mountains
by itself without any vertigo.
Enoch Powell

Foreword

Unlike the Labour movement, Conservatism is said to have no ideology. The Labour party was formed to bring about socialism, defined as the nationalisation of the means of production, distribution and exchange; though it claims socialist origins that predate Marx by a hundred years and more, the marxist analysis of society gives it doctrinal coherence and purpose. The Conservative evolutionary and instinctual view of society is harder to define. Indeed it calls for periodic redefinition. Conservative principles are admitted to need restatement in contemporary terms, their application to current conditions to need adjustment. Successive writers on conservatism hold this to be an advantage; 'change is our ally'. At times the leadership itself updates the party's aim – one thinks of Disraeli. Sometimes committees do it – one thinks of R. A. Butler's charters. And from the ranks there arise men who recall the party to fundamentals and demand a new approach when it seems to be losing its way in expedients for the sake of power and office. In the past fifteen years this has preeminently been the task of the Rt Hon J. Enoch Powell, MBE, MP. He has put forward criteria for policy and for conduct that, taken as a whole, come nearer to a conservative ideology than anything propounded since Edmund Burke.

A politician's ideas become an 'ism' when they are sufficiently cohesive, comprehensive and distinctive to require a label. This is a recognition of impact. 'Powellism' is used as a synonym for the race prejudice and hatred which he abjures; his analysis of the immigration phenomenon and of racial conflict is only a part, though an integral one, of his total political argument. Not many politicians can publish collections of speeches as an ordered exposition of political fundamentals – lucid, eloquent, taut and readable, and re-readable after the immediacy of the occasion has passed. Powell has published eight* – perhaps thus demonstrating his view that a politician's business is with words – and this is only a small proportion of his writings, speeches, and addresses which show him to be an indefatigable natural educator as well as 'communicator'.

Much has been said of his powers as a communicator in the modern sense – as a master of the art of public speaking and of House of Commons debate – while in the narrower sense his rhetoric has been likened to Gladstone's. To compel the House to listen, however unwelcome your argument, to be a permanent draw on television especially in a battle of wits with the tougher TV interrogators,

*Nation or No Nation (Batsford, 1978) was published as this book went to press.

attests exceptional power to sustain your case in and out of season. But there is a more powerful quality to powellism than its presentation. This resides in the fact that Powell lives uncompromisingly his own powellian logic. His ideas are not a professor's constructs; they are a public drama of which he is sometimes both protagonist and stage manager. He lives his ideas. They live him.

This puts a would-be biographer and expositor of the history of powellism in a quandary. It is easiest to take the elements and themes that make up a system of thought separately for statement and analysis of how they grew, irrespective of the chronological order of events and personal history. The man, however, lives chronologically with his whole growing system, but to follow the statement and restatement of his ideas from event to event is to lose the logic of the thinking and to present it in snippets. The career of a man of action is best followed chronologically, that of a thinker analytically. Powell as politician and theoretician is both of these. In presenting the development of his ideas I have not kept strictly to chronology; there is overlap. But powellism was a nearly complete system by 1970. It led to the duel with Heath on several fronts between 1968 and 1975; so I have largely returned to chronology at that point, hoping to show how principles and ideas, not a pure power game, generated political action.

This seems the best approach to the question: is Powell mainly an opportunist who takes up causes to win power, as his detractors allege (notably Paul Foot upon his involvement with immigration), or is he a politician whose motives can be inferred from his publicly stated principles, such as he projects himself and as the public sees him? The more Powell's thinking is subordinated to the events of his political career, the greater the emphasis on his ambition, his striving for power. Failure to become prime minister then becomes a study of failure – Dr Rhodes James (who has judged Powell also) subtitled his biography of Churchill to 1939 a study in failure. Political scientists quantify the standing and influence of leading politicians by the percentage in opinion polls; politics becomes then a competitive game of 'ratings', of popularity, the race to the top job.

By what then does one measure the achievement of a politician like Richard Cobden, between whom and Powell parallels could be drawn; or even Robert Lowe, who was better at social and political forecasting than most? The reasons behind Powell's failure to attain the party leadership are the reasons why his campaign to reform the party's thinking was partly successful. Only his commitment to his ideas, and his commitment of his political fate to their rightness could provide the fulcrum on which one man, with no parliamentary following, could lever the party out of office and change its leadership. (Whether he feels that was enough is another question.)

Major contributions to political thought do not come from specialists. The range of Powell's interests, erudition and experience outside politics is that of a renaissance or perhaps eighteenth-century personality. Polyglot, polymath, he has never permitted himself to be wholly consumed in politics; he sets an example of resistance to the most depressing threat to civilisation – the politicisation of all human activity, the impending encroachment of the collective on the private life. The first example of opportunism of which he is sometimes accused is his abandonment, on entering politics, of the atheism, anti-sacerdotalism, will-to-power or *élan vital* of his Nietzschean period for (rather spiky) Anglicanism where he could be seen at prayer with the Tory party. He has given his own account of how pure thought, periods not of prayer nor of meditation, but of self-propelled intellection, brought about his reconciliation with the Christian phenomenon. His political position is fully congruous with his theology. When he left parliament in 1974 he expected, briefly, to be absorbed in other interests. He shields his private life from the X-ray publicity in which, he said, Members of Parliament cannot but live; but the enviable range of interests in the background of the public man – so delightful to anyone who has the good fortune to meet and converse with the private man – enliven and inform his politics. A political and above all constitutional philosophy of, and for, Britain is his Great Work, but not his only life. The relation of Powell and Britain sometimes makes one think of the relation between Jacob and the Angel: my attempt has been to put this epic match into perspective both in time and range.

The chronology of Powell's career that follows should make it easy to set the working out of particular developments or statements of powellism against the succession of events.

Any opinions expressed in this book, and the necessary selection of the material from the great body of powelliana are entirely my responsibility; my grateful thanks are, however, due to Mr Powell for his careful and constructive reading of the manuscript and his readiness to answer almost all my questions. I have his *nihil obstat* on this book but certainly not his *imprimatur*. He is still hotly engaged politically; the Powell story is still a 'running story', and the summing up is provisional. Among those who have also helped me I must specially mention Mrs B. Carthew who gave me her large collection of speeches, cuttings and files of 'Powellight'; Mr Philip Norton and Dr K. W. Watkins; and Mr William Rees-Mogg and my colleagues in the Information Department of the *The Times*.

Chronology

16 June 1912   Born at Stechford to Albert Enoch and Ellen Mary Powell
1925   Wins scholarship to King Edward School, Birmingham
1929   Wins classical scholarship to Trinity College, Cambridge
1933   First Class, Classical Tripos
1934   Elected Fellow of Trinity
1937   Appointed Professor of Greek, Sydney University, Australia
1939   Appointed Professor of Greek, University of Durham, as from 1 January
            1940
4 September 1939   Resigns Sydney professorship
October 1939   Enlists as private in Royal Warwickshire Regt
1940   Commissioned 2/Lt. Posted 1 Armd Div, later 9 Armd Div
1942   Promoted Major, then Lt-Colonel, Secretary to Jt Intelligence Commit-
            tee, Middle East
1943   Military MBE. Posted to India, Secretary to Jt Intelligence Committee
            India and SE Asia
1944   Promoted Colonel. Assistant Director, Military Intelligence; promoted
            Brigadier, Member, Reorganisation Committee, Indian Army
          Resigns Durham professorship. Decides to enter politics
1946   Joins Conservative Parliamentary Secretariat
1947   Defeated in Normanton by-election
1948   Briefs Maxwell Fyfe against British Nationality Bill
          Writes Conservative Charter for Wales
          Adopted candidate Wolverhampton South-West
1950   Wins Wolverhampton S-W by 691 votes; maiden speech on Imperial
            Defence after India
          Opposes British entry to Coal and Steel Community
          Member 'One Nation' group for clarifying Tory ideas
1951   Attacks Bevan's Health Service plans, publishes *Social Services: needs
            and means* with Iain Macleod
          Holds Wolverhampton S-W with majority of 3,196
          Opposes Diplomatic Immunities Bill
1952   Marries Pamela Wilson, daughter of Lt-Col J. E. Wilson, Indian Army
          Gives up fox-hunting
          Declines Churchill's offer of Under-Secretaryship, Home Office

1953 Joins Suez Group pressing for retention of Suez base
       Elected to 1922 Committee executive
       Opposes Churchill's Royal Titles Bill
       Vice-Chairman, Backbench Committee on Housing
       Masterminds *Change is Our Ally* for 'One Nation' group
1954 Votes against Government on Suez base withdrawal
       Withdraws from Suez group
1955 Votes for abolition of capital punishment
       Retains Wolverhampton S-W with majority of 8,420
       Publishes *Biography of a Nation* with Angus Maude
       Elected Vice-Chairman, 1922 Committee
       Appointed by Eden Parliamentary Secretary to Ministry of Housing and
           Local Government
1956 Pilots Rent Bill for partial abolition of rent control
       Supports Butler for succession to Eden as prime minister
1957 *January* Appointed Financial Secretary to Treasury
1958 *January* Resigns with Thorneycroft and Birch on holding ceiling in
           estimates – '£50 million'
       Opposes Life Peerages Bill
       Appointed to board of Bestwood Co
1959 Attacks increased borrowing powers for electricity authorities
       Speech on the Hola Camp (Mau Mau) deaths scandal
       Holds Wolverhampton S-W by 11,167 majority
       Refuses offer of Parliamentary Secretary to Ministry of Education
       Attacks Radcliffe report on finance; opposes housing subsidy
1960 Appointed Minister of Health at same time as Thorneycroft rejoins
           government
1962 Announces ten-year hospital building plan and concentration of facilities
       Refuses nurses' wage demands, under pay pause
       July Raised to Cabinet after Macmillan's government reorganisation
1963 Defends Macmillan over Profumo
       Backs Butler for succession to Macmillan. Refuses to join Lord Home's
           government
       Begins campaign on Party rethinking in public speeches and newspaper
           articles
       Calls for trade union reform
1964 Holds Wolverhampton S-W with 9,856 majority
       Shadow Minister of Transport under Home
       Joins board of National Discount Co
1965 Calls for curbs on immigration and new citizenship laws
       Gets 15 votes in leadership election
       Shadow Minister of Defence under Heath
1966 Holds Wolverhampton S-W with majority of 6,585
       Visits Nato HQ

Calls for a floating pound sterling

1967   Heath opposes Powell's policy for withdrawal east of Suez; vetoes his
      CPC pamphlet

Opposes entry of Kenya Asians

1968   *February*   Heath objects to tone of immigration speech in Walsall

April   Speech in Birmingham. Powell dropped from Shadow Cabinet

Joins with Michael Foot to defeat Lords reform

1969   First speech against joining European Community

First speech on Ulster

1970   Powell holds Wolverhampton S-W with 14,467 majority

Conservatives win with majority of 30 seats

1971   Supports Commonwealth Immigration Bill, but demands massive
      voluntary repatriation

Opposes reversal of Selsdon policy

Speaking tour in Europe against British entry to EEC

Opposes nationalisation of Rolls-Royce, etc.

1972   Opposes abolition of Stormont constitution

Defeated in fight against European Communities Bill

Opposes entry of Ugandan Asians

Opposes statutory price-wage controls

1973   *June*   Warns that principle may come before party loyalty on EEC issue

Opposition to government spending; attacked by Barber at party
      conference

Opposes Government's policy to miners as useless

Attacks Heath as unbalanced

December   Welcomes Barber's expenditure cuts

1974   *February*   Declines to stand for Wolverhampton S-W. Heath defeated. Wilson Prime Minister

September   Adopted as UU candidate for South Down

October   Wins South Down with 51·8 per cent of votes

1975   Heath replaced by Mrs Thatcher as Conservative leader

Fights EEC referendum campaign

1976   Opposes devolution white paper and bill

1977   Devolution bill defeated February, reintroduced November

Demand for full Ulster representation in Parliament conceded

Opposes direct elections to EEC Assembly

1978   Government Bill to give Ulster seventeen or eighteen seats in Parliament

Chapter 1

The Crisis, 1974

1   The Refusal to Stand

On 7 February 1974, the Prime Minister, Mr Edward Heath, called a general election for 28 February. His purpose was to obtain the electorate's emphatic endorsement of the Government, backed by the Conservative majority in the House of Commons, in its contest over pay with the National Union of Miners, who had called a full official strike two days previously: the miners' work-to-rule had reduced coal and power supplies so much that the country was on a three-day working week under emergency regulations. The election had been a possibility for a month, but up to the last moment it was not certain whether Mr Heath, who had sixteen months of Parliament's term in hand and a majority of twenty-seven, would accede to the urgings of his close coterie of advisers and go for a new mandate, or fight out the issue on the Government's authority.

The same evening the Chairman of the Wolverhampton South-West Conservative Constituency Association, Mr G. Wilkes, opened a letter from that constituency's Member of Parliament, Mr J. Enoch Powell, announcing that he would not stand; its contents had just come on the evening news. The Chairman had received some warning of the eventuality of Powell's decision, but had been hoping that it could be averted. Speculation about Powell's position in the event of Heath appealing to the country for its support had occurred. Powell had publicly opposed an election; but apart from Mrs Powell and a few intimates, nobody had an inkling of his precise intentions.

The terms in which he resigned provided a sensation for the press and media only second to the election news itself. Powell told his constituents:

> I consider it an act of gross irresponsibility that this general election has been called in the face of the current and impending industrial situation.
>
> The election will in any case be essentially fraudulent; for the object of those who have called it is to secure the electorate's approval for a position which the Government itself knows to be untenable, in order to make it easier to abandon that position subsequently. It is unworthy of British politics, and dangerous to Parliament itself, for a government to try to steal success by telling the public one thing during an election and doing the opposite afterwards. Obviously – and I am sure this will not surprise you – I cannot

personally ask electors to vote for policies which are directly opposite to those we all stood for in 1970, and which I have myself consistently condemned as being inherently impracticable and bound to create the very difficulties in which the nation now finds itself.

I shall not therefore be seeking re-election for Wolverhampton South-West at this election as the Conservative candidate and I have no intention of standing otherwise.

Few would have been surprised if Powell had failed to ask his constituents to vote for the Government, and in particular for Heath's leadership. Nearly everyone, however, was surprised that he should find this an insurmountable barrier to his standing himself, defiantly Tory, for his own powellite policies, and to continuing his campaign to substitute true conservatism for false. Mixed with this astonishment was the horror of his friends, the embarrassment of his allies in the House, and the pleasure of his foes. The local embarrassment was made much of by his critics in the party establishment. Three weeks before polling day he had left his constituents without a Conservative candidate and without any attempt at consultation to discover in what, if any, capacity they could support him as an unofficial or semi-official Conservative, or even as an Independent.

His Conservative supporters woke up to find that they had lost a representative in whom they (with a small dissident minority) reposed immense confidence, indicated by the increases in his majority at almost all elections since he first stood in 1950 (though the swing to Powell had not always exceeded the general swing in 'Powell country' in the Midlands generally). They had been loyal to him through all his frequent disagreements with his own party, government and colleagues. They had either accepted his arguments – which he was punctilious in explaining to them in constituency meetings – or set aside their doubts in deference to his brilliance of mind, the distinction of his ministerial career, and the unquestionably large following in the country beyond Wolverhampton – notably, though not exclusively, as the result of his campaign to limit coloured immigration in these areas. They stuck with him notwithstanding his idiosyncrasies, his occasional high-handedness; proud of him as a national figure and in a growing faith that destiny had reserved him for special purposes, possibly for the prime ministership. They approved his ambition for the highest office, his confidence that he had the soul and guts for it. They knew they could have no more careful constituency member. Suddenly with a brusque letter, without a personal word, he resigned. The terms of the letter were final. They had to find someone else. However, such is politics that this proved easy, and the hitherto *sotto voce* pro-Heath section of the party moved in swiftly. A hundred applicants leapt forward, 'feasting their eyes', as the *Sunday Times* put it on 10 February, 'on his 14,000 majority'.

Bereft also of his leadership was the following that he had attracted throughout the country since the mid-sixties, but especially since his dismissal by Heath from the Shadow Cabinet in 1968 for the tone of his Birmingham speech on immigration. Since 1965 he was able to attract audiences larger than any other parliamentarian could muster, save only the prime minister of the day; he spoke, and was usually reported, two to four times a week, at every kind of gathering, the length and breadth of the kingdom, putting his arguments with an eloquence and charm unmatched since the death of Ian Macleod in 1970.[1] The size of this national constituency was in dispute. His supporters believed, and Powell concurred, that it was large enough to have turned the tide for Heath in 1970 in the last week or so of the election campaign. The psephologists at the time doubted if the 'Powell effect' had been decisive, but later sifting of the opinion poll evidence by academics like Dr Douglas Schoen and Dr Dudley Studlar[2] confirmed the grassroots feeling that the Conservative deference to Heath as sole architect of their victory, whence stemmed his presidential assumption of authority, was misplaced.

In 1974 nobody knew what the Powell-Heath duel had done to this body of support (or how it was composed). The polls showed Powell ahead of Heath in public regard in 1973. But Conservative Central Office was not impressed, and considered that this new demonstration that Powell was a 'resigner' whenever the going got sticky would destroy him with a pragmatical British electorate, faced with a choice in the middle of a national crisis. The voters would, it was thought, rally to authority.

Nobody could find a satisfactory precedent for such an act of self-immolation. No Member of Parliament, however estranged from his party, had done such a thing. A few people knew that his close friends had tried to argue him out of it, only to find him adamant, his letter written and ready to go. For thirteen days silence supervened while Heath struggled with the crisis of the campaign, notably the backsliding of the Director-General of the Confederation of British Industry, and the Relativities Board Report of differentials that indicated that the miners' demands were not excessive; indeed conceded that this issue was irrelevant by pledging himself to accept the Board's final recommendations.[3] But on the slogan 'Who runs Britain?' few had doubts of the result – Wilson was with the majority in this, opposing the election as strenuously as Powell. The only doubt was whether Heath had acted too late, missing the tide of public indignation at the full. Powell was assumed to have made his gesture. Later his political future, if any in a Heath-dominated scene, could be considered. A few observers felt there must be more to come from Enoch Powell.

2 Changing Sides

On 23 February Powell broke silence. He captured the headlines with a speech in Birmingham almost as sensationally as he had done there in April 1968. In it he greatly enlarged on his letter to his former constituents. He turned to the Conservative manifesto and pointed out that, after all that had happened over the Common Market, in the abbreviated version there was no mention of it, and in the full version, a passage of 750 words did not explain that Britain was committed to full economic and monetary union in 1980: 'so here we have the most . . . revolutionary act of policy that can be imagined – and the Conservative Party does not think it necessary to tell the electorate, let alone seek the electorate's approval.'[4] There followed an excoriating attack on Heath's record of deception over the entry to the Common Market in 1970–73; 'and now at a general election Mr Heath gives us to understand that Europe is not a subject he wants to talk about' – in 1970 it was a commitment only to negotiate; now it was a *fait accompli.*

Powell made clear that though the Common Market had not been the reason for his refusal to stand, he had now gone further and transferred his weight to the opposition side because his party treated British membership as a *fait accompli* whereas Labour was pledged to renegotiate the Treaty and put it to the electorate by referendum. There was a choice, a critical choice on a real issue; a choice which, for those who considered the surrender of independence a disaster, country must come before party allegiance. The implication was plain – such Conservative voters must vote Labour.

The second shock was greater than the first. The speech, and the one that followed it two days later at Shipley, received immense publicity. As Wilson's press secretary later revealed, arrangements had been made between Wilson and Powell to ensure there was no Labour statement on those two days to detract from the impact of Powell's repudiation of the Conservative leadership. Powell had first called the election fraudulent; now, after the Conservative manifesto and Labour's election pledge to renegotiate had given him the opportunity to point to a real choice, he made a statement that a clear good did come of the election – the issue of the Common Market had been decisively kept open. The Powell intervention was clinched when, asked how he would himself vote, he stated that he had already done so with his postal vote – for Labour.[5]

Members of Parliament have changed sides, crossed the floor, and turned against former colleagues out of conscience – and have duly been denounced as turncoats or Judases. The ever-quotable events of 1931 and 1886 were to hand. In his speeches on Ulster, Powell had recalled warningly Joseph Chamberlain's revolt against Gladstone. But nobody had ever done as Powell did: first stripping himself of all parliamentary power, then, alone and without allies – as a private citizen without a political future – as it were, totally disarmed, set himself to defeat the Government of his own party and to enthrone those he had fought since 1946.

He put down in advance the full price of his revolt. At the polls, Heath was defeated and after a futile bid for a Lib–Con pact, the Conservatives were driven into that powerlessness which they are supposed to find so excruciatingly unnatural (and Powell has described it mordantly). But Powell cast himself into the outer darkness, cut off from the fount of political influence – that House of Commons to which he was devoted. The reasons he gave at Birmingham and Shipley he reiterated: to substitute one seat for another would blur the reasons for his not standing for Wolverhampton South-West, and also detract from the advice he intended to give before the campaign ended. Few accepted the explanation. Incomprehension lingers despite his further explanations. Doubt has been kept alive partly by his re-entry into Westminster as an Ulster Unionist six months later – the immediate reaction was that he must have planned it all along, never made a sacrifice, had a line of retreat prepared.

Yet it was also thought in February 1974 that he had made a disastrous mistake, one of those Himalayan miscalculations to which all great political careers are liable. His own followers ask – still – why he had to be so pedantically scrupulous. He gave them guidance for one election, but deprived them of a greater boon – all hope in the Conservative Party. He found a new *point d'appui* in Ulster, but those who had put their faith in him in Great Britain were left with nothing. At lectures they were still asking him what they should do in 1977. (His reply in effect was: vote against the Conservatives until they reformed on the Common Market, and badger their MPs with letters in the meanwhile.) His friends refused to accept the logic of his refusal to stand as an Independent Conservative (as Taverne in Lincoln stood – and actually won – as Independent Labour) in opposition to Heathian heresy but *in the House* witnessing the true Tory faith. For on all issues apart from the EEC he still seemed further from Wilson than from Edward Heath. If he had taken that stand Central Office would not dare to disown him, or split his vote with a Heathite candidate.

It has been pointed out that members of all parties have rebelled against what they considered the abandonment of principle yet stayed in their seats. Aneurin Bevan regarded Hugh Gaitskell, the ascendant influence in Attlee's cabinet, with as much distrust as Powell felt for Heath (Powell regarded Bevan as an admirable parliamentarian notwithstanding their total opposition). Wilson resigned with Bevan, and became leader. Eden resigned more or less on a point of principle from Chamberlain's government and ended as Prime Minister. And Powell had particularly studied the career of Churchill, who had fought his party on national survival – on India, on the King, above all on rearmament – as a voice crying in the wilderness of the back benches (which is less of a wilderness than outside the House) until his hour struck and he became dominant in his party for fifteen years, as well as Britain's greatest war leader. Surely, dedicated Powellites asked, what was possible to Churchill was possible to Powell?

Those who had more or less consistently supported Powell from 1971 to 1974 in the House found no stumbling block in standing as Conservatives and therefore swallowing the manifesto – John Biffen, Richard Body, Hugh Fraser, Neil Marten, Harold Soref, Ronald Bell. There seemed something disproportionate, egregious, about Powell's line, argue as he might. The general seemed to have lost sight of the campaign in leading a skirmish. And these judgements upon Powell the political tactician were confirmed in many minds when the leadership was put to the vote again in 1975, and Margaret Thatcher took it, no Powell available as an alternative. He seemed to be one of the parliamentarians who had missed his destiny; the case of Lord Randolph Churchill and the 'Orange Card' obtruded itself.

A few speculated that he was retiring to his Colombey-les-Deux-Eglises to await the call that would come when (for example) Weimar-scale inflation began. But whatever else he was, Powell was (and is) a dedicated House of Commons man and a devoted francophile, both. He knew better, indeed had expounded better than most, the difference in the genius of the two oldest nations in Europe; these required that an Olympian De Gaulle should withdraw from the Assembly while a bulldog Churchill should fight for his corner in the House of Commons. That argument made no sense.

The Conservative establishment settled for an overweening conceit suitably put down, and it solaced the Party counsels that they were well rid of a bounder who would have been a disastrous leader. They mulled over a theory that Powell had anticipated that the Party would lose, as it did, and then he would return, forgiven, at a by-election to claim his inheritance. Others thought that he supposed Heath would win but thereafter be repudiated, so opening the door for the only alternative. All this dissection of powellian logic or motivation breaks down on Powell's profound understanding of the Tory Party. He knew his treason would be unforgivable as Peel's; he could scheme for anything, provided he did not say or imply 'vote Labour'. But he did, and he did it unconditionally, not knowing whether it would have any real effect on the result.

Powell's own pungent comment was never given enough weight: 'the trigger was pulled and I was there.'[6] Those words go to the heart of Powell and powellism. One might say his whole life had been a preparation for February 1974. In Derby[7] on 9 January he pictured Heath's administration as a Greek tragedy in which the victim, in his ignorance which the audience does not share, is seen bringing disaster step by step upon himself. But the metaphor also fitted Powell. During his thirteen-day silence he ironically gave a prearranged sermon on the meaning of Christian sacrifice, the road to Calvary.[8] It was not noticed in the hurly-burly. For everyone knows that it is the business – the first business – of the politician NOT to be there when the trigger is pulled. If he is, it is sheer incompetence, especially when he passes the square marked 'announce a new situation.'

3   The Logic of It

There is good evidence that Powell knew the risks he was running and did what he could, in prudence, to reduce them. But they were great. He had consistently opposed the government from 1971 for breaking its specific election pledges, and, quite apart from the key issue of taking Britain into the Common Market without the 'full-hearted consent of the British people', which Heath had pledged as the condition of so doing, the succession of broken undertakings had been elevated by Powell into a constitutional disaster brought about by the party to whom above all the constitution should be sacrosanct: the sundering of the fiduciary relationship between the Member of Parliament and his constituents, the undermining of the validity of party government which was, in Powell's view, the engine of British parliamentary democracy – without which it degenerated into mere faction.

By 1972 Powell already saw the trap fate could be preparing for him. In the long struggle over the Communities Bill from second reading onwards he always quoted Heath's own concessions about voting according to conscience for the purpose of retaining a distinction between defeating the bill and defeating the government. This was some personal insurance, even if it was mainly designed to offset the pressure Heath and Pym, the Chief Whip, were putting on waverers. Heath, if he lost the bill, was indeed virtually forced by his European record to resign the premiership; but powellian logic did not require him to call an election. There was other business to be done, other leadership available. When the Act came into force, Powell began to pin the guilt of betraying the nation and its sovereignty upon the Party as well as its unprincipled and time-serving leadership; but he avoided saying so. In 1973, though he assiduously pointed to the fulfilment of the first of his prophesies about the effects of membership, he seemed to put the issue of reversal of membership into the future. He did not foreclose anything; he kept responsibility (for 'economic and monetary union by 1980') tied to Heath personally; he spoke and acted as if the Party could change its attitude. Even when Labour came out with a definite pledge to give the electorate a chance to reverse the Act, he continued to present Heath as a mesmeric influence like those thralls to unreality from which he had laboured to release the national will since 1963. The rebellions in the Party, including the most humiliating revolt against the whips in November 1972, that had been sustained by any government since 1945, gave Powell some hope that the Party could yet repudiate Heath and his policy before the next election was due (in 1975). While he could hope that, he need not endorse Labour.

The possibility of an election took shape towards the end of 1973, when the miners, strengthened by the soaring price of oil after the Yom Kippur war, challenged Heath's interpretation of the authority of the Prices and Incomes Board. Powell sensed the danger of a confrontation on this issue which might precipitate an election in which the Common Market issue could not be avoided. On 3 December he was at last able to welcome a change in the Government's economic policy – Barber's emergency budget which made the drastic cuts in public expenditure for which Powell had pressed. Over the Christmas recess, however, he learned that Heath was discussing with some of his ministers the possibility of an appeal to the country on 7 February, the earliest practicable date. Heath was, however, hesitating, and Powell tried to influence the decision in the speech in Derby, during which he said that an election would exacerbate an already tense situation in which one part of the country was 'learning' (by events and press comment) to look upon another part as the enemy of its peace and well-being. This was destructive of national unity, but all that was necessary was to deflate a bogus crisis: those who had led the country into it should sacrifice their pride and the Prime Minister should have the courage 'to order the about-turn'.

On 15 January Powell decided to bring matters to a head by issuing a statement – not waiting for an occasion to put it in a speech. This decision speaks for his confidence in his influence as a voice in the Party and the country. It duly received great publicity, enhanced by an interview with Robin Day on the BBC. Powell stated that the 'sole purpose of an election would be to obtain a larger majority and an extended lease of office by false pretences.'[9] He shared the view of those who were urging Heath to dissolve because the moment looked electorally so favourable, but declared that the Government's majority was adequate to budget for the increase in taxation necessary to brake the growing inflation:

> Nor do they need an election to get the country back to full-time work. Neither the miners nor the other trade unionists have broken the law or threatened to break it . . . it would be fraudulent or worse to fight an election on 'Who governs the Country?' when the Government's first action after the poll would be to scrap the . . . impracticable 'stage III'. It is . . . dangerous to Parliament to try to steal success by telling the public one thing and doing the opposite afterwards.[10]

He was faced with the possibility that he would not only have to make the Government's double-dealing over the Common Market a vital issue at such an election, but he would have to warn the nation not to be taken in, as it had been in 1970. In November he had declared that Heath's defence of the pay code as a responsibility which Parliament had given the Government, unasked, was so unconstitutional as seriously to reflect upon 'the mental and emotional stability of a Head of Government to whom such language can appear rational'.[11] Yet this Head of Government seemed to be seizing upon a crisis to prolong his ascendancy for another five years. On 14 December, with no election yet rumoured, Powell told his constituents, to explain his record of opposition to Heath, that

> It has never been suggested that to recognise a person as the leader of a party confers on him the right to the agreement and support of all its members for all his words and actions . . . there is not only no claim of loyalty or duty which constrains a member to support policies contrary to those on which the government and he were elected, but there is a duty on him to expostulate, and if need be to oppose. Otherwise all faith between Parliament and people is destroyed . . .[12]

Thus in January Powell was opposed to an election over the miners' claims; he was pledged to support any party that would give the electorate a choice over joining Europe; he had publicly expressed no confidence in Heath. To outsiders this seemed a challenge to and for the leadership. When the magazine *Newsweek* asked him if he intended this attitude to be so understood, Powell cautiously answered that the means did not exist to end his current isolation, but added, 'this isn't to say that the means do not exist, and it isn't to say that they are not now being prepared in what they call "the arsenals of divine vengeance".' Robin Day tried to improve on Powell's reply to *Newsweek*, but he declined to define his decisions on the hypothesis of an election which he hoped his statement had averted; if he had failed and there were an election, 'my answer is ready.'[13]

He thought indeed that he had succeeded. On 23 January he told an audience at the Overseas Women's Club with obvious relief that a fortnight earlier 'the nation actually did stand on the brink of the precipice. One step further – the one step that was not taken – would have plunged it into a political conflict upon lines which would have created the maximum division and animosity between one class and another, in order to approve policies which all concerned knew to be impracticable and about to be abandoned by their own authors.'[14] These remarks incensed, among others, the *Daily Mail*, which was as disappointed as the Cabinet hawks that Heath had shied away from the February 7 date. It unveiled a Machiavellian scheme to force the 'dogmas of powellism' on the country: 'All it takes is for the Prime Minister to turn away once more from an election. Then the whole idea of sharing burdens by agreed restraint of spending power would be overwhelmed by sledge-hammer economics' – i.e. deflation and unemployment – while Heath would have shown himself no more effective than Wilson in 1969 when he abandoned the attempt to reform the unions and industrial relations by Barbara Castle's scheme 'In Place of Strife'.

Nevertheless Powell evidently hoped that the election had been averted. Early in February he reported to an audience in Aberystwyth that the danger of an election fought 'to decide a pay claim or defeat a strike' was over.[15] He then put forward his own policy for ending the coal emergency. This was to withdraw government intervention, to allow the Coal Board to make its own deal with the miners on pay on the strict condition that both sides realised that the whole cost of the award would have to be defrayed from prices, with no subsidy, 'thus restoring responsibility to the bargaining parties' (and of course meeting the 1970 election undertaking). Powell accepted that as oil prices had gone up, nothing could prevent the miners getting more, or coal costing much more – a redistribution of the national income in favour of the miners at the expense of other members of the community – for just so long as coal had this competitive advantage.

Powell's hopes collapsed when Heath called the election. No matter how he reviewed the succession of statements he had made in the past two months – let alone his earlier opposition over the EEC – the logic of his strict application of principle and honour dictated that he could not stand as an official Conservative. A different kind of politician would not, of course, have made such statements, would perhaps have fallen silent, or ill, when the possibility of an election began to open up. As things were, had Heath designed to rid himself and his party of Powell, he could not have managed it more neatly: soon he would be in office with a large majority, a greater personal dominance, and free of his pestilent critic.

When Powell told William Buckley, the American radio commentator, on 25

February, that to have helped to return Heath by standing in the election but keeping silent would have resulted in his own 'moral and intellectual self-destruction' he was envisaging what would have been said, how his entire case against Heath for three years, his defence of Parliament and the nation, would have been laughed to scorn – with his own armaments turned against himself. The first person to have repudiated powellism would have been – Enoch Powell. He told Buckley:

> A man cannot stand up in the election – not at least if he is going to be heard – and say 'I disagree with the very issue on which this election is being fought; I think it is an absurdity; but nevertheless vote for me as an official candidate', because then the next question would be 'You are standing as an official Conservative candidate: does this mean that you want to see a Conservative majority in the next Parliament?'
>
> 'Yes, I suppose so', would be the answer. 'So you want to see a majority in favour of the very policy which you have been denouncing for fifteen or eighteen months, which in speech after speech you have pointed out is absurd?' one cannot then say 'Well, never mind that; just vote me in'. I cannot do that.[16]

He may have hoped he would not have to face the choice – that the election would not come. But long before December he had made it. For he told an interviewer subsequently that from the time the Communities Bill was passed in 1972 he could not see how he could be returned as a Conservative member, 'because to be re-elected meant approving and reinforcing that decision to which I was fundamentally opposed. There always hung over me the shadow of saying to my constituents, "I cannot be your candidate any longer".'[17] In one of his retrospects upon the political morals to be drawn from those events, in 1976, he told the Young Conservatives that he had fixed May 1974 as the latest date by which he must do so. His one hope, in fact, was that Heath would be forced from within the Party to modify his course during his term of office – not an impossible development but an unlikely one.[18]

But it was not enough merely to refuse to be an official candidate. He could not stand as an unofficial candidate or Independent ('A single imaginary question settles that point. "Mr Candidate, if you find you have the deciding vote in an evenly balanced new House of Commons, will you use it to turn the Government out or keep them in?" The candidate cannot refuse to answer. When he does so, he ceases to be an independent candidate'). He could not be silent. He had voted in 104 divisions with the bulk of Labour MPs against the Communities Bill; inexorably his position required him to turn against his party and support Labour publicly. When he broke silence on 23 February, he explained why he had to reject the arguments of the 'many hundreds' who wanted him to stand as an Independent or 'to manufacture my own party and stand for that'.

> There is here a profound and dangerous misconception which I wish to dispel ... Politics and Parliament in this country are about party. Without party

neither responsible government nor responsible democracy is possible . . . the elector votes not for a person, and not for a party in the abstract, but for a party majority in the House of Commons . . . he must decide what matters most to him, and then he must help to give a majority to the party that has that to offer.[19]

This view, which also makes clear why and when a party member must reject his party – when it adopts a different policy from that for which it was expressly given its majority – excluded him from standing as a no-party man, a man who would be asking to be elected simply as a lone voice, a powerless tribune. But it also excluded him from refraining from advising how others should vote. The next step was that a man who, though not standing himself but still evidently in politics (for he did not say he had retired), from whom so many expected guidance as well as explanations of his decision, had to declare himself. He put it to his Shipley audience:

On one side we have a certainty: if the Conservative party has a majority in the next parliament, then . . . the question of Britain in the Community will be . . . irreversible. . . . On the other side there is more than an open chance. There is commitment . . . underwritten no less by Roy Jenkins than by Michael Foot. It commands the general assent and support of the whole Labour party. Unlike 1970, when many Conservative candidates were openly against British entry, there are no Labour candidates at this election who repudiate this commitment and . . . it would be supported by a section of the Conservatives. . . .[20]

This was powellism politics lived in action. Its links hold inexorably from his pledge to fight to keep Britain out of the Market in his 1970 election address to his call in 1974 to his audience to vote Labour. Iain Macleod once said of Powell's logic that he went a long way with it, but got off the train a few stations before it crashed into the buffers. In February 1974 it sent the political buffers flying in all directions.

Enough voters in marginal constituencies voted Labour, or abstained from voting Conservative, to deny Heath another five years of personal ascendancy. But what the electorate had voted *for* remained in dispute. Most commentators concluded that it reacted in the time-honoured way of blaming the government of the day for the mess of the day – inflation, the oil crisis, the three-day week, the quarrel with the miners that should have been avoided.

On the constitutional issue the oracle was ambiguous. On the question who ruled Britain – Parliament or unions, Heath or McGahey – the outcome has favoured the unions. Since more electors voted for the Conservatives than for Labour, it could be argued that the prevailing attitude of loyal anti-market Conservatives was that whilst they went a long way with Powell's argument about the loss of British independence to the Community, they would rather lose their independence than vote Socialist; they did not buy Powell's point that with independence they could vote the unions down at any subsequent election, but independence was irrecoverable. It was in the marginals, where the first-past-the-post system destroyed the Conservative majority, Powell could say that he had won the election; that he had put Heath in and had put him out again.[21] But could he say that powellism had done so? Some Conservatives had no doubt who was to blame, at least; they cried 'Judas!' Powell retorted 'Judas was paid.'[22]

4   Party and Patriotism

Still the search went on for an explanation of his behaviour, on the face of it 'so quixotic that it had to be supposed a subtle and tortuous machination for self-advancement',[23] as Powell wryly described it. As he was still a political person, therefore he must have somehow planned exactly this result, Labour in by a whisker, Heath out of favour with his party, all that was needed was a by-election in a powellite constituency and there he would be, the leadership in full view. Churchill had said while anyone could rat, it took a man to re-rat, and Powell was just the man to play the Churchill.

But Powell could hardly be unaware in 1974 that the process whereby Churchill ratted on the Conservatives and then re-ratted back took not one election and a few months, but the whole period of basic party realignments from 1903 to 1923. Later Powell recalled, if in vain, that on the eve of the poll he thought he was probably finished in politics and only when he saw the results realised that he probably wasn't.[24] To his own surprise, his sacrifice was not in vain – or not yet. He had a role, if only as a former MP of prominence, in the Keep Britain Out Movement; but he began publicly to intimate that he would get back to the Commons; the fates would find a way. This may be a vindication of the inherent dynamism of powellism, but it does not alter the fact that, when the future was unknowable, Powell risked everything for its – for his own – primary article of faith.

That primary article is the preservation of the nation, of nationhood, as Britain's instinctual life force, 'will to power', developed and trained in its inner conflicts and resulting institutions; the English style, the English thing, fought for and died for repeatedly; the British nation-state without which Britain becomes unrecognisable, disintegrated, a page of history, like the Venetian republic or the Roman Empire.

By an irony of fate, it was that central Tory article of belief that brought Powell to repudiate the Conservative Party. It is supposed to be the roots of the Conservative and Unionist credo; but it is the taproot of Powell's alternative conservatism, the first premise of all powellian logic, the assumption which constitutes the only rug that can be pulled from beneath the structure of powellism – as the socialists seek to do. Primary in thought, it proved (it still proves) the last issue. Powell's logic could have permitted him to have stayed silent after 8 February; but not over the betrayal of the nation. On this he had to stand, he could do no other.

Of course there is, somewhere, an alternative Powell. Goethe spoke for all men when he complained 'two hearts beat within my breast'. Powell has always insisted that he has never put forward any political programme which his party could not – subject to the exigencies of the situation – put into practice in office. He would deny any charge that he was a brilliant political theoretician, though this description of him is common. Because he lives his ideas, he believes the Party, and the nation, can do so. It does mean, however, that he is prepared to take the responsibility; and logic requires that one who advocates a supreme, and perfectly practicable, policy of national survival, should seek office. Tactical requirements then obtrude, and no programme, no alternative policy, is likely to carry weight if it does not come from a man with experience of office – of successful use of power. Powell notes that 'only in politics does personal experience make up so large a part of the material used to form judgements'.[25] The most valuable material is the experience of office, the highest possible, most powerful obtainable, office. But to that, many are called but few are chosen. That must not only be deserved but usually fought for, intrigued for. The distinction between winning office as a means, and going for it as an end in itself, is narrow. It excites, it exhilarates, it is even addictive. Churchill is reported to have said he would have joined Chamberlain's government if he had been offered a place in it; and Powell would hardly have refused office in 1970 if Heath had offered it. How long either would have thereafter stayed in office is academic – one of the 'ifs' of history. Within Powell there is, and remains, a full-blooded politician, and his career would not fascinate and instruct, let alone remain relevant, had he not used the political arts to his fullest ability, including a capacity to personify his principles, and to use opportunity to gain power, or its sibling in a democracy, publicity. It is not usually convenient in politics to admit a change of mind, or even of emphasis; a politician is always pleased to find a passage in an old speech to cite as evidence of consistency, and the phrase 'we are in a new situation' is at the back of every politician's mind. Powell sought to combine a systematic and logical approach to policy with a career in a party that prides itself on not being too logical and is inclined to dismiss its thinkers as 'too clever by half', a party that is solemn about principle, but is quick to dismiss as a 'resigner' those who stand on principle, reserving its deference for those who stay in the kitchen and sweat out the heat of it. In 1974 principle and party allegiance became irreconcilable, and he ceased to be a Conservative. The link that justifies the title Conservative and Unionist party also snapped at that moment, and it became open to him to become an anti-Conservative Ulster Unionist. But, as he said himself, he remained throughout the turmoil a Tory: 'I was born a Tory, I am a Tory, and I shall die a Tory!'

Chapter 2

The Making of a Tory Intellectual, 1912–1963

1 Triumphs of a Scholar

It was as a little Liberal, however, that he was born into this world alive – on 16 June 1912, to two elementary school teachers in Stechford, Birmingham. For they belonged to that section of the lower middle class which voted Liberal before 1931 and Conservative after. His ancestry was subsequently researched by his enemies, but proved disappointingly autochthonous. It goes back, as the name indicates, to Welsh forbears. For the little it signifies, Welsh history being what it is, he is rather more Celtic than Anglo-Saxon. From that bank of genes he was issued with an exceptional brain, his reading ability at four being almost comparable with that of the infant John Stuart Mill; he was reading Harmsworth's Encyclopaedia. With the brain went an exceptionally sturdy constitution.

The environmentalists have had more luck with his upbringing. The only offspring of devoted parents, his mother (as with many successful men) was the greater influence, the father the lesser but balancing factor. To this circumstance he owed his capacity for practical achievement. Having given up teaching upon marriage, his mother made him her single pupil. Loving, intelligent, ambitious but endowed with common sense as well as womanly insight, she gently but insistently shaped a gifted child as a mental athlete, trained to scale the ladders of opportunity – the scholarship system of the twenties. His father gave him the sense of fun and playfulness that underlie a personality imbued with seriousness and self-sufficiency. The teachers of that time were also prone to emphasise meticulous attention to detail and tidiness of mind and appearance. (Educational theory has reversed this now.)

He had middle-class security. His father progressed in a safe profession to the top, a headmastership. Materially there was always enough; nothing to excess. The wretchedness of unemployment, financial anxiety, was around the house, but not in it. Plain living and high thinking taught him to respect, value and husband money. There was no smoking or drinking, but shelves of books and the countryside to explore. His holidays coincided with theirs. So between them they almost completely furnished his childhood and adolescent world, a republic of three persons. School was for him a workplace, not another community. He returned to his home base with intellectual plunder more often than with noisy comrades.

His biographer, Mr Roth,[1] whose researches one can but summarise and supplement, noted the reinforcing effect of his Dame school, run by a teacher friend of his mother. The local secondary school led to a scholarship to King Edward VI School, Birmingham, one of the best of the 1553 foundations. He has expressed gratitude for its unashamed intellectual competitiveness – for its élitism. Wedged between New Street and the LNWR station, it had an Oundelian science 'side', and to this he was initially 'streamed'. Had he stayed there he might have become one of the great research scientists of the present day, for he has all the qualities of analytic capacity, precision in method, intellectual curiosity and poetic imagination, as well as powers of concentration, that make great scientists.

But the classics side happened to be rather low in numbers; there were more rungs in the classics career ladder, and after his first term he was drafted to classics. His mother, who had once taught herself Greek in a small Shropshire town, brought him up to second-year standard in Greek from nil during the Christmas holidays. At King Edward's everything but classwork was voluntary, and he confined himself to it, abandoning, in order to put more time into texts, some early prowess with the clarinet – in 1974 he demonstrated his surviving skill on a recorder to children during his election tour in South Down. The curriculum imposed French as well as Latin and Greek; but he also took voluntary German; 'I remember, as sharply as Keats looking into Chapman's Homer, the moment, it must have been in 1927, when I opened my first German book. Here was the language I had dreamed of but never knew existed: sharp, hard, strict, but with words that were romance in themselves, words in which poetry and music vibrated together.'[2] He thus laid the base for his linguistic prowess. He has also Welsh, Italian, Russian, Urdu and some others: but Greek was his passion. At school he began a new translation of Herodotus which in later years he revised and published. It was especially but not only for Greek books that he frequented Birmingham's then worthwhile second-hand bookshops.

German not only opened the classical commentaries to him, but also German philosophy *via* Carlyle. It offered the young mind, fenced with Midlands conformity, new vistas. A year or two later, the reading of Nietzsche put Christianity into a new focus; he became an atheist as a matter of course, revelling in new freedom to think and question the conventional wisdom. Nazism had not then suppurated on German idealism. Nietzsche denounces Bismarck, as Schopenhauer (a favourite of Powell's) does Hegel. Whatever influence German chauvinism had on young Powell's mind he was already an anti-German patriot and recalls among his first memories the accounts of the Coronel and Falkland Islands battles.[3] He was not influenced by the surge of anti-war writing, like that of Graves, Sassoon and Lawrence. Those who learn to versify in Latin can compose workmanlike English verses: Powell was soon writing competent poetry.

He published four slim collections between his Cambridge days and his marriage in 1952. They have been ransacked for clues to his personal and emotional, not to say public life, invariably a foolish procedure. The earlier work, well-constructed as it was, inevitably reflects the uncertainties of youth in the forest of the productions and pronouncements of the great and established; but the lyrics and epigrams are neatly turned. If Nietzsche inspired some, the English countryside informed others, and Housman whose lectures he attended and whom he knew as another fellow of Trinity, Cambridge, was not the only influence. The effect of writing poetry comes out in the eloquence and counterpoint of his political speeches.

It needs no poetry to perceive that a youth with Powell's surroundings, intense family life, and delight in the mastery of difficult subjects, found companionship outside his family, let alone intimacy with the young of either sex, extremely difficult and even discouraging. He knew his mind was diamond-hard, but girls respond to charm and to the language that is found in no grammar. Between Powell and people there was a curtain of shyness and sensitivity thicker than most shy and sensitive people have to pierce; nor is such shyness a single fortification but tends to be a defence in depth. But it is, as Powell was moved to shift it into poetry when once he was lying next to a soldier in an agony of asthma in hospital during the war, a universal condition which varies only in degree:

> That strange destiny
> Which makes one thing impossible to man
> Of all things most desired, by word or act
> To help another, has condemned us here,
> Lying a yard or two apart, to weep
> In uncommunicable loneliness . . .

The reaction-formation is often hardness, social gracelessness, insensitivity – even cultivated insensitivity. The will to power in men of short stature is proverbially strong; it may also be so in those handicapped in some of the social skills.

At Trinity, Cambridge, he was almost a recluse; he even politely declined an invitation by the Master to the usual scholars' dinner on plea of work. But he made good that excuse by capturing virtually all the University and College prizes in classics: an eremite behind his doors, overcoated in winter because coal fires made him sleepy, he achieved a resounding reputation. His energy took him beyond the Cambridge hunting-grounds. In Selly Oak College, in Birmingham, he unearthed the Rendel Harris papyri dealing with life in Roman Egypt and lectured on them in Italian in Italy. He collaborated in writing the code of the Welsh lawgiver-king Hywel. He began a lexicon to Herodotus, later to become the standard work. His ambition was to become that rare classicist, a great textual critic, and to become a professor as young as Nietzsche. He almost did. He made a competence from his prizes and stipend as a Fellow of Trinity. The classical world lay open when, at twenty-five, he took up his professorship of

Greek in Sydney, Australia, in 1938. The scholarship was kept in working order, and, as reviews and articles from his hand show, is still in full use.

This was the 'Professor of Greek' to whom slighting reference was sometimes later made (most hurtfully by Iain Macleod when their friendship was ruptured) on occasions in which he made detailed and expert analysis of a bill in committee which bored a journalist or a party hack. But he regarded Greek as a no less practical, and more civilising, discipline than science or mathematics: a necessary foundation for political perspective and that exercise of 'taste' which alone can keep the mind discriminating in a time of corruption. He told the Australians (but Oxford University distributed his views more widely) in his inaugural lecture:

> In their passage through two and a half millennia, Greek texts have reached us, not in their pristine condition, but admixed with a dross of interpolation and corruption. Their purification has been the labour of innumerable scholars . . . since, and even before, the renaissance. Yet the humblest pass-degree student who has to read a book of Sophocles or Plato is still confronted on every other page with open questions. Many of these, especially where authenticity or interpolation is at issue, are in the last resort questions of taste; and every reader has to form for himself an idea of the standards of the age and author under consideration, and then judge the particular passages in the light of these.[4]

He went on to point out that the process by which the Greek classics have come down to us through 2,500 years, unlike Latin or Sanskrit texts, compels the student to have present to his mind the cultural history of all those ages of transition. 'In other words he must cultivate not only an independent and critical judgement, but a sense of history', a point which enabled the Professor to find relevant to his story the case of 'a great empire deliberately taking every possible step to secure its own destruction because its citizens were so obsessed by prejudice . . . as never to perform the few logical steps necessary for proving they would shortly be involved' in a life-or-death war. The germ of Powell's political style, approach and rhetoric is here.

2   The Fortunes and Lessons of War

Everything, he has said, had for him a provisional quality from 1934, when Hitler's purge of the Brownshirts signalled the true nature of the Nazi regime, and uncovered the extent to which it had distorted Nietzsche's concept of the *Uebermensch*. The German dream had dissolved. On taking up his appointment in Sydney, Powell warned the Vice-Chancellor that on the outbreak of war he would leave at once. By 1939 he had the appointment of a chair in Durham as from New Year 1940; but he returned in September 1939 to enlist as a private in the Royal Warwickshire Regiment.

The sensitive and solitary personality found the same ready-made sanctuary in the Army as in the College – a framework, demand for method and routine, and a similar challenge to understand and use its managerial set-up. He mastered the grammar first: he ensured initial recognition as the best-turned-out private soldier, the most conscientious on duty, in the company. Off-duty he studied Field Service Regulations and Clausewitz *On War*. The fortunes of war were reduced by him to an either-or. Either he would be eliminated by death or wounds, or his talents would carry him to the rank of major-general. After six and a half years' service he was still one rank short, as Brigadier.

But this was because the war ended a year sooner than he anticipated. When he went into the Army he made a strategic appreciation which was correct in most anticipations, except the nuclear bomb. The sense of history derived from scholarship and military experience enabled him to predict (it is said) in a lecture, to which he was called as last-minute fill-in, to brother officers of the 9th Armoured Division during the gloomier days of 1941, that the United States would be drawn into the war by conflict with Japan, that an Anglo-American war machine would defeat Germany and Japan; but that the price to be paid would be domination of the post-war world by Russia and America – even a third world war.

Promotion in the field was what he desired, but he was spotted as a natural intelligence officer. His personal contribution to victory was at its greatest (recognised by the military MBE) when as a lieutenant-colonel and Secretary to the Joint Intelligence Committee, Middle East, Cairo, his assignment was to predict Rommel's moves in the North African theatre. To the study of Rommel and the Afrika Korps he brought a matching Germanic *Tüchtigkeit* as well as a British imaginativeness. In Algiers in 1943 he saw his predictions of American preponderance realised in the decisions on allied strategy which did not follow Churchill's political priorities. He tried hard to join Wingate's Burma operations, but was posted to India Command as Secretary of the Joint Intelligence Committee for South-East Asia, planning the British advance eastwards, which Hiroshima was to make unnecessary.

He tried again to get active service in the coming push, and wrote afterwards of his feelings of guilt at being kept 'this side of the separating flame' from so many comrades; he was relegated to a planning group to consider the shape, role, and officering of the post-war Indian Army. This amounted to forecasting the future defence of India, which in turn involved assumptions about the future relationship between India and Britain. These went awry. For he pre-supposed that the old Anglo-Indian relationship would remain after India achieved a status like Canada; that the sub-continent as one unit would remain the core of a still-evolving British Commonwealth and Empire; and that it would have to face the old Russian expansionism on a larger scale. His group deduced that half the officers of this reconstructed army would still be British. Such miscalculations have been quoted against Powell with relish when he began to prophesy future conflict in Britain. Perhaps it made a mark on him, for he has repeatedly shown how predictions and detailed planning in national affairs are usually falsified by the shortcomings of the data. But in an army an order to make contingency plans is an order. He gave it his usual unremitting effort. His plan for a future Indian Army might well have fitted it a good deal better to meet the Chinese when the test came from that unexpected frontier.

Though he practiced his Urdu among Indian villagers, he was not familiar with the Indian intellectuals, journalists and Congress politicians whom in different circumstances he might have met on the New Delhi cocktail round, and so he received no powerful impression of the intense undercurrents of nationalist sentiment, which Auchinleck could not miss. But in 1944–5 Powell was far from exceptional in thinking that somehow or other the unique partnership between the island and the sub-continent would continue, since both parties seemed to need it. Most of the ICS thought so (they were still recruiting British material) as did the Princes, the expatriate business communities, the *banyia* and mercantile castes. The Army, inevitably Powell's *milieu* (critical as he sometimes was of it), thought so. The strength of Congress was misunderstood even after the 1942 disturbances and the 1943 famine. The Hindu-Muslim, Nehru-Jinnah confrontation seemed to require a British presence. Nobody foresaw Mr Attlee as the Labour Prime Minister in 1945.

Thus when the nuclear detonations transformed the framework of the post-war world, at least to appearances, Brigadier Powell was still an imperialist. The grandeur of the Empire had impressed him more from the foothills of the Himalayas than from the Blue Mountains. When he realised that his Army career was over, and that he had to start a new one, it had grown on him that the most urgent issue for Britain was to preserve the imperial connexion, to retain a world role, and to avoid the moral disintegration of 1918–22. If he was to play any part in this work, he had to go into politics: most Viceroys had started so. He resigned the professorship of Greek which had been kept open for him in Durham, and began reading economics before he quitted India.

3   Member for Wolverhampton South-West

His career as a classical scholar had shown that he had an intellect of the highest order combined with a self-discipline that could extract its full potential: he had met the best scholars the country could produce and had beaten them all. Called to the profession of arms he had shown himself able to meet with distinction every demand made upon him; his combativeness had been trained; and he had looked upon the kingdoms of the earth. The withdrawn, shy, but forceful academic had become the single-minded, uncompromising military logistician – a brasshat who exacted every tittle of respect due to rank, and gave it with punctilio to whosoever outranked him. His army career grew as rich a crop of anecdotes as had his academic one.

Competing in politics meant going for the biggest prize, the most coveted pot of all. He knew he had some of the qualities for it. He would only find if he had enough of them by measuring himself against the establishment and the ambitious new men coming into the power game from the services. In full uniform, he reported to Conservative headquarters in February 1946, to offer the 'patriotic party' his brains in the time of its greatest need.

R. A. Butler was recruiting talent to rebuild the shattered Party. In 1939 the Conservatives had led an ill-prepared country into a disastrous war, emerging with bare survival and a little honour under a leader who had been rejected until all seemed lost and there was no one else to take over; and even then, many of them had to dissemble their dislike.

Now they were out, disgusted at not cashing in on Churchill's war leadership, and incapable of functioning even as an effective opposition unless they could call in the brains and ideas to underpin them. They needed, they thought, devillers to work up for them the briefs that, when ministers, they were used to getting from their civil servants. Butler was assembling a staff in the research department to provide the needed ammunition for the day to day battle. After an interview with an impressed Lord Clithero (Sir Ralph Assheton) Powell was signed on.

Butler also wanted to put out a new Tamworth manifesto calling for a total reorganisation of the social structure on which the Party had so long rested, an explicit acceptance of redistributive taxation, and a repudiation of *laissez-faire* economics in favour of a system in which the State acted as a trustee for the interests of the community and as a balancing force between different interests. He envisaged codes of behaviour for industries like professions, and a spirit of partnership between management and men, though not, of course, workers' control or even representation at board level. This programme was thought far ahead of the run-of-the-mill Tory MP. Churchill himself feared that when an opposition spells out its position in detail, the Government becomes the opposition and attacks the opposition which, having failed to win the sweets of office, also forfeits the benefits of irresponsibility. Indeed this did happen.

Butler's designs read oddly against the later tenets of powellism. But to the cause of working out Conservative ideas, Powell devoted himself. He had to prove his value as a backroom boy and so earn a winnable constituency when the pendulum began to swing back. On a salary of £900 a year (he had saved out of his Army pay) he joined a trio of top researchers, the other two being Reginald Maudling and Iain Macleod, both out of the forces. But Butler considered Powell 'the most intellectually formidable, with strong and pungently-expressed views on all subjects'. They were all overworked, but the ex-brigadier revelled in the long hours and intense analysis of each topic, as well as the study of parliamentary law and procedure. He tackled social legislation as he would the syntax and texts of a new language, and equipped his seniors to ask questions and fire off well-informed speeches on housing, health, town planning, local government, redistributive taxation, national insurance and nationalisation. His main contact with foreign policy was through his secretaryship of the Party India Committee, which in 1947 he resigned when Churchill decided not to oppose the granting of independence. The linchpin of his political thinking was out. In the following year he provided Maxwell Fyfe with a case against the British

Nationality Act of 1948, pointing out some of the unfortunate legal consequences, at which the great man scoffed. The change in the definition of British nationality and subjecthood was the *fons et origo* of coloured immigration, though Powell did not foresee this. Fyfe also helped to saddle Britain with the European Court of Human Rights, to Powell's later disgust.

In the secretariat in Old Queen Street he was as brusque and unforthcoming as he had been in Cairo, but joined in more relaxed though closely argued discussions on party principle with the others after hours, and particularly with Macleod who often stayed in his Earls Court flat. From the first there obtruded the question: what was post-war, post-welfare state Conservatism? Butler persuaded Churchill that it was not enough to reserve one's position, and wait for the electorate to tire of Labour: there had to be a specific policy, programme, pledges. He felt that Conservatism, which could claim to have originated so much social reform in the past – the rather remote past admittedly – must now absorb the welfare state, and undertake to accept National Health and nationalised industries.[5] The issue, in 1947–9, was – how far did one go? Or, to put it the other way, how many controls, how much state management, did one 'consign to the flames'? Though it took time to emerge, Powell was basically opposed to Butlerian tendencies. The seeds of his alternative conservatism were planted then, though perhaps they did not germinate until the era of Butskellism.

The ambitious young men (Powell, Maudling, Macleod – but also others like Heath, Alport and Maude) studied the constituency form-book. Powell was blooded in a hopeless by-election at Normanton in February 1947, where he found he could speak to miners as well as lecture to students, and fought as an exponent of imperialism and *laissez-faire*. The result showed the first slight post-war swing against Labour, but Powell needed to get a winnable seat. Butler felt that in many marginal seats victory was possible if the candidate appealed to the Conservative working class voter, an element which normally makes up about a third of the Conservative vote, but which has been less reliable in the post-war years from the Conservative point of view because of the lamentable decline in 'deference' – the belief among many older and more skilled working class people that it is better for them if the country is led by 'gentlemen', or at least by more educated people whatever their origin – a propensity psephologists try to measure. Whereas in the less 'deferential' section of the skilled and conservative working class, the vote can merely stay at home, even if it does not go to Labour, Wolverhampton South-West looked like a seat that the right kind of Conservative candidate could win, and the wrong kind could unnecessarily lose. The seat had been 'improved' by redistribution, and the candidacy was therefore open again. The former candidate was upper class and, in a decision that left some bitterness, was passed over by the local association with Central Office goodwill (it could not be more) in order to adopt Powell, who came from the region, spoke with its accent, knew its ways and could impressively prove that under the Tories a local lad could go to the top. The selectors felt, one said later, 'we had a potential prime minister on our hands'.

Powell had promised to give his whole time to the fight. This was the decisive factor. He moved to Wolverhampton, and camped there, much as he had camped in the war, or even in Sydney, 'doing for himself' and working all hours knocking on doors to make himself, his antecedents and the new Conservatism (no abolition of the popular free Health Service) known: talking without condescension and taking snubs with sportsmanship. In his favour was a general irritation with controls in an area that has lived by small enterprises or partnerships – where traditionally a craftsman out of a job would set up a workshop or even run a mini-factory in the outhouse after a day's work. It was still Adam Smith (or Marshall) country in the 1940s, where *laissez-faire* worked partly because people liked to stand on their own feet and be beholden to none.

In the 1950 election he won the seat by some 700 votes, proving that hard work in canvassing, and organising the postal vote can do as well as familiarity with a four-ale bar. He thus joined the famous 'class of '50' which was the embodiment of the new model Conservatism. Even Bevan admired it. Nearly half of that hundred became ministers. It was well placed to sharpen its parliamentary teeth on the remnants of Attlee's government, but it also set itself to force the gates of the Party's citadel of power, the county and City insiders. The new boys were determined to get in and try out their ideas. A struggle for control of the party ensued, and after a dozen years the grammar school boys had won – and were fighting among themselves.

The first need of the ambitious new member is to draw the right kind of attention to himself in the House, especially from his own front bench. He must as soon as possible show he is ministerial timber. He must be seen to be useful, in some subjects indispensable. Effective attacks on the other side are essential. But the art of advancement includes choice of the right moment to disagree with your own side, if you feel overlooked, and a sense of which of the shifting cabals to join and leave; which of the streams of party thinking to swim with; and when and if to rebel in divisions.

For rebellion, not only are persuasive points of principle and conscience needful but one needs friends and influence. Powell was one of those with no 'power base' in the shires, in the old boys' network, in local government. He did not remedy the handicap, seeking no friends nor showing clubbability in the House. He felt happy, again working within an institution with complex rules and procedures to become versed in, wearing a new uniform – the distinctive black coat and striped trousers. He was noticed moving with an intent expression between chamber and library as he had done between classroom and library. He was working up his special subjects, so that he could quote his authorities, word-perfect, from official papers, from the statute books and the Official Report: an effective parliamentarian's constant reading is back numbers of Hansard. When Powell got up a subject, he knew it, every intricacy, every statistic, what everyone had said about it. Brick by brick he dealt with the minutiae of housing, planning, local government, school meals, nurses' grants, Welsh development, mineral licences. He soon established his gift for lucid exposition as well as oratorical cut and thrust. He and Macleod were the outstanding pair; their nuisance value was recognised by the other side who nicknamed them Tweedledum and Tweedledee.

Powell had only words and performance to establish himself, but he quickly demonstrated that an independent judgement, a voice for principle, a fiery particle, had arrived on the backbenches. In his maiden speech he took up the burdens of defence (see p. 98). His sensitivity to American presumption led him to oppose British participation in the United Nations, but overwhelmingly American, force in Korea. He did not challenge his front bench on this issue in the lobbies; but that came when he abstained in a division on joining the Coal and Steel Community, which the Conservative leadership supported – his first moment of cooperation with Labour on a question of national sovereignty. Another keynote in his subsequent career was touched in his criticism of the Royal Titles Bill in March 1953 when he justified his opposition to his own side: 'We have a meaning in this place only insofar as in our time and generation we represent great principles, great elements in the national life, great strands in our society and national being' (see p. 75).

He became a member of the One Nation group founded by Cuthbert Alport and Angus Maude to carry forward the rethinking of the Conservative position on every aspect of domestic policy initiated by Butler. The men who had worked on the charters were nearly all in Parliament, but he did not want the momentum to be lost; the manifesto *One Nation*[6] was prepared for the 1950 party conference. The label of course recalled Disraeli's warning against a nation divided – in Queen Victoria's reign between rich and poor. The new Young England wanted to make clear to the electorate, and possibly even more to the unreconstructed members of the party, that a clear break with the nineteen-thirties had been made. (An electorate, as Ivor Jennings showed, is imbued with the political stereotypes of the previous generation.)

Among the new Young Englanders, Powell provided a corrective: he offered the guideline that when one had strayed from the path (and the Tories supposed they somehow had in the thirties) the only thing to do was to retrace one's step to the point of divergence and take new bearings. He argued for principle (he would go back even to Bolinbroke), for the postulation of logical objectives for all policy. He remarked later that practical people found it irritating to be reminded that a philosophical problem has first to be solved in facing fundamentals, 'But in the end fundamentals win just because they are fundamental.'[7] He and Macleod in 1951 examined the fundamentals of the social services, more searchingly than One Nation had done, the relation of needs and means (see p. 30).

These educational enterprises helped Macleod before Powell. In Churchill's 1951 administration Maudling and Heath got junior posts at once. Macleod and Powell had worked together on the Conservative amending bill to introduce prescription and other charges in the free Health Service; and when Bevan, who had intended to do the same, attacked it Macleod was called to speak as they both rose. Macleod's destruction of Bevan thereupon marked him for early promotion, and when Henry Crookshank was soon after moved from the Ministry of Health, Macleod got it without any apprenticeship in a junior post. Powell would have done exactly the same if he had been the one to be called; his chagrin was noticed. The friendship between them endured for fifteen years, even if it changed; they still thought that they would have made an unbeatable politician if rolled into one. Powell helped Macleod deal with a grave illness in his family while learning his new job; and he passed to Powell the directorship of the London Municipal Society. Six months after Powell was offered a junior post in the Home Office which he rejected much as he had once rejected lectureships when looking for a professorship. He was learning to wait; he was known.

Churchill's offer of the post was due to a miscalculation of the number of ministers in the Commons which was, and is, limited by statute. Had Powell accepted a compensation would doubtless have been offered as soon as possible; as it was continued back-bencherdom permitted him to join the Suez group of MPs led by Charles Waterhouse and Sir Harry Legge-Bourke opposed to the decision to withdraw from the Suez base (and the Sudan). Churchill pleaded that the H-bomb had made the base militarily irrelevant as well as financially and politically too expensive. Powell believed that the unusability of nuclear weapons left conventional strategy little changed; if this pivotal base could not be held Britain's entire world system was shown to be untenable. He could not reconcile the Government's decision with the Treaty which nonetheless provided for reoccupation by agreement. The Suez group was surprised when, as logic required, he thereafter declined to join them in opposing the evacuation of Cyprus.

In the reshuffle which followed Churchill's retirement in March 1955 he was passed over like others of the Suez group, but found consolation in election as vice-chairman of the 1922 Committee, the standing organisation of Conservative back-benchers. His offence was considered purged at the end of the year, however, when Eden made him Parliamentary Secretary to the Ministry of Housing and Local Government: his first big job. His speeches against Bevan on housing subsidies had commended him not only to Eden but to Duncan Sandys, the Minister, with whom he began work on the – partial – derestricting of rents (see p. 35). At work on this bill, Powell could remain silent on the Suez crisis which preoccupied Sandys as a member of the Cabinet. Powell did not have to say 'I told you so', but neither did he go around saying the Government had prevented World War III, as some ministers did to keep unhappy constituents and sceptical financiers quiet. His silence, his prowess with the bill, recommended him to Macmillan, who included him in his ministry of reconciliation and recovery, in January 1957.

4   Macmillan and After

Macmillan put together his Treasury team to find specifics for stimulating the economy by tax reductions but without inflation, appointing Peter Thorneycroft Chancellor, Powell Financial Secretary and Nigel Birch Economic Secretary. The trio were like-minded on financial orthodoxy, and Powell attained a position from which in time he might become an obvious choice for the Chancellorship. But in a year they were all out, their policy overruled.

'Stagflation' was the in-word of that time, expressing a tendency for prices to rise, sterling to be subject to strain, yet without much growth in production. The run of Butler's budgets had injected money into the system; imports were buoyant, unemployment was growing, the pound weakly, the Bank of England worried by by-elections going against the Conservative vote. Thorneycroft put control of inflation and strength of the pound abroad, as first priority; lower taxation meant tight control over expenditure. Over their second budget the Treasury ministers found themselves opposed to the rest of the Cabinet, and in January 1958 the public learnt that there was a crisis over the gap between what the spending departments wanted and the Treasury ministers' insistence that there could be no increase over the level of 1957–8. The gap was alleged (later denied by the ministers) to be a mere £50 million; yet the ministers stood on what they said was principle, and resigned.

Macmillan had the better of it for the moment. An adventitious and sharp improvement in American trade underpinned British exports so that as activity increased, employment improved, yet inflation did not immediately accelerate.

Perhaps for this reason, and because Powell remained punctiliously loyal, Macmillan offered him a more junior government post – Parliamentary Secretary to the Ministry of Education – after the 1959 election. Powell refused office until Thorneycroft had been brought back; both joined the government again in the reshuffle of 1960. Powell was Minister of Health, without cabinet rank; he became a Privy Councillor with which goes the privilege that thereafter he could ask to be called in any debate in which he wished to speak – a great advantage when in opposition or out of office. He was Minister of Health for over three years, of which he was in the Cabinet for fifteen months until Macmillan resigned in October 1963.

At the Ministry he proved, once again, capable and decisive; the medical professions liked him, at least at first, and his civil servants found him a model boss, better than Macleod. He introduced a hospital building programme then costed at £500 million, 1961–70, and thought well within the country's means – but, significantly, still not completed. His most controversial political decision was to come down on the side of those who advised that the small hospital, even if specialised, was unsuited to scientific medicine; it meant that family doctors lost contacts with consultants as well as 'beds'. He reorganised the approach to mental illness; but it is a thorny subject for any layman, even a minister, and though in theory it is right for mental patients whenever possible to live in the community, the structure of home life and morality in the last half of the twentieth century made this a hazardous norm to promote, or retrieve. Powell fought to preserve the humane tradition that in hospitals the patient's interests come first; only later did he perceive how proliferating bureaucracy undermines that tradition (see p. 43).

After three years he knew he had come to the end of his usefulness as a maker of political decisions in the Department.[8] The most invidious of these was the application of the Government's 'pay pause' to medical staff at the very moment when they were pressing long overdue claims justified by the rise in prices produced by Macmillan's financial policy after 1957. Powell could only offer $2\frac{1}{2}$ per cent, and found himself embroiled in a distasteful wrangle with discontented nurses. The truth that a high proportion of these were male, tough, Irish and unreasonable did not get into the newspapers. He was sternly loyal to Cabinet decisions; then to his disgust saw the ground cut from under his feet when the port employers, without government restraint, conceded the dockers 9 per cent. His reputation for cheeseparing and insensitivity was thus dexterously increased by Macmillan, as part of the whole art of Cabinet management which he played according to his own rules. Powell reflected deeply on the episode; it contributed to his analysis of the reasons why incomes policies must be short-lived and usually boomerang on the governments that rely on them.

Macmillan, however, elevated Powell to the Cabinet after the 'massacre' of 1962, when the Chancellor, Selwyn Lloyd, was sacked, mainly for not being expansionist enough for Macmillan's taste. Powell thus joined a Cabinet already committed to taking Britain into the Common Market, but the Nassau meeting between Macmillan and President Kennedy, from which Britain obtained the ambiguous gift of the Skybolt missile called down De Gaulle's veto on the negotiations. Accordingly Powell played no role at this juncture in the European debate beyond a general support for the Government's abortive attempt.

At forty-eight, as a cabinet minister, Powell had reached the stage in a rising politician's career when the great offices of state are within grasp if his performance is sustained and his luck holds. He ran fourth in the quartet of the 'class of '50' which were close to the top: Heath, Chief Whip in 1959 was now Lord Privy Seal and a Macmillan intimate, Maudling and Macleod had more senior ministerial experience. Powell on the other hand had emerged as a clear-cut and respected political personality. Sometimes called 'the sea-green incorruptible', his adherence to first principles in policy and conduct had recommended him to the whole House. His remarkable intervention in the debate on the Kenya 'Hola Camp' scandal, where he called for acceptance of Parliament's ultimate responsibility for such events and the punishment of those culpable, showed the humanity under a somewhat flinty exterior. Labour members gave him credit for this as they did (until the racial issue) for his support for the abolition of capital punishment and for homosexual law reform. The business community applauded a minister who saved candle-ends, and his caricature as the man with the axe in Vicky's left wing cartoons helped to establish his political personality. He was regarded as a brilliant man whose full powers had yet to be disclosed by events and responsibility.

But events turned baleful. The failure of Macmillan's monetary and incomes policy was manifest in rising prices by 1963. Macmillan's posture was then further weakened by the Profumo affair. To the question whether Macmillan, the worldly-wise aristo, whose jokes in White's hardly argued an unsophisticated mentality, could really have been totally unaware of what was going on, was added press speculation whether Powell's puritanism (imputed to him because presumably the press could find no gossip to suggest hypocrisy) would permit him to serve in an atmosphere of equivocation and dubiety. He personally and meticulously satisfied himself that the Prime Minister had not been a party to concealment or falsification, and on this basis came out with a carefully calculated speech of unconditional support on the eve of the crucial censure debate on 17 June 1963. Despite the damaging outcome of the Profumo tragedy Macmillan decided to stay in office and outface a campaign of innuendo. But he was also preparing to choose a moment when he could determine the succession.

Powell's inner distrust of Macmillan's Machiavellism proved well founded in the leadership crisis in October. Macmillan had determined to lead the Party in the looming general election when his unexpected incapacitation by a prostate operation made unavoidable his resignation during the Party annual conference which he was to round off with a key policy speech. He was removed to hospital, and there followed the celebrated episode in which that conference took on the character of an American presidential convention. The story has been told by most of those who played lead parts; Macleod's version, put forward in the following year when he was editor of the *Spectator*,[9] is the one endorsed as most accurate by Powell, who subsequently added his own authority to Macleod's accusation that Macmillan had acted unconstitutionally. This was the charge that Macmillan used the authority of a prime minister (though in hospital) to carry through a process designed to identify his successor in such a way that the Queen would be obliged to take his advice and no other, and to make no check upon the facts which Macmillan gave her as to the Cabinet's preferences: information which he misrepresented as a majority for Lord Home, who up to then had been studiously neutral and enjoyed no such majority when Macmillan induced him suddenly to come forward as the compromise candidate.[10]

Macmillan, according to Macleod, had been thinking in terms of Maudling, Heath or Macleod himself for the Party leadership eventually, but he had been so successful in putting them all in balk meanwhile that when his health gave way it was R. A. Butler, newly designated deputy prime minister, whom the Party was ready to support as the obvious outcome of the 'customary processes'. Powell thought that Butler could have and should have refused to serve under Lord Home, thus forcing him to return to the Queen and advise her that, after all, he was unable to form an administration; in which event she would have used her prerogative properly to send for Butler. Butler shrank from a course of action that would have seemed perfectly proper a hundred years previously. He reasoned that he must not disrupt the party unity to which he had devoted and subordinated his career. Macmillan's comment[11] on this self-abnegation was that it showed Butler was never fit for the job; Macleod's comment on Macmillan's comment was that Butler did every job far better than his gnomic style indicated; nor did Macmillan deny Macleod's flat assertion that from the days he elbowed Butler aside in 1955 he was determined never to allow him to become Prime Minister.

Macleod and Powell were the only outgoing ministers to refuse to serve in Lord Home's administration. The wisdom of their decision has been questioned. When Butler threw in the towel, and Maudling, a no less ardent Butlerite (Powell hardly was, yet he had said 'on the rules it has to be Rab') the critics could not see why they should not have bowed to events and rallied to the new leader, instead of seeming to add to his task of pulling the Party together. (Neither foresaw that Home would come so near to winning in October; they perhaps supposed that the Party would soon be swept into the wilderness after a few months in office under a leader of no great pulling-power with the public, so that Home's offers were for short leases anyway.) But they had both already refused to serve under Home before Butler caved in; and they were assumed to believe not merely that Home lacked the requisite party support, but that he had been wrong to change his mind, disclaim his peerage, and reduce himself to Macmillan's cat's paw to keep Butler out. Powell made the reason for his own refusal to serve in Home's government no more explicit than the remark that he would not have been able to look at himself in the mirror; but the meaning was clear after Macleod's exposé.

In personal terms, both Macleod and Powell liked Home, and accepted places in his shadow cabinet once his offence had been purged by defeat in 1964. Macleod's biographer[12] reached the judgement that his refusal of office fatally precluded him contesting the leadership in 1965. Powell, who knew him so well, dissented, giving his view that Macleod reckoned that he had lost the end-game much earlier, because of the unpopularity he incurred with the Party's right wing for the part he played in liquidating the African empire, and also because other stars were rising faster while his own health was declining ominously.

Macleod missed office, which he loved with all the passion of an uncomplicated political animal, and enjoyed it again for only a few weeks before he died in 1970. Powell forfeited the opportunity to add experience in another ministry, doubtless in one he would have preferred such as Defence. But his destiny was being shaped differently. He was beginning to question the direction the Party was taking, a direction which did not change when Macmillan was replaced by Sir Alec Douglas-Home (as he became after resigning his peerage and entering the House of Commons after winning a by-election). In July 1963, while still in Macmillan's Cabinet, Powell told an audience in Bromsgrove that 'there is the sense of an era passing, of one phase of our party's life yielding place to another. What we want most at this moment is to speak out boldly, defiantly, even blatantly, the basic things we believe in and stand for.'[13] Twelve years of administration had deadened political vision: 'We have seen some of our aspirations defeated or deferred; some of our faith in things and persons tarnished; some of our purposes blunted or modified.' The Party must, he said, rise above day-to-day exigencies and say what it wished for the nation in the future. It was with hopes of such a 'recap and rethink' that Powell attended a conference to review strategy at Chequers that summer under the guidance of Heath, Macleod and Maudling. He found it futile and frustrating, though Macmillan, who called it for his own purposes, took care that the press should hear that Powell's contribution had been outstanding and much appreciated by one and all.[14]

Since the leadership would not speak out, it fell to Powell to do so – defiantly, even blatantly – in the five years ahead. He was well equipped to do so. He had not only made a mark as a parliamentarian, a minister and a personality in public life; he had pondered on parliamentary institutions and their relation to the life of a nation that seemed to so many (not excluding 'Supermac') to be declining. He had briefed himself on the spate of failures that had overtaken the apparent success story of the fifties, and there now was (as Gerald Nabarro jocularly put it) 'a Powell policy for everything'. Perhaps not everything: but when the unexpected happened he had a firm bed of political, moral, administrative and social principle from which a reference produced a logical standpoint in harmony with the rest. He was ready for the Age of Harold Wilson.

Chapter 3

A Rationale of Welfare.
1950–1963; 1975

1 Tory Welfare v. Welfare Socialism

It was one thing for the Conservative leadership, primed by the Butler think-tank, to make promises in the years 1945–51 that when they regained power they would dismantle the war-derived controls, end the rationing, restore competition which would lower prices, unleash private enterprise to generate jobs – all within the new framework of humane codes and charters. It was another thing to work out and offer the electorate a Conservative programme for the social services that would conform to other national priorities, and to Tory principles.

The Conservatives are fond of claiming that they, not the Liberals, or the not yet-existent Labour party, initiated the social reforms in the nineteenth century which bridled the right of employers to do as they liked over hours, conditions, child-employment, machinery-fencing, sanitation and so on, in the name of such doctrines as the wages fund; that it was Disraeli who in 1867 foresaw the Tory working-class voter; that it was the Tories (long before the radicals joined them) who started compulsory state education, and so on. Bones fifty years old are dry. What was remembered against them was unemployment and means tests. Were the Tories merely 'me too' about health, or had they something new on offer?

This question reached down to bedrock Tory feelings about the nature of man, naturally selfish and not perfectible by doctrinaire systems of human rights, claims and privileges, in contrast with the socialist view of humans as intrinsically good, perfectible indeed by the application of a legal structure of rights and claims on society called social justice. The spirit of the age seemed to be against Tory compromise – the social services could be built up the quicker in an expanding economy trimmed of their extravagance. Powell saw here a fundamental and difficult question of political philosophy which had to be thought out if policy was to make sense, however unwelcome the conclusions reached. His conclusions considerably shaped the One Nation manifesto. He was credited in particular with the section entitled 'The redistribution of wealth: rights and duties'; these were developed in detail in the pamphlet 'Social Services: Needs and Means'[1] which, published by the Conservative Political Centre under the joint authorship of Macleod and Powell, is mostly Powell's work. Both subtitles were significant.

Since 1945 political writers have presented the argument between Conservatives and Labour as a question of the placing of the frontier between state and private enterprise, between the share of the state and of private provision for life's hazards; between the rights of private property and the community's interests or priorities, between the so-called private sector and public sector. The Butlerian approach envisaged the setting of this frontier as a matter of bargaining, a form of treaty making, a business deal based on underlying consensus, an acceptance of a mixed economy. Powell never did. To him, where that frontier was set had to be defined firstly in terms of a free society: how big dared you permit the state to become?

Secondly, he did not regard the two parties as simple opposites, the one the negative of the other. The difference was not to be defined in a way that would imply underlying likeness. Socialism (he wrote later, in 1968) is a theory which would be the same for all branches of mankind since its validity (if it has any) must derive from general characteristics of the human species.[2] But conservatism was not the dogma of a right wing party in any continental sense; it was unique, because rooted in British institutions which are unique – a uniqueness derived from 1,000 years of continuous history, which is true of no other nation-state.

A conservative approach to social services has therefore to be rooted in British (or English) experience, and it must take into account the need to conserve the national uniqueness. The starting-point for a difference between the Labour (socialist) approach and the Conservative approach he found in the attitude taken to the redistribution of wealth and income – that is all fiscal and social law which impinges on the structure of the British nation – the attitude to the extent to which it was right to alleviate the condition of the currently poorer, less fortunate, disadvantaged part of the population by distraining upon the wealth, the income, and indeed the less tangible assets of the privileged, or luckier, or better-off sections (not necessarily classes) of the population. Powell examined the social legislation that was justified or defended on this central principle, and rejected it as a universalism whose logic was 'eliminating poverty by providing the same to everybody, with the corollary of forbidding anyone to have anything but the same.'[3] He deplored the insidious permeation of conservative thinking by this socialist doctrine. His destiny as a minister was to wrestle with it, largely in vain.

2   The Insurance Fallacy Exposed

The provision of social services is a particular case of the role of the state. Powell always accepted that the extent of that role was a matter of judgement, and judgement was affected by the circumstances, including technological progress. His concern was to make the frontier between state and non-state very sharp; on one side the criterion was political judgement and administrative control; on the other profit-making and personal effort in competition with everyone else. On one side the minister (ultimately) decided, on the other the market, untrammelled, decided. The Conservative should make the distinction as absolute as possible, wherever the frontier lay; socialists blurred it as a matter of strategy.

On the state side of the frontier, Powell accepted the fact that the provision of social services is redistributive, and that this is true of every service – state education, health, old-age pensions, housing, legal aid and also that element of the 'social wage' represented by subsidies on food, or assistance for children or families. Indeed, the question of who gets most out of, and who pays most for, social services – the net advantage and disadvantage – has become in our time a matter of statistical measurement, and a complex one. Herein lies the essential difference between state services and individual insurance. A person who pays a premium to a company to cover himself against sickness, old age, loss of employment, the education of children, must pay according to actuarial calculations the whole cost of what he gets under an enforcible and invariable contract within the private sector. The more income he has at his disposal after paying for conventional necessities, the more extensive the provision he is able to make. The income available is a function in the main of the taxes of all kinds levied upon him, including that taxation exacted by the government's depreciation of the currency.

Theoretical sink-or-swim *laissez-faire* leaves it to the individual to make *all* provision both for self-improvement and survival. From the first some services – defence, policing functions without which the state is anarchy – are wholly compulsory, financed by tax, delivered to all. Powell made clear 'if *laissez-faire* means that government withdraws from those functions in society which citizens must not or cannot try to perform for themselves, then the Tory party . . . never can be the party of *laissez-faire*'.[4]

The concept that beyond this point – wherever located – the citizen was on his own, influenced the provision of such services as health and old-age pensions. To maintain the principle of 'self-help' the 'insurance principle' was imported into statutory and compulsory arrangement. This meant that even when the state financed the fund out of general taxation before contributions (usually by the stamps method) were sufficient to defray the outpayments to claimants, the payment, even though compulsory, established a right to benefit for all contributors. Powell argued that from the first this 'principle' was a fiction which put many social services on the wrong footing, even though the self-help principle which the schemes imitated fitted conservative principles. The reason was that, as matters worked out, the contribution could *never* provide for the benefit envisaged, which was in practice defrayed from general taxation. The contribution lost its actuarial and contractual status; logically it was just another tax; yet it was treated as conferring entitlement to the full benefit. There are two reasons for this development. The first is that it is the nature of state aid not to be true insurance, because the state is everybody; it is its own insurance; it cannot insure itself with anybody but itself. True insurance is made by an individual or a section. The second reason is that the secular rise in expectations means that old age pensions are no longer fixed at bare subsistence level, as was first done early in the century partly on the presumption that it would encourage people to save for contingencies ('a rainy day') beyond the amount of the compulsory premium or contribution. In western affluent societies voters expect, after a lifetime of work (or availability for work), to live in dignity and some comfort – and in a degree not to be calculated at the point they 'enter the scheme'. The pensioner, in short, expects to have the telly that was not invented when he stuck on his first stamps. This demand may well increase the amount of current production to be diverted to the pensioners; an ageing population affects matters more. Powell analysed the element of subsidy from general revenue in health and pensions insurance benefits and found it overwhelmingly the greater part. He noted the further complication of inflation, even at the level of the fifties, which necessitates the topping up of benefit which cannot be matched in past or in increased current contributions.

It follows that services supplied as of right upon the insurance principle by 'a pantomime of stamp-licking', but financed in reality from taxation, approximate more and more closely in nature to those services which are wholly financed by the taxation of everybody to meet the needs of an unproductive minority – as with education – or by means of subsidies where the minority thus assisted may be less easily identified. 'There is no basis whereby the scheme can be used for its original purpose, to achieve complete independence in old age.'[5] As he showed, one-fifth of those getting benefit from their insurance stamps were already having to be granted supplementary benefit too; and this meant that, considered as poor relief, supplementary benefit had become a larger element in providing for old age in 1952 than in 1900.

Powell drew the conclusion: To regard the financing of the social services as an insurance operation was nonsense. The solution was to recognise the plain truth that *all* social services were paid out of taxation, even if for administrative convenience some was levied by compulsory purchase of stamps, as a 'poll tax'. In such a straightened-out, honest system, the state should only provide 'a minimum but decent sufficiency',[6] which should not be of right but related to means. He went back to the means tests of the nineteen-thirties with a new formula: 'any service that was free should be means tested, any service that was not means tested should be actuarily sound.'[7] Benefits, and tax, should be a minimum, for the more the state did, the less choice was left for the individual, the less incentive to self-help which, *via* investment, would encourage wealth production for the whole nation. Such a principle – the provision of a simple safety net for the unlucky and inadequate – implied that those who put in good money to provide for their own old age or misfortune, should not find that when they needed it, it was bad money, without the purchasing-power to buy the benefits in real terms originally planned for: and this depended on a healthy economy, a sound stock exchange, a supply of state securities in which savings could safely be invested. Then everyone could choose what sacrifices to make now, to provide for what scale of benefit in future. Implicit in this principle was the wrongness of nationalisation which narrowed the choice of investments, and of inflation, which destroys savings.

He believed reform was still possible. 'I see,' he told an interviewer in 1971, 'the automatic old age pension as something which gradually disappears – certainly as a prime instrument of maintenance of the elderly. It would be replaced by a great growth of self-provisions – which includes collective provision. At the other end could be the safeguard of a guarantee of a minimum income. The flat rate benefit is obsolete, repressive of real saving, and a great deal of real saving does take place via insurance'.[8] Powell's conclusions and proposals stand out as the antithesis of socialist theory, and re-read today, measure how far down the road to collectivism the British people have been taken.

The Conservatives were never prepared to face the rigour of his arguments. Instead, they compounded the illogicality and byzantine complexities of the system; they themselves opened the door to further socialism. As the annual cost of paying out benefits rose in the way Powell predicted, the Government in 1961 were constrained to introduce a graduated contributions and benefits scheme simply because the rise in flat-rate benefits would bear more heavily upon the poorer contributors. This entailed the contracting-out by people who had better private schemes than the state graduated scheme. Crossman was thus duly enabled to extend state control under the guise of the insurance principle. Powell brutally took it apart:

> Still masquerading as a glorified insurance scheme like the graduated and flat-rate schemes that went before, it reveals the cloven hoof of rising taxation to meet state-determined claims. 'The rates of contribution,' runs the telltale sentence, 'for any period will be fixed to meet the expected expenditure in that period.' After that almost anything can be called insurance, and we are not surprised to hear that 'among risks . . . which must be pooled is the risk that money will change its value'. Anyone who can be persuaded to regard inflation over the next forty years as an insurable risk, will swallow anything.[9]

Under socialism equality in services is produced by inequality in contribution through taxation. A rising degree of compulsion to use state provision by making impossible or illegal private arrangements, any opting out of the state scheme, in education, health or anything else, logically follows. The destruction of savings by the inflation which these growing state expenditures tends to promote completes the circle: and the logic of socialist thinking leads, as Labour thinkers like Mr Kilroy Silk and Mr Heffer have explained, to the state providing all needs compulsorily out of taxation 'stoppages' – on such a scale as to leave the citizen only pocket-money with which to exercise his choice in the (probably state cooperative) supermarkets. The two systems of thought on welfare stand in stark contrast.

The reality remains blurred and confused. The Conservatives no longer dare talk of safety nets, and means tests are rude words though a regrettable necessity in practice; while Labour is still divided over making all housing and banking a state service. The costly and inefficient compromise which Powell said would have the advantage of neither clear-cut logical scheme, prevails.

3   The Scandal of Housing Subsidy

Powell's first chance to apply his logical analysis to the social services came not in dealing with the insurance principle, but in housing. Powell declared that the 'giant evils' of government rent control[10] and the housing subsidy were responsible for misery and squalor on a scale that baffled calculation. Labour's view was precisely the opposite, that these two marvellous tools of social engineering had ensured cheap accommodation for the needy and homeless on a scale that merely fell short of the ideal; that the persistence of the housing shortage simply argued that there had not been enough subsidy to local authorities to build for rent, and not enough restrictions of the giant evils of private renting and construction for owner-occupation (though it was impolitic to mention the latter point).

The emphatic statement in *One Nation*, influenced by Powell's analysis, that if controls were removed 100,000 more local authority and private (speculatively built) houses could be provided annually led at the party conference of 1950 to the floor forcing the platform to accept a pledge to build the 300,000 a year so shown as possible; and it was Harold Macmillan's forceful fulfilment of this promise after 1951 which set him on the road to the premiership.

But a housing equation in which old, and privately rented houses decayed almost as fast as new houses were rushed up hardly solved the shortage. Powell argued that only if rent restriction was abolished would private landlords have the incentive to build for renting once again, and put money into the maintenance and modernisation of the large stock of decaying rented houses. Powell wanted all housing out of government control: a free market in housing in which demand would naturally generate supply. He was unperturbed by the arguments that no such market could be created, and did not exist anywhere – witness the slums and overcrowding everywhere, in any country, capitalist or socialist. Powell contended[11] that a free market could not produce Rachmanism or rack renting; it would produce the up-to-date, modern, socially acceptable houses that the public wanted, just as the motor industry improved automobiles model by model by model. He contrasted how all other consumer goods had improved as the result of market forces – food, clothing, transport, amusement, furniture, and other durables. The failure of housing was symbolised by the television aerials over rows of obsolete houses, with new washing machines inside and new cars standing outside. For decades people had been prevented from making effective their demand for the one thing they wanted most after food and clothing, in the numbers and choice of quality and style they wanted – houses and flats. As he put it: 'imagine what would have been the fate of our motor industry if the majority of its output since 1920 had been purchased for provision at subsidised prices to persons on 1,500 waiting lists, while all existing cars were compulsorily priced far below replacement cost. You then have some faint and distant conception of the havoc which the nation had inflicted on its house-building industry.'[12] In the teeth of Labour assertions that the private rented house market is 'naturally' disappearing, Powell said that what people most wanted at that time were houses and flats to rent, and it was government interference that artificially choked off the supply. To the assertion that market forces would merely produce speculative profits, harassment and evictions, but no increase in accommodation or modernisation, Powell replied that fifty years of subsidies and rent restriction had created an Augean Stable that could not be flushed out quickly. If housing had commanded its market price in that half-century, the stock in general would have been kept in repair, modernised or replaced like any other 'consumer durable'. Tenants would not occupy houses they could not really afford; everyone would get what he paid for, and there would be no situation in which some were happy beyond their means and even deserts, while as many had nothing at all, or a mere place on a housing list. To the argument that the slums were the product of market forces, he retorted that when 'bad' houses were newly built, there were bad food, bad clothing and other living conditions (though even these might be an improvement on what went before). In some ways 1850 was a nadir; but 'of all that Charles Booth described in London, only housing remains remotely recognisable to-day.'[13] Moreover, the more the subsidisation, the worse the housing often was. In 1970 he told an East Lothian audience, in surveying exceptionally bad conditions, 'You have pretended too long that houses cost less than they really do. Your pretence has been on a vast scale compared even with the pretence in England.'[14]

Neither he nor Sandys at the Ministry of Housing in 1956 were authorised to release market forces in one swoop, however tempting was the prospect that a sweeping declaration that the 1939 emergency was ended would have terminated all rent control, introduced in war-time conditions. Simultaneous contraction of subsidy would have forced local authorities to set rents of council houses at market rates, or to sell them off; at the same time construction for rental would have begun – along with the demolition of bad and obsolescent housing – because such investment would have been made profitable once more.

Powell was therefore compelled to make the best of a half measure. Even so, he introduced the second reading with much pride, though to a rather thin House of Commons as everyone was preoccupied with the aftermath of the Suez fiasco. To him and the rather lack-lustre civil servants at his disposal it seemed that even a half measure might exert disproportionate leverage. They unwisely accepted the Labour claim that there was a near balance in the country *as a whole* between housing and households.[15] But before the bill went into committee both Sandys and Powell had left the Ministry, Powell to the Treasury. The Act had not long been in force before there were complaints that rents and prices were going up, but there was no more accommodation, and that the Tories' perpetual friends, the property developers and speculators, were the real beneficiaries. Powell has always denied that the Act was a foredoomed failure.[16] Indeed without it, he wrote in the *Sunday Times* in 1965, 'housing conditions would be worse to-day than they are' (he could offer no proof). But he agreed that the Act had two weaknesses. The first was that decontrol was partial and gradual. The second was that it did not provide for 'the dramatic and continuing fall in the age of marriage and the rise in the birth-rate which began about 1956 and swept over the limits, low as they were in any case pitched, which the Act fixed for permitted rents, and which there was no mechanism for adjusting if the value of money fell, or demand rose.'[17]

In the result the Party leadership backed down and tied its own hands with a promise that there would be no further decontrol – which was what was needed to remedy the Act's inefficacy. Powell sadly concluded that 'no political party can yet make the restoration of a free market in housing' its policy.[18]

The history of housing from 1964 to 1978 has, nonetheless, confirmed Powell's diagnosis. The privately rented sector has continued to shrink from organised unprofitability, so that the legitimate demands of, for example, transients, visitors and persons who must be mobile, as well as those who cannot yet buy a house or get a council letting, are frustrated. The same nostrum, animated by a doctrinaire loathing for 'landlordism', has been applied to furnished accommodation even in private houses; the security of tenure given by statute to tenants, their ability to keep owners out of all or part of their property, to break contracts by appeals to housing tribunals on grounds of 'need' and to thus become another privileged class, has caused a further huge slice of accommodation to be withdrawn from the market and left more or less idle (or offered surreptitiously to foreign visitors who must leave on a due date). The subsidisation of council house rents has had to increase as costs of building have risen; rent arrears increase the burden of rates; and the result of massive interference has increased homelessless and the scandals of squatting. Powell pointed out in the 1950s that housing should not be in politics at all – it should be a market function only.[19] Today it has become an intense and bitter political issue, with resulting illwill, lawlessness, misery and squalor. This has if anything increased the Labour belief that housing ought to be a social service wholly provided by the state.

Since 1964, the Labour solution has been the nationalisation of development land. Powell destroyed the argument that this would make housing cheaper on the plain fact that the price of houses depends on supply and demand for them, and that it is this which determines the value of the land on which they are erected. Labour's objective was to acquire – to nationalise – all owner-occupier houses by restricting the residual right of freehold only to the immediate heirs of the occupier, suitably defined. 'The site is to belong to the owner-occupier as long as the house stands, but only so long. How many houses will be pulled down and replaced on those terms? No more powerful inducement can be imagined to keep worn-out and obsolete property in existence and in use'[20] – the slumdom of the socialist future.

Labour's concession to owner-occupiers was dictated by their voting-power. Just as the Conservatives shrank from the interim unpopularity of restoring a free market in housing, and confessing the egregious errors made by all subsidy-minded governments since 1919, so the Socialists could not convert housing into an institutionalised social service at one blow by nationalising millions of owner-occupiers who might vote them out (including a growing number of black Labour-minded owner-occupiers). Such an action would remove almost the last protection that the ordinary citizen ineligible for a fully index-linked, inflation-proof pension has against the destruction of his savings by inflation. The Labour plan must be to take over the owner-occupied sector by the same means whereby they successfully destroyed the rented private sector, and liquidated the landlord classes. Restriction would destroy the market in freeholds, and prepare the way for compulsory purchase of unsellable or deteriorating property.

4   State and Private Medicine

Powell's argument that only a free market in housing could provide adequate accommodation for everyone, and his acceptance of responsibility for the nationalised health and hospital services, may seem inconsistent. But all that Powell has admitted about the National Health Service is that

> the general public interest in seeing that medical care is provided for the members of society in a great range of situations is not open to dispute and has been long and widely recognised. . . . As medical care by its nature may be a necessity of life no less than food or shelter, the medical needs of the individual are to that extent a necessary subject of public concern; and the step from public concern to public provision is an easy one.[21]

His experiences as Minister of Health enabled him to see what social and administrative consequences followed that step from concern to provision by nationalisation. His analysis of the workings of the system, *Medicine and Politics*, which appeared in 1966, posed the inherent conflict between needs and means; it has been much quoted for and against equivalent forms of public provisions, such as Medicare in the USA.

Surprise was occasioned by the pessimism the book expressed about the future of private medicine, and he provided in it an *ex post facto* defence of his own rejection, when minister, of the Conservative Party's proposals for subsidising or sustaining the private sector specifically to maintain an alternative to the state near-monopoly.[22] In 1975 Powell did not oppose the Labour Party policy of ending pay beds and excising the remaining overlap between state and private medicine which among others he had accepted as a British compromise when he first became Minister of Health.

His reasons for endorsing a complete separation between the public and private sectors show that *Medicine and Politics* is no fatalistic acquiescence in nationalisation, but a deadly critique of it. In 1966 Powell faced the factors which made the future for a competitive commercial medical sector seem dubious then. But in 1975 the further development of the state service towards a near-monopoly, and the growing dissatisfaction with its bureaucratisation, led him to think that a commercial alternative was becoming viable, and also, just as important, that a completely separate service would be much harder insidiously to absorb into the state system, ultimately leading to the denial of the right for an individual, however qualified, to sell (or buy) medical care. The construction of such a bulwark he regarded as being of first importance. Its counterpart in education, the choice between going fully independent and surrendering to comprehensivisation which was put to maintained schools, made private education a viable and defensible competitor to the growing inflexibilities and the declining performance (however disputed by educationalists) of much of the state system. There was an obvious moral in both cases for the legal professions. He had exposed the 'phenomena' of free medical care, particularly the open and covert rationing of it, and in *Medicine and Politics* he prefaced his rejection of the alternatives then proposed with the words:

> A great part of my argument has been to show that these phenomena are implicit in such an organisation and are not the accidental or incidental results of 'blemishes' which can be reformed away while leaving the system as such intact. If those phenomena are judged unacceptable, the rejoinder must be Hamlet's 'Oh, reform it altogether'.[23]

It was not appreciated in 1966 what Powell meant, but by 1975 it *was* clearer: competition by a quality of service worth paying for.

Macmillan's choice of Powell for Minister of Health in 1960 was acclaimed as an example of the Prime Minister's knowledge of men. It was part of a reshuffle that brought pro-marketeers in strength into the Cabinet (to which Powell, unlike Macleod before him was not immediately elevated, so he was not closely concerned with Europe at first) while Macleod was entrusted with the liquidation of the African Empire. Powell's membership of the government silenced his dangerous commentaries on financial policy, and he was kept away from the Treasury. He had a spending department, but his reputation for economy was enlisted to hold down the rising cost of health. Thus everything fitted.

Powell was set the task of doing something to the service within a tight budget if he was to emerge as an outstanding minister; he seemed to have a clear field for little had been done to the service since Macleod, and Macleod did very little.

5 Free State Health is Rationed Health

The Tory recipe for the Health Service in *One Nation* was written by Macleod; it was hardly distinguished by clarity of purpose, or by insight into the implications of nationalisation. It had not taken in the lesson of the school dentist service which it proposed to revive; it urged an increase in aftercare and rehabilitation through welfare clinics, and the inclusion of industrial health in a comprehensive service. Formally right in saying that 'we have at present a service to cure ill-health. We need a service to promote good health',[24] it did not analyse the cost or consequences. It was left to Powell to make this analysis of what was a socialist compromise: a centralised state service headed by a minister responsible to Parliament taking policy decisions carried out by an administrative machine, but with elements of independence built into it in the form of the contractual status of general practitioners, and in some other ways.

The service, praised by Powell initially at least for its fine old English illogicality,[25] became the channel through which by 1960 the overwhelming proportion of that fraction of the national income devoted to the cure of sickness and protection of health was directed. Powell's first question, to get down to fundamentals again, was exactly what that fraction *ought* to be – he found the question meaningless. The idea that resources devoted to health had any direct influence on wealth did not stand up: the NHS was designed to do something not utilitarian (as the veterinary services do); what it does is to meet part of the obligation of a civilised society to take care of its sick, old, handicapped, unfortunate and its children. This definition of the NHS fitted his criterion for a Tory approach to welfare: health had been placed within the frontier where state provision must rule, as in education, defence or even sewerage; though its exclusivity was a matter for argument. This principle initially conceded, the problem was one of efficiency and method; until the working of a system of free medical aid was understood, no final judgement could be made.

The question of assessing need and resources, however, could not be judged in isolation. The more one social service has, the less another. In his study of the Welfare State in 1961 Powell quoted with approval words from the Plowden Report on the Control of Public Expenditure: 'The social changes in the last fifteen years have altered the incidence of hardship, so that there may now well be excessive social services for some purposes and inadequate ones for others.' He noted that the allocation of resources between forms of welfare dated from 1942–4, and this had underestimated some post-war needs, particularly those of the prison service and the care of the aged.

> It may not be a popular view, but I would dare to say that prisons are our most important and also our most deficient social service. Here, whatever else is obscure, the need . . . is indisputable . . . and [new] methods cry out for more and more exploration.[26]

The passage of a further fifteen years, the secular rise in the crime rate by 8–10 per cent a year, has shown these words to be prophetic. No less prescient was his argument that an almost new service needed to be designed for the old in a fast-ageing population:

the problem of how the necessary support, which in different circumstances the old would obtain in the setting of a family or closely-knit village community, can be available to these millions of ageing individuals isolated in a modern industrial society.[27]

He saw it as being as much a physical and moral as a financial problem – and the conditions of the geriatric departments in the NHS have grimly shown how right he was.

The appetite of the Health Service for funds is voracious; unique among the social services, it

is rendered free to the consumer at the point of consumption – apart, that is, from spectacles and certain dental treatment and appliances. Consequently supply and demand are not kept in balance by price. Since, therefore, resources are limited . . . while demand is unlimited supply has to be rationed by other means than price.[28]

Earlier assumptions (by Beveridge, for example) that a fixed quantity of medical care was needed (about £400 million worth in the scheme's inception) and, once met, no more would be demanded, proved wildly wrong. Statistical limits can be set to education or old age – by for example demography. But Powell realised that not only is there 'virtually no limit to the amount of medical care an individual is capable of absorbing' in any one period, but in addition 'every advance in medical science creates new needs that did not exist until the means of meeting them came into existence'. Many of these new needs, like kidney or other organ transplants, relate to preserving or lengthening that most precious thing of all, life itself.

During his term of office the disaster of the prescription of thalidomide to pregnant women occurred, but it was a decision made entirely out of ministerial purview, confined to the provision of resources. The advice on the drug came from the West Hendon Research Centre. Powell resisted the call for a state drug testing and authorising authority, and set up the expert Dunlop Committee which exercised surveillance on behalf of the profession over the introduction of new drugs.

Two consequences follow for the minister from an unlimited demand for 'health'. One is that he is made responsible for the inevitable rationing, and urged to ease it – to reduce waiting lists – and secondly he is under unceasing pressure by the doctors for more facilities – equipment, hospital beds, staff – both to reduce this rationing and to make possible the new treatments which create still newer needs, new waiting lists; and once the service is nationalised, all idea of conserving resources, as in other government operations, promptly disappears.

Powell summed it up in the story of his visit to a privately financed laboratory. It was cramped and crowded. With his tongue in his cheek Powell reported

> As Minister of Health I instinctively expected to be assailed before crossing the theshold with complaints of inadequacy and underpayment of staff ('How can people be expected to work in conditions like these?' 'How can we recruit staff on the rates we are allowed to offer?'). To my bewilderment the chemist in charge proceeded to demonstrate with pride and pleasure a series of devices by which he had contrived to get a quart out of a pint pot, and appeared highly satisfied with the opportunities his position afforded him and his assistants. I could not help reflecting sadly how all this would change if the Exchequer ever took responsibility for maintaining or even assisting the work.[29]

In consequence Powell found that the only subject he was ever destined to discuss with the medical profession was money – not even salaries, but the demand for resources; even Ministers of Education could, he said bitterly, sometimes discuss education.

Like other Ministers of Health, Powell at first thought it was his duty to try to reduce waiting lists; he soon saw that waiting lists were essential to a free medical service. (Just as they are to a subsidised housing service.) Some waiting is necessary to the efficient use of hospital resources, but it

> can be viewed as a kind of iceberg: the significant part is that below the surface – the patients who are not on the list at all, either because they are not accepted on the grounds that the list is too long already or because they take a look at the queue and go away. . . . It might be thought macabre to observe that if people are on a waiting list long enough they will die – usually from some cause other than that for which they joined the queue. Short of dying, however, they frequently get bored or better, and vanish . . . time on the waiting list is a commutation not only for money – measurable by the cost of private treatment with little or no delay – but also for the other good things of life.[30]

Powell found that however much was spent, whatever changes were made, waiting lists between 1951 and 1965 were steady at around 480,000 on 31 December each year. By 1978 waiting lists for serious operations or treatments had begun to develop.

The waiting list expresses the balance between the capacity of a free service and the potential demand upon it. The lower the point of balance falls, the slower the treatment of 'less urgent' cases until, in certain conditions, hospitals may accept life-or-death cases only. This is all much clearer to all of us than when Powell analysed the service as the result of unionised hospital workers' and doctors' 'industrial action', strikes or work-to-rule.

> What are called the 'deficiencies' of the NHS . . . are those consequences of the quantity and quality of medical care being purchased by the state that help

to equate the demand with the supply. The supply of medical care of all kinds through the NHS is rationed by forcing the potential consumer to choose between accepting the quantity and quality offered or declining the care offered. If he declines . . . he can either renounce or defer treatment . . . or . . . endeavour to purchase it outside the NHS.[31]

6 Powell and Bureaucracy

But even the additional resources supplied were misused and partly wasted by the growth of bureaucracy, of which, as Minister in 1960–1963 Powell only saw an early phase – but he was early alarmed, as was natural in a friend of C. Northcote Parkinson. He saw in 1963 that 'policies which are formed centrally and executed administratively are bound to be slower to change and less adaptable . . . than if responsibility was diffused and decisions were independent,[32] and for this reason he applauded even the illogicality of the NHS which allowed elements of independence to be built into the service – the contractual status of the GPs, the separate representation of the doctors in the structure of the hospital and executive council services, the power of the professional colleges (he ought to have added the autonomy of the teaching hospitals), everything that, in the 1970s was eroded or swept away.

Even by 1965, however, Powell was pessimistic about stopping the march to a monolithic state system, which would give nobody satisfaction except the well-paid ever-proliferating administrators (and union shop stewards). He noted that the administration through local boards of governors and management committees was enhancing centralisation, their independence nominal. And all his efforts to find a measure for efficiency were baffled by the complexity of hospital operations.

Powell put his finger on an abiding reason for professional discontent; it was not that the decisions were lay decisions – they had to be, since they involved taxpayers' money – it was the uniform application of the decisions, right or wrong. It was rigidity, the end of experiment and improvision, and of the local variety that would teach better methods. It was precisely the flexibility of the old hospitals' lay governors that had met the doctors' approval under the old system; and, though Powell and other ministers did not always accept this plea, the petty rigidity of the local government hospitals made them a byword for bad treatment and the subordination of new ideas to the seniority rule. Indeed, it was the pride that the unwitting local officials and public felt in 'their' hospitals that misled him: bumbledom can be a miniaturised version of nationalisation. The position is now inevitably worse. The other source of professional irritation – loss of morale – is the slowness of decisions, which continually grows, as the committee system proliferates under Whitehall rules.

So potent is the thrall of a so-called 'free' service, so ignorant must public and patients be of its shortcomings (to the point of disintegration) and so great the state's near monopoly (98 per cent of the country's total health expenditure) that

Powell in 1966 could see no hope of ameliorating its inherent defects by providing alternatives. He rejected subsidies to private medicine (by tax relief or access to free prescriptions) on the grounds that even to double the private sector would leave it ineffective to force state medicine to provide a better service, yet would require money that would be either withdrawn from state medicine – which was impossible in view of the magnitudes and pressures – or be a net addition to the total cost of all medicine.

For similar reasons he rejected the arguments for allowing taxpayers who were going to private doctors to contract out of the NHS element of the contribution. This represented only 13 per cent of the cost of the service, and even patients who had renounced it would still remain dependent on it in many respects. Moreover, were it allowed, it would have the effect of excluding the 'good risks' of the service, leaving it with an undue proportion of chronically sick and dependent. This would mean levying more taxation to make up the loss.

Powell ended his period at the Ministry gloomy about the prospects of the service, but convinced that it could not be improved by piecemeal reforms or tinkering; lack of the competitive factor rendered dissatisfaction with the service endemic, frustrating for the profession and bound to remain a political battlefield, with the public and the professionals ranged against the minister and the civil servants. He pondered on the possibility of an alternative system, and found that neither of the candidates offered an escape. In the first place he did not see any prospect for denationalising health and returning it to private enterprise or even to a better 'mixed economy'. He examined first the proposals that private medicine should in various ways (by subsidies, by tax relief, by paying for prescriptions) be made a less expensive alternative than it was, and of course still is. He rejected this on the grounds that the amount of private medical care is barely 2 per cent of the NHS, and that even if it greatly increased, the NHS would still need the same budget; therefore the money given to the private sector would be a net increase to that budget, or a reduction in the quality of the NHS, to compensate for the cuts. When a Conservative delegation came to Powell in 1962 to urge that private patients should have their prescriptions met by the NHS, which they thought he favoured, he told them bluntly that he did not think such a subsidy would increase the size of the private sector enough to relieve the public system.

'As long as the decision stands to make a service or benefit available at the public charge,' he contended, 'no group of taxpayers can contract out of their implied share of the burden.'[33] This reasoning could only be overturned if the whole service were financed by contributions on an adequate actuarial basis, which is impossible as he had shown in his book with Iain Macleod.

For the same reason, it was impossible to reduce the subsidy to state health by, for example, making everybody pay the full (or a larger) cost of prescriptions, for existing charges, while a slight deterrent to waste, do not affect the huge general budget: the extra charge would amount only to a minor tax. It would not make private medicine competitive, he concluded, because that competition 'takes place across the barrier of the difference in cost between virtually nil and a market price, and is confronted by the embodiment in the nationalised service of virtually all the pre-existing hospitals.' And, as he anticipated, these circumstances have brought about the gradual decline in private medicine. But the deterioration in the state service accelerated too, for reasons Powell did not mention. One is competition – the competition for good British doctors and nurses by American hospitals and clinics, and after 1976, of the EEC medical services, offering larger salaries and lower taxes.

Powell pointed out that at a given remuneration the state service got a given quantity and quality of medical professional (and other) staff. His concern was to show that the service did not 'value' their work at so much; this was a condition of offer and acceptance. But equally if remuneration lags behind, quantity and quality fall off; more doctors emigrate, less well qualified doctors are imported from the New Commonwealth (see p. 110).

He did not discuss why the remuneration given to the administrators had to be so much higher than the professionals (which produces the complaint 'that's all you think our life-and-death work is worth'), though in a state bureaucracy it is inevitable that the civil servants will pay themselves better than anybody else; this was not true of the voluntary hospitals. By 1975 Powell saw, on the other hand, that trade union interference in hospitals was so bad for the 'free' service that new possibilities were opening up for the 'commercial' service.

In 1973 the process of nationalisation was brought almost to the limits that Powell had feared were inevitable. Health was taken out of the hands of local government entirely. New area authorities became agents of the minister. Powell had always thought there were some elements of independence in the decentralised system; in the event the new authorities have slowed down decisions even more, and the capacity of the teaching hospitals – amalgamated with the rest in 1973 – to search for excellence is being destroyed in the dead level of uniformity, congenitally preferred by an administration to awkward excrescences of excellence. It is now predicted that the international reputation of British medicine has been fatally undermined.

Depressed by this picture, some legislators suggested that the new larger local authorities created in 1972 could now take over the local health services, leaving the Ministry to coordinate, on the lines of education. Powell, who had opposed the local government bill as unnecessary, pointed out that no conceivable system of block grants or local taxation could enable such authorities to finance the health services. He was gloomy, and told the House of Commons:

These then are the three major losses – the growth of bureaucracy, the loss of independent sources of initiative and authority in the health services, and the removal of a major function from local government . . . the loss of things which once destroyed cannot easily be restored.[34]

The depressed condition of the family doctor, Powell in 1966 ascribed to the dilemmas posed by the system: the GP on his own combined private enterprise and state service without the advantage of either. Contrary to the original hopes of the BMA, the GP cannot build up a practice and reputation that enables him to reap the rewards of his effort in either income or satisfaction. The better he does his work, the worse off he is. If he improves his facilities or reduces his list to give better service to patients, he loses financially, and doctors who do neither – who are downright unscrupulous – gain, and even at his expense. The capitation fee denies him a salary, paid-for premises, and promotion. He cannot often have a private practice, unlike the consultants who (in London) can do so on top of the other advantages. In satisfaction, he had lost his traditional partnership and equal status with consultants, for they are not obliged to him for patients, and he has no access to beds – or even information. Powell predicted that the loss of the cash nexus would make the GP's embodiment in the salaried service inevitable; it might be hastened even by the separation of state from private medicine.

7   Against a State Monopoly of Health

But Powell's hopes from that separation may also be dashed. He does not believe – as so many doctors do – that the interplay of private and state practice helps both: that private practice, pay beds, and the former peculiarities of the teaching hospital were the 'leaven that leavened the lump'. Private medicine does rely on the ever more costly special equipment reserved to the state hospitals, with which it can rarely compete; it largely exists to jump the queue, get round the rationing, besides living on the reputation for British medicine that brings in high fee payers from the newly affluent countries (and the foreign abortion-seekers). Undoubtedly the egalitarians in the Labour Party, and the marxists in the trade unions, wish to end this remnant of the privilege of money to buy health. 'All to the wall – all to the general ward', is their cry – except, of course, for the TUC's own private clinics. It is here, as Powell points out, that politics and medicine find a new context for struggle: the liberty of the qualified individual to sell, and the patient to buy, medicine. 'The main battlefield,' Powell remarks in his 1975 postscript, 'is thereby marked out in stark ideological terms.'[35] Thus, after thirty years, the nationalisation of health care ends in a fight on principle, private enterprise versus monopoly socialism.

Powell's analysis of the NHS is an integral element in his case for the market, for choice, for individual freedom, for, in fact, capitalism. Down the ages, in laying out their resources, men have traditionally been prepared to pay for health, and pay in some conditions almost anything to avoid death; are such reactions, reflected in a cash nexus, so wrong? The place of commercial medicine is still undetermined: the frontier between what the state takes on economic considerations and the private sector where the market registers the balance of supply and demand, is unsettled. But Powell recognises that there is considerable political high potential behind the concept of the welfare state, and of course he accepts that legislation must reflect ultimately the will of the electorate, wise or unwise. In his Morecambe 'budget' of 1968, in which he reduced income tax to 4s 3d ($21\frac{1}{2}$ p) in the £ by handing back state operations to private enterprise, he pointed out that he had made the reductions without cutting a single one of the social services. Vicky's powellian axe fell entirely outside the welfare state.

Chapter 4

The Cause and Cure of Inflation, 1950–1968

1 Delimiting *Laissez-faire* and State Control

'An almost unlimited faith in the ability of people to get what they want through price, capital, profit and a competitive market,' was Powell's own definition of powellism. He explained that 'this mode of self-expression is congenial to Toryism, not because of any theoretical beauty or academic precision in such a system, but because it enables a great range of changes to be absorbed currently, *ambulando*, by people themselves . . . it recognises and seeks to live with, a built-in dilemma of human nature and human society'.[1] For the market overcomes the resistance to change – which has its legitimacy and is rather strong in British society – with a minimum of compulsion and regulation; it keeps law-making down.

This proposition lies at the bottom of Powell's often repeated and as often deprecated assertion that the Conservative Party is the party of capitalism, and should glory in it, because capitalism is an integral constituent of free institutions, of modern mass democracy.[2] Powell (perhaps a little carried away by what he knew was the theoretical elegance of 'this wonderful, silent automative system – this computer') always enjoyed being solemnly adjured that *laissez-faire* was not a Tory but a Liberal–Radical ideal; that the Tories, as opposed to the Whigs, were the regulators and interferers in defence of principles based on property and order and not on competition and market forces. His answer was that what was congenial to Toryism before the industrial revolution is necessarily different after such a revolution (what are revolutions for?). The defences of liberty change, not the defence of it.

Powell always returned to the proper role of the state: only to make non-economic decisions appropriate to its own sector – defence, external and internal, the social services, humane correctives, overriding policies like the redistribution of income, and not to take, or interfere in, economic decisions in the private sector. He defined permissible state interference in the economic field as a set of Queensbury rules – not itself entering the ring and knocking out the boxers, without gloves on; he was precise:

> The division between the kind of non-economic decision which limits the economic field and that which denies its existence is that between general

prescription and particular instruction. No woman shall work underground in a mine; every employer shall provide towels with washbasins; every employer and employee shall provide 10s a week for the sick, retired and unemployed; no one shall build in the green belt. By all these decisions a boundary line is drawn within which economic criteria apply. . . . On the other hand decisions taken on non economic grounds – that steamship companies shall build a lot more large liners, or motor cars be manufactured on Snowdon . . . require . . . that economic criteria shall be displaced altogether and the actions of individuals positively determined.[3]

General prescription was in the unfolding Tory tradition of uniting the 'two nations' by factory and truck acts and all that followed on. Particular instruction was the active principle of socialism, leading towards totalitarianism. Or, to modify Hayek, the road *back* to serfdom; *from* contract *to* status. In logic the two were mutually exclusive. Powell stated that 'to get the best results in the economic field decisions must be wholly centralised or left wholly to the interplay of individual choice.'[4] Hence followed his famous axiom, quoted often out of context: 'The Conservative in principle denies, in practice minimises, Government intervention in the economic field.'[5]

His party preferred fuzziness to such cold fundamental thinking. The Conservatives felt apologetic about the depression; Macmillan found it good politics to parade his bleeding conscience in the matter. Keynes was the talisman, because he was reputed to have reconciled a measure of capitalism with overall government control, full employment with a conditional but considerable business freedom: the 'mixed economy', the middle way. Conservative MPs might not have read or grasped Keynes, but it was assumed Powell did not either. However, Powell in 1954 persuaded the One Nation group to examine the 'mixed economy', arguing that the extent to which Government interference by both parties before and since the war needed to be set out and subjected to a critique.

He wanted to identify just how far down the road to serfdom Britain had gone. He was the moving spirit in *Change is Our Ally*, published by One Nation in May 1954.[6] It had a clear purpose, to assess the practice and performance of 'planning' and consider how far market forces could be restored, and the state evacuate the field of economic decisions. It is fundamental to Powell's arguments – to powellism.

The book, based on an impressively detailed reading of reports, statutes and Royal Commission findings, if not on Keynes, defined the amalgamations and 'rationalisation' of industry from 1919 to 1939 under state pressure which prefigured nationalisation later, especially in coal. It described and passed judgement on wartime planning and controls; it went on to examine the nationalisation of coal, transport, steel, land and power. Powell found no evidence that the enforced concentrations of the inter-war years had done anything to prevent the incipient 'English sickness', the national industrial decline. The war could not have been won without centralised control: but

Powell pointed inexorably to the reason for its comparative success: compulsory direction of labour. He denied that planning had necessarily made the best of national presources, and he dissected the mistakes made during the war in post-war forecasting: that is, he identified the previous failures of the planners and forecasters and their techniques which were to play such a role in the post-war period; it was the first of many such exercises he was to undertake.

Change is Our Ally recommended denationalisation of steel, and praised, but critically, the partial unscrambling of transport and town and country planning: it opposed the subsidy of any part of the transport system by any other part – but did not attempt to take account of the 'social costs' of transferring more and more transport to the road system; it was an accountancy solution. For coal, it accepted nationalisation with something of the resignation that Powell subsequently felt for nationalised health; the solution it offered was competition between coalfields and collieries in delivered prices, so that the weaker could fail. The problem was not so tackled and remains unsolved to this day, the Coal Board forced to subsidise too many uneconomic units.

Powell's analysis showed that Britain needed more new industries – new small inventive firms by the thousand – to adjust to and compensate for the decline that was accelerating in shipbuilding and textiles and the former engineering stables. It did not foresee the rise of Japan and Asia in electronics, or realise that the British car industry was reaching its peak: few businessmen did. But change involved new firms, and new firms meant profitable investment: 'the essential condition for future stability in this country is industrial flexibility. . . . Our great anxiety now is the future earning power of . . . industry.'

And indeed, that was the coming trouble – the continued long decline in the share of profits, and therefore, of investment in the national share-out. The book also asked if management was enterprising enough, and union leadership expansion-minded; these points were facets of each other and on both Britain was to fail in the later sixties. Everything Powell later said was foreshadowed in the conclusion of 1954: 'if change is to be effective it must be a gradual process, an organic growth of existing institutions'. The elements of the process were competition, profit, risk-taking and investment. Conservatism had to put all of them back into the capitalism which Powell insisted it stood for.

2   With Keynes in the Treasury

Powell came to his appointment as Financial Secretary to the Treasury in 1957 with a firm grounding in (what are called) classical economics; and now, among other things, he began to bring his mind to bear upon the prevailing orthodoxy of finance: the theories of J. M. Keynes. The Treasury in 1957 had not then recruited the hundreds of young economists from the universities that now provide its expertise. Powell mostly found civil servants whose training was in the classics, and who had picked up their economics, their understanding of finance and accountancy, currency and credit, on the job. They had absorbed the doctrine that full employment could be maintained by credit policy (as did the One Nation group). What others came to call 'stop-go' later, had then the ambitious Keynesian term 'fine tuning'. The economy was seen as a well trained orchestra for the Treasury to conduct. Keynes's proposals were formulated to deal with an economy in which much unemployed labour, capital and other resources persisted against a background of stable or falling world price levels; accordingly his prescription (less original than is sometimes supposed) was a delicately controlled credit expansion by a regime of budgetary deficits. It fell to Powell to argue, against the Treasury orthodoxy, how inapposite such treatment was in the inflationary post-war period.

That period was a turning point, as *Change is Our Ally* had sensed. The forties had been a period of growth in non-economic expenditure. The fifties had seen the 'bonfire of controls' which had 'set the people free'. There had been full, some thought overfull, employment for a decade (immigrants were pouring in, indeed being recruited, to fill vacancies which British workers could not or would not.) An economy growing at 3 per cent a year would double in size in twenty-five years, by 36 per cent in ten; politicians' hopes were high – Powell shared them – that rising production and standards of living would keep social tensions low. But to promote commercial expansion, the drain on resources and profits by central and local government should be kept down; and this, it seemed to the new Chancellor, Peter Thorneycroft, to Powell and Nigel Birch (who was the Economic Secretary), was the task Macmillan had given to them. Macmillan, it seems, was thinking simply of getting the economy into order for rapid re-expansion according to the formula of Keynes.

But there was a big difference between 1937 and 1957. Powell did his calculations against a background of rising prices. Between 1952 and 1957 the general price level had risen on average by $3\frac{1}{2}$ per cent a year; this was inflation – an expansion in money unbacked by a proportionate increase in production. The reasons for this inflation were much debated. To many observers, noting full employment and rising production, it seemed tolerable. To others it looked dangerous, especially because there was no agreement on its causality. There were two identifiable schools of thought, which exist today. The first thought that wages and prices chased each other upwards in a 'vicious spiral'. The answer was either restraint by the trade unions of 'leapfrogging' wage claims, or an incomes policy.

The second school was the monetarist one, which believed that the expansion of the money supply should be restricted to the volume growth of the economy. But the prescriptions of this school were complicated by Britain's balance of payments in a period when the value of the pound against external currencies, notably the dollar, was fixed. In 1957–8 Thorneycroft and Powell were to live through a case history of this condition. The demand for imports was strong – because monetary expansion in previous years had made general consumption expansive (the revolution of rising expectations). The British economy was unable to produce and sell enough exports to pay for the imports that consumers and industry demanded, or to provide enough home-made goods to sop up much of the extra demand, which indeed competed with exporters for a slow-growing supply. The trade gap widened, foreigners sold sterling, and reserves began to flow rapidly out (in payment in part of bills falling due). The Treasury's answer was to raise the bank rate, restrict credit, reduce business activity, slow the demand for labour and halt wage demands – artificially induce a fall in imports and a rise in exports. Though a clumsy way of restoring balance, it was the only one known to the Treasury, since it was unthinkable either to devalue the pound, or 'float' it and let it find its own level at which imports and exports balanced. In the autumn of 1957 the familiar sterling crisis recurred; but Macmillan and the Cabinet, fearful of unpopularity, did not want corrective measures to be drastic.

But in November, in a speech at Newcastle, the Financial Secretary emphasised the requirements of a non-inflationary budget which he amplified in articles and speeches in the years ahead. 'There are three main classes of exchequer commitment: current expenditure, investment financed by the exchequer, and maturing debt. Unless all three are met – if not more than met – by taxation or non-inflationary borrowing, inflation is promoted.'[7] If the government reduced taxation, as its policy was to continue to do, it must either reduce expenditure or borrow by tapping the savings of the community with government stock that individuals and institutions would buy for its intrinsic worth in competition with the rest of the market for savings. Such borrowing became maturing debt to be later paid off out of revenue – from taxation ultimately. He urged the public to become more responsible about expenditure, to stop asking for cuts in general and to start opposing particular items. 'I suggest that until inflation is definitely halted every proposal that means higher expenditure in the Budget ought instantly to be met by critical questioning, and if need be by protest and contradiction. It is by this test of self-discipline that we shall succeed or fail in restoring for ourselves . . . honest money.'[8] There needed to be no doubt that within the Treasury the Financial Secretary was setting the public an example.

Powell at this stage, however, was not as completely convinced that inflation was entirely and exclusively related to the budget as he later became. He had to account for the objection that inflation was worldwide, and could, so it was thought, be imported and exported along with goods and capital funds. In December 1957 he discussed the contrast between the stable monetary values that prevailed before 1914, and to a great extent between the wars, as an argument that stable prices did not inhibit growth, that Keynesian credit policies were not the sole prophylactic against stagnation. But he noted in 1965 that

With the second world war there began what we can now see to have been a new phase in which a downward trend in money value has operated more strongly . . . than in any period since the sixteenth century. Not all the causes of this new phase are yet known or understood. Nor are all of them directly within the control of governments, still less the outcome of deliberate government decisions. What is clear is that our contemporary monetary system lends itself more readily than those of earlier periods to action by governments and others which results in debasement of the currency . . .[9]

When this speech was republished for a second time in his collection *Freedom and Reality* in 1969 he put brackets round the words 'and others', and appended a note to explain that he had subsequently come to reject the conventional view that public consumption or banking decisions could be a cause (rather than one of the consequences of) inflation: only governments were responsible for inflation and for currency debasement; they made the effective decisions, whatever the pressures on them. Powell already considered that Keynesianism, or rather its contemporary version, produced the temptation to finance by inflation the demand for more and more social services and higher material standards 'at a greater rate than the nation is willing to make possible out of its production by taxes and saving'. This message he was trying to get across to the Prime Minister.

Macmillan believed that Powell had the Chancellor of the Exchequer in some baleful thrall, and that the Treasury had been put into hair shirts, when after Christmas Throneycroft told the Cabinet that he was not prepared to approve estimates for government expenditure for the coming year (1958–9) at a total higher than was spent in the current (1957–8) year, because he regarded limitation of state expenditure as the prerequisite for the stabilisation of prices. This was therefore to be the second orthodox budget in succession. It meant that if one department spent more another had to spend less – and all had ideas for expansion. But none more so than Duncan Sandys, now defence minister, who needed a large capital expenditure to carry through his plan to substitute reliance upon nuclear weaponry for conventional forces; his claims that there would be ultimate economies left the Treasury with heavy costs in the year ahead. After horse trading between departments, there remained a gap (afterwards alleged by the Treasury ministers' opponents to be as little as £50 million) between Thorneycroft's 'cash limits' and those of his colleagues. He resigned on the point of principle, not the sum, but told his juniors they need not. They did: they were both identified with a policy in which the government could not support them. They refused to rebel; they remained firmly loyal; theirs was an old-fashioned resignation on a point of policy.

3 Basics of Monetarism

In the end they proved to be right. But not immediately. In 1958–9 world trade recovered and Britain's balance of payments with it. The new Chancellor obediently reflated, and far beyond £50 million, but Powell was able to show that the money and credit so created had lain idle and 'once again we have been denied the privilege of observing a government coping with a recession on Keynesian lines'.[10] Macmillan, finding no disaster followed from the Treasury resignations, was thus able genially to dispose of his 'little local difficulties', and was prepared to allow the trio to 'work their passage back', less than two years afterwards offering Powell a minor ministerial post, which he rejected, not because it was minor, but because he felt he could not accept a new appointment until Thorneycroft also enjoyed the Prime Minister's confidence again.

Honours were thus even; but Powell had become an acknowledged expert on public finance and on the problem of inflation which made him a valued contributor to the *Investor's Chronicle* and the *Financial Times*; the City's doors opened to him; he became a director of the Bestwood Company and the Commonwealth Unit Trust.

But the intellectual problem remained to be solved, in or out of office: the relation between government finance, the money supply and inflation. It is a problem on which economists continue to disagree enjoyably. Powell concentrated on the way in which government manufactured money by bogus borrowing. He watched the reality of the 'net borrowing requirement' by successive chancellors, and in 1965 summed up the true relationship between savings and government borrowing:

> Every Chancellor of the Exchequer . . . sets out to raise less in taxes than he proposes to lend and spend, and professes that he will borrow the difference . . . known in the jargon as his 'net borrowing requirement' . . . talking about it in the sort of terms a young man might apply to his sports car and even going so far as to claim that without it they would not be able to 'steer the economy' ('look where they steered it' did you say?) . . . government now lacks the prime requirement of all borrowers – credit. In the six years from 1958–9 to 1963–4 inclusive, how much do you think the Government succeeded in borrowing net from the public by the sale of marketable securities or 'gilt edged'? Just £3 million. Yes, sir, £3 million.[11]

He demonstrated that the rest of the government's borrowing came from national savings, quite genuine, of £100 million, while the rest, some £833 million, represented the sheer manufacture of money – credit, ultimately translatable into cash. He gave an authoritative explanation of the process, arcane to the general, how the Treasury created by fiat in the banking system the credit which it then solemnly borrowed to pay its bills: 'lending to itself, which means in crude terms using the printing press'.

Convinced that it was wrong for the government (whether Conservative or Labour) to finance in this inflationary way services and objectives for which there was only one honest method of payment – taxation – Powell asked himself what the real savings of the community were from which growth was sustained; or, in other words, what was the true growth willed by the community. In 1960 the Institute of Economic Affairs published his detailed findings, *Saving in a Free Society*.[12] He itemised all the ways in which the ultimate saver – the individual earner and taxpayer – saves, and concluded that while interest rates affected the direction of saving, they did not necessarily affect its total; he denied that government could promote saving very much in total, though it might in direction. 'Forced saving' by taxation or inflation (another form of tax) merely discouraged 'normal' or natural saving. This book, specialist in its calculations and meticulous detail, is in its argument central to his economic thinking, as those who criticised his 'Morecambe Budget' of 1968 should have known. Economic growth in a free society depends on the rate of saving and investment reciprocally; it is a question of the *propensity* to save, whether in house mortgages, building societies, hire-purchase, life insurance, national savings, premium bonds, bank deposits, stocks and shares, government securities or physical assets (now including gold). He showed that the private saving was inelastic, relatively unchanging, in response to various influences that were supposed to manipulate it, such as rates of interest and ever growing re-distributive taxation: though obviously if individual incomes fell steeply, some reduction in saving would occur, but had not done so by 1960. The malign effect of inflation on individual people was spelled out and the conclusion was never truer than in 1975-8:

> The decision of the saver in a climate of inflation reflects not only his choice between certain alternative forms of reward for savings . . . but also a view upon the likely behaviour of the currency which is not an economic judgement . . . but essentially a political judgement or guess.[13]

Chronic inflation, he wrote, is irreconcilable with the acceptance of a free economy. Growth in a free society required the humble acceptance of the community's decision, not the bureaucrats' judgement, what growth is necessary. If growth is centrally determined, then saving has to be centrally determined. Inflation is the instrument chosen, almost inevitably, by the socialist state for this purpose; and a negative rate of interest acts both as a wealth tax and a means of phasing the private saver out. (The national savings scheme becomes little more than a government swindle.)

Powell's monetarism was filled out by these studies and reflections on his experiences in the Treasury. The practice of the state lending to itself as a camouflage for printing money he sought to pin down on every occasion – to explain the 'cash factory' to the uninitiated: 'it consists in selling Government securities to the money market and at the same time providing the money market with the wherewithal to purchase them. The net effect is that additional money is churned out';[14] in other words, the government does not borrow from true abstention from current consumption. The debauching of the currency, by both political parties, became for him a central evil, affecting many if not most other political issues; and he repeatedly called on his audiences to demand from the politicians the one thing these could provide: honest money of stable value. It was seen almost as a paradox that Powell could say that politicians had it in their power 'to operate upon monetary demand with the object of keeping [it] as nearly as may be in line with total production'.[15] He pinned the responsibility for inflation upon the government of the day: 'it is politician-made', 'it is willed by governments', as he so frequently categorised the public's misfortunes.[16] His repudiation of the Keynesian attitude had a moral dimension for him, as was perhaps to be expected. In 1964, when commenting upon Maudling's last budget, which was to produce the deficit Wilson never allowed the Tories to forget, he remarked:

> It is not only false, it is dangerous, to inculcate into any nation that prosperity is something which can be engineered by financial arrangements . . . that it is within the power of governments to set a specific rate of advance and to guarantee by their policies that it will be achieved. The creative forces within a nation lie in the people themselves, in their . . . hope, thrift and enterprise.[17]

This indeed, is the basis for Powell's frequent denunciation of comparisons of Britain's growth rate unfavourably with that of other countries as meaningless, even impudent. He stigmatised the demand for 'greater growth' as essentially socialist in philosophy.

But it is one thing to show by argument that money creation is solely the result of government action; it is another to demonstrate a mechanism of direct linkage between price increases and budgetary deficits that will convince people. If one admits there is a time lag, people want it defined, and any other inflationary factors excluded. When in 1964 Powell said that Maudling's £800 million borrowing requirement – money creation in intent since he proposed to lend it to himself as Chancellor – 'is the utmost limit to which prudence can go', he was pointing to the risk the Chancellor was taking that he would not be able to borrow the money without its being inflationary, because production would not rise proportionately; it was a stricture, politely phrased.[18]

This statement of the variables, however, accords with the Keynesian position, as first stated. The quantity theory of money – money supply – is deceptively simple; in the equation $n = pk$, where n is the amount of money (in all forms), p is the *general* price level, and k is the quantity of goods and services flowing on to the market to be bought. Double n and you logically double p unless k alters too. But as n is a complex entity (not a quantity of gold coins), and k even more so, while p is an abstraction (since prices vary in relation to each other) this relationship between p and n and is only true, Keynes sadly admitted, in the long run – about 80 years – and in this particular context, 'in the long run we are all dead'.[19]

But by 1952 Keynes was dead, and the long run had practically become the short run. Between 1952 and 1958 prices (p) rose by $3\frac{1}{2}$ per cent a year, at the rate of 5 per cent a year by 1965; by 8 per cent in 1969 and by 25 per cent in 1974–5. The deduction was inescapable when set against Powell's dissection of government 'borrowing' by deficit. It nonetheless took nearly fifteen years for the monetarist argument to make headway. Initially Powell was regarded as a right-wing troglodyte in monetary policy as in everything else.

Moreover there was a missing variable in Powell's equation of government money creation and inflation. Britain is not a self-sufficient entity but an open economy tied to the world economy by trade and monetary flows. When he was at the Treasury and the pound was brought under strain the only resource the Treasury knew was to raise the bank rate – higher interest rates – attract money from abroad and choke off expansion. The biennial autumn sterling crisis was a byword. When the British economy was expanded under Treasury stimulus the balance between exports and imports, in- and out-payments, was disturbed and pressure on the pound at its fixed parity forced the Treasury to raise bank rate, to ease the selling of pounds but, by discouraging enterprise, to produce un-employment and depression.

4 Freeing the Pound

Between 1958 and 1964 Powell came round to the view that the proper remedy was to allow the value of sterling to fluctuate: unpegged from the dollar or any other external standard of value. (Maudling reached this conclusion ahead of Powell, but he made no attempt when Chancellor to put it into operation.) A floating exchange rate was the natural concomitant of budgetary policy. If that policy was inflationary, but was promoting full employment, the rate would tend to fall, and rising import prices, falling export prices, would restore the economy to equilibrium – balancing payments in and out. Governments who inflated the currency grossly would quickly encounter rapidly falling values for their currencies. But balancing the budget would stop the growth in money supply, tend, perhaps only slowly at first, to push up the rate of exchange: import prices would fall, exports be trimmed back, a new balance at a new level be reached. Honest money, maintaining its value internally would mean stronger exchanges, foreigners would bring their money in on deposit, or for investment in new production.

When in 1967 the Wilson Government was forced reluctantly to devalue the pound from $2.80 to $2.40, they made just this adjustment, but clumsily and in a jerk, and at great cost to the reserves of gold and dollars, which a floating rate would perform continuously and without loss. Powell became convinced that the floating rate was the natural regulator of economic relations with the outside world for a free economy. He explained to an audience of Birmingham businessmen in homely metaphors:

> If the rudder of a ship is lashed in one position, it takes a deuce of a lot of rowing to steer the ship between the rocks. With a fixed exchange rate, that balance, which would have been maintained automatically, has to be contrived artificially. . . . The attempt has to be made to keep the supply and demand for sterling . . . at a level corresponding to a fixed rate of exchange. This means that the internal value of money must not be allowed to fall faster than in other countries concerned in the equation. This is something which it is impossible to gauge or predict accurately. . . . It means that imports and exports (in the widest sense) have to be adjusted so as if possible to balance at

a predetermined exchange rate. . . . So long as the price mechanism is out of action, there will always be balance of payments trouble every few years simply because there is nothing to keep exports and imports in balance. . . .[20]

– and all that could be done was to work directly on business men, changing interest rates, encouraging exporters and discouraging importers, interfering with banking rules, and above all resorting to control of wages and prices: all with the sole object of riveting the pound at $2.80 or $2.40. Powell's arguments were resisted by the Treasury and by eminent economists like Paul Einzig. After the pound *was* floated in 1971, just as he said it should be, he explained the resistance:

When a position has been embraced officially, and that by more than one party in the state, all the forces of authority are automatically aligned on it. This is the more so when the proposition in question refers to external, not internal, affairs and when therefore international as well as national respectability is mobilised in its support. As time passes, and more and more sacrifices have been offered up on the altar of the said proposition, its sanctity is proportionately enhanced. Only outsiders and bounders will then discuss or question it, the sort of people not to be found in official or banking circles.[21]

Just before the pound was floated Lord Cromer telegraphed a denial to a press story that he had taught Powell to favour a floating pound, or that he wanted it himself.

Other states had floating rates. In the Treasury's irrational fear of the pound losing its 'unique' position as an international currency, Powell suspected just the 'prestige' arguments, derived from the out-dated great-power mentality, which in other directions were weighing down post-war Britain with unnecessary burdens, and sapping its resurgent energies. Hence his objection to the idea of 'weak' and 'strong' currencies as emotional, not scientific, terms: 'Allow me to alter the parity of a currency,' he said at Bournemouth in the aftermath of the 1967 devaluation over which Wilson and Cromer presided, 'and I will guarantee to put any country you care to name into surplus or deficit. . . . I will make it "strong" or "weak" almost overnight.'[22] And, two years later, he was able to point out that in six weeks the Germans – of all people – had converted themselves from a creditor to a debtor nation by exactly such a procedure. As he noted later, a floating pound was quite impossible – until it happened. Much the same had occurred over leaving the gold standard in 1931 – with Keynes in Powell's place.[23]

5   Putting Trade Unions in Their Proper Place

But in the meantime, the politicians, fortified by Treasury adherence to their interpretation of Keynes, sought everywhere but in unbalanced budgets and the 'net borrowing requirement' for the causes of the 'stagflation' which extinguished most of the rather modest progress Britain had achieved up to 1959. Macmillan blamed his ministers and sacked them. Under Harold Wilson, a whining note of complaint that it was all the fault of the people, of their morals and materialism, that things were going wrong, began to creep into the politicians' speeches. They were encouraged to take this line by the general sense of depression and defeatism. Politicians are quick to express the national mood, be it of confidence or the reverse. Thus encouraged, many politicians ventured upon little homilies on the nation's shortcomings, when the recourse of blaming the other party became threadbare or unconvincing. Periodic hortatory 'we must pull up our socks' speeches had often, when nicely judged, gone down well, though more with the middle than with the working classes. But Powell scented a search by politicians for diversionary tactics; what he termed 'a deafening chorus of denigratory comment' and which he thought, dinned into the people's ears in and out of season, was very harmful to the nation.[24]

He was aware of the country's weaknesses, as his speeches (particularly on trade unionism) showed. But that these should be exploited by politicians – he used this term at times widely, and included in it trade union leaders and businessmen who insinuated themselves into a public role – affronted his belief in the creativity and uniqueness of the nation; a belief without which British politicians had no right to practise their profession at all. Certainly not Tories. His monetarism, like that of the Hayek-Freidman school, was dismissed as simplistic, without the unremitting intellectual examination he felt it demanded. From 1964 he began a sustained campaign to put the blame back on the politicians, and to stand forth more strongly as champion of the people. He did it with facts and statistics as well as theories. For example it was typical of his attacks that he analysed the balance of payments at a time when sterling was under strain and ministers were reproving the nation for exporting too little and importing too much, and showed conclusively that while private business-management, proprietors and workpeople – had 'by the sweat of your brows' produced a surplus of exports over imports, as well as investing in overseas assets, the government by its foreign spending and financial mismanagement had turned this surplus into the very deficit they were deploring. 'You were in the black; they put you in the red,' was his message, angrily dubbed as populism.[25]

His campaign was aimed at his own party as well as at the incoming Labour government; but Labour's belief in the efficacy of centralised planning, and in an administrative right to interfere in every aspect of public and private behaviour, made them a much more vulnerable target for his exposures. He thus dealt with the Minister of Labour, Mr Gunter, in 1965, when he

> told the world that 'we had shrunk away from the facts of life and have been, though people may not like strong words, dishonest and thriftless'. Now if by 'we' in that sentence Mr Gunter was referring to himself and his colleagues, he was perfectly right. . . . I am afraid, however, that it is all too clear that his 'we' meant the people at large – not the government but the governed. Being so the statement was not only insulting but an impudent bid to escape

responsibility.... Our economic troubles – our inflation, our balance of payments, our growing indebtedness – are politician-made.... Theirs is the dishonesty, theirs the thriftlessness, theirs the unwillingness to face the facts of life. There is no mystery about inflation: it is willed by governments.... It is 'dishonest', to use Mr Gunter's favourite epithet again, to go round blaming private citizens for asking and being paid higher incomes. The individual cannot help himself.... The prices and incomes policy and the prices and incomes freeze are cynical manoeuvres designed to transfer blame from the guilty to the guiltless.[26]

Powell, who had loyally acquiesced in, and come (as a departmental minister) much worse than anyone out of Macmillan's pay-pause, now concluded that incomes policies were an escape, a piece of politicians' wishful thinking. He had to get their attention back somehow to the unstaunched wound in the nation's side, the net borrowing requirement and the pegged exchange rate. In this endeavour, he had to formulate and state a radical view of trade unionism.

Since governments alone could produce inflation it followed that trade unions could not. It further followed that incomes policies were useless. Since trade union action could not raise wages, their privileges, built up over a century, but developed after the legislation of 1906, lacked their supposed justification in either economics or politics. Indeed, the upshot was that 'trade unionism, as we know it in this country, on both sides of the table, is a collusion to keep the living standards of the workers down. There's nothing novel or secret about that fact'. Union monopoly was a particular case of restriction in any factor of production, top-hatted or cloth-capped. Unions were interested in keeping numbers up. That meant keeping wages down – as well as the general 'luddism' that Powell came increasingly to see as a menace to competitiveness and market forces working to benefit everybody.[27]

These propositions, which did not recommend themselves to the union leadership or to fellow politicians, Conservative or Labour, were derived from Powell's stalwart belief in classical economics; and that he knew his stuff was shown when he quoted from Royal Commission reports from 1869 onwards, quite apart from repeated paraphrases of Adam Smith. It sounded too extreme to be formidable; but, as Powell kept saying in this and other contexts, old truths may shock but do not get out of date.

He did not deny that restrictive actions by one or another union (or monopoly) could briefly put the wage-level of a particular group ahead of the rest; but while they enjoyed such an advantage it was at the expense of the rest, because

wages, profits, prices are determined, always have been determined, and always will be determined until we go Communist, by the market – by supply and demand working through the market. While we tie ourselves into knots trying to invent non-market criteria for our commissions to use, the market is there, noiselessly, efficiently, irresistibly doing the job for us all the time....[28]

The rise in workers' living standards, like the rise of the general standard, over a century and more, was not the consequence of trade union action and intervention, but of rising productivity (capital, invention, discovery, organisation). Anyone, Powell challenged, who believed the trade unions had anything to do with it, would believe anything. To which Frank Cousins was constrained to reply at a mineworkers' meeting that, in that case, Mr Cousins *was* a man who would believe anything.[29]

Powell retorted cheerfully that the activities of the union leaders only resulted in the market price being paid in the end. Non-unionised occupations were the standing proof of it: they got the market price for their labour just the same without paying union subscriptions; the trade union official's function was, if not parasitic, essentially that of a medicine man in primitive society, a rain-maker whose purpose was 'to dramatise and personalise the abstract and impersonal forces by which man's life is governed'.

> Millions of trade union members want to believe that their subscriptions, their solidarity, their doughty leaders wring an annual rise in real wages from flinty employers. They do not wish to know that similar or larger rises are being obtained by millions of other employees who have no unions and no collective bargaining. Their own employers could not long pay them either more or less than the marginal value of their services in the market; but how much more satisfying to the dramatic and sporting instinct which is in all of us to see this cold impersonal fact transmuted into the clash of personalities on the national stage, the comings and goings at ministries, the conferences and stirring resolutions . . . the strikes and threats of strikes. . . .[30]

The idea that labour is a commodity just like any other, that one kind of labour (that of a brain surgeon) is subject to the same marginal utility laws as another (like a bulldozer driver), meets ancient, and medieval, resistances. The idea that unions expensively register bargains that would have been concluded anyway (dramatised in Galsworthy's play *Strife*) remained unacceptable, despite the fact that 'the hoary allegation that the seller of labour is at a natural disadvantage because he "cannot wait" whereas the purchaser can, has been shot to pieces again and again' (and strikes continued to disprove it). Powell argued that it was the shop steward who alone perhaps was worthy of his hire, ensuring that the haggling of the market produced just the market rate on the shop floor, where the final bargains were made.

The conclusion was not merely that incomes policies were fallacious and deceitful, but that as trade union privilege had no economic effects, the whole structure of trade union law needed overhaul. Unions needed no more power to protect their members; the protection of the freedoms of the public required unions to be brought within the ordinary law of the land. Powell's challenge came at a moment when the trade union leadership was changing. So far from being prepared to relinquish powers, they now wished to increase them. Left wing infiltration in union leadership at all levels had been preceding apace and Mr

Wilson's 'tightly knit group of politically motivated men' was busy preparing to use union controls for political ends – to radicalise the Labour Party and to accelerate the process of socialisation. This tightly-knit group was by the media called militants or the New Left. So far from agreeing with Powell that non-unionised workpeople did as well as unionised occupations, they were determined to unionise everybody shop by shop, to extend the closed shop as fast as possible (even to the self-employed in some trades) and by any means fair or foul; even to control the actual supply of labour – to deliver it as if it was a raw material or piece of machinery, exactly as Powell forecast they would. A new phase had begun, and was to provide impetus to inflation, but only because government cooperated as tamely as Hayek believed it would.

Hayek argued that the continual growth of the public sector – the nationalised industries, the bureaucracy and the penumbra of regulated industries and institutions – of whose personnel the government was the ultimate employer implied that the government would not resist excessive wage claims; rather, it would yield after a show of resistance, and then, instead of making the taxpayer pay, would print the money to meet the wage bills. This would generate inflation, and lead to incomes policy and to compulsion; this would in turn erode democracy.[31] The Hayekian foreboding was turned on its head by Powell's critics who argued that the wages demands came first and of themselves produced the expansion in money supply; hence incomes policies were the correct solution by governments intent on containing the inflationary process.

Powell accepted Hayek's point as a political not an economic judgement. It was by yielding to the wage demands by printing money (through bogus borrowing) and so allowing money supply to outrun the volume of production that the government caused inflation. But a resolute government need not be so constrained. If it yielded to wage demands it could finance them out of higher taxation or true borrowing (borrowing only from the true savings of the community) or both; and by thus refusing to inflate the government left it to employers in the private sector to reject undue wage demands or pay them strictly out of profits or out of more efficient production. If this resistance produced strikes all that was necessary was 'the courage to do nothing',[32] except in the limited cases where the survival of the community was threatend, when the honest retort was not inflation, but the imposition of a state of emergency to break the strike.

The money supply, not the monopoly power of the unions, was the key to inflation, and the government alone held that key: to persuade parliament and the public of this basic truth about monetary and fiscal policy, became from the sixties the consistent theme of all his speeches on successive budgets and finance bills, on every development in the nation's economic fortunes; to read them from 1960 to 1978 is to be reminded of Cobden's speeches against the corn laws and for free trade. He identified the incipient inflation of the early sixties as the symptoms of a new era in state management of economic affairs. In the past, the ability of a union to force up wages produced unemployment which in time restored the natural balance of production by new relativities; each worker got the differentials their trade or industry had to pay to get their skills; those turned off went elsewhere. But in the modern state such corrections, as the result of technical or other changes, were made,

> not, as in the past, by unemployment and the forcing down of wages, but by inflation and the devaluation of money; if one group succeeds in raising the price of its services by restrictive methods, then everyone else will get around to being paid more for theirs, until a pattern which corresponds with the balance of supply and demand is restored. The resultant inflation not only has the familiar inconvenient consequences for a country with a fixed parity of exchange. It also increases injustice for those persons and classes whose expectations are defined in fixed money terms.[33]

This statement, made in 1965, precisely described the process that was to bring the country to crisis after crisis, and to the repeated attempts of governments to stave off the results by prices and incomes policies, when the powellian answer was to let bargaining take place, but force the public sector to recoup by raising prices, and (if necessary) pay the civil servants out of more taxation. The corrective would come through unemployment and falling values of sterling. The distortion of the British economy would make it harder for Britain to supply the goods in the quantity and quality foreigners would buy, and this in turn presaged the fall in the standard of living, achieved through inflation, which eventually would affect everyone – even indexed officials and miners.

The result was visible by 1965: steadily to lower British real earnings in comparison with those of workpeople on the continent. Powell called for a reform of laws that had made British trade unions uniquely maleficent, not to be compared with American or German: 'The use to which the restrictionist, work-spreading egalitarian mentality of this country puts trade union law . . . consecrates the very weaknesses and handicaps we suffer from as a nation.'[34]

He did not underestimate the difficulties of reversing the 'work-spreading, profit-hating, almost Luddite attitude' that had been rooted in Britain for decades. But he wanted to bring the unions within that same legal framework in which 'citizens regulate their mutual dealings in accord with public opinion and the general sense of what is right and fair'.[35] This ruled out the closed shop. The right to associate must not exclude the right not to associate – if it did, right itself disappeared in a framework of compulsion, whether by law or by individual agreement. When employers offered total unionism in return for pledges to end unofficial strikes, it necessarily meant that if the unions were to be able to enforce their bargain they must have the power to deprive any recalcitrant member of his livelihood, as it would be intolerable if members could be held to a bargain but non-members could not be. The logic was that all workpeople would be disciplined totally by the unions, and all employers in trade associations: socialism in the guise of the corporate, the fascist state. Such arguments were dismissed as 'extreme' in the sixties.

Nevertheless the process continued. In October 1965 Powell told an audience in Weston-super-Mare that coercion and intimidation were growing, and gave instances.[36] In one case a union organiser told the managers of a Wolverhampton firm that unless all their employees joined the union (apparently the management was expected to apply any needed pressure) the union would see to it that orders from a large customer would cease; the firm told the employees that unless they wished to have their employer ruined and the jobs terminated, they had better join. Such arm-twisting became very frequent, as closed shops proliferated and employers bowed to marxist-minded officials to avoid trouble. In the Wilson government of 1974 the unions exacted a great increase in their powers to enforce closed shops. Powell warned his own party in the sixties – which he declared was more embarrassed by the union problem than many others – that 'what is not open to two opinions is that such a system is inconsistent with all that the Conservative party has ever said about the right of a man to belong to any union or none'; and he foresaw the danger of 'giving the closed shop legislative sanction, by converting the contract between employer and employee into a contract between the employers' union and the employees' union'.[37] Like inflation, he declared that the tyranny of union organisation was politician-made, and could only be politician-cured.

'What is in question,' Powell declared in 1966, when, as a member of the Shadow Cabinet he was involved in the early stages of Conservative policy re-thinking, 'is a state of the law which places trade disputes and trade unions outside and above the general law.' This the Heath administration tried to change in their Industrial Relations Act of 1971. Powell gave it, with considerable reservations, his support.[38] It need not have failed, if the government had not rejected the rest of the powellian recipe for dealing with the unions – allowing wages to find their own level in a free market in which the government declined to print the money to pay for the leapfrogging wage settlements that ensued. Powell saw trade union policy in the whole context of a return to the market – to competition and capitalism. In the event the Conservative débâcle left the unions stronger than ever, able to defy even such law as still supposedly bound them.

6   Opposing the Inevitability of Socialism

A Labour Government, said Powell, is a government which expands public expenditure regardless, unless and until it strikes some exterior obstacle. That obstacle in the first Wilson administration was, of course, the fixed parity of sterling. Like Orestes hunted by the Furies, Labour lost control of its policies on the morrow of victory, dominated by its conviction that it had to maintain the overvaluation of the pound, until, when it devalued, it conceded without realising it the arguments for a floating rate. Meanwhile, however, inflation continued, and Powell noted that inflation was a valuable tool of socialism, since it inevitably produced the requirement for all sorts of compulsory devices – prices and incomes policies, pressures on businessmen and trade associations, all of which developed a climate of centralised control and dependence on official directives.

Powell, like other advocates of a market economy, was provided with a classic example of the absurdity of planning in the early stages of the Wilson administration in the form of George Brown's ill conceived and humiliatingly ineffective National Plan 'to equip the community to take charge of its own destiny and no longer be ruled by market forces beyond its control.'[39]

Powell relentlessly followed the plan episode (which finds no niche in Lord George-Brown's own political memoirs) from its inherently unsound conception to its inevitable collapse and abandonment.[40] He showed that it was a laborious attempt to produce for 1970 'a pattern of production which the despised working of market forces and decentralised business decisions would do far better,' and he found it 'pathetic' to see Wilson and Brown setting their puny strength to make the myriad calculations involved. First they assumed overall output would rise 25 per cent; then thousands of questionnaires went out to firms to show how much they would produce by 1970 on that assumption; they had to ignore world economic forces that they could not predict, and other developments that might throw everything out – who before 1960 would have included North Sea oil in a five-year plan? He showed that all previous forecasts even of so predictable an internal product as steel had proved wrong.

He drew the same moral that he had drawn in *Change is Our Ally* from war-time experience: 'unless the government is to enforce compliance with the plan by detailed allocation of all the available supply of labour, capital and materials to individual units, managements cannot be prevented from conforming to commercial circumstances as they find them, regardless of any plan.' It was, indeed, the rigidity of plans and controls which ensured (as Hayek noted) that communist utilisation of resources was far less efficient (30 per cent less) than in market economies in the west; and Powell made his point with the news that Russian planners were injecting commercial criteria into their calculations and accounting systems.

The failure of the National Plan did not, of course, cure the Government of planning. Socialism is planning because it is not *laissez-faire*, and planning, compulsion and nationalisation remain its credo. The objective is conscious control in place of reliance on 'blind forces' *alias* Adam Smith's 'invisible hand'. Powell was soon exposing and dissecting, usually with devastating wit, the subtler essays in coercion and persuasion that succeeded Brown's downfall. He noted a campaign to condition people to believe that whatever its merits or failures, socialism was inevitable; phrases like '*laissez-faire*', 'wasteful competition', the 'jungle of competition' relegated capitalism to a passing phase.

> In the last analysis all power rests upon opinion. The great object of the Socialist is therefore to get people to believe that management, ownership and control by the state are inevitable. . . . Once that belief has taken hold in a sufficient part of the nation, the task is done. The safest prisoners are those who are convinced that they could not live outside the gaol. . . .[41]

He itemised some of the propositions being sedulously propagated: only the state could raise enough capital for electricity and atomic power; the state must promote and assist in export expansion; it must provide homes; it must control or oversee prices and wages; it must end a free market in land.

We had only seen 'the first wavelets of socialism'.[42] Every advance of socialism created new dependants of the state, and vested interests in state control. He urged industries not to be seduced into voluntary cooperation with the state, advice that seemed irresponsible to some timid business magnates, who also did not like being told they would lose their shirts in any contest with politicians and their officials.[43] He warned them to avoid the National Industrial Reorganisation Corporation, exhorted them not to fill in questionnaires not backed by statutory authority, and identified trade associations (even the CBI) as ready-made instruments for government interference, 'choking and drowning Britain in a mass of paper planning' – 'an enormous and steadily increasing deadweight of organization and constraint'[44] that killed initiative and hope:

> There is the whole range of nationalised industries. There is the whole gamut of government intervention in non-nationalised industry. There is the great and growing host of organizations advising, exhorting, cajoling, planning, interfering with our industry and commerce. There is the system of a welfare state designed to produce uniformity . . . the range of policies from incomes and prices to industrial location, which aim at averaging everything and everybody. No wonder people say '. . . there is no escaping, no reversing it, so let us acquiesce and drift along with the tide which is taking us on to the predestined Socialist society.'[45]

In these speeches Powell was beginning to sound a warning against the insidious spread of what he was later to categorise as 'non-law' masquerading as law, in systematic attempts by the government and the departments to exploit voluntary agreements to secure compliance with arrangements for which they had no statutory authority, and for which they would find it hard or impossible to get such authority. His exposure of this practice, his calls on citizens and firms not to cooperate as a matter of public duty and principle, struck hard at bureaucratic pretensions and at Wilson's new model *dirigisme*. It was to have a sequel in the Heath regime.

Otherwise Powell's speeches might seem good knockabout party polemics, not so different from other Tory speeches, if more elegant and furnished with more effective parables and topical allusions. But they *were* different, for they called for a plan of counter-attack, or perhaps counter-reformation, in which socialism should not merely be stopped, but rolled back; the private sector and its area of genuine competition and choice should not merely be preserved, but should be enlarged at the expense of the public sector.

Powell was consistent; having advocated *laissez-faire* within a specified economic field, he wanted to remove most if not all the restrictions on its unhampered operation. All forms of monopoly should be extirpated, trade union monopoly and nationalised monopoly, and the whole penumbra of monopolistic practices of lesser note.

He called on the Party to act on its principles, as well as unashamedly to proclaim them. He shocked many, and tied a new label of extremism round his neck when in 1963 he said at Bromley:

> . . . we are a capitalist party. We believe in capitalism. When we look at the astonishing material achievements of the West, at our own high and rising physical standard of living, we see these things as the result not of compulsion or government action, . . . but of that system of competition and free enterprise, rewarding success and penalising failure, which enables every individual to participate by his private decisions in shaping the future of society. Because we believe this, we honour profit competitively earned; we respect the ownership of property, great or small; we accept the differences of wealth and income without which competition and free enterprise are impossible.[46]

He denied absolutely that men had to acquiesce in socialism just because a climate of opinion, like a fatalistic miasma, inculcated the notion that resistance was a futile struggle against the *zeitgeist*.

But he warned that at a certain point the momentum of socialism and nationalisation *would* become irreversible, the private sector would become too debilitated – 'atrophied' – to retain either independence or powers of recovery.

> It is another dangerous delusion to think that there is no harm in trying a bit more Socialism experimentally and that if after a while we do not like the consequences, we can stop and go back where we started from. As in an individual's life, so in that of a nation, with every step you take in a particular direction it becomes harder to return or change . . . there are some mistakes which, once made, can never be undone; some decisions, and these often of the gravest, which are irreversible. One is free to nationalise an industry, but not so free thereafter to denationalise it. One is free to cast away an independent means of defence, but not so free thereafter to get it back again. We are not like scientists doing an experiment. . . . The electorate is always taking decisions which will inexorably govern their lives and those of generations after. It is this solemn responsibility which gives to politics meaning and dignity.[47]

This was said in October 1963, when he had just ceased to be a minister. It is a speech with many echoes – of the EEC and immigration issues, for example. The emphasis is upon 'not so free'; Powell insisted that mistakes could always be rectified by Parliament if the electorate demanded. Free will existed – though a penalty for error was always exacted. His intent was to preserve space for such rectification, reversal and repentence.

At a time when Wilson was talking science and Heath was talking modernisation, Powell tried to keep the public debate to realities. 'We uphold the capitalist free economy . . . as the counterpart of a free society which guarantees as no other can that men shall be free to make their own choices . . . to obey their own consciences,'[48] a matter of politics as much as economics: for 'it is no accident that whenever the state has taken economic decisions away from the citizen, it has deprived him of other liberties as well.'

Powell deplored the 'ratchet effect' of socialist measures under semi-socialist Conservative governments: Labour nationalised, controlled and socialised but, under consensus politics, the Conservative party reversed only a small number of such measures. This ratchet effect, which made Conservatives fatalistic, was their own fault. In 1963–4 he renewed his earlier demands for the rolling-back of socialism, calling for a thought-out programme of denationalisation, before it became too late; he insisted that the ratchet could be made to work in the opposite direction.

7   Bringing Back Capitalism: Denationalisation

He reminded audiences[49] that he had opposed in the House the Churchill government in 1954 when it made the British nuclear power industry, which then led the world, a nationalised concern; by 1967, under civil service management, it was far behind other such industries abroad and still losing ground. An earlier mistaken Conservative decision had been to put the telegraph under the Post Office – Disraeli's mistake in 1874 from which stemmed the state's control and dead-hand on the telephone; this, too, should be challenged by the Party, and be put right; for he now proclaimed that it was possible to denationalise virtually everything, going much farther than *One Nation* on the subject. It would be intellectual dishonesty for Tories at one and the same time to disapprove and reverse the nationalisation of steel and at the same time to acquiesce in continued state ownership of the coal, gas, electricity and transport industries.[50] Tactics were important, but he wanted prior commitment by the Party to the principle:

> I admit, of course, that there are a number of nationalised industries and public enterprises which it may be necessary to put up with for varying times yet. But there are many disagreeable and basically wrong things which we have to put up with until we can replace them . . . that makes it still more our duty to remind ourselves and others that these things *are* disagreeable and wrong.[51]

He reminded the Road Haulage Association, for example, that it had been possible to denationalise their industry and he instanced a particular reason for thinking the ratchet not irreversible: the visible preference of the vast majority of consumers for competition over government compulsion, government price-fixing, prohibition of newcomers with upsetting ideas; witness to this was the fact that socialists did not dare attack competition openly; 'they say there is no such thing as perfect competition, which is true, and want to trick people into assuming that therefore imperfect competition is worse than no competition –

which is not true'.[52] They talked of 'cut-throat' competition, 'unfair' competition, always attaching pejorative adjectives. Powell liked to point out that the housewife welcomed a 'price war' in the high street, and that attacks on the 'jungle' of competition showed ignorance of the delicate set of checks and balances that preserved equilibrium in such an ecosystem. He said that 'a whole new theoretical framework' had to be worked out to reintegrate nationalised industries to a free economy. Later, he proceeded to demonstrate that this could be done: that the state's assets could be sold back to entrepreneurs, and the fact that nominal capital would be 'lost' in the transaction, merely indicated how far a state undertaking was from making profits, and prospects of profits, a condition necessarily reflected in its capitalisation.

He brought together his programme for a true Tory economic policy in a remarkable 'demonstration model' in a speech at Morecambe in October 1968.[53] The spotlights were on him at the height of the immigration controversy; the Conservatives had just completed their party conference at which the strength of Powell's support was manifested for the first time. Powell put his ideas for a return to market forces in the form of a budget, which was so drastically to reduce government expenditure that it would achieve a twin purpose: to stop inflation by making true borrowing possible once more and to eradicate all government interference in the economy. On the basis of the 1968–9 financial year he showed how income tax could be halved: reduced to 4s 3d ($21\frac{1}{2}$p) in the £ at standard rate 'solely by removing from Government the functions which it has usurped from private enterprise and, by stopping it from doing, or interfering with, those things which price and profit and the market do far better'. He explained that his was a true budget, showing both expenditure and revenue. He set himself to reduce both sides of the account by £2,855 million, and achieved it principally by removing the exchequer payment of £375 million to local authorities for housing, and £800 million of advances to gas, electricity, Post Office and other state concerns. He made a clean sweep of activities like National Economic Development Councils, location of industry, regional funds, the Ministry of Technology, all agricultural price guarantees, and foreign aid. It was an exposition, almost Gladstonian, of putting money back into the pockets of the people to fructify.

The response by the financial journalists gave Powell a field-day for an exposition of how nationalisation worked and could be reversed; for after calling the ex-Financial Secretary of the Exchequer an economic illiterate (a man whose mastery of finance bills' complexities was universally admired in the House of Commons), they recklessly declared that it was impossible to sell back state industries to the public; and that even if it were possible, such industries in private hands could never find the capital needed for development.

The retort might be described as Powell's fork. He argued, first, suppose coal, railways, steel and telecommunications had never been nationalised: are we then saying that they would now cease to exist because nobody had put any money into them? The reply obviously was that they would have hired the money at the appropriate price for that degree of development which the market made profitable. The second prong: suppose instead of coal, steel, transport, etc., Attlee had nationalised ICI and similar large prosperous corporations, 'the same dreary people would be telling you to-day that nobody would put money, or enough money, into automobiles, cement, chemicals, steel and the rest. And you know it is not so'. The suggestion that the remission in tax which he envisaged would all be spent on fripperies, and none in investing in these industries under private management, he found offensive: it suggested that the British, in the view of journalists and professors, were thriftless. He paraphrased their objections: 'The industry used to be financed without compulsion, but from now on compulsion must continue, for if we remit what is now taken from you in taxation and spent on investment, you will only save 10 per cent of your new added disposable income and will spend the rest.'

To those experts who objected that if the state did not tax the nation and reinvest the proceeds in 'adequately' planned growth, growth would be 'inadequate', Powell retorted that the essence of a free economy was that its growth could not be predicted; but that did not mean that because growth could not be predicted it would not happen. He had already explained the function of personal and corporate savings in a free society as a mechanism of financial incentives; now he bluntly added

> I find myself quite out of sympathy with those who say we ought to be having more capital investment. . . . Just as I do not know how one can decide as between one form of consumption and another – or one form of investment and another – except by the test of the market, so I do not see how any test other than the market can decide the right proportion of total investment to total consumption.[54]

If there was a diminished propensity to save (in comparison with Germany or America) the cause, he said, was inflation, negative rates of interest, and socialism. Of course, if the market were destroyed it would no longer give the appropriate signals. The alternative to the market was the decisions of the men in Whitehall, imposing their patterns of savings and investment: an unfree society. In the present halfway house, schemes like Concorde, Maplin Airport and the Chunnel were thrown up by the planners, and not tested by the market (i.e. the willingness of the public and the institutions to subscribe to finance them) and inevitably Powell condemned them when they were announced.

The Morecambe budget was, of course, a 'model' such as academics use to simplify the complex workings of economic (or social) life; 'I was giving a whole parliament of budgets telescoped into one,' he said: but it was his programme for a Tory administration to restore freedom. Industries had been denationalised, and the process could be repeated. However 'poor a bag of assets' some of them had been reduced to (this was how the railway companies were described before arranging terms of compulsory acquisition from their shareholders) they each had a market price, and any paper losses this price showed against its book value represented past mismanagement and prospective unprofitable operations until reconstruction could be carried out. Even 'a poor bag of assets' can be turned into a paying service by somebody at a price (Powell did not discuss whether the price might be nil, or even that the acquirer might have to be 'paid to take it away').

He saw no problems in turning the state's title-deed into equity shares; it was then for the shareholders to hire management. Powell castigated the wave of prejudice in favour of state planning, state boards, state decision-making which had been generated under Macmillan since 1958; he professed to see signs of a reaction by 1968, 'and it was with the object not so much of encouraging it as of doing an exercise in quantifying the possibilities that I conceived my Morecambe budget'. He did not deny that there had to be state expenditure; he only required it be justified 'If you can convince me a policy is right and necessary, I'll fork out, tax me! It is because I think the state takes wrong decisions, which are infinitely impoverished compared with those you can get from the spontaneous action of members of the community, that I want to see the expenditure on these harmful policies eliminated.'

The greatest scoffing had come not from the socialists, but from the Conservatives. He sometimes showed mild astonishment when he found he had to remind Conservatives that their creed was free choice, free competition and free enterprise:

Some people commented as if I had said that the Conservative Party is nothing but a capitalist party (which is quite a different proposition). Others accused me of being doctrinaire and explained that the Conservative Party is bound to no fixed principles but picks up good ideas where it finds them. Others protested again that all this about capitalism was out of date . . . 'why,' they said, 'this is *laissez-faire*', as if incantation of those two French words . . . were sufficient to consign to perdition anyone to whom they are applied. 'Mr Powell', said one commentator, 'often gives the impression of having been dragged screaming from the nineteenth century.'[55]

That had been the reaction in 1964. In 1968, as he well knew, Heath's working parties preparing the Party for its next period of office were not contemplating a return to more capitalism; to Powell's protests Heath said widespread denationalisation would not be possible. They were examining 'indicative planning' which Powell in advance condemned as a meaningless phrase. The committee chaired by Iain Macleod was not thinking of income tax at 4s 3d; indeed, it had abandoned hope that government expenditure could be significantly reduced. To make the traditional Conservative cuts in income tax as well as redeem the pledge to businessmen that the Selective Employment Tax should go, it was looking for other imposts to counterbalance these window-dressings: notably VAT.

In 1970, with the election in full view, Powell told his audiences that if the past five years of state encroachments continued for another five on the same scale, a point of no return might be reached.[56] There was not to be another five years of Labour power. What lay ahead were the nationalisations and the Industries Act of Edward Heath, and then the minority socialist regimes from 1974–8. The ratchet continued to operate. But Powell does not yet agree that socialism is inevitable, or private enterprise yet incapable of resuming the management, for profit, of the state-owned industries. In the decade of further nationalisation and rising losses in the public sector that followed his Morecambe budget he did not repeat that exposition – there has been no further such 'model' to fit current conditions – but he has consistently fought each successive transfer of undertakings from private to state control, and has demanded reductions in public expenditure on that scale of Morecambe. By 1976 he called for cuts of £4,000 million in two successive years – 'a massive moratorium on capital expenditure in the public sector' which would switch £8,000 million into private demand, arguing that this would at once reduce unemployment and inflation. 'Take a hammer to it,' he said.[57]

Chapter 5

The Myth of Empire, 1945–1965

1 From 'Ind. Imp.' to 'Head of the Commonwealth'

To resign an Empire, to be superseded in the senior councils of mankind, is a moment charged with danger for a nation. No epigram has so reverberated in British thinking as Dean Acheson's 'Britain has lost an Empire and not yet found a role'. Classical history has its examples, modern history has Spain and Austria to prompt the anxious question: *how far down*? When Powell said that the abandonment of India in 1947 seemed for some days to have deprived his life of meaning, this was not merely hurt pride or patriotic grief: it contained a judicious element of proper foreboding. His career turns upon the need to find that new role, or new equipoise, for the nation, disencumbered of obsolete fixations, of overcostly and irrelevant overheads. The preceding argument for unfettered private enterprise, for competition, for rolling back the state's control, was a necessary condition for releasing the nation's energies to find that new role.

He was not the only politician to have presentiments. Attlee, in giving independence to India, used all his influence with Nehru to ensure it did not go the way of Burma; he saw in the Commonwealth a substitute – a worthy one – for the imperial concept in British *amour propre*. Socialists, of course, already had a ready-made post-imperial role: an egalitarian socialist society whose influence in the world would be great because based on morality and example rather than on navies and colonies; a state of affairs in which, so to speak, foreign governments would amend their ways when admonished by the leading articles of the *New Statesman*. Between 1945 and 1960 Powell came to hope for a more organic development of British genius; he did not think an ideology could prescribe it, or politicians organise it, but history suggested that the conditions for its most effective, indeed triumphant expression included *laissez-faire*.

At his first parliamentary contest, however, at Normanton, Powell laid emphasis on the preservation of the empire, on which, he said, the recovery of Britain's debilitated economy depended. This view was consistent with his decision in India to take up politics to defend Britain's imperial role. Not many Tories in 1945 realised that the empire was perfectly dead. It looked imposing if heterogeneous on the map, on the flagpoles, on the postage stamps. It seemed to many of them to have achieved a new cohesion in fighting Germany and Japan as a single unit – even South Africa had fought, even Irishmen had, on a personal basis, put on the King-Emperor's uniform; Africans, Indians, West Indians, Solomon Islanders – contingent after contingent – had marched past in the victory parade. Winston Churchill thundered that he had not become the King's first minister to preside over the dissolution of the empire.

Powell's imperialism, moreover, was nourished on his special, perhaps romantic, reactions to India; it may have had some parallel with his earlier attachment to German philosophy and culture. 'India claimed me,' he wrote later, 'almost from my first moment there. I started to love and learn thirstily. I bought and read omnivorously anything about India I could lay hands on.'[1] The more he studied, the less he felt such an organic achievement as the Indian empire could be passing away, and he returned home to fight for it, just before the mutiny of the Indian navy served an almost classic notice of its end. He could find 'no parallel to the handful of civilians and soldiers from an island oceans away who stepped into the shoes of Moghul and Mahratta and felt themselves to be both Indian and British'. That relationship of caste and *noblesse oblige* could be no hallucination, no vulgar colonisation like that of the French in Algeria or the Dutch in Indonesia. R. A. Butler recounted that Powell put to Churchill in 1946 a plan to take (or, according to other accounts, to hold along the lines of his memorandum to Auchinleck) India with ten divisions. It was dismissed as a sign of crankiness.[2]

Powell appreciated that with the links to India severed the empire lost its structure. It had almost been a dual monarchy, turning on the fulcrum of India's central defence, on the world role implied by India's interests, and on the power conferred by the Indian army. Yet he did not immediately accept that the world role had disappeared. He sought new cohesive forces.

Nonetheless, it was a mirage. Those who had studied the empire from the turn of the century, who had pondered the failure of Milner and Curtis, who had realised that what Britain had sown was not a Roman uniformity but a divergent nationalism, that the fissures of separation ran from 1776, through Irish nationalism, to Congress non-cooperation, and to African self-assertion (who knew that the African nationalists met to plan their independences in Liverpool in 1946?) – those who had followed these processes knew that there was no empire; that, indeed, Roosevelt was pushing a yielding door in his determination that the anti-Nazi war was not fought to restore European colonialism. Nor could a professor of Greek in Sydney be expected to ponder the implications of the reports of the Australian Tariff Board. The hegemony, based on sea power, economic mutual interest, and white technological prowess, was dissolving naturally. In 1955 Powell dropped all reference to empire or Commonwealth in his election address, as these facts were borne in upon him. Characteristically, he proceeded to read up and reassess the entire British imperial and expansionist episode, and relate it to the nation's current and urgent needs.

Until the late nineteen-forties important issues could arise in few parts of the world without involving imperial interests. Without such world relevance, how would Britain fare among the superpowers? Powell's first reaction had been to advocate a colonial army capable of the role of the Indian army ('the greatest non-European army the world has ever seen'); he also called in his maiden speech for a greater Canadian and Australian commitment 'if what we are defending is indeed a unity'.[3] He still saw the Commonwealth connexion as a high British interest – including the earning of dollars for food. He envisaged a new type of military world role based upon positions, on bases, rather than on colonised areas,[4] and on corresponding defence arrangements (not unlike that provided by the Simonstown agreement of 1952). The Suez base was preeminently such a position. It was also a symbol of a stand against the long retreat from the commanding position held in 1945, a retreat which encouraged Mossadeq to humiliate Britain, and strengthened the Egyptian view that Britain was 'a nation used to being driven out'. In his election campaign of 1951 Powell threw out the idea of a new sort of conclave for a new sort of texture of interests, using the words of Edward I in 1295 'what affects all should be approved by all'.

As the new strategic map unfolded he abandoned such speculations. Nor did he ever subscribe to the school of thought that a new empire in Africa endowed with resources that modern technology would make accessible (like the groundnuts scheme) could replace the Anglo-Indian condominium. When the Suez position was abandoned in favour of membership of 'the hydrogen bomb club' to keep Britain in the superpower class (*aut imperator aut nihil*), Powell discarded the whole concept of a world role and began to rethink the national status.

When he parted with the Suez group upon the abandonment of the Suez base, they misread his motives as a move to make himself eligible for office. But Powell had turned to the new priority in a new situation: the freeing of Britain's energies to find a new role. When in 1956 Nasser's challenge and Eisenhower's veto – and the incompetence of Operation Musketeer – produced an even more disastrous national humiliation, his military appreciation in 1954 was vindicated.

'If what we are defending is indeed a unity.' His doubts had been growing before the Suez withdrawal and fiasco. In 1953 his growing feeling that Britain had to return into itself, and his instinctive distrust of the airy concepts of Commonwealth, were fused together by the Royal Titles Bill. That enactment broke the last real tie that gave any reality to British hegemony: allegiance to the same monarch. Now a bogus title was invented to conceal the reality that the new nations could only be kept as members of a successor association by giving them republican status nominally linked to the British crown as 'Head of the Commonwealth', while the dominions became crowned republics with a nominal British monarch to wear the crown. It completed the process begun by the British Nationality Act of 1948, which he opposed from the Research Department, and the subsequent Act of 1949 which gave the citizens of the Irish Republic all British rights. (Rights that were not reciprocated.) Now there was erected on the vacant pedestal of empire a mere *conversazione*, something he was to define as 'a gigantic farce' when its peculiarities became clearer.

The Act of 1953, taken together with the Acts of 1948 and 1949, Powell called, in a speech in the House, 'an immense constitutional revolution, an entire alteration of the basis of our subjecthood and nationality, and, since allegiance to the Crown was the unifying element of the whole Empire and Commonwealth, it brought about a corresponding revolution in the nature of the unity of HM dominions'.[5] He first pointed out that when the Statute of Westminster in 1931 gave statutory recognition to the legislative independence of the Parliaments of the empire, it recognised in its preamble two voluntary limitations to that independence. Any alteration in the succession or in the title of the crown would only be made with the agreement of all; it preserved the unity of the person of the monarch by maintaining that the succession if changed should be changed simultaneously. But in 1953 alterations in the title had been left unspecified with no statutory basis. Queen Elizabeth II had a new style, under new arrangements 'all of which seem to be evil'. These admitted the divisibility of the crown; they suppressed 'British' from the words 'her other realms and territories', and they introduced the new concept, 'Head of the Commonwealth', 'unknown to the law'.

Powell pointed out[6] that under the Act of Union, 1707 the British Isles became a single realm, the kingdoms of England and Ireland, and of Scotland, with one imperial crown, together with 'territories belonging' to that crown. The unity thus imposed made the growth of those territories into a single imperial realm possible: a unit because, whatever its various forms of government, it had one sovereign. This unity was not impaired when the monarch governed different territories with different ministries. Instead of this organic union of selfgoverning (and partially selfgoverning) lands, there was left only 'a fortuitous aggregation of territories', and Powell poured scorn on the style 'Queen of the United Kingdom and of her other realms', a tautological statement that she was king of her kingdom, a solecism perpetrated out of the abject desire to get rid of the word British for the sake of a nominal union that was in fact rejected by the insistence upon republicanism by the new Commonwealth members.

To those who saw the invention of the Commonwealth as a means of featherbedding the British ego in its fall from imperial state, Powell seemed to be quibbling and pettifogging, forgetting that forms and titles are the façade; it was the good British compromise that kept us all together that mattered. Powell retorted that 'The Indians say they recognise the Queen as Head of the Commonwealth. Well, I recognise the Rt Hon Member for Walthamstow [Mr Attlee] as Leader of the Opposition. But that does not make me a member of the Opposition.'[7] What, he asked, was the content of unity? It was that the parts recognise that in certain circumstances they would sacrifice themselves to the interests of the whole. Unless there is some such determination, there is no unity – there may be an alliance – and under the new legislation India had, and was recognised to have, no unity with the United Kingdom. Yet, he pointed out, though without then foreseeing all the consequences, the 1948 Act substituted for allegiance to the crown the concept of a number of separate citizenships, but retained the status of a 'Commonwealth citizen' endowed in Britain, and only in Britain, with all a subject's rights.

Powell was writing with Angus Maude a short history of the British people which was published in 1955 as a *Biography of a Nation*; it summed up the Commonwealth in the words 'the people of the United Kingdom congratulated themselves upon this achievement as the highest flight of constructive states-manship – on rare occasions, that is to say, when the matter received their attention at all.'[8] It was to Powell's mind a delusion, an escape from reality. It worried him because he saw it standing in the way of the British people coming to terms with their new status, preventing them from closing ranks and sitting out a necessary psychological trauma preparatory to realising anew their identity – as in the fifteenth century the nation had to do when its French dimension vanished. With foreboding Powell and Maude described in their *Biography* 'how the consciousness of being a nation began among the English, how it grew and changed, embracing with various intensity and various meaning the inhabitants not only of these islands but of countries and continents across the world; and how that consciousness is again waning and its limits shrinking as if some natural span were nearing its close'.[9]

For a few years the Commonwealth idea reflected some pale consequence upon British prime ministers; the way ex-colonies accepted the Queen as their 'Head of Commonwealth' was thought (and the British people were assured it was) immensely impressive to the Americans and foreigners generally, even amidst shouts of 'neo-colonialism' and the rapid disappearance of the liberties of the liberated colonial subjects.

Macmillan played with the notion of the three intersecting circles – the Commonwealth, Europe and the 'special relationship' with the United States. In the early sixties Macleod dismantled, with the aid of Sandys and Maudling, the African empire that never was. About the same time the limits to Britain's 'independent deterrent' were brutally revealed, as technology required ever newer means of delivery and special warheads that had to be got from the USA. The European movement won recruits; by 1962 a Commonwealth conference was told that Britain wanted to join the Common Market – to mixed reactions. One thing was significant: the British decision was only constitutionally possible because there was no constitutional unity. Under the protestations of love, the cries of 'don't leave us', there was no echo of the Britons' feelings at the departure of Rome and her legions in AD 404. The shadow of the Common Agricultural Policy lengthened over the ex-empire.

2   The Baleful Commonwealth

Since the empire collapsed and the Commonwealth proved a disappointment, historians seem to have vied with each other in seeking to prove that it never amounted to an empire in any definable sense. Disappointment seems to have bred hatred and self-contempt. Powell may seem to have absorbed these judgements, suffered the same revulsion. He found he had to turn against the Germans in 1934; against the British Empire in the 1960s; and against the Conservative Party in 1974. It is easy to impose a pattern: the mortification of a person who had been taken in, deceived by an ideal, let down by friends.

But a politician, a man in public life, is in a different position from a historian or philosopher; he has to be practical. Powell came to see the empire of his youth and war-time experience in a new light; but he would hardly have bothered so much if he had not perceived in the Commonwealth a serious danger in the present and the future, for the British people. The Commonwealth became an excuse for refusal to face hard facts about the economy, public expenditure and inflation just as much as facts about Britain's shrinking and doomed 'world role'. He supposed in 1945 that he could help to save that role from American and other maleficent forces; he found in 1965 that the task was to save Britain itself; and that the Commonwealth and the mental image of the British Empire as the culmination of Britain's 1,000-year history were obstacles. A demolition job was required.

So he told audiences and wrote in the press that in the national consciousness the Empire bulked large for little more than forty years – from the jubilee of 1897 with men like Chamberlain, Curzon and Rhodes as its exponents, even though Seeley's *Expansion of England* had earlier provided the gospel. 'The Empire', until those men took the stage, meant to the average Englishman only the United Kingdom with its three capitals in London, Edinburgh and Dublin; 'the colonies' meant places like Canada, New South Wales, New Zealand or Natal whither he could emigrate, often to the homesteads of relatives.[10] India was a separate empire, until 1857 a chartered company's administrative area. Until the Queen became Empress many Victorians thought of it as temporary, even an embarrassment. Africa came later: initially a periphery for naval positions on sea routes, then a field for humanitarian and missionary endeavour. The lesson to moderns was: 'no longer to possess an Empire of which at its supposed zenith the rulers were either unconscious, or conscious only as a puzzling embarrassment of accidental origin, is no very strong argument for national decline or decadence'.[11] Britain's golden age was as legendary as other golden ages. Powell asserted that you could search contemporary records and find no sign of it – only a familiar sense of insecurity about an uncertain future, an anxiety about entaglements in Egypt or Africa flowing in turn from the greatest entanglement of all, the defence of India, which weakened Britain's proper role in Europe.

He belittled the imperial idea as a thing of Birmingham manufacture by Joseph Chamberlain, who sold it to the Conservative Party, which was forced to buy it in order to keep the support of the Liberal Unionists, of which he was leader; opposing Home Rule and upholding imperial interests being part of the same policy. To these were added tariff reform, as an essential ingredient of some sort of *Zollverein* to cement the heterogeneous structure together by mutual benefits:

and in the years in the wilderness after the landslide of 1906, years when a party needs a policy, the Conservative Party took them both on board, but especially the Empire, because about that one could make stirring speeches without needing actually to alter anything. And so it was that just in the very last years when Britain's relationship with her overseas colonies could by any stretch of fiction be represented as imperial, the Conservative Party first, and then the British people, came to believe instinctively, implicitly, that they had an Empire – a belief that was to colour their thoughts, emotions and actions for nearly seventy years, and to set a gulf between them and the rest of the world: the same gulf which exists between a man in the grip of a hallucination and those around him who do not share it.[12]

In his biography of Chamberlain which appeared in 1977 Powell said of this ideal of a federal empire that it 'was indeed nothing. His labour was vain and the years have condemned it'.[13]

The raj in India he reduced to 'a sort of dream which was dreamed jointly for two centuries by the inhabitants of the Indian subcontinent and by what Curzon called "the speck of white foam upon a dark and thunderous ocean" . . . even to the very end the shared hallucination persisted'.[14] Powell recalled how Indian villagers had smiled and said 'He is a Hindu', because so conscious was he of their caste rules that he had known to break his earthen *loti* immediately after drinking from it: 'There is a sense in which it had been true: the British were married to India as Venice was married to the sea.'

Powell did not dissociate himself from this national hallucination, to which he gave the Conservative Party pride of place in fostering. But he was the first public man not only to try publicly to break it, but quite deliberately to do what was not done: to say what so many thought, using in public the language that so many parliamentarians and others used in private. He tried to break the spell, desecrate the idol, smash it violently. While so many thanked heaven that Britain had not had any such experience as that of the French in Algeria, and condemned complacently France's *folie de grandeur*, Powell came to envy France's constructive and creative agony in Algeria, and subsequently wrote of it:

> It was the firm conception, and the perilous execution, of the severance of Algeria which confirmed de Gaulle's position and gave him the basis for everything else that he was to do. Indeed the psychological renewal of France . . . could not begin until the French had proved that they had the ability, by a decisive act of will, to put their imperial and colonial past behind them . . . they were spared that weary and perhaps, in some of its consequences, fatal course of self-deception with which the British were fain to beguile themselves in corresponding circumstances. . . .[15]

The hallucination was cauterised with powellian thoroughness in the course of the three sensational *Times* turnover articles by 'A Conservative' in March 1964. Their impact on politics is considered below (Chapter 6). Their authorship remains unclaimed, but on the Commonwealth in particular they have the powellian ring. They stated that most Conservatives knew the Commonwealth was 'a gigantic farce' and despised the politicians who kept it going. But the author added that, so far from being a harmless club for nostalgic get-togethers, the farce had become an entanglement for Britain in the same sense that India was an entanglement for Victorian England. It had, for example, caused Britain, hag-ridden by Commonwealth preferential tariffs, to delay entering into 'closer commercial relations with western Europe'.

The use of the monarchy as one of the characters in the Commonwealth charade was vitiating the 'subtle emotions of loyalty and affection' of which the British heritage – the soil of the necessary national renaissance – consisted. But the articles granted that 'The unravelling of the tissue of law and practice which constitutes the Commonwealth fiction need not, indeed could not, be a sudden act'; they envisaged that the next batch of colonies would be completely independent, and not allowed to become Commonwealth countries endowed with the various privileges this gave their citizens in Britain. Gradually a 'new basis' would emerge for relations with individual countries in the Commonwealth. The thinking here was that a relationship subsisted with the white Commonwealth which should be distinguished from the different and often unfriendly relationship with grievance-prone Asian and African ex-colonies. But the irreversible damage of giving the monarch different titles in different realms was done. The concept of allegiance and subjecthood was beyond recall.

In subsequent years, despite such plain speaking, the thrall of the Commonwealth held surprisingly well, at least to outward appearance. Few other notabilities cried out that the Emperor had no clothes on. The 'pathetic pictures of the Queen posed among the ever-widening ranks of her prime ministers'[16] (not to mention presidents and beribboned military dictators) became a biennial event, quite falsifying Mr Macmillan's fear in 1961 that another such conference would be impossible to stage.

Powell blamed the Conservatives for agreeing to set up the Commonwealth Secretariat as another vested interest in perpetuating the illusion. And indeed it was due to indefatigable efforts by Mr Arnold Smith that the Commonwealth countries were brought to realise that it was against their interest to resign; out of the British hallucination they were getting trade preferences, aid, places for their own people to settle in permanently (and send remittances home from) and above all an influence upon British foreign policy, especially over Rhodesia and South Africa. 'A Conservative's' hopes of a cut-off in membership were firmly squashed. Powell observed:[17]

> To sustain the pretence that nations are associated which are not associated, that they hold principles in common which some do not hold at all, that they are friendly when they are bitterly hostile, that they have mutual interests when some have opposing interests – the effect of all this is not merely neutral: it is positively harmful.

Of course harmful to British interests. Powell realised that it was race which between 1961 and 1971 had come to form the content of the Commonwealth relationship; perhaps that the tension and friction produced by race was actually becoming the cement of the Commonwealth.

> If the United Kingdom twenty years ago had treated the citizens of the rest of the Commonwealth as what they were and are – no different from the citizens of other independent countries – the result, far from increasing antagonism, would have been to prevent the creation of a problem (call it racial or minority or what you will) which provides endless matter for friction and hostility between Britain and other countries. The reason why Britain, and not France or Germany or Italy, is arraigned and badgered by a score of countries round the world, is not because she washed her hands of her former dependencies when they became independent, but because she wanted to pretend that they still belonged to one and the same Commonwealth, and thus created undefined claims and presumptions which would always be disappointed.[18]

But which were valuable political properties, like grievances, a point that African governments came to appreciate. Powell said that the question is not whether we preserved the Commonwealth, but whether we preserved the pretence. He saw Britain impaled on its own outworn (statutory) words: hooked.[19] In 1971 he was asking how we could get off that hook. He saw it, momentarily, as possible through a realisation of the absurdity of trying to treat differently would-be visitors and entrants who should be treated the same: the absurdity of patriality whereby 'one UK-born grandparent sanctified an Indian but not an American, or the instant conferment on a Sikh with no English of the franchise withheld from a European admitted on the same terms'.[20] If this absurdity were recognised and ended, 'the pretence of the Commonwealth would have gone, and soon everyone would be saying that they meant that all the time' (as happened in 1971 over the floating of the unfloatable pound).

The strangest part of the pretence was, of course, that British governments could be influenced by threats from Africa of resignations from the Commonwealth; for the sake of the pretence, Whitehall yielded to pressure. This form of blackmail was rather short-lived; Commonwealth leaders were notified that British public opinion was changing – due in part to Mr Powell – and they would lose the Commonwealth leverage if their bluff was called. As Powell put it,

> The people of Britain observe that a number of these [Commonwealth] countries are antipathetic to each other even to the extent of breaking off relations and going to war. They note that an antipathy towards Britain is a marked feature of the visible behaviour of these countries at the United Nations and elsewhere, and none of them appears to recognise any common interest with Britain where it would override or conflict with their own . . .[21]

When told that there was a risk of the Commonwealth breaking up, unless Britain made concessions, 'those who merely judge by what is said publicly or printed in the newspapers might be astonished to know how many people on being told this say to their neighbours or under their breath: Let it break up then, so much the better'.

3   The Rhodesian Make-believe

Particular examples of the way in which the Commonwealth entanglement led Britain to lose sight of its true interests and the reality of its position were the cases of Aid to underdeveloped – Commonwealth – countries and of Rhodesia.

His views on Rhodesia were widely shared by a minority of Conservatives, by many Labour MPs surreptitiously, and of course by a wide section of the informed public. Powell's particular approach to the Rhodesian imbroglio was strictly deducible from his reactions to the abandonment of the Suez base in 1954. Responsibility implies power, and Powell declared[22] that Britain had no power in Rhodesia (where it has never exercised direct political control); accordingly it could not accept and attempt to discharge any responsibility. When attempts by Sir Alec Douglas-Home's and Wilson's governments to persuade the white Rhodesians to open up a process of conceding power to the blacks by degrees had failed, in Powell's view there was nothing left for Britain to do but warn them of their dangers, indicate that they could expect no help or sympathy, pass an Act recognising their independence, and then let this new state of 250,000 white Spartiates and four million black helots work out its destiny for good or ill. In 1964 such a decision would probably have produced the resignations that would have dissolved the Commonwealth pretence in the way Powell desired.

Even Sir Alec Douglas Home had no intention of taking this controversial if realist line at the time of his electoral defeat in 1964, to judge by his enunciation of the 'five principles' for granting Rhodesia independence – principles for that advance to African rule which the Ian Smith government had been specifically elected to prevent. Whether Powell was right about Britain's military incapacity to coerce the white Rhodesians (as the Kenyan settlers had been overawed) may be disputed; but to have attempted to exercise it would indisputably have been to risk a colossal military disaster, ranging anywhere from outright defeat to a mutiny in the British Army and the RAF – even a sort of British version of Algeria. The decision to declare independence illegally was taken on a carefully thought-out conclusion by Smith and his coadjutors that the will to take any such risk was totally lacking in the make-up of Harold Wilson and the rest of the British establishment. In this sense Powell was right and 'Bomber Thorpe' was a bletherer whose notions merely exposed that lack of will. The ensuring blusterings and humiliations of Britain were mordantly examined by Powell after a year of 'throwing the book' at the Rhodesians, as Wilson called sanctions.

They embarked on a course of attempting to overpower by sanctions a government in the heart of another continent. It is not an operation for which even Lord North and George III can be appealed to for precedent. In consequence they have led the nation down a cul-de-sac from one contradiction and breach of faith to another, with a prospect at the end of appalling confusion and tragedy . . .

They declared that Rhodesia was a wholly British responsibility, and then called on other nations to assist in terminating a rebellion. They said that an oil embargo 'bristled with difficulties' and then they tried to apply it. The Prime Minister undertook solemnly and repeatedly to the House of Commons that this country would not seek a United Nations resolution to enforce the embargo; then . . . did exactly what he said we should not.

The Government put the RAF into Zambia; and then they took the RAF out of Zambia. The Government talked about a period of direct rule in Rhodesia from Whitehall; and then said it 'might last only for minutes'. The Government told the Commonwealth conference at Lagos in January 'on expert advice' that it would be a matter of weeks rather than months before their measures terminated the rebellion, and now in September at the Commonwealth Conference in London they asked for another three months . . . after which this country would join in going to the United Nations for mandatory sanctions.[23]

In 1966 he called it a case of the Sorcerer's Apprentice; and in 1978 the confusion and tragedy was still growing. By December 1966 the Conservatives voted against the Rhodesian policy, and Powell said he was proud to be in the division lobby with them. He anticipated a firm opposition henceforth, which implied, of course, that when the Convervatives regained power, they would extricate the country – and in Powell's logic that meant abandoning responsibility and nominal sovereignty together.

It is anyone's guess what would have happened in Africa if Britain had taken the powellite line. But rejecting it bought Britain no friends in Africa; and did not prevent the Portuguese revolution from forcing the pace. Powell regarded the discussion of Russian or Cuban penetration as irrelevant to British policies, and in 1976 he predicted

Unless the surrounding omens are all misleading, something very nasty is going to happen in Rhodesia . . . more likely sooner than later. There is nothing that Britain can do to avert or delay this; but by attempting to do so she could easily bring humiliation upon herself and actually increase the loss and sufferings of others . . . if catastrophe occurs and precipitates an outflow of refugees, Europeans or non-Europeans, then, as elsewhere in Africa, our responsibility for rendering succour will be no greater than falls on all other civilised nations and we can be expected to take no more than our proportionate share in it.[24]

It remains to be seen if, in the event of a Rhodesian *sauve qui peut*, the laws on passports and patriality that Powell opposed would facilitate such an inflow on a Uganda 1972 scale.

4 The Economics and Theology of Aid

The cost to Britain of resisting Rhodesia's declaration of independence is incalculable, the price paid in national humiliation. On the other hand the cost of the aid programme was about £200 million a year when Powell cut it from his Morecambe budget. He recognised that the whole episode of aid to developing countries, which he later said would rank high in the annals of human folly, was not solely a Commonwealth entanglement – though naturally British aid flowed mainly to the poorer Commonwealth – it was an international obsession; and it is still a firm article of faith among western governments, enshrined in the EEC in the form of the Lomé Convention.

In 1965 Powell decided to add his voice to that of others who were arguing that aid was futile and even harmful to the developing countries.[25] His position followed logically from his belief in free competition, which he considered should as nearly as possible be applied to international as to domestic economic activities. 'As nearly as possible' took into account the fact that the sort of labour mobility possible within homogeneous nations is not possible internationally; or not uncontrolled, because cultural preference – for staying where you are among your own kin and not being forced to receive strangers from anywhere – is as much a good as any increase in material living standards. With this limitation – the limitations on the mobility of human beings, which may apply within a national economy in limited degree – the proposition holds that in the global interchange market forces best determine what is produced, and, in so doing, maximise all round the returns from trade and investment.

Once it is accepted that the resources diverted to aid programmes are diverted from their most productive use in overseas countries as expressed by relative return or rates of interest, they become counter-productive. They hold countries longer in the grip of poverty than need be; nor did he doubt (any more than the World Bank does) that the local governments will put much of them to the least productive uses, not merely out of ignorance, but for political and prestige reasons.

In the classical economist's judgement it is therefore usually kindest to be most mercenary. But those who appeal to market forces to support this view must as human beings show how they react to the cry of misery that rises from the poorest of human kind, the poor that they say, as Jesus does, we have always with us. Powell does not duck the question. On the contrary,

> the question deserves a serious, a solemn, above all a truthful answer. First, then, there is not a happy ending to every story in real life, nor a solution at all, let alone a happy one, to every problem. History at least shows us that, and we have not yet walked out of history. Because millions of human beings are hungry and appear to us wretched, it does not follow that therefore it is within our power to make them full and, in our own rather peculiar application of the term, happy. If the western nations were to confer on the rest of mankind not, as at present, just a tiny fraction of their goods and capital, but were, literally,

in the words of the epistle, to 'bestow all their goods to feed the poor', their wealth would only disappear, like a snowflake on boiling water, into the maw of these vast and astronomically increasing populations, and the outcome would be a common level of poverty and incompetence.[26]

This is the international application of Powell's argument (notably in *One Nation*) that the redistribution of national income from the 'rich' to the 'poor' has already gone so far as to be inimical to growth, investment and wealth-formation. The same reasoning required him to oppose regional subsidies in Britain designed to raise the investment in areas of high unemployment and declining industries at the expense of the Midlands or the South East. He pointed out that people were moving of their own accord from the worse to the better markets for their skills, far outweighing the artificial forces trying to keep them immobile. In international economics a comparable massive if gradual movement was taking place from the poorer countries into industrial Europe and industrial America; it was economically right, though under social and political priorities to be resisted or limited. A reverse movement was concurrently taking place – the movement of light, and even very advanced, industries from the affluent high-wage economies of the west to the poorer countries, notably to the Asian 'golden crescent' which swings from Korea round through Japan, Taiwan, and Hong Kong to Singapore. These were complex cross-currents for Powell to chart.

His views brought him into conflict with churchmen and Christian opinion which felt that its responsibility to the poor of the world called for much increased allocations of aid, and that to argue otherwise was to cling to 'unjust economics'. Powell felt he had to put them right. He admonished the Archbishop of Canterbury that trade did not impoverish but enrich the poor – Britain's trade with America did not impoverish Britons; and Britain's trade with poorer countries did not impoverish them. Trade was for mutual advantage and Aid was in restraint of trade. Charity was for individuals: an individual could meritoriously give his entire life and talent to the world's poor as a moral decision; Powell never withheld admiration for those who do. But when it came to aid given by governments by means of taxing their citizens it was a form of compulsion from which religion and morality were by definition excluded:

> Those who advocate aid or more aid do so not in order to be charitable themselves but in order to bring compulsion to bear upon others to perform what, in the case of those others, cannot be a moral act. As for Christianity, I confess it seems to me little short of blasphemy to seek arguments from it in favour of a compulsory levy of 1 per cent rather than 0·7 per cent. Whatever Christianity is about, it is not about decimal fractions of a percentage point.[27]

To the humanitarians he gave a practical answer: growth in the poorer countries had to come 'essentially from within': from slow but sure local capital formation such as Japan had shown to be possible in the nineteenth century when everything depended on a return upon investment and nothing on grants, soft loans or other hand-outs. 'It was due to the character of the people'; and a similar character has been shown by the people of Korea, Taiwan and Singapore. They have adopted what Powell called our only western gift: capitalism and enterprise. The recipe will vary with national character; but a modern malthusianism persists. Western investment in hygiene and chemotherapy for a small and easily afforded outlay produces an exponential growth in population while investment in agriculture produces a linear growth in food for consumption. Unless the curves themselves are changed, then, however pitched, they ensure catastrophe – a story without a happy ending.

Of the argument for Aid to keep poor countries 'from going communist' he wrote scornfully,

> Leaving aside the fact that there is no visible correlation between standards of living and liability to Communism. . . . If inter-governmental aid is inefficacious to produce the results held out for it, the outcome is more likely to be disenchantment and recrimination than gratitude and a common front against the alternative philosophy of Communism.[28]

And indeed Somalia, which came under Russian influence in the seventies, is one of the most heavily 'aided' countries in the world – and still one of the poorest, and warlike to boot.

Powell also pointed out that if aid is deleterious, and if it is undertaken merely for self-interest or for political ends by the donor, it must be immoral as well as uneconomic; and he dismissed the argument (in the Conservative as well as the Labour Party manifestos of 1964) that the gap between rich and poor countries, accentuated by race and colour, required subventions and aid from the industrial nations, as the argument for Danegeld. He added that poor and weak nations do not attack rich and powerful nations, or if they do, pose a smaller threat than that from strong countries: 'it is not China's poverty but the prospect of her becoming rich enough to afford nuclear weapons' he said in 1964 'that scares both Russia and the west'. The gap is a defensive wall so long as it lasts. Aid given to secure an ally, furthermore, suffers from all the disabilities of the relationships based on patronage and blackmail; indeed the World Bank has to study continuously ways of meeting donor-beneficiary resentments. He dismisses also the idea that Aid costs nothing to the donor because it is 'tied'. The government used 6d in the £ of tax money taken from the public to buy goods to give away; these, being free, do not add to exports (though counted as such) but are in reality imports. The raw materials in them have to be imported and paid for, while the added value is withdrawn from profitable production in the rest of the economy: they are waste, in the sense that warships are waste, but with no such defensive value. They are worse than waste, insofar as they inhibit the ability of less developed countries to help themselves: 'The introduction of cheap or free capital lowers the price of savings and thus represses indigenous saving on which sound future development must eventually be founded.'

5 The Answer to Dean Acheson

The delusions of an imperial or a world role cleared away, the Recessional sung, what then was Britain to be? Powell's reply was essentially to trust the people to provide the answer; once freed economically, morally, spiritually they would do so – and if, so freed, they would not, then no politician, not even 'the higher wisdom of a little group of men somewhere in the centre', could do it for them. In 1963, still in government, and in similar vein in the run-up to the election, Powell was taking pride in what the Tory principle, put into practice, had so far done:

> We dismantled ... the economic controls ... and powers of direction inherited from the war and post-war Socialism; we restored a market for savings and abandoned the rigging of artificial rates of interest which had been a fruitful cause of inflation ...[29]

He praised the Tory record, so far, on nationalisation – and even on inflation. But,

> society is more than a collection of individuals acting together even through the complex and subtle mechanism of the free economy for material advantage. It has an existence of its own; it thinks and feels; it looks inwards, as a community to its own members; it looks outwards as a nation.[30]

It was the sense of the nation's life, posture and destiny which gave meaning and purport to the individual, whatever his contribution to the community. 'If you care to call this patriotism, so much the better; I would like to see the word in use again; we surely need the thing.'[31]

In the mid-sixties he offered a basis for a renewal of the sense of nationhood and for pride in it.

> I suppose few nations have had, in a single generation, to confront the fact and the effects of such tremendous changes in their world situation as Britain has had to do in the last 30 years. In so short a space of time have a globe with one quarter of the land surface coloured red, our naval and air predominance, and our commercial, industrial and financial primacy become things of the past. History is littered with nations that have been destroyed for ever by the stress of lesser changes than these. But greatness does not consist in mere size, mere power. It lies in a realistic appraisal of the true stature of a nation, neither exaggerated, nor underestimated, and a faith in the unique possibilities for the future with which our history and our position have endowed us.[32]

The appeal to a unique history was to become a recurring theme, as Powell appraised the position in the later sixties and the seventies. He had long seen in that uniqueness a source of regrowth, a store of vitality. It is the marriage of hard-headed economic *laissez-faire*, practiced as far as possible in the private sector with a belief, mystic or romantic as it is usually and dismissively described, about the nation, that is distinctive in Powell's recipe for Britain, his answer to Dean Acheson. It can be discerned in his thinking and writing from early on. It emerged, for example, in his speech opposing the change in the Royal titles:

> Sometimes elements which are essential to the life, growth and existence of Britain seem for a time to be cast into shadow, obscured and even destroyed. Yet in the past they have remained alive; they have survived; and they have been the means of a new flowering which no one had suspected. It is because I believe that, in a sense, for a brief moment, I represent and speak for an indispensable element in the British constitution and in British life, I have spoken. I pray, not entirely in vain.[33]

It would be easier to recover these origins if it could be shown that the empire was an episode, not a culmination; and it was to that end that in 1964 he went back to history (he frequently enjoined the reading of history upon politicians) to illustrate his argument. He ended a reappraisal of the imperial episode in a lecture to Dublin academics on the same moral:

> Happiness and success are likeliest to come to nations that know themselves as they really are . . . if Britain could only free herself from the long servitude of her seventy-year-old dreams, how much that now seems impossible might be within her power. But that is another story that has not yet begun.[34]

It could begin, because he discerned a 'deep and providential difference' between the British and other world imperiums. The nationhood of the mother country was unaltered amid the strange, fantastic structure built around her. 'The citizenship of Rome dissolved into the citizenship of the whole ancient world, Spain learned to live on the treasure of the Americas, the Hapsburgs and Hohenzollerns extended their polity with their power.' In contrast, he told the Royal Society of St George in April 1964, in often-quoted phrases, that the thousand-year-old continuity of English history was unbroken when her connexions with other continents and other races fell away. He may have been speaking for himself and his war-time travels, as well as for the proconsuls and their entourages, when he suggested that this generation had come home to 'discover affinities with earlier generations of English, generations before the "Expansion of England" who felt no country but this to be their own'. His political argument was warmed by the feelings that had moved some of his poetry before he went to India, when he wrote of the host of living presences of the 'old English' who, in 1940

> . . . filled
> The broad air with their company
> And hovering in the fields that once they tilled
> Brooded on England's destiny.

Now, after the climacteric, he turned to the classics for a parallel, or perhaps parable, poetic but more adapted to a later audience:

Herodotus related how the Athenians, returning to their city after it had been sacked and burnt by the Persian army, were astonished to find in the midst of the blackened ruins, the sacred olive tree, the native symbol of their country, alive and flourishing. So we to-day at the heart of a vanished empire, seem to find, like one of her own oak trees, standing and growing, the sap still rising from her ancient roots to meet the spring, England herself.[35]

Such imagery, such attitudes, enabled those bent on internationalism to dismiss him as a little Englander, as irrelevant as his own insistence on freer markets, free enterprise. To him freedom *was* the condition of that rising sap, that growth; and he never ceased to say so. A decade later, out of Parliament, his future all at risk, he stormed at the falser myths that had enthralled national energies even more than those of imperial nostalgia. Britain needed 'more than ever to be itself, more deliberately, more self-confidently, more defiantly even, but with more self-understanding ... Britain will not thereby have less to contribute to the life of other nations, neighbouring or distant, for always, throughout history, it is when Britain has been most herself, she has had most to offer'.[36]

But Harold Wilson in 1964 certainly did not see himself becoming prime minister to preside over a state of the third order: with men like Kwame Nkrumah beside him, he dreamed of such feats of world statesmanship emanating from No 10 as Commonwealth mediation in Vietnam. The pro-Europeans of the European movement thought (despite the Gaullist ban) of British leadership of Europe. The New Left, eating its way into the Labour Party and unions from constituency grassroots or factory floor, saw the future as 'Finlandisation' – better still, a People's Republic within the great Soviet hegemony. Powell's immediate concern, however, was with the Conservative Party, its thinking and leadership.

Chapter 6

Powell *v.* Heath I:
The Party; Defence.
1965–1968; 1975–1977

1   Self-made Tory and Grassroots Conservative

After their voluntary exile on the back benches during Sir Alec Douglas-Home's twelve-month premiership, Powell and Macleod accepted invitations to join his Shadow Cabinet following the narrow defeat in October 1964 – Powell in charge of Transport – but both with explicit right to range over policy in general. Sir Alec resigned the leadership in July 1965 and in the leadership elections, Heath won against Maudling and Powell, and then invited Powell to serve on the new opposition front bench as spokesman on defence. Powell accepted readily: 'to carry responsibility, although it is only for the present shadow responsibility, for the defence of this country is the fulfilment of an almost lifelong ambition' he told the Conservative Party conference in Brighton in 1966. Defence was the first priority in Tory policy.[1]

This responsibility provided continuity and standing to Powell in his unabated campaign to reassess Britain's position in foreign affairs. In office he had been confined to housing, finance and the social services; he stood now to receive very senior office in the next Conservative government under Heath's leadership. Then in 1968, after the Birmingham immigration speech, Heath dropped him, and, after further disagreements, indicated he would never serve in a Heath administration. Powell's campaign to persuade the public to come to terms with the changed facts of the nation's position – to abandon a whole series of 'sham positions' in home and foreign affairs – thus grew into a struggle between Powell and Heath for the soul of the Conservative Party. To Powell it was an assertion, or reassertion, of principles and fundamentals. To Heath it was a question of legitimacy and loyalty.

Similarities in their backgrounds, even in their characters, may have contributed to the incompatibility. Powell's reason for refusing to serve in Lord Home's administration was that he had committed himself without reserve to Butler as Macmillan's proper successor, but he also considered that Home, stepping down from the Lords, perpetuated the backward-looking, great-power-minded image which needed at all costs to be exorcised from party and nation; the demonstration in 1963 of Sir Alec's popularity in the constituencies only proved his point in Powell's mind. Yet Home's departure opened the way to the era of Conservative grammar school modernising leadership with which Powell was to struggle much more bitterly. The grammar school ambience was to please him not more than the Eton ascendancy. Whether it would have been different if Maudling – or Macleod – had won in 1965 may be doubted. All were products of the Macmillan period. But Heath was the most closely associated with Macmillan; Heath, with Redmayne, played an important part in promoting Home's candidacy against Butler's, notably in providing the 'evidence' that the majority in the Cabinet preferred Home. Heath could see that Home was, as the compromise candidate, a brief barrier to a later bid by himself for the leadership: a short Home interlude was the best means for becoming an alternative to Maudling or any other contender.

Men who serve in the Whips' Office, as Heath did from 1950 to 1959, become influential, understand the party machinery, but rarely enter the running for the leadership; they do not speak in debate, push through legislation, prove their worth in departmental administration; all of which, in as much variety as possible, are the main qualifications for the highest office. In 1963 Heath's experience in such matters was no greater than Powell's. He knew the party sentiment, the cross-currents of feeling, the personalities, private strengths and weaknesses of members. These are obvious reasons why too long experience of the Whips' Office is not a recommendation to party members for the leadership. Heath knew Powell's distinctive position. He had helped to handle the Thorneycroft resignation; the seeds of later antagonism lie in that period. But it is widely agreed that Heath's personality as a whip was easier, more relaxed, more outgoing, more friendly than it was as leader and Prime Minister. Necessarily so perhaps, but the transformation into a tense, defensive, intolerant and domineering character seemed very marked. Whips must be bonhomous but listen more than they speak, know more than they tell, persuade and squeeze gently rather than browbeat. They are artists in means rather than identifiers of ends: tacticians rather than strategists; field rather than staff officers. Heath's leadership of the Conservatives could not but reflect his House of Commons experience. He had to become what he had not been; it seemed to put his self-confidence under strain.

Heath and Powell both rose from social obscurity. Heath came from an artisan family, Powell the same at one remove. Both had devoted mothers who spurred their ambitions and equipped them to rise socially by merit. Heath, whose family was hit by the Depression, felt the need to provide for them; Powell felt the need to be a credit to his. Heath was more straitened for means. Both were perseverative and industrious, Powell the more so. Both were noted for obstinacy, both rather withdrawn from other boys and family-centred, but Powell the more so since Heath had a younger brother which developed his sense of protectiveness. Both repressed their emotion, became self-contained, self-insulating, with a preference for older people as companions. Neither were Boy Scouts or cared for games. Heath responded to religion, perhaps strengthened in this by his musical prowess; Powell reacted from religion under the influence of philosophy, abandoning music for concentration on study. Heath's shyness and introspection placed an icy barrier between him and women; Powell having suffered (on the evidence of his poems) and having served an apprenticeship to woman's power, won through to love, a happy marriage and devoted parenthood.

Both climbed the scholarship ladder, Powell far faster. Both went to grammar schools, Powell's the more famous. At school Powell's intellectual promise shone out; except in music Heath was an average performer, almost vocational in his subjects, a keen debater, a tough prefect, winner of the prize for character. His headmaster claimed he saw a future prime minister in the boy. At Trinity, Cambridge, Powell proved the unbeatable competitive quality of his mind; Heath, at Balliol, Oxford, became a social figure, taking a Second in politics, philosophy and economics; the stuff of his career. He was president of the JCR, of the Union, he campaigned in a by-election for A. D. Lindsay against Quintin Hogg, became known as a promising young man, a pro-Churchill critic of Chamberlain; he visited republican Spain. His career was launched before he volunteered for the army in 1939, escaping at the last moment from Poland.

Heath displayed his qualities of leadership in action as a battery commander, was wounded, rose to the rank of lieutenant-colonel. He did not serve his political apprenticeship in the party organisation like Powell: after a spell in journalism, banking and the Civil Service, he got through his widening contacts, and with Woolton's approval, the nomination for Bexley – like Wolverhampton South-West a Labour-held seat thought to be vulnerable to a non-U Conservative candidate.[2]

So they entered the House together in 1950, and were fellow-members of the One Nation group until Heath received promotion to Junior Whip in 1950. They both fought the 'kissing ring' which controlled the Party, Heath from inside, Powell from outside (until he too achieved office); both despised the leisured class. Both aimed at the top, and neither were immediately popular with their Hon Friends, though respected for their obvious toughness and survival capacity.

These not unalike influences, not dissimilar conditioning, produced contrasting political qualities. Heath's were those of organizer and moderniser; Powell's those of a theoretician and traditionalist. Heath endorsed the view that Powell was pernickety and over-logical; Powell thought Heath shallow-rooted, though he generously conceded to him that he had the makings of a great prime minister, and this at the moment when their differences had become an open breach. These differences might be said to have begun when Heath approved and Powell rejected the Schuman plan for a European coal and steel community – or cartel – in 1950. Heath backed the Americans in Vietnam; Powell correctly identified the war as one the Americans could not win, and therefore one of which Britain should keep clear.

Powell's dissatisfaction with Butskellite Conservatism developed during his service under Macmillan as a modernising Health Minister. He came to believe that the Treasury resignations of 1958 were the watershed; Macmillan, who as Chancellor had threatened to resign on restraining expenditure, found his own Chancellor's precisely similar stand that of a fanatic, and thereafter swept the Party along on a tide of inflationary expansionism, experimenting with all sorts of novelties and expedients devoid of any real strategy of change or reform or fundamental thinking. Heath on the other hand was one of Macmillan's closest coadjutors, shared his interest in experiment, and accepted a basic belief that the nation was under-performing and had to be galvanised, chivvied, and excited into greater effort. His views on growth were the exact opposite of those of the author of *Saving in a Free Society*; his approach was that of the Whitehall statistical econometrist, the devotee of the 'League Table' in which Britain ranked shockingly low – a view with which, though on a different assessment, Harold Wilson and George Brown agreed. Heath agreed with Powell on the Commonwealth connexion, but he had sought to negotiate Britain's entry into the Common Market; he saw Britain's new role as European leadership.

To strengthen his claim to the reversion of the leadership, Heath needed something more on his record than the whip's office and his unsuccessful common market negotiation. He needed to show himself capable of getting an important modernising measure through the House. Sir Alec offered him the portfolio of Industry, Trade and Regional Development; and Heath hastily produced and ultimately piloted through legislation to end retail (or resale) price maintenance, the price-fixing system under which manufacturers fixed the price at which the retailer could sell their products to the public, and they policed this system, which no law invalidated, by the threat to deprive of supplies any retailer who sold at a lower – or higher – price. This was a thoroughly Powellite measure for restoring competition and prohibiting restrictive covenants, and Powell supported Heath in the fight for it, attacking the Labour Party for withholding support.[3] It split the Party, upsetting the small shopkeepers whose cause was defended by the back bench Committee on Trade and by the 1922 Committee. Heath miscalculated and had to compromise on amendment, indeed he had nearly to resign. For though the bill promoted competition, it increased the competitiveness of the big stores and chains against the small trader; the 'shoppocracy' of small towns is a kind of Tory peasantry with comparable influence; Heath and Powell had shown their underlying radicalism, even ruthlessness.

But Powell was at odds with Heath over a more significant issue. This was Heath's determination to extend the National Economic Development Council by creating subordinate 'Neddies' to prod businessmen, especially exporters, into growth policies. Powell had already condemned, as undue interference with business decision or market assessments, the location of industry policy developed under Macmillan – the Conservative attempt to develop the regions and limit the 'congestion' of the Midlands and South East. In the *Observer*, in December 1963, he warned that the 'Neddy' policy, and others like it, were providing Labour with excuses for a vast expansion of plans and planning – as witness their complaint that the Conservative Neddies had no teeth. Labour had promised to overbid this halfway house by a plan setting 'targets' for businessmen to achieve (as in Russia). One of Powell's first attacks on the whole concept of planning as inferior to the price mechanism and a free market was mounted against the bad forecasts of the NEDC on motor industry output, which grew thrice as fast as had been predicted; under full planning Powell wondered if the 'excess' output would have been curbed, the cars not built. In March 1964 he attacked the nine little Neddies and noted that while Douglas Jay was lamenting the loss to the next Labour government of the war-time apparatus of compulsory planning 'perfected during the war and available in 1945' to the Attlee government, because the Tories had dismantled it, Sir Alec's government was in effect reconstructing it. Powell satirised NEDC's performance over the gas industry as 'authentic glimpses into a Socialist Britain'.[4]

2   The Alternative Conservatism

In July 1963, while still in Macmillan's cabinet, Powell called for a restatement of Conservative principles, which when the Party had been long in office tended to get submerged under the exigencies of day-to-day administration. 'There come from time to time moments in the life of a party . . . when it once again needs to tell itself and others, loud and clear, what it stands for, when it needs to say plainly what it . . . aims at and what kind of future it wishes for the nation.'[5]

In April 1964 there appeared precisely such a restatement, reviewing the entire Conservative experience since 1945, in the three turnovers in *The Times* signed by 'A Conservative'. Besides demolishing the Commonwealth and Empire myth, they summed up succinctly Powell's own views on the Welfare State, the social services, free enterprise and the distinction between the areas where economic criteria apply and those where the state applies its own criteria. The guessing-game that ensued enhanced the sensation they made, a Haleyesque touch. Nobody has ever claimed authorship of this *tour de force*, though Powell said he had an idea whose it was; and whether Powell wrote, or 'A Conservative' ghosted them licitly or illicitly (they contained whole phrases from Powell's canon), there can be no doubt today that they constituted the Powellite Manifesto. They challenged the Party to go back to fundamentals before it wrote its own manifesto for the coming election, and it was a jolt for the *dirigistes* and indicative planners in the administration. In its final condemnation of the 'Neddies' it was aimed at Heath directly. Since Powell still had every reason to expect to return, in government or in opposition, to the senior counsels of the Party, he was no doubt wise not to sign – or countersign – it. Its statement of a Tory credo prefigured much that Powell would have to say, stand by and suffer for in the years ahead, if he was to be true to his beliefs. It was not a complete statement of powellism; but nearly so, when it is re-read in 1978. It is the alternative conservatism which Lord Coleraine was to acclaim in his book *For Conservatives Only*, issued when Powell became a household name.

'A Conservative', with powellian candour, began by declaring that humbug was necessary in politics to ease the electorate into unpleasant realities, but 'there come moments in the life of a party when it needs to wash off that application of humbug and start afresh. For fundamentally any party depends for its survival on clean hands and a good conscience. Such a moment has come for the Conservative party.'

His principal target was the undiscriminating 'modernisation' to which the party had become wedded under Macmillan's leadership; and his demand was for the drawing of a clear distinction in purpose and philosophy between what conservativism and socialism offered the country: an end to the blurring of basic issues which occurred when Socialists, committed to Point Four nationalisation and coercive planning, in practice took refuge in a mixed economy to evade the rigour of their principles, while Conservatives used 'indicative planning' to escape from their commitment to freedom, economic and individual.

Macmillan, the articles implied, was no Conservative behind his tactical mask of fuddy-duddyism. He was unconservative and innovating by temperament, attracted to novelty for its own sake. 'The contradictory term "new tradition" which when Minister of Housing he personally insisted on applying to non-traditional forms of construction, was a gem-like reflection of his cynicism.' In foreign affairs, he quietly abandoned the Commonwealth myth for Europeanism; in home affairs he encouraged modernism and a cult of newness which persisted after his departure; under the 'politically neutral' figure of Sir Alec 'the Cabinet contained a bigger proportion than before of the technocrats, ministers who would be doing for the doing's sake'. The writer added pointedly, 'Perhaps somewhere here lies the key to that unsolved riddle, the decision (if it was a decision) to deal with resale price maintenance in the last months of the Parliament.' He called, in conclusion, for a resolution of the dilemma posed by the spread of the NEDC, regional planning and location of industry bodies, exactly as Powell was doing in speeches: was the party for capitalism or for planning for growth? The Government's policies – and the articles pointed at the Department of Industry – 'represent a shift in policy as definite as it is recent. The difficulty is to reconcile it with the convictions of a party which bases itself on the belief that economic ends are best achieved by the mechanisms of competitive enterprise.'

'A Conservative' did not deal in detail with inflation and the trade unions as Powell was now doing. His ideas were not fully formed in 1964. He was not yet ready to advocate the floating of the pound as a means of keeping the balance of payments in equilibrium. The Maudling budget of 1964, and the way in which the economic upturn preceded Maudling's expansion of credit ('The patient was up and playing golf before he swallowed his medicine') required Powell to reflect upon the imprecise relationship in the real world between money-creation as he had analysed it and prices. This relationship seemed to be complicated by the velocity of circulation of 'money' in all its forms – the capacity of the money supply to stay idle in stagnant pools or pass more rapidly from hand to hand speeding up business transactions: 'numerous variables and complexities in the connection between Government financing of expenditure and the increase in the quantity of money', as he put it in 1973. He conceded that 'Forces deeper, wider and more embracing' than the budget alone affected economic activity in 1964. He was unshaken in the belief that control of incomes, to which both parties seemed committed, was wrong; but notwithstanding the deficiencies in his recipe 'we do all know one alternative, though neither perfect nor pleasant nor as yet at all precise or delicate in its operation. That is to operate on money demand [and keep it] in line with total production. Incomes can then find their own relativities within this total'.[6] He argued that 'a cause can be certain and demonstrable without being precisely definable or predicatable in its operation. The doctor in the 1840s who traced typhoid to water supply and arrested it by removing a pump handle was unaware of bacteria . . . yet he was right about cause and effect'. Powell never did find the precise process – but neither did the economists.

Labour entered on office with its expansionist plans, only to be frustrated by the familiar symptoms of inflation – heavy sales of sterling by foreigners. Wilson blamed Maudling's deficit, but he could only use the Treasury placebo – raising interest rates and proclaiming a pay pause. Events were beginning to bear out Powell's analysis. As an opposition front bench spokesman he called for a fresh start before another election presented the opportunity of getting back into power. He told an Aylesbury audience:

> I wish we could change the phrase and talk instead of 'getting forward into power'. Neither individuals nor nations can ever go back. . . . What we as a party ought to want to say and do today should be as fresh in spirit and as different as the world of 1965 is different from the world of 1951. Unless it is to say new things and do new things that we want the power and opportunity, then the power and opportunity will not be worth having.[7]

Few politicians would agree with that last sentiment, one feels – power at any price is what politicians want – but Heath could not quarrel with the call for 'new things'. Sir Alec might be committed to what the Conservatives did between 1951 and 1964, but he would not be. Powell asked a 'stern but simple' question:

> Have we the courage to accept that it is out of our own abilities and resources here, such as they are, that our future must be fashioned? And if so, have we the courage to put [them] to . . . the only acid test – that of competition between man and man, company and company, industry and industry, country and country?
>
> The Conservative party, if it presumes in the name of the nation to answer Yes to these questions, must submit every department of policy and of the national life to an unsparing analysis in the light of that answer before it dare claim the opportunity to govern.

Powell's message was however widely misunderstood as an outré back-to-the-nineteenth century call; the up-to-date thing was the elimination of 'uneconomic competition' – as in the nineteen-thirties. But Powell did have a new thought for his party: to eat that most disgusting of meals, one's own past words. He wanted profit, competition and enterprise to be the Tory manifesto. It would not have won the election; but Heath was to lose it anyway, outbid by Wilson's call 'You know Labour Government works', and the 'white-hot technological revolution'.

By the summer of 1965 Powell had been urging a distinctive alternative to Macmillan's modernising conservatism for two years. Sir Alec Douglas-Home had replaced the 'customary procedures' by a system of election which in 1963 would undoubtedly have made R. A. Butler Prime Minister. When Sir Alec realised that a large number of his colleagues thought that he was the wrong man to lead them in the 1966 election, he was too proud to resist the Party feeling, though he could have put himself up for election and, on his remarkable performance of 1964, even won. As it was, Heath and Maudling were the obvious choice before the party. Powell's obviously hopeless candidature surprised many. In fact it was dictated to him by his own conduct. He had called, over and over again, for a new policy, which neither Maudling nor Heath were likely to offer in place of 'modernisation'; therefore he had to offer it in his own person, even if he was humiliated; and even though he was hardly likely to advance his future chances of leadership by exposing his lack of following.

In the event he got only fifteen votes, though he probably had a larger following among the younger Tories. Heath's experience in party management won the day for his brand of modernisation; Maudling's greater popularity as a man of the centre was thrown away by his unaggressive canvassing style. The Party wanted someone to match Wilson. Wilson himself feared only one Tory leader – Macleod, but reposed on his belief that the Conservatives were too stupid to have him.

3 Defence: Where, Wherewith and How Much?

After the leadership elections Heath had no easy choice over Powell. Either he brought him into his Shadow Cabinet to help in 'submitting every department of policy and national life to an unsparing analysis' such as the new leader had announced he intended to carry out before the next election, or he left him out, notwithstanding his service under Home and his senior status, to become a focus of Tory dissent on the back benches. As Powell had already begun the 'unsparing analysis' it would look odd to leave him out; but if he was in, the explosive quality of his logic might have awkward results during the analytical process. Heath decided to have him in, at least for the time being.

The first misunderstanding between the two men arose from Heath's managerial intention to follow Gaitskell's, rather than Home's, precedent, and to confine his shadow ministers to their portfolios, only more strictly. He may have recalled the disputes during the much earlier period of Conservative opposition when R. A. Butler complained of Harold Macmillan's 'kleptomania' in pinching his colleagues' subjects and headlines. Powell took the traditional view that while he shouldered the responsibility of subjecting the Government's defence policy to unsparing analysis from the Opposition front bench, he was free of any inhibitions to talk on any subject in the country that he liked. He soon found that audiences were regrettably less interested in the agonising reappraisals to be made in defence than in other topics of the day.

Powell had become one of the most popular speakers at Conservative constituency meetings, Young Conservative conferences, trade functions and the like, and his views were sought on current topics appropriate to the occasion. In 1965 his first book of collected speeches, covering the period when he was out of office, appeared and was widely discussed. But he made defence first priority, visited NATO, and gave it the thoroughgoing reassessment that Heath apparently wanted.

Inevitably he adumbrated a defence policy in keeping with the much reduced role in world affairs which he had said post-imperial Britain must accept. The first question to be answered was the relation of British conventional armaments to nuclear strategy. Some Labour thinkers considered that as any war in Europe would quickly involve the nuclear exchange, conventional weapons and forces had become unnecessary; Sandys's 1958 defence white paper had promoted the notion that in Europe all that was needed by way of 'deterrent' was a 'tripwire' to the 'nukes'. This prospect at least released money for social welfare. Other left-wingers felt that as Britain could never match Russia and the United States in nuclear capacity, we needed neither nuclear nor conventional arms. Against this thinking, there were Conservatives who saw Britain's world defence role as one of dealing with 'brush-fire' wars, for which we needed bases, garrisons, a large fleet and amphibious capability almost everywhere, and certainly enough to carry out our commitments to the South-East Asian Treaty Organisation.

Powell brought a new order into this confusion. Britain had not only 'come home' from a world role; history had shown that it always had been first and foremost a European power. The threats to its survival as a nation had always come from over the Channel. British commitments to NATO came first, but with the proviso that as an island Britain had to retain the power of independent action. In 1940 this had meant defending the moat; but in 1965 it also meant that use of 'our own strategic nuclear weapon must be retained until circumstances were quite different'.[8] The fact that it was purchased in part abroad was irrelevant: 'with a weapon so catastrophic it is possession and the right to use it which count'. This thinking, in 1965, assumed that however rapid technical advances in warheads, targetting, and delivery systems became, even an out-of-date system constituted an effective *'force de frappe'*, deadly enough to deter because of its capacity to inflict unacceptable damage without an ally's nuclear support. But Powell at that time considered that the weaponry for the conventional forces must be made in Britain, so industry had to remain technically adequate to keep them up to date.

Outside Europe and the Atlantic, Powell saw no such requirement. At the Party Conference in 1965 he pointed out to his colleagues who thought trade had to be guarded that those who were taking it away from us kept no such forces abroad as we did. He advocated reliance upon the balance of power and of military forces throughout the world, rather than on military presences which might be counter-productive and cost too much.

In 1966 he told the Conference that a balance of defence expenditure which was 40 per cent for Europe and 60 per cent for 'world commitments' was wrong. The 60 per cent converted a surplus in the balance of payments into the chronic deficit which kept sterling under strain. He denied there was a defence commitment to the Commonweath (unlike the empire which had contributed to its own defence and cost nothing in foreign currency). Anzus proved the point. It was a cardinal need

> neither to undertake nor to appear to undertake more than we can physically perform . . . Capabilities in terms of the East have to be looked at realistically. Even the colossal strength of the United States is being put under strain in the effort to uphold the status quo in Vietnam . . . our own capabilities have been altering . . . dramatically. In a few months the positions we occupy East of Suez will be restricted, apart from Singapore itself, to one or two places in the Persian Gulf and some islands in the Indian Ocean . . . I have no patience with the pseudo-realists who imply that because Britain no longer has battalions or bases on which the sun never sets, therefore she can have no influence in the world and nothing to contribute to the defence of her friends outside Europe. This country, unique in its position, in its resources and its institutions, can never be negligible anywhere if she will provide herself with those forces which befit a nation essentially maritime and at the same time part of Europe.[9]

The implications of Powell's thinking were distasteful to many Conservatives, while giving no joy to Labour disarmers. In 1965 he told the Shadow Cabinet that the Americans would be defeated in Vietnam; eliciting the retort that they had the ability and will to stay there for twenty years if necessary.[10] Powell's prediction was based on a military axiom that was applicable to the United States as much as to Britain – that military power is relative to distance: it is effective in inverse ratio to the distance at which it is exercised. Missiles annihilated distance – but they could not be used to win wars. In 1967, in an address to the Monday Club, he used the case histories of the six-day Israeli-Arab war and the 1962 Cuba confrontation to demonstrate to the doubters that military power does not exist in the abstract – in the statistics of *Jane's Fighting Ships* for example – but is a function of place. (His intelligence record in North Africa gave him an authority hard to dispute.)

Krushchev's gamble had not come off because he was not prepared for mutual nuclear suicide; once it was clear that the Americans could and would sink any vessel trying to reach Cuba, and could, and were ready to, occupy Cuba, he had to retreat in good order. Similarly,

Israel inflicted a decisive defeat on Egypt and Jordan. She did what Britain could not have done, and what the United States would have had the greatest difficulty in doing . . . This does not mean that Israel is a greater military power than Britain. It only means, what we could see anyhow by looking at a map, that Israel lives there and we do not. Israel is now the principal military power in the Middle East excluding Turkey. But she has no military power at all in the Straits of Dover or in the Low Countries. She doesn't live there.[11]

And the Americans did not live in Vietnam. In the days of the Empire, however, Britain did live in India as well as in Britain, and was therefore an Asian and world power by dint of that occupation. It followed that

the insight into the relationship between geography and military power is vital to a restoration of our confidence in ourselves, and of a rational basis for our armed forces . . . Any nation which is strong where it can be, and needs to be, strong, and has successfully married space with force, may be as formidable and secure as those numerically much larger,[12]

and therefore Britain should make itself strong where it could be strong – in the Atlantic and Western Europe. 'A pound spent on arms and preparations relevant to these theatres produces a higher return in military strength than a pound spent anywhere else . . .' It would produce a military power inferior to none. 'We should not need to buttress our self-esteem by talking about its role and importance in the world. It would have them.'

The Arab-Israeli war proved his point: the expensive bases in Cyprus, Libya and Malta merely exposed Britain's inability in the Mediterranean to influence the outcome. That being demonstrated in a real conflict, Powell proposed that Britain should save the expense of bases, forces and naval patrols anywhere East of Suez. For

it promptly appeared that the so called British 'presence', either in the Mediterranean or in the Persian Gulf, was powerless to protect our interests either in oil or in sterling. From the Government of Iraq to the Sheikh of Abu Dhabi, those who wanted to, just turned the taps off, and we . . . never dreamed we could do anything to prevent it by our military presence any more than we could have used force to prevent sterling deposits being withdrawn.[13]

He rebutted chatter in the House of Commons that Lord Caradon had obtained the cease-fire in the United Nations or that Britain, one of the Big Four, was organising a Middle East settlement. Such wanton deceptions led to the waste of taxpayers' money on the wrong weapons – on bases, types of warship and the purchase of costly aircraft for roles we could not sustain and so should not try to sustain. He attacked Denis Healey, the Minister of Defence, for not seeing so proven a proposition and tailoring military logistics to the Atlantic-European theatre. This redeployment was only partly a choice of weapons; an army had to have a role, to understand it, to know where it would fight, and how. When the last garrisons returned home, Britain's essentially European army would have to stay permanently in Europe, its base and home there, quite unlike the posture in 1914 and 1939: it was no longer an expeditionary force, but an extension of home defence as much as were troops in Aldershot. Powell considered defence and the army depended therefore on a Western European Alliance, even more than NATO, vital as NATO was at this time. But he made no observations, as it happened, on the failure of the NATO armies to standardise their equipment and become logistically interdependent; this might not fit his stipulation that Britain must retain 'the possibility of independent action'.

Circumstances had demolished Powell's arguments of the early fifties for holding bases round the world's peripheries derived from a maritime supremacy that belonged to history. He now ruthlessly discarded costly relics of that past – the African ports, Aden, Hong Kong, Singapore, which, without India had become meaningless in terms of defending them. All Britain now needed was 'friendly ports' to be secured by wise foreign policies. He dismissed the defence of the Cape Route as a relic of outdated thinking (and hence the Simonstown arrangements, destined to give Heath trouble in 1971). But he also questioned the nuclear assumptions, quoting Macnamara's statement that 'the threat of an incredible action is not an effective deterrent'.[14] This implied that lesser wars could occur, perhaps even major wars, under the nuclear umbrella.

Hence the defence of Europe had to be defence in depth and in time. The trip-wire theory was replaced by the strategy of buying time with space and casualties, of delaying the moment when the West would be faced with the choice between accepting defeat and embracing communism or proceeding to mutual annihilation. The latter strategy required a different sort of army. Powell at first called it a citizen army, perhaps thinking of Switzerland and Israel; in 1975[15] he refined this idea to a 'cadre army', one that would provide the leadership and training for the reserves and conscripts to be thrown into a defence in depth, analogous to the procedures of 1914 and 1940. He attacked the Government, in furious exchanges with Healey in the sixties, for systematically destroying all possibilities of any home defence, beginning with the wrecking of the Territorial Army.

The concept of a long – or at least a longer than nuclear – war, implied also a sea war; and this in the American view in the later sixties might be drawn out. It would also be worldwide, and by the seventies it was clear that the Russians, perhaps converts to Admiral Mahan, were building an oceanic navy to challenge the West everywhere and strangle it everywhere. Powell, however, considered Britain's naval contribution must henceforth be confined to winning the battle of the Atlantic (for which the Falklands in British hands had relevance). His axiom required two riders: that the Americans must maintain the equivalent of the Britannic naval supremacy of 1800–1926; and that the Russians were themselves in error in seeking to be strong everywhere at sea, setting out to take over the British Navy's former role. Powell wanted the Royal Navy, and the air-sea army, to be specialised in, and adequate to, Atlantic control.

It followed that by 1967 Britain's presence east of Suez was preventing this increasingly urgent reshaping of forces to keep the country strong where it only could be strong. Powell was at war on two fronts; he had to argue his case as strongly with the 'east of Suez brigade' in the Tory ranks as in the House of Commons:

> Why are we startled by Russian warships in the Mediterranean and not by Russian warships in the Baltic? Answer: because we still think the Mediterranean is the route to India . . . the vital link of that strange, unique, fantastic bi-polar state that was India cum Britain, the spinal cord of which did indeed run through [it]. . . . You asked, did my appointment have an educative purpose? Of course, all serious politics is. . . . You are trying to provide people with words and ideas which will fit their predicament better than the words and ideas which they are using at the moment, and I am sure that Ted Heath when he asked me, to my great delight, to speak for the Party on defence, knew very well what my outlook was on the shape of the present and future world and on Britain's place in it. It's an outlook which I believe to be close kin to his own.[16]

That interview appeared in 1968, but the kinship had already vanished. Until 1967 Heath accepted Powell's defence logic; then he reversed himself after a visit to South-East Asia and Australia. He found men like Lee Kuan Yew of Singapore strongly of the view that Powell's analysis was premature. On his return he stepped in and committed the party to a continuing role east of Suez; as luck would have it, just at the moment when Powell's arguments had converted Denis Healey himself. Crossman and Wilson took the opportunity to drop the east of Suez commitment and so to conciliate their own anti-defence Tribunite left. Powell had prepared a pamphlet for the Conservative Political Centre setting forth his arguments – already in essence given to the party annual conferences – whereupon Heath forbade its publication, at least as a quasi-official party document. Powell's position as Opposition front bench spokesman on defence was hopelessly compromised.

Heath stated the grounds for his sudden and total rejection of Powell's views, 1965–7, in an article that appeared in *Foreign Affairs* in 1969, referring not to Powell by name but implicating him as 'one of those who argued that the British defence effort must henceforth be confined to our own islands and the continent of Europe'. He wrote that this argument did not stand up to 'serious examination'. His examination amounted to asserting that while there had been some cases of British military power failing to achieve the purpose for which it was deployed (could this have been Operation Musketeer?), there was ample proof that it could be and has been effective world-wide: his examples were the suppression of the mutinies in East Africa that followed the marxist revolution in Zanzibar in 1964; the deployment of troops in Kuwait to prevent the Iraqi take-over in 1961, and the frustration of the communist Sukarno's designs on Borneo. He reiterated that British forces in the Persian Gulf and Singapore/Malaysia were 'part of the landscape' and 'helped ensure stability' without which British trade (as opposed to German and Japanese) could not flourish. He might have done better to state that while our principal NATO ally was engaged, for good or ill in Vietnam, we were undertaking a subordinate job for him even against our better judgement. Powell might have respected an argument based on loyalty to an ally in trouble – the underlying truth. In due course, the east of Suez role was abandoned on the sheer powellian logistics of it, though Powell himself remained unsatisfied that the ghost of world-wide imperial commitments was entirely laid even by 1977. On the other hand the corollary of Powell's axiom was not followed up either; Russian strength increased in Europe and throughout the world, but Britain's increased nowhere.

> Year after year the whole course of these debates has been that as each instalment of cuts of prospective expenditure . . . has come along, the proposal has been opposed by Her Majesty's opposition; but the next time there has been no question of reverting to the previous level or to the level before that[17]

he told the House of Commons in 1977, and introduced a new element into his priorities, with a plea

> to establish the primacy of the maritime element – I include the air as well as the naval forces of all kinds – and to treat our domination over that air and sea area which is indisputably ours as the basis for thinking, for training, and for the military ambitions of our people.

The implication seems to be that an attenuated budget for defence allows Britain now only to think of the defence of its own lands and waters – the 200-mile zone – with anything left over going to NATO; a different emphasis to Powell's assertions on Britain's part in a continental army.

> I do not believe that . . . we should in any way be reducing the true effectiveness of our contribution to the alliance . . . for in the last resort the impregnability, if we can make it so, of these islands to invasion and domination of their sea and air space could again be in future, as it has several time been in the past, the guarantee of the liberty and ultimate victory of our allies upon the continent of Europe.[18]

He asked for more discussion, but at least it can be said that such a concept is a long way from the world commitments of twenty-five years ago. What defence it offers an island that imports half the food of 60 million may be for argument, but it is related to Powell's belief that the reason why Russia has so far refrained from invading Western Europe is not the nuclear deterrent, which he regards as irrelevant; it has not gone to war for traditional reasons of its own: 'advancing when you can do so cheaply, and not advancing when the price becomes too high'. It follows that, on Powell's logic, the problem of western defence is to keep the price just too high.

But whose is the decision to make? Powell pointed out that a province has no defence policy, and that he heard voices already urging that the day when the EEC should have a defence policy should be hastened. As part of a centralised defence system Britain would stand or fall with the rest of the land mass. 'However, we have not got to that point yet and there are some of us who are determined to see we never do,' he said in 1976. While Britain was sovereign in defence policy his answer was still a reorganised force to enable Britain, alone if need be, somehow to hold out; and that such a redirection of the defence effort need not represent a diminished contribution to NATO, 'though plainly it would involve renegotiation and redefinition of the terms of that contribution'.[19]

Chapter 7

Powell *v*. Heath II:
Immigration; the Break.
1962–1970

1   The Birmingham Speech

The parting of the ways was reached over immigration, not defence. Nobody – at least nobody outside the Party leadership – expected it. Powell's speech on immigration in Birmingham on Saturday 20 April, which now ranks with the most celebrated orations in British political history, was followed the day after by his dismissal by Heath from the Shadow Cabinet.[1] The speech received enormous publicity and produced a sensation; it was obviously intended to make a decisive impact. But Powell's dismissal from the Opposition front bench multiplied the effect a hundredfold. It transformed his own political position overnight.

His reputation had been rising with the public, if unevenly, for years. But he still received less attention outside political circles than Macleod or Maudling. In the Macmillan resignation drama of 1963 he had appeared as a secondary figure. His standing in the Party was higher than the votes he received in the leadership election: he was respected as a thinker on the radical right, recognised as a formidable parliamentarian, known to be intolerant at times but reckoned a valuable ingredient in the Party 'coalition'. Suddenly he was a national figure, a household name, and destined to remain so. To the masses, especially to the race relations industry, 'powellism', from being an alternative blueprint for Tory policy,* was narrowed by the mass media to an immigration policy, indeed to racial prejudice, racialism, racism. The fulcrum of his influence was transferred from inside Party counsels to a national constituency outside Parliament.

The contents of the speech were consonant, carefully so, with race relations policy under discussion in the Shadow Cabinet. Callaghan, as Home Secretary, was introducing a new Race Relations bill to strengthen the law against inciting racial hatred and against discrimination, as a counterweight to the curbs the Government had placed on East African immigration earlier in the year to the dismay and affront of the Labour left. Powell's speech was timed to get in ahead

* And remains used in that context in this book, notwithstanding any new dictionary definitions.

of the debate in order to drive home the Tory view that such laws amounted to lighting matches near gunpowder. Heath condemned the speech not on its content but solely on its tone – which he called racialist.

Subsidiary charges, not made public until later, were soon on the rounds. Powell, it was said, had been calculatedly disloyal: he had sedulously avoided giving Heath an advance text and Heath (who had written up the same policy in measured language for a Sunday newspaper to appear the following day) had known of it only after delivery. Powell had made elaborate preparations to ensure press and television publicity. He had, therefore, challenged his leader's authority.

The facts were that the occasion was a West Midlands Area Conservative Associations meeting, arranged long before, at which Powell might be expected to report on the Party's race relations policy; the Area agent, as representing Central Office, properly requested and took over the publicity for a local speech by a Shadow Cabinet minister; through area distribution the press and media picked up the story. So though Powell was reported to have sent out some of the handouts himself, he had personally nothing to do with the reporters' attendance in force.

It was put about that the Conservative amendment to Callaghan's bill, which was to be put forward by Quintin Hogg, had been drafted with Powell's assent in terms which proved very different from those in Powell's public utterance. There were stories of his having sat 'silent, tense and white-faced', saying nothing of the tone of the speech he intended himself to make. Powell, it was implied, knew exactly what effect his speech would have, planned the whole sensation, and was thus making virtually a speech that did diverge from the party line, and so should have been shown to, and passed by, Heath. Subsequently Quintin Hogg wrote up his own version, which was that he had asked Powell if he had explained the situation fairly, and received the reply 'You could not have been fairer'.[2] In Hogg's view this reply implied that Powell would make no speech in any other terms than those Hogg used in Shadow Cabinet (which he does not disclose). Apparently neither he nor anyone else realised the West Midlands Meeting was on and that Powell was billed to speak. Powell had not reminded them, and Hogg was, he said, 'outraged': he was no longer prepared to serve in the same Shadow Cabinet with Powell.

But it quickly became evident that Powell was not guilty of anything but 'bad taste' in the language he used to state the Party's – and the country's – position; and that there was enormous support for the way in which he stated that position, tasteless or not. So new explanations were soon on the rounds. Powell had for a long time shown contempt for consultation with his colleagues; they no longer wanted to serve with him; the language if not the substance of what he said was designed to sabotage the party line – and particularly the leader's decision that immigration was to be kept out of party politics as much as possible because of the danger of turning it into a major issue, embarrassing or diversionary.

Powell waited until November to rebut publicly the charge of disloyalty;

perhaps too long, because in choosing a date and place to make a considered defence of his actions he had to pass over an opportunity to participate a few days earlier in a debate on the Expiring Laws Continuance Bill, for which he was charged with cowardice. But what he had first to say on disloyalty could hardly be said in Parliament:

> There is no substance in this charge [of disloyalty]. No rule or convention forbids front benchers to advocate or defend, even before parliamentary debate, the line which the leadership of the party has publicly decided to take. There is none which requires them before doing so to consult or even inform their colleagues. . . . It is different if they intend to recommend a divergent policy; but this it was not suggested I had done. It was to the 'tone' of my speech that objection was taken. . . . Now 'tone' is a matter of personal taste . . . and a leader is entitled to be guided by his own taste in the choice of colleagues. What is matter of fact and not of opinion is that neither in making the speech nor in the circumstances attendant upon it, did I neglect or break any of the rules or conventions which govern honourable behaviour between colleagues.[3]

Much, in fact, lay behind this speech. It was known, or at least said, in party circles that Heath was hoping for an excuse to get rid of Powell, and that in this feeling he had most of the Shadow Cabinet with him. They had found his dissection of party policy proposals uncomfortable; and he was finding that Heath ignored his views or prevented him increasingly from putting them forward. Powell certainly knew his tenure was not easy, but plainly he was taken aback at being sacked on such a charge. Nicholas Tomalin, in an article in the *Sunday Times* in December 1968, recalled from memory a conversation with Powell prior to the Birmingham speech, in which Powell said he always included in his speeches 'at least one startling assertion . . . in order to give me a power base in the Tory Party. Provided I keep that going Ted Heath can never sack me from the Shadow Cabinet'. Such a remark is consistent with Powell's knowledge that Heath wanted to get rid of him, but is hardly consistent with any wish by Powell to stay, since 'startling assertions' were likely to produce an excuse for Heath to sack him but most unlikely to build a 'power base' in the party; nor is such language powellian, since he has often made fun of power bases for politicians 'rooted like Antaeus in the soil'.[4]

What Powell was doing – legitimately, he supposed – was to push his colleagues from within, but getting their backs up more than he realised. Heath was able to say that Powell had been warned once before about his language – that is, on the occasion of his speech in Walsall in February. This speech was made between two meetings of the Shadow Cabinet, at a juncture when the Home Secretary, James Callaghan, was becoming anxious and himself pushing his own colleagues to do something about immigration lest public anger and resentment boiled over against the Government. Powell felt that the Tories could not appear less concerned when the Government was in a position to take some action – in fact, Callaghan put the brake upon the inflow of Asians from East Africa. The Walsall speech produced 800 letters, which revealed how far the politicians of both parties were from understanding public sentiment. Powell could feel he had then saved his party from presenting an impression of trailing Government initiatives. But for his speech, *The Guardian* considered, Callaghan's Act would not have passed in a week.

Heath disliked being pushed. He wanted to appear master in his house. He had already dismissed Angus Maude for an article in *Encounter* which did only a little more than elaborate what 'A Conservative' had said in *The Times* about the undue influence of the technocrats in the Party. Yet when Sir Edward Boyle disregarded a three-line whip, he was not dismissed from the Shadow Cabinet, nor yet when he advocated comprehensive education along lines incompatible with party views – views in this instance shared by Powell and Heath. Boyle did not make Heath feel insecure. The exceptions made for him revealed to Party and political commentators that Heath's sense of insecurity in his leadership, as much as Party requirements, decided who was acceptable. The future, it began to be grimly said, was 'Ted-shaped'. When forty-four Conservatives voted against the third reading of Callaghan's Race Relations Bill, rejecting their own whip, in protest against consensus politics, after the whole party voted against the second reading, Powell's dismissal looked even more unfair.

Heath could not forgive Powell. His reaction was never to mention him by name if he could avoid it, so far as possible reducing him to a little local difficulty, a role of minor if sometimes embarrassing eccentricity. But Powell found most of his colleagues turned against him – a noteworthy exception was Lord Home. Quintin Hogg became a scathing critic. Iain Macleod's rejection and subsequent hostility was a greater pain and surprise, because Macleod well knew that his erstwhile flat-mate was no racialist, and he had supported Macleod when his policy of dismantling the African empire earned him such lasting unpopularity with the Party right wing that it cost him the chance of the leadership.

Two questions remained: why had Powell made such an emotional speech, which was bound to unite the liberals of all parties in condemnation? And had he actually planned to become a populist hero to the millions who were longing to have their fears and revulsion articulated: what Powell called 'the astonishing manifestation from all classes of people and all areas of the community, expressing relief and gratitude that such a speech was made', which had borne him up?

It is difficult to believe that he knew what would happen with any precision. He may have known he was taking risks. But he was taking them because the logic of events and of his own thinking drove him to take them. After the explosion, in hindsight, his enemies were quick to find a pattern in it all – a deliberate exploitation of racial prejudice for his own ends after his other attempts to shake the nation from its illusions had brought scant dividends. This thesis, argued in detail by Paul Foot in his book *The Rise of Enoch Powell*,[5] requires that Powell should by 1968 have decided that he had a better chance to lead Party and country from a populist position outside Heath's Shadow Cabinet than by pushing within it – with all the implications for such a choice by a man well versed in the discouraging precedents of British parliamentary history.

2 The Peaceful Invasion, 1948–68, and the Politicians

Powell lacked the prevision on immigration that he displayed on so much else. The roots of the problem lay in the British Nationality Act of 1948 which he criticised, but without realising that it would keep open doors to immigration from the New Commonwealth which it would later prove impossible to shut. His initial criticism was aimed at the meaninglessness of the concept of Commonwealth. Had he been able to warn of its practical effects, those criticisms would not so easily have been brushed aside as technical or irrelevant. In 1948 the inflow from the West Indies had hardly begun; the McCarron Act, which closed the United States to West Indians, had not yet taken effect. The substantial negro settlement of the eighteenth century had been bred out or repatriated. The decisive differences after 1945 were cheap and easy communication and the welfare state which enabled migrants to survive the initial period. Overfull employment (at under 2 per cent unemployment) had produced a demand for cheap labour and jobs were generally available. Employers, including the nationalised industries, actively recruited labour in the West Indies, there being no immigration bar. They boasted to each other that the availability of West Indian and Pakistani labour enabled them to keep wages from rising as fast as they otherwise might, at least in some industries. This application of the principles of classical economics to the international field was approved by the Treasury as counter-inflationary in effect.

By the early fifties the impact of coloured immigrants on social conditions in areas where they settled was giving trouble to MPs for Midland and some other constituencies. Powell could not have been unaware of it. But the numbers were still small; there was still an imperial sentiment, up to 1954 at least; and control presupposed a fundamental change in immemorial English law. Those few who looked ahead observed that the whole population of the West Indies was under three million; uneasiness only began to take hold of middle class and intellectual people when it became clearer that Indians and Pakistanis were establishing themselves in a steady stream through joint family structure, and that the whole weight of the subcontinent, and its poverty, pressed behind them with no barriers in front.

A group of MPs led by Cyril Osborne and Norman Pannell first began to articulate rising fears about the inflow of coloured people. Then came the shock of the Notting Hill riots in 1958, when exemplary sentences were handed out amid general establishment satisfaction. For the idea that Britain managed race relations better than the United States was a valued tradition to upper-class Britons who resented American criticism of the British Empire. Parliamentarians reflected a reluctance to admit that Britain could not handle a small race relations problem: that we were as liable to 'prejudice' as South Africans or whites south of the Mason–Dixon line.

Powell did not support the pioneers of immigration control. He was precluded by office for part of the time between 1955 and 1963; he also disliked the racist overtones in some of their comments – and when the problem still looked small, racism was particularly inexcusable. Powell, in a much-quoted comment, said he would set his face like flint against any legal discrimination between one citizen and another, not did he see in 'the management's right to refuse admission' in working mens' clubs any discrimination which could be objected to. Much of the friction alleged was not over dance halls or being refused a drink.[6] It was mostly over housing, and Powell believed he knew the formula for ending the subsidy-produced housing shortage.

Even before the Birmingham speech, however, he admitted that for ten years, from about 1954, Commonwealth immigration was the principal and at times the only political issue in Wolverhampton South-West. He had his answer:

> 'Why' people used to ask me, 'is the Government bringing these people into our country in ever growing numbers and where is it all to end?' I tried to explain that the law of England could not distinguish between one British subject and another and that therefore the inhabitants of India, Africa and the West Indies were all the same in law as the inhabitants of Wolverhampton.[7]

He could undertake to try to change that law, and he claimed that 'in government and out of it, I begged colleagues to bring the law into line with reality'. His difficulty was that so few ministers or MPs had any personal knowledge of what was happening in a few stricken areas; but Powell's complaints opened up a division in the party, with Powell supporting a worried group against Macleod, Boyle, Sinclair and other liberals. This hardly helped him with Heath, who wanted, in an autocratic way, to give himself an aura of liberality and enlightenment.

After the explosion of 1968, Powell was accused of having, as Minister of Health, presided over the encouragement of an important sector of immigration. As he had already explained (even complained) a Minister of Health has no power over recruitment (see pp. 41–2). The supply of nurses and medical workers is set by the negotiated going rate for the job, which may be limited by the Service's budget provision, and the minister can do nothing about the attraction the conditions may have for Irish, and in recent years, for New Commonwealth nurses. In the case of doctors, the General Medical Council decides at what standards doctors, home-produced or foreign, may practice. As Minister, Powell had to put up with the fact that the Willinck recommendations had generated a shortage of home-produced doctors, and that the GMC had decided that the qualifications of Indian and other medical schools were equivalent to those in Britain, when they were not, and the GMC knew they were not. Powell knew this in 1960, but could do nothing about it, any more than his predecessors or successors could. When the full facts emerged in the Merrison Inquiry he charged the GMC with the betrayal of standards.[8] In 1963, the year he ceased to be Minister, 360 New Commonwealth doctors entered the service with qualifications accepted by the GMC; in 1973 the annual intake was between 2,500 and 3,000.

By 1966 the Census estimated that there were a million coloured settlers and their dependants and offspring. Powell later calculated that this 'dark million' figure was reached earlier, perhaps by 1960.[9] The big inflow occurred between 1958 and 1962; before 1955 it had not reached 50,000 a year. But by 1961 the Government was under bombardment from party associations to bring in controls despite the reluctance of ministers like Macleod and establishment opinion like *The Times*. In 1962 the Immigration Act set up limits which at the time Powell thought effective. Though it made no change in the definition of British nationality it did seek to correct the results of the 1948 Act by limiting 'right of residence' to those British subjects who had or were issued with passports from the British Government and it introduced a work-voucher quota for aliens and British subjects from the New Commonwealth of about 8,500 a year. Those already here retained their right to bring in dependants. In a rough-and-ready way the 1962 Act defined those who 'belonged' to Britain and imposed restrictions on all others – in fact, it deprived them of a right that the 1948 Act had – in Powell's view disastrously – conferred.

After 1963 Powell directed his criticisms against 'the tissue of law and practice' which (as 'A Conservative' put it) was 'the cause of the massive coloured immigration in the last decade which has inflicted social and political damage that will take decades to obliterate'. In 1965, he assumed that the roots of the damage had been cut; consequences would take time to treat. As a result, when the first opportunity arose to make immigration an election issue, Powell rejected it. His constitutional instincts were always to give the electorate an opportunity to show their feelings – which means that a candidate must put into his election address a policy the voters can react to. This possibility was discussed by the Midlands Conservative candidates in 1964. Only Peter Griffiths, opposing Gordon Walker in Smethwick, made explicit pledges on stricter controls. He defeated Walker, but how far the result was affected by racism as opposed to a reasoned explanation why the Act of 1962 was inadequate – or indeed by Gordon Walker's mishandling of his campaign – was not very clear to Powell, who had been campaigning on the threat posed by socialism to a free society: but he was not surprised at the result.

Between September 1964 and March 1966 his attitude changed. So did everybody's after the Smethwick and Perry Bar results. Wilson put Maurice Foley in charge of immigrants' affairs and he duly reported that they were all sitting on a volcano. Wilson tightened up the administration of the 1962 Act, reduced the numbers of work vouchers issued and cut back the range of dependants – while at the same time cooling the liberals in his party with a White Paper promising laws against incitement to race hatred and the prohibition of discrimination. It was a bid to depoliticise race and immigration this time round, and Heath was ready to cooperate. But Powell now realised that the 1962 Act was not working as expected, either because it was laxly administered or for other unknown reasons. He had been alerted to the 'generation effect' by the local Medical Officer of Health, Dr Galloway, who drew his attention to statistics which showed that something like a quarter of the births in Wolverhampton were now coloured: and that this, if it formed a settled pattern, inexorably ensured a future in which one quarter of the whole Wolverhampton population would be coloured since, without making allowance for population movements (more likely to favour black than white numbers in an inner city) births must determine the composition of the population in the course of a generation or so.[9] Ten per cent of Powell's own constituents were already black; the pattern of births ensured that at least 25 per cent of the voters whose MPs represented the district in 1985–90 would be black. So he spoke out:

> It is absolutely absurd to say that immigration either is not, or ought not to be, an issue . . . especially for Wolverhampton and other parts of the black country. If by an issue we mean a problem which is felt to affect the welfare of every section of the community – repeat, every section – then immigration is pre-eminently such, and has been for the last decade or more. It would be quite wrong that the policies on this matter of those presenting themselves for election to parliament should not be known to their prospective constituents.[10]

It had not been an issue hitherto because, though its magnitude was not known, action – the 1962 Act – had been taken, and the results were awaited. Now he was saying that the full extent of the problem was being quantified; the figures were coming in; and he and other candidates could no longer avoid telling the electors where they stood. Nobody could deny the propriety of this without denying the basic principle of democracy.

There were (and remain) two problems for Powell: the first was the assimilation or integration of the immigrants of diverse skin pigment, language and culture already here. The second was the reduction of future immigration 'in a period of years' to a level at which 'the inflow and the outflow is roughly balanced'.[11] In March 1966 Powell considered that, at about one million, there were already enough immigrants in the country if integration was to succeed in the decades ahead. At that stage repatriation was a question of a 'small minority' which could not make a success of life here; and he expressed satisfaction over the Conservative policy of making help available 'to such of those as voluntarily desire it' to return whence they came. It would be a humane provision, which could do nothing but good all round. Of course I stress the word "voluntary". . . .'[12]

Powell reassured his black constituents that he was determined that 'they should so far as is humanly possible have the same rights and treatment as anyone else'. This was a condition of assimilation and integration, which he like everyone else at that period presumed that the immigrants desired, but which 'would only come about gradually over many years of mutual tolerance, as the immigrants slowly filter into all the classes and callings of society'. Powell continued for some time to repeat that, in the right conditions, history had shown that British society had immense powers of absorption of newcomers. But there was another condition: the 'anxiety and apprehension for the future in the minds not only of the native-born citizens but of the existing immigrant population' that a never-ending inflow would hinder the process of growing together.[13] Powell believed, and believes, that intermarriage is a prime mark of this process.[14]

Thus Powell established his central proposition on immigration into Britain: it was not primarily a question of race and colour: it was primarily a coefficient of number. As Lord Elton had put it, one archbishop in a village was welcome; five began to be a bit much, fifty became intolerable. This argument was derided by the Liberals, the Labour left and the increasingly influential immigrants' leaders as 'the numbers game'. They retorted that numbers did not matter; they were exaggerated; they were small; the real problem was the re-education of the natives by race relations legislation. Powell, in an article in the *Daily Telegraph* in 1967, denied that any imputations could be sensibly made against the natives in terms of what was happening in some areas: within twelve years whole areas of Wolverhampton had been transformed by the substitution of a wholly or predominantly coloured population for the natives as completely as other areas were cleared by the bulldozer:

> My uppermost feeling on looking back on these years is of astonishment that this event, which altered the appearance and life of a town and had shattering effects on the lives of many families and persons, could take place with virtually no physical manifestations of antipathy. This speaks volumes for the steadiness and tolerance of the natives.[15]

With this statement the race relations lobby disagreed.

So far, there had been no extensive violence since 1958. Later that year Mr and Mrs Powell visited the United States at a time when racial, along with student, violence had reached a peak, as the blacks pressed for the reality of civil liberties enshrined in the Constitution and the students reacted against the call-up for a war many of them thought unjust. Powell saw what happened when passions were stirred not merely over real but over invented grievances, and by the territorial instinct. He saw the effects of southern black immigration into the northern cities in a period only a little longer than that of immigration into the Midlands, but not by people from afar, by a people who had lived for over 200 years as Americans and knew no other language, culture or tradition. It deepened his forebodings, for all it was a snapshot impression, not derived from the historical perspective that he had of British social evolution.

Powell thenceforward collected all the figures he could, as they became available, on the magnitude of demographic change in Britain, asking questions in Parliament from time to time to add to public information on the subject (other MPs assisted in this task). In 1967, putting the coloured intake at not far short of 50,000 a year, which would if sustained amount to $1\frac{3}{4}$ million between 1968 and

2000, and making a guess at the effects of natural increase, he concluded that 'one estimate is that by the end of the century it will have been sufficient to raise the coloured population to about $3\frac{1}{2}$ millions or 5 per cent of the whole'. The percentage took into account an annual outwards movement of 120,000 natives which was projected for 1975 by the Registrar-General, in which year inwards and outwards movement were expected to balance. Of the inwards movement Powell expected half to be coloured, and the rest to be roughly equally divided between southern Irish and aliens (mostly, of course, Caucasian). In a stable population, such substitution would raise the coloured population more rapidly.[16]

In the ensuing ten years, Powell periodically revised this picture, which was the statistical basis of his assertion that the British were heaping their own funeral pyre. He concluded, as more information became available, that he had underestimated in 1967. In 1968 he projected, failing new controls, the coloured population in 2000 at 'five to seven millions'. But in 1976, taking into account the effect of the restriction in the 1968 and 1971 Immigration Acts, and other new factors, he predicted 4 million as 'the lower limit of estimates'. This figure was adopted by Mrs Thatcher in February 1978; she was rebuked by demographers who asseverated that, as the fertility of Asian marriages was precipitately falling, the total would be only 3,300,000 by 2000 and would not increase much subsequently. The natural increase of the native population, however, was also falling (see pp. 118, 175–7, 235–7).[17]

From the first, however, Powell placed much less emphasis on the total number of the eventual immigrant and immigrant-descended population – which liberals found unimpressive – than their concentration in a few big cities. Long before the coloured population reached 5 per cent of the total, a proportion would have merged almost indistinguishably with the general population; but by far the greater part would be concentrated in distinct 'colonies' or 'encampments' (words he always preferred to ghettos). It was 'for these colonies, and the problems thereby entailed on our descendants, that they will curse the improvident years now gone, when we could have avoided it all'. Consequently between 1967 and 1968 Powell felt a new urgency about 'virtually terminating net immigration', hoping that if the 1962 Act was reinforced to achieve this result 'a small but significant net emigration might soon follow, especially given aid and inducements to immigrants to rejoin their families in their countries of origin, or to return thither when they encounter prolonged unemployment or other difficulties.' He added to this programme measures, as yet unspecified, to encourage dispersal, which would hasten absorption; yet

> The best I can dare hope for is that by the end of the century we shall not be left with a growing and more menacing phenomenon but with fixed and almost traditional 'foreign' areas in certain towns and cities which will remain as the lasting monument of a moment of national aberration.[18]

Almost all that Powell ever said about immigration he said in principle in 1966 and 1967. In 1967 he thought the 'first phase' was over, but added 'I am going to prophesy, however, that there will be subsequent phases, when the problem will resume its place in public concern and in a more intractable form'. Nor did he exempt himself from blame for the aberration, the failure of foresight. In November 1968, when he had become a national figure – but before Paul Foot or critics like Smithies and Fiddick[19] had accused him of exploiting British racism for his self-aggrandisement, he remarked 'even those of us who inveighed against the British Nationality Act from the outset, and who from inside and outside government urged legislation over the years, feel an oppressive sense of guilt and humiliation'.[20] No other politician joined him in that. Most of them continued to tell the public that immigration was very good for it.

3 The East African Asian Passports

The new phase that he had prophesied was not long in happening. In 1967 it emerged that there was a large reservoir of British subjects (Commonwealth citizens) who, though not connected by birth or naturalisation with the United Kingdom itself, had the legal right to settle in Britain free of all restrictions under the 1962 Act. These were the Asians of East Africa. They possessed or were eligible for passports issued by the British Government. So long as the inhabitants of the African or other colonies held passports issued by the respective colonial authorities, the 1962 regulations debarred them from automatic entry into Britain. No problem arose when a colony of homogeneous ethnic composition, such as Nigeria, became independent; for virtually the entire population (with exceptions whose significance should, however, have been noticed) became citizens of a new independent Commonwealth country.[20]

But in Kenya and Uganda there were white and Asian settlements (and some in Tanganyika, though its trusteee status was rather different) dating from the turn of the century. In the independence legislation which was passed when Britain withdrew its authority provision was made for these non-Africans to remain 'citizens of UK and colonies' if they so opted within certain time limits. But as the British Governor was gone, the passports for which they became eligible were then issued by the local British High Commission, and were thus passports issued by HM Government in the UK, which the local High Commission represented – and conferred immunity from the Immigration Act, just as passports issued by British embassies in foreign countries did.

Duncan Sandys, who was Secretary of State for Commonwealth Affairs when Kenya's independence was negotiated in 1965, Powell and others argued that, as ministers were not told in 1962 of the effect of the Immigration Act in giving rights of entry to British passport holders in ex-colonies, and as there was nothing on paper about this liability, which was never raised in Parliament, a 'loophole' existed that should be closed. It was never intended that this should happen, and therefore the so-called rights could be withdrawn. This view was strengthened by the knowledge that when the Labour government took office, pledged to repeal the 1962 Immigration Act, the Cabinet was shocked to discover what the granting of independence in East Africa entailed under the law, and hastily revised their plans, shelving the pledge and reducing the number of vouchers issued to below the 8,000 then in force.

But can ministers blame anyone but themselves for even unwanted effects of legislation over which they preside? Powell has extensively criticised the civil servants over immigration. But Sandys was the minister; he could have bargained with Kenyatta to require everyone in Kenya on independence to have Kenyan nationality unless they held a passport issued in Britain or elsewhere. This would have forced some 20,000 white settlers to become Kenyans – or get new passports in London before independence day. This did not suit the whites who wanted to stay on and see how they fared under 'the Squire', but with an option to resettle in Britain if it did not work out. This Sandys gave them, and as no distinction could be made between whites and Asians in providing such a choice, the Asians also were eligible for passports to Britain issued by the High Commissioner. Their leaders were gratified, and checked that they were so privileged. Many Asians immediately applied for such passports, and others did so when the Kenyan Government began to withdraw their licences to trade because they had not become Kenyan citizens.

Powell, drawn in to the controversy, made as good a case as possible for Sandys's protests that no such 'loophole' was intended, arguing that people who had one status – citizens of a colony with residential rights only locally – could not overnight have another status, citizens of the UK with the same right to live, work, vote and produce a new generation there, as if they had been born there and the 1962 Act, and its intentions, had never existed. He argued that there never had been such a pledge, which would have had to have had full discussion and documentation. Macleod disagreed and specifically declared that the 'loophole' had been known, and the rights had been intended, but he produced no other evidence that this was so. 'Honour the passports' became a slogan.

It was too late – someone had blundered, and the right of entry, exercisable by several hundred thousand Asian families (the total numbers were not clear) proved irreversible. In his Walsall speech, which was followed next day by Sandys's demand for withdrawal of right of entry conferred by the passports, Powell said

> There is a sense of hopelessness and helplessness which comes over persons who are trapped or imprisoned, when all their efforts to attract attention and assistance brings no response. This is the kind of feeling which you in Walsall and we in Wolverhampton are experiencing in the face of the continued immigration into our towns. . . . Out of over 600 parliamentary constituencies perhaps less than 60 are affected in any way like ourselves. The rest know little or nothing and, we might sometimes be tempted to feel, care little or nothing.[21]

This was a criticism not merely of the Labour government, which Powell knew was going to take some action, but of those members of his own party who were putting on the brakes. He spelled out what the continued issue of 8,000 vouchers annually would mean – an additional million immigrants in twenty years, on a basis of five dependants per voucher-holder; he noted that under the current law it was impossible to prevent 40,000 to 50,000 'actual or alleged dependants' mostly of school age or below entering Britain and its school system every year (and he asserted for the first time that official assurances that this number would tail off in a few years were dubious); he referred to the 200,000 Asian passport-holders that the Government did not feel they could exclude; and he added in the effects of the law of summary jurisdiction that enabled illegal immigrants to stay once they avoided action against them for six months. The people of other Commonwealth countries whose governments deported unwanted non-nations must think that 'to use a famous phrase, we are "stark, staring bonkers" to offer all illegal immigrants a prize for breaking the law'. The phrase was Quintin Hogg's, and the implication was that he was one of those who were indifferent to the plight of the sixty stricken areas. Thus Powell was pushing his colleagues into more forthright attitudes and commitments; Heath cautioned him – but Hogg, whatever he did, did not refuse on this occasion to serve with him in the Shadow Cabinet.

The Labour government pushed through in a few days an amending act which took away in future all residential rights from passports issued by British High Commissions to New Commonwealth citizens; but it put, in effect, the East African Asians on a special basis. It put them on a quota; their arrivals were slowed down to meet Britain's 'capacity for absorption'. Thousands poured in to beat the new act. The rest had to form a queue. It became well organised, with many Asian families split deliberately between the two countries, obtaining the best of both worlds; the undertaking to take them all in time remained, however, augmented by time and personal arrangements.

4   The Accusation of Racialism

Though the outspokenness of the Walsall speech kept the lead on immigration with the Conservatives, Heath complained later that it had undermined 'our whole strategy', which was, like Wilson's, to find a policy or approach that would not split his liberals from his right wing. But Powell was not satisfied with what had been achieved even by Callaghan's immigration act. There was still not the sense of urgency or even understanding among parliamentarians that Powell felt necessary. He and other Conservatives could remember how the resolutions pouring in from Constituency Associations in 1961 had overcome the rearguard in the Government still resisting the preparation of the 1962 Immigration Act. The Midlands Area April meeting gave him the occasion for a new speech. But he had nothing new to say beyond stating Conservative opposition to the Callaghan race relations bill. To get bigger results his only recourse lay in presentation and rhetoric, and in still stronger implications of neglect by the national leadership. In February he had noticed that the citing of figures had little effect, whereas the illustration of what the figures meant in terms of an anecdote, like an anecdote in the February speech of a class with only a single white pupil, did drive the point home: not a very new discovery by a politician or a preacher. A certain undertone of desperation in the speech testifies to Powell's own anxiety about the position. It was intended in some measure to appeal over the heads of the politicians of all parties to the people; to encourage the people to round upon the politicians to reciprocate their alarm. Even in this Powell was doing nothing in principle that he had not done before in his campaign to recall his party to fundamentals: 'blatantly' to restate the conditions of freedom and individual liberty, and to break 'the spell' that gripped the country. He felt, he explained later, that 'a lead would only come from words that startle; the sleeping nation will not be awakened by lullabies'.[22]

At the beginning of the Birmingham speech he warned of the curses that followed politicians who succumbed to the temptation to concern themselves with the present at the expense of the future, and noted that it was the function of 'statesmanship' to provide against preventable evils. At the end of the speech, having set out the evil that was being neglected and ignored by the politicians, he concluded: 'Only resolute and urgent action will avert it even now. Whether there will be the public will to demand and obtain that action, I do not know. All that I know is that to see, and not to speak, would be the ultimate betrayal.' This was the central message of the speech; and it was this which outraged the political consensus – and the media who had been as eager as the Conservative Research Department to play down, even deny, 'the evil'.

The substance of the speech was again that 'numbers were of the essence'. As Powell invariably said, 'all I have ever talked about is numbers'. Though he put forward a revised estimate of a population of 3,500,000 immigrants and their descendants in Britain in twenty years (1988), and of ten per cent of the population of England and Wales coloured by 2000 'on present trends', he did not state that this in itself was intolerable or a threat to peace: it was the concentration of this population in a few areas that would cause the explosion, a matter of critical masses, because such concentration must imply that in some areas the coloured new population would progressively outnumber the white natives. Nobody ever contested this, Powell's central point. When the Ugandan Asians arrived in 1972 systematic efforts to settle them in dispersed areas failed: they homed in on Leicester and a few other areas of Asian development.

These were the areas where the people, Powell averred, 'found themselves made strangers in their own country'.

> They found their wives unable to obtain hospital beds in childbirth, their children unable to obtain school places, their homes and neighbourhoods changed beyond recognition, their plans and prospects for the future defeated; at work they found that employers hesitated to apply to the immigrant worker the standards of discipline and competence required of the native-born

worker, they began to hear as time went by more and more voices which told them they were now the unwanted.[23]

In this Powell was speaking for the sixty constituencies. He then turned to the topic which launched the speech, the forthcoming Race Relations Bill:

They now learn that a one-way privilege is to be established by Act of Parliament; a law which cannot, and is not intended to, operate to protect them or redress their grievances, is to be enacted to give the stranger, the disgruntled and the *agent provocateur* the power to pillory them for their private actions.[24]

He repeated his February warning that the sense of being the persecuted minority would be dangerously heightened by the communalism indicated by the Sikh demands for special treatment. From this argument he deduced the dangers of growing racial tension and hostility, which he carefully did not make concrete, but left to the imagination (in Latin, then English) from Virgil: the Sybil's vision of the Tiber foaming with blood.

He made a stronger plea for the Conservative policy of 're-emigration', using this coinage for the first time (though Labour was accepting the general idea) but he put it in a far more comprehensive form by implication. There should, he repeated, be no discrimination between citizens of Britain under law or by public authority; but, while it could be no part of any policy that existing families should be kept divided,

there are two directions in which families can be reunited, and if our former and present immigration policies have brought about a division of families, albeit voluntary ... we ought to be prepared to arrange for them to be reunited in their country of origin.

This proposition in particular was received with alarm and indignation by the immigrant organisations. They rejected the status of *gastärbeiter*, of transient or contract workers such as they had known in colonial history. They now had rights, civic status, a grip on Britain; and some said they would be 'repatriated only over our dead bodies'. Most settlers, as opposed to transients, move first to improve their immediate prospects and then, when established, to bring in their families and ensure that their children do still better in the new environment. They wanted for their families the superior British welfare and education. To some extent, Powell felt, Asians emigrate as a way of life, taking their way of life with them and implanting it as a separate self-sustaining culture, a condition of mind and motive dissimilar in root, and therefore in social fruit, to the migrations of Europeans to other lands.

But it was not his repatriation suggestions which produced the attack on the speech or the charge of fomenting racial conflict such as had not followed the Walsall speech in February. What set off the outcry was the two or three harrowing case-histories which Powell had inserted in order to 'reflect the mood, the experiences of people who do live in these areas', as he put it to David Frost on television,[25] to bring the realities home to the millions who lived in areas where no such impact could be seen or understood.

Frost denied these case-histories were typical – the old lady who had excrement pushed through her letter box, the constituent who said that in twenty years' time the black man in Wolverhampton would have the whip hand over the white man, the single white child in the class (the Walsall speech was now under intense scrutiny not given it in February). It was asserted that the white child was alone in class only one day (Powell had given no time limit), the old lady whose ordeal had been reported to Powell in a letter was never found by investigative journalists, and Powell refused to identify her: Frost insisted 'You have only one story, and you don't give evidence of it.' Powell's reply that a speech, not being a book, can only give instances, was rejected by Frost on the ground they were unacceptable instances. Powell replied that the typicality of the cases had been confirmed to him by Dr Bamford, a South London general practitioner, quite apart from letters he had received himself by the hundred. He referred Frost to the Milner-Holland and other reports on landlord-tenant disputes. Messrs Smithies and Fiddick, in their extended analysis of the speech, pointed out that of the 790 cases of this kind reported, only one was of mistreatment of a white tenant by a coloured landlord. The argument continued to fascinate journalists for some time.[25]

The debate with Frost enabled Powell to explain that he had never used an argument about race as such; if racialist, however, is a term applied to people conscious of race differences 'then we are all racialists'. He rebuffed Frost's (and others') attempts to lure him into pronouncing on controversies among scientists about the inherent superiority of one race over another, whether in all or in some qualities, because he had not studied the evidence: what he was discussing was the displacement of one population by another population with distinctive differences of colour, culture, language and norms of behaviour. Because of these differences, the process of assimilation or integration would be slower than would suffice to absorb Poles, Huguenots or Jews; it followed that those who wanted that process to take place must accept a limitation upon numbers of newcomers being injected into the host society.

Few people have contested Powell's statements that the New Commonwealth immigration has been out of proportion to any previous intake, or that in terms of assimilability it cannot be compared with previous migrations. The most honest reply to Powell's contention has come from those who, like Bishop Huddleston, believe it is morally good for the British people to have an almost unlimited number of Asian and African newcomers thrust upon them, and that they will only reveal un-Christian and immoral characteristics if they cannot peacefully yield up part of their homeland and possessions to them. In debate with Powell, the Bishop retorted to his forecast of a 10 per cent coloured population in 2000 that a Christian people ought to be glad to have at least as many: immigration, he implied, was a God-given opportunity to show virtue. He gave the impression that white people might not be morally capable of such feats as non-white, but he challenged Powell, as a professing Christian, to put his religion into practice in the matter. To which Powell's reply (frequently stated on many issues) was that Christianity and politics are distinct: that a politician who places on people burdens to which they are unequal is responsible for the consequences; churchmen have no such responsibility. They preach to men to practise virtue, they do not pass laws to enforce virtue.[26]

(Powell carried the war into the Church's camp on subsequent occasions, asking, for example, if it was Christian doctrine, as distinct from the practice of race relations, for a priest to attend – as one did – the rites of Hindu deities when celebrated in England.)

There was another reaction to Powell's speech from those who (like Sir Edward Boyle, his erstwhile colleague) believed in multi-racial, plural, culturally diverse, societies as inherently good, precisely and particularly because they weaken a sense of nationhood which such people regard as unduly exclusive. Powell likened such professions of enlightenment to the man who jumps off a tower saying 'look, I have become an angel'.

He had the whole establishment against him. To Labour he was a God-given pariah, political leper; though when Labour MPs were lobbied by the dockers demonstrating for Powell, some of them were reported to have come close to abandoning the proletarian convictions of a lifetime. As for the press, Powell declared that 'No imputation, no innuendo has been too vile for supposedly reputable journals to invent or repeat.'[27] He had exposed not only the gap between political leadership and the feelings of the people, but between journalists and the facts. An opinion poll showed that 74 per cent of the sample agreed with the speech, 69 per cent thought Heath wrong to dismiss him for making it, and 24 per cent thought he would make the best leader for the Tories – against 1 per cent who thought so before 20 April.[28]

Powell made a short impenitent speech at the Party Conference in October. He had stressed the crucial importance of concentration; but he surprisingly diminished his previously expressed confidence in the community's absorptive powers by doubting if even a coloured community of 5 per cent spread evenly over the country 'could be contemplated with equanimity'. He feared the distraction of attention from his own prescription – a party commitment to massive repatriation. 'A large part, a greater part, of the present coloured immigrants and their families do not yet regard this country as a place of permanent settlement.' Quintin Hogg retorted, 'what numerical contribution to the problem does he expect from the policy of repatriation to which he is committed and we are committed?' Macleod called him a pedlar of panaceas. In short, there was to be no big commitment to repatriation in the coming election manifesto. The platform carried the voting, but the applause went to Powell, who had himself to quieten it.[29]

5   The Argument for Repatriation

At Eastbourne in November he not only defended the Birmingham speech and his behaviour towards his colleagues, but he also began the process of showing, in successive speeches henceforward, that his statistics were well founded, his statements about conditions in the afflicted areas not exaggerated: 'In September the very newspapers which had attacked me [for the story of one white child in a class] had the ignominy of having to report the existence not only in Wolverhampton but in Birmingham of such classes, as well as the 90 per cent immigrant school in my own constituency. So quickly does the incredible turn into what everyone knew all the time.' (Soon after local authorities introduced bussing lest they had more such powellian conditions to report.) To support the instance he had given of the 'typical situation of the last and usually elderly white inhabitants' of a street passing into immigrant occupation he quoted three similar cases reported to him by Dr Bamford.

He also dealt with the years when he, along with most other Conservatives, had failed to take action. The taunt 'you did the wrong, you have no right to talk about it now', levelled by Conservative as well as Labour leaders and critics like Paul Foot, offended against his concept of Parliament's sovereignty – the all-important circumstance that one parliament can undo what another did and afford redress. 'Woe betide that nation that will not let its rulers admit their errors and try to remedy the consequences: there is no surer way to persist in a disastrous course . . . than to attach the penalty of mockery to those who say "we have done wrong".' Nobody but Powell had the least intention of admitting they had done wrong.

Powell rejected Quintin Hogg's assertion that the repatriation policy which they could undertake would have little numerical effect. He demanded a party commitment to an ambitious programme for the election. He conceded that it would become progressively more difficult as the proportion of immigrant-descended coloured people increased, even though they often would retain their parent's nationality as well as British-born citizenship. In 1968 this 'first generation of black British' was still small; but it would not long stay so: in Wolverhampton an immigrant population consisting of 5·2 per cent, or one in twenty inhabitants, was producing 23 per cent of the births, one in four. Re-emigration, as he rechristened repatriation, was only feasible so long as the immigrants had a home overseas with which to identify. The elderly might well retire there; it was the young people that he wanted to find their careers there and not here. Early in 1969 Heath appeared with Powell and other Midland MPs on the platform of an area meeting at which he agreed that provision for repatriation was part of the policy for the election, and promised that a government of his would insist on finding out the facts and figures of the immigration, and its implications for the future. He was embarrassed when he was asked from the floor why, if that was his policy, he would not take Powell back into the Shadow Cabinet.[30]

It was a matter of emphasis and sincerity; Powell believed that hundreds of thousands of families could be given inducements to re-emigrate ('a bullies' charter' *The Times* called such a policy). He pointed out that the West Indians, and even more the Asians, maintained a network of family and social relations with their places of origin; many when they first arrived intended to return when they had made enough money; they therefore had communities with which they could be reunited humanely by providing adequate inducements, which would be increased if further immigration were halted and the uniting of families should be in the homeward direction rather than Britainward.[31] He quoted a survey for the BBC that suggested that 20 per cent would so respond, and on this analysis he suggested that an active Ministry of Repatriation could reduce the prospective immigrant population in 1985 by no less than 500,000; in effect he wanted to cut off reinforcement of the immigrant colonies and cut down the rate of increase of British-born who would mostly claim they had no other home.

> At present large numbers of the offspring of immigrants, even those born here in Britain remain integrated in the immigrant community which links them with their homeland overseas. With every passing year this will diminish.[32]

He then went on to say that, for the majority, assimilation would not come about. Alienation would.

> The West Indian or Asian does not, by being born in England, become an Englishman. In law he becomes a United Kingdom citizen by birth; in fact he is a West Indian or Asian still. Unless he be one of the small minority – for number, I repeat again and again, is of the essence – he will by the very nature of things have lost one country without acquiring a new one. Time is running against us and them. With the lapse of a generation we shall at last have succeeded – to the benefit of nobody – in reproducing in England's green and pleasant land the haunting tragedy of the United States.[33]

The dislodgement of the indigenous population on a scale that would convert whole towns in Yorkshire and the Midlands, whole areas of Inner London, into 'preponderantly or exclusively' Afro-Asian settlements must eventually produce violence: 'I do not believe that it is in human nature that a country, and such a country as ours, should passively watch the transformation of whole areas which lie at the heart of it into alien territory.'[34] Yet so far, as Powell had shown, the natives had surrendered – moved out – passively; and the establishment were anxious that this submissiveness should not change.

His assertion that immigrants could not become Englishmen was held an insult to coloured people by the liberals, who also had a great belief in the retention of cultures other than the English one; the coloured people had indeed been saying this for years and were happy to quote Powell as a good reason why they should remain themselves. Black spokesmen maintain that the Englishman has to be re-made, surgically operated upon for his racial and cultural prejudice; and that it is the mission of the black man to do just this, for it is the challenge of

British society that provides the black man with the means to throw off in battle his slave or colonial mentality. Hence the black – or West Indian – argument that freedom is to be in the battle of Britain, in the front-line of race conflict, rather than in the stagnant West Indies. As one has written, 'England is heaven even when they don't admit it'.[35]

The first report of the Community Relations Commission gave assurances, however, that assimilation was proceeding steadily as the school system worked upon the rising immigrant generation, 'English in every respect except the colour of their skins'. Powell called such talk an intolerable arrogance from people who would not dream of saying that the second generation of English born abroad are Chinese or Indians in all respects except the colour of their skins.[36]

Numbers remained of the essence; using the birth figures kept separately in some cities for the immigrant and native populations, surveys of the use of maternity services, and statistics kept by some education authorities of the proportion of native and immigrant children in schools, he pieced together a profile of the future adult population of certain areas when the new coloured population grew up, reporting his findings to a sceptical and sometimes abusive House of Commons in November 1969. He established that 19·5 per cent of the twelve Inner London boroughs with a combined population of 3 million would be coloured – because one birth in five was coloured (Hon. Members: 'So what?'). He examined the figures for Leicester and Huddersfield and showed that the proportion of coloured births was rising and showing no sign of reaching any peak; in Birmingham the proportion had risen from 7 to 21 per cent between 1958 and 1968, while in Wolverhampton the proportion had reached 25 per cent. He pointed out that the native population was moving out, and would do so even more. He showed that he had underestimated the trend. His forecast of internecine violence was received with angry shouts, but he concluded:

> The Home Secretary . . . asked me to appeal for understanding, for tolerance, for restraint, for patience. The Right Hon. Gentleman has it exactly wrong. It is not to the people of this country that we in this House should be appealing for tolerance, restraint and understanding. The people . . . have shown tolerance. There can be no criticism of the people . . . for the way in which this unexpected, even uncomprehended event has been received by them. It is not from us to them that the appeal goes. The appeal is from the people . . . to this House – and this House has not heard them yet. Let this House do so while there is still time.[37]

The House hardly disputed his figures; and Powell told audiences that his deliberately understated figures, previously 'treated with ridicule and abuse', had now been 'removed from the realm of conjecture and placed firmly in the realm of fact'.[38] He dealt with those who insisted that the only danger of internecine violence was his own instigation of it by quoting from local newspapers and Community Relations officers to show that violence was beginning to simmer under the surface. Those who had first derided his figures now promised that the roots of any incipient violence lay not in the dislodging of white by black in particular areas, or fears of the whites for their jobs, but simply in bad housing or a total lack of enough jobs for all.

Heath had proposed, and Labour broadly agreed, that funds should be made available to those local authorities which had an 'immigrant problem' defined in such material terms: whereupon Powell attacked the proposal. Attitudes and human nature would not be changed, he said, by spending money on health, housing, schools or development:

> Except as an integral part of a policy of voluntary and assisted repatriation, measures of financial and other alleviation to the administration of the areas specially affected, measures to . . . facilitate the absorption . . . of that part of the coloured population which will eventually make a permanent home here and become a part of national life, are worse than merely neutral in effect. They are positively harmful in their nett effect, because they encourage all concerned to deceive themselves . . . and they squander these few precious remaining years when it still might be possible to avoid disaster.[39]

Heath saw in this piece of powellian logic ('tortuous' Boyle called it) an opportunity to put his own policies in a liberal and humanitarian light. He publicly said Powell's argument that 'to help coloured people was positively harmful is an example of man's inhumanity to man which is absolutely intolerable in a civilised society'. Powell protested that Heath's condensation of his actual words was completely misleading, to which Heath replied that he had spoken only after carefully reading the speech 'and I have nothing to add or alter to what I have said'. Attempts to paper over this new breach failed; Heath seemed determined to leave the impression that Powell wanted to hound out the immigrants.[40]

This version of Powell's intentions found a ready ear among the liberals. Praful Patel, the prominent spokesman for immigrant interests, urged that he should be called to appear before the Parliamentary Select Committee on Race Relations and asked to be constructive. Powell had supposed he was being constructive; but the Committee lacked the gammon to invite him. He found himself shouted down or refused a hearing when invited to university gatherings; but taxi drivers refused to accept fares from him. A group of businessmen had offered finance for a 'Powell for Premier' campaign, which he had rejected in September 1969; the offer was to be renewed from time to time. He invariably replied that Heath was the elected Party leader. Heath had the satisfaction of observing that the numbers agreeing with Powell's views in opinion polls had dropped from 74 per cent after the Birmingham speech to 48 per cent at the time of Heath's second reprimand. Heath, having attacked Powell on 'tone' and 'humanity', and on making a difficult job worse in an irresponsible manner, quietly began to emulate Powell on content, calling for tighter controls on dependants and in no way watering down his party's repatriation scheme.

Before the election Powell was able to point to the admission by the Registrar

General that the number of births to immigrant parents in 1969, put at 35,000 earlier, was in fact 51,863, or around 52,000 with Scotland added, and on very restrictive assumptions about the coloured illegitimacy rate. It was an error of practically 50 per cent ('Imagine', he remarked in an aside, 'what would have been said if the trade deficit had turned out to be 50 per cent larger than the government had estimated!').

The error[41] could not be dismissed as minor because it related to one year. In a paper to the Institute of Population Registration he brought all the figures together to show that such an error invalidated *all* the current official projections. Taking those for Birmingham alone, and without taking fresh arrivals into account, the records implied that a complete generation would be 20 per cent coloured by 1979, which meant that 25 or so years on, the population of Birmingham as whole would be 20 per cent coloured. The same analysis of the figures showed that the annual addition to the coloured population in Britain was nearly 60 per cent greater than the official estimate, and on reasonable assumptions more like 100 per cent. In one of his election speeches he mentioned these errors as implying that 'the size of the present immigrant population, or its birthrate, or the two combined, are twice what the government have assured us.'[42] Hence the coloured population in 1970 must be nearer two million than the 1,250,000 officially estimated. The subsequent analysis of the 1971 Census admitted, however, only a error sufficient to raise the total to 1,500,000 (which would mean only $1\frac{3}{4}$ million by 1975). But Powell had reservations about the Census returns. In any case they did not take into account the effect of white emigration. The small coloured population was already increasing numerically as fast as the large white one: 'at that rate the proportion between the two is altering very rapidly'.

Reviewing the work on statistics between the Birmingham speech and the election of 1970 he noted 'those who mocked two years ago have taken refuge either in silence or abuse. What I said is ceasing to be a prediction and is becoming current fact. There are at this moment parts of this town [Wolverhampton] which have ceased to be part of England except in the sense that they are situated in it geographically.'[42]

To those who accused him of making self-fulfilling prophecies by asserting stridently that the newcomers were unassimilable he retorted, 'I can be mistaken about the consequences, or, if I am not mistaken about these, then I can be mistaken about the possibility of averting them. What is certain is that, whatever the consequences are, my words could not cause them and my silence could not avert them.' His critics often spoke as if Powell alone had created racial tension; had he been silent inter-racial harmony would have occurred naturally. He retorted that as the colonies of aliens grew and solidified, as they took in each other's washing in every way and moved to cultural self-sufficiency, so would their alienness; and this process would give them the appearance, both to themselves and to those they progressively supplanted in area after area, of victorious invaders, and would impart to the natives a sense of being worsted.

Powell thought this would intensify resentment. The liberals denied that it would: arguing that with suitable help people would happily rearrange themselves.[43]

Between 1968 and 1970 Powell, from a protesting insider had become an influential outsider in party politics. His unpopularity was proportionate to the destruction of his critics' arguments by statistics and facts. In pushing him out of the party's counsels, Heath pushed him into a populist experience. He had to appeal to and react to the national constituency. He could not be unaffected by the letters, the applause, the tumultuous receptions; by the touching offerings of humble people; by the contempt and vilification of the intelligentsia; by the howlings-down in places of learning; by the attacks from the pulpit and the magisterial condemnation of *The Times*. He was struck; he saw people fighting savagely; he could judge how the herd reacts; it all fed his apprehensions for the future.

When, however, one looks not at the Birmingham speech in isolation, but at the whole sequence of Powell's speeches, his diligent assembly of the demographic and social facts as they became available, in the five years up to the election of 1970, it becomes harder to imagine that he could ever have spoken very differently, give or take an anecdote. Nor is it easy to see how any discussion of these facts could have done other than divide him, however reluctantly, from the Heath–Hogg–Macleod–Boyle viewpoint. He once said that he did not find the immigration issue, it found him. One could almost add, it chased him – a sort of hound of heaven. In retrospect he seemed to feel there was a destiny in it, the destiny of his inherited make-up, of that Hardyian sense that character is fate. For once he intervened it was decisive in a way that a Griffiths election victory never could be. He had set the politicians' teeth on edge, and he was a man apart. His earlier reluctance becomes then as significant as the rhetoric at the Birmingham meeting. It is an indispensable equipment of politicians to have premonitions.

Chapter 8

Powell *v.* Heath III: The Lords and the Constitution; the 1970 Election. 1969–1970

1   Populist and Parliamentarian

Just over two years elapsed between Powell's dismissal from Heath's Shadow Cabinet and the acid test of his influence on public opinion in June 1970. They were important years. The experience of being execrated by almost the entire leadership of society – by the best, the cleverest, the wittiest, by the most powerful and articulate, both inside Parliament and outside, across all party lines and degrees of civility from Andrew Faulds to Quintin Hogg – yet at the same time being applauded by the '*canaille*' in their millions, could leave no man unaffected. Insofar as a man can be detached, at least outwardly, Powell was such a man. The press photographers, the cameramen, above all the cartoonists brought his features into everyone's home, cast into demonic, mischievous, urbane, quizzical or other expressions as occasion suggested. His audiences, already large, increased still further; now halls were packed and overflow arrangements had to be made. He was overwhelmed with requests. Often militants cat-called at the doors, while police stood guard. 'I have been heard,' he remarked, 'as no politician has been heard since the war.' He made one hundred speeches between April and December, 1968.

He was not only heard on immigration. In these years he added important new themes to powellism, notably those of the Common Market and the defence of Ulster. But the events of 1968 and 1969, the showdown with Heath, gave amplification to all that he had been saying about free enterprise, common sense in social services, trade unions and inflation. Powell was not unknown before 1968: he was, as politicians go who are not right under the spotlight, well known. His impact over immigration was so great precisely because of his reputation as a political thinker, an outspoken man of original mind and intellectual integrity; Cyril Osborne could hardly have achieved it, for all his standard-bearing in the fifties. Along with Powell's stand over immigration there grew in the public consciousness a broader, if fuzzier, picture of a man with an alternative policy, a man (whether you always liked what he said or not) who stood apart from the consensus, a word to be translatable into the cynical vernacular about politicians, 'they're all the same really'. Powell was not the same; people began to see he never had been; and from 1968 onwards he had only to speak on any aspect of powellism to strengthen this impression. His solitary position, attacked by all the parties and pundits in these years, enhance d his appeal. But many of the pundits denied that such a position conferred any influence where it mattered – in Westminster, in power politics.

The first subject to which he gave new attention was the growth of violence. 1968 was a violent year – Paris, Chicago and Grosvenor Square were salient episodes. He had a taste of the upsurge in his reception by students and staff at universities. Unprepared to listen to reason, they made meetings into such a travesty of academic discussion that he finally declined invitations to what was often designed to be a free-for-all. But he sought to rationalise: to find the underlying reasons for this almost unattached unreasoning explosiveness – almost 'panic' in the classical sense. He found one cause in the lawlessness of the state itself under socialist rule, and indeed, going further back, under Macmillan's directive interference.

> The state has failed, or ceased, to perform its most elementary function, which is the protection of the physical safety of its members. Politics has become so engrossed with the functions of government as interfering with individuals and rearranging society, with its functions in organising the life and activities of citizens, deciding how they shall be housed and educated, cared for in sickness and maintained in age – so much so that its first duty of all, to protect them from violence, has almost atrophied.[1]

An endemic propensity to violence, so analysed, lent emphasis to his warning about being myopic about the combustible material of race rivalries in cities; and it was soon exemplified again in Ulster. Weakness, whether in men or states, is usually challenged. Powell found this challenge in the working-up of a new technique to 'radicalise' protests and grievances. He identified 'a great innovation, which, like all other major inventions of mankind, looks so simple that the wonder afterwards is that it was not thought of long before.'

> Like all inventions it is essentially a method of getting large results with disproportionately small effort. . . . Into a normal situation inject a new element of purposeless violence and aggression. . . . Suddenly news exists where there was none before – pictures, action, reports. As the violence was purposeless, everyone is bound to set to work on discovering its purpose . . . Grievances are found to exist, which therefore by definition ought to have been removed before . . . with the speed of an explosion roles are reversed: the blame for the violence is discovered to lie with authority: government, law, society itself, are put in the dock by the criminal: the simple fact of the violent aggression becomes proof that those who are attacked are guilty.[2]

Ulster became the outstanding example of this process in 1969, but defiance of authority at the universities provided other case-histories of Powell's theory, which so angered the professors that Lord Annan, whose subsequent report broadly confirmed Powell's analysis, referred to him as a 'renegade don'.

Aggro would not have got far if the forces of authority, moral and physical (a frightened Home Office was hurriedly trying to strengthen the neglected police) were not in disarray. Powell found one cause of this moral confusion in the concept of 'human rights', non-justiciable rights, inflated to an absurd degree. Such human rights, passionately proclaimed in the abstract, but negated and disappointed in real life, provided an endless supply of grievances to exploit – even to gunpoint – and inevitably to put authority on the defensive. Hence grew a miasma of guilt in the establishment, a guilt that produced its own reversed intolerance, so that, as Powell noted, people became afraid (under social and other pressures) to speak their minds about taboo subjects, even though what they wished to discuss was entirely legal. 'The Permissive Society' meant anything but true freedom of speech.

His experience in housing enabled him to dissect the fell consequences of one of these: the 'right' in the UN Charter of everyone to a standard of living adequate to the health and welfare of his family. There cannot be such a right enforceable at law; but it became in the mouths of the radicals a 'right' to housing of a standard (unspecified) adequate to health and welfare; which in turn permits Shelter and other bodies to accuse Britain of denying people the basic 'right' – a decent home. Inevitably subsidy and compulsion were invoked to fulfil the right, and this, as Powell had showed (see pp. 35–6) in fact led to a shortage of housing and worse conditions than an absence of 'right' and the presence of a free market would deliver. 'Not only does the unlimited role of the state provide unlimited fuel for dissatisfaction; it provides unlimited scope for the fostering of animosities between one section of potential recipients and another.' And this led by easy stages to terrorism.

Anarchy comes in thought, in the use of words and terms, before it comes in the street. Powell exposed the shoddy thinking behind the lofty words of Lord Hill, Chairman of the BBC when he said (to applause) that 'a man who speaks in favour of racial intolerance cannot have the same rights as he who defends tolerance', a proposition in which neither race nor tolerance were defined (or even could be); it was a piece of double-think under which the BBC could apply its liberal 'partiality' to those who supported the race relations acts of 1965 and 1968, and suppress other views, often by distorting them.[3] Powell had said, provided numbers were controlled 'There is no limit, over the years and generations, to the changes we can undergo – yes, or to the strangers we can absorb – and still remain throughout it all ourselves.'[4] The *Daily Mail* encapsulated his views as, 'Powell: They'll never be English'.

The immigration debate had revealed an anarchy in culture, a tendency to sentimentalism, a confusion in logic and meaning of law and authority, which prejudiced the country's future (though not only Britain's) as much as the myths of empire and world role. It was a climate that many saw as ripe for a populist leader, and many looked expectantly at Enoch Powell. Foolishly: for Powell saw the country's safety in its institutions, above all in the subtle, always varying but dynamic relation between people and Parliament. The year that began with his taking the immigration issue to the people ended with him in the centre of House of Commons argument, demonstrating to general admiration his skills as a parliamentarian over a constitutional issue to which the people were indifferent. There was no inconsistency. And nobody who listened to his constitutional theory in the debates on House of Lords reform between November 1968 and April 1969 would be likely to think he would make any alliances with the National Front which claimed parentage of his ideas (quite wrongly) and would have liked his name. (Oswald Mosley shrewdly recognised how far apart were powellism and such a movement.)

2   The Lords and the Constitution

The battles over the Parliament No. 2 Bill picked up and restated the essential strand in all Powell's thinking: a unique Parliament for a unique people (one might add, and a unique Conservative Party to complete a stable triune structure). To defend that citadel of polity, Powell was prepared when necessary to override party; and over the Lords he made a successful albeit informal alliance with the left wing of the Labour Party. It was a prelude to his opposition to the Communities Bill in 1971–2, and the devolution bills in 1976–8. In all three campaigns party rules and conventions were broken in favour of higher loyalties to principle. In all three extremes met: the so-called right wing of the Tories, which included those often called Powellites, making common cause with the far left, the socialist fellow-travelling elements of the Labour Party. In all three cases Powell articulated, and to a lesser extent helped to organise, an inter-party revolt on the floor of the House, against the government of the day – indeed against a consensus of the party leadership. Differing in form, the three campaigns were alike in this: they opposed basic changes in the constitution.

The long-term aims of the allies were incompatible: Powell wanted to keep the checks and balances of the constitution, the integrity and sovereignty of Parliament, because these were the defences of freedom; the Labour left opposed change only because they desired the unalloyed power of Parliament, sovereign and unicameral, to make the far more drastic changes that would dispose of mere 'bourgeois liberties'. Though they loathed Powell's principles and politics, they gladly cooperated with his skills in their tactical needs: thus displaying their mastery of historical-objective dialectic.

To Powell, as to any high Tory, the slow evolution of British institutions is what gives them their authority. This was also the argument against the Reform Bill of 1832: Burke defended the rotten boroughs by his doctrine of prescription – that what worked in one age excellently was not to be condemned merely because its origins offended natural justice. Powell pointed out that most cherished British institutions had been evolved rather than designed by Lockean logic: trial by jury, the House of Commons, even a constitutional monarchy. In February 1958, when out of office, he opposed his party on the creation of life peers. The arguments that he then put forward he developed in greater detail in opposition to the further round of 'Lords Reform' ten years later. In 1958 he was completing the first part of his historical study of the House of Lords, subsequently published in 1968 as *The House of Lords in the Middle Ages*.[5] He was well-equipped to tell friends and opponents alike with complete candour,

> There is no possibility of arguing that the present composition of the House of Lords can be justified by logic or preconceived constitutional theory. . . . It is the result of a long, even a tortuous process of historical evolution. Its authority rests on the result of that historical process.[6]

But in 1958 (as in 1832, he could have added) the House of Commons rested on no logic in the principles whereby members are elected or the House formed, either: 'it rests on acceptance by the nation of an institution, the history of which cannot be torn out of the context of the history of the nation itself'.

But history means change; change is the theme of Powell's career; and change he did not deny to the House of Lords any more than to the Commons. It was not the hereditary principle alone, but also the notion of conferring dignity by patent, that had preserved the House of Peers for 500 years. Powell approached the Life Peerages Bill simply in the Burkean spirit that one should not interfere except under the necessity of avoiding an evil that is clear and imminent, and in such a way as to obviate it – as Reform in 1832 avoided the threat of civil war, justifying the Whigs and others who carried it. But in 1958 Powell argued that the reasons given for interfering with the prescriptive principle were not convincing; no danger impended of an overriding sort. The object was to enable the Socialist point of view to be put more effectively in the House of Lords and to give the Prime Minister a wider range of ministerial and expert talent to draw upon. To which Powell's answer was that the Prime Minister of the day could always make enough hereditary peers to take its whip in the Lords and that, as Lord Tweedsmuir had shown in a notable speech, the Upper House was already one of great variety, and of all ages and types of experience. He said that the bill was desired by neither party, an intimation of the 1968 situation. The real feeling on the Labour left in 1958 was, as in 1968, for outright abolition.

The Life Peerages Bill went through, however; it was complemented in 1963 by the Renunciation of Titles Act passed largely if not explicitly to meet the desire of Anthony Wedgwood Benn not to inherit his father's title (Lord Stansgate) and to avoid his enforced transfer from the House of Commons, where he sensed that he had a brilliant future, to the Lords where he had none. Designed for a Socialist's convenience, the Act, Macmillan was to note with amusement later, enabled Lords Home and Hailsham to renounce their peerages and become candidates for leadership later in that year; it might have been designed as a custom-built tool to ditch R. A. Butler. Later both became peers again. The episode was a remarkable blurring of differences between peers and commoners, though Benn did not so acclaim it. When Powell joined the Cabinet he found the decision made; but he took the opportunity of going on record against it. It may be one thing for peers to decide not to use their titles; it is another to hop from one house to the other as prospects of offices and dignities suggested.

The plan to extend further the 'democratising' of the House of Lords followed the lines of the interparty conference of 1948 which had failed to reach agreement. The object, both in 1948 and 1968, was to fashion out of the husk of the Upper House a new sort of revising and delaying second chamber which did not depend on the hereditary peerage, which was to be phased out. The institution of 'life peers' had still left the House with a majority of hereditary peers who, however circumspectly, mostly voted Conservative and above all *felt* conservative, as did many of the life peers who started their political lives as Labour MPs. The Lords' powers to delay legislation, though truncated, remained; this amounted to a veto in the last year of a Labour government's life, unless it was re-elected. What made this veto appear a matter of mere prejudice was that the Lords so rarely treated a Conservative government in this way, natural as such conduct usually was when Parliament consists of an innovating and a revising chamber.

The 1968 bill was designed to change all this. It was introduced by agreement with the Conservative and Liberal oppositions. It was, therefore, another example of the consensus politics that Powell found suspect. The Conservatives under Heath were ready for change, but mainly because they did not want to give Labour an excuse to make outright abolition their policy. R. H. S. Crossman, who introduced the bill,[7] admitted that he would have preferred abolition, but said that when he had examined its implications he had come down for a reform which reduced the powers of the Lords but provided the government of the day with a built-in majority of life peers, a kind of aldermanic majority for the party which won the election, analogous to the system long in use in local government. The aldermen were to be 'Lords of Parliament', but nonetheless placemen. One of Crossman's arguments to his own back benches was that the House of Lords had the virtue of being the weakest second chamber in the democratic world, and his plan would institutionalise this weakness. The sop to the Conservatives was to allow existing hereditary peers to sit, and speak, but not to vote, until their deaths; voting would be confined to the appointed peers, the government retaining a right always to adjust by creation their number to a level that gave it a small majority.

Such a plan violated Powell's conception of the constitution even more than the introduction of an auxiliary life peerage. The battle that ensued was confined to Westminster. The public was not aroused, and in the press of his speaking engagements up and down the land, Powell made it the theme of only one. Public disinterest encouraged the front benches to think they could push through a deal that suited them both. They underestimated back-bench dislike of both bill and front-bench collusion. The result was a series of debates on second reading and in committee which qualified for Powell's criterion of a 'great parliamentary occasion', though it came too late for inclusion in his broadcast series under that title.[8]

Having decided that the inherent impracticability, inconsistency and sheer opportunism of the Parliament No. 2 Bill rendered it destructible in committee, Powell began his second reading speech by predicting its collapse:

> I believe that long before the end of this debate, let alone of any proceedings which are to follow, the Government will have been undeceived as to . . . the degree of agreement about it. Indeed it is a symptom of what is to come that I find myself in unwonted and far-reaching concurrence with . . . [Sir Dingle Foot] who already . . . has shot away in ridicule considerable portions of the scheme. Reform is commended to us on two distinct and contradictory grounds. One is in order to prevent the Upper House from frustrating or unduly delaying the decisions . . . of this House. The other ground, which is contradictory to it, is to enable the Upper House to be a more effective check upon . . . this House . . . both these notions are chimerical. . . .[9]

He argued that the present Lords could not frustrate the firm intention of the Commons because to do so was to risk a crisis and their own abolition. He added that this was still true in respect of their power to veto a statutory instrument, where their powers were not limited by the reforms of 1911 and 1949. Nor was there any need to provide a greater check, such as the bill actually proposed, on the Commons; and he did not think that the Commons, if they found a sharper check was operating, would tolerate it, 'and would not again seek to overthrow the legislation which had made it possible.' A greater check on the Commons could only be exercised by an elective house or a nominated one. What was valid in a federation, where the upper house represented the units separately from the numerical population at large, was not possible in Britain. Either, therefore, one concocted a chamber capable of claiming far more authority than a hereditary peerage could do nowadays, or an assembly of placemen who would owe debts of gratitude to the governments and parties which had ennobled them, and would vote not on merit but on party loyalty. (The Supreme Court of the United States is perhaps an example of the difficulties of packing a body whose membership is terminal for a man's ambition.) An elective upper house in a unitary state posed a basic conundrum:

> If we were to establish another chamber representing the same electorate we should be faced with the insoluble conundrum 'who are the true representatives of the wishes and party affiliations of that electorate?' One or the other would have to concede . . . However the method [of voting] was rigged, we would never escape from this dilemma: how can the same electorate be represented in two ways so that the two sets of representatives can conflict and disagree with each other?[10]

This being so, Powell turned to the alternative, nomination, and easily demonstrated that it was a device inferior to the prescriptive system they had happily inherited from the vicissitudes of the past. He pointed out that under Crossman's scheme the transfer of a mere six votes from government to opposition among the Lords of Parliament would checkmate government business. To ensure that the nominees of either party did not change sides they would have to swear to vote like robots, a precondition which would ensure that only Tadpoles and Tapers would wish to be ennobled. If the dummies voted like statesmen on some critical issue, breaking their bond, they would lack the 'built-in respect which would give the other place a counterbalancing influence that would make it a complement to this House'. Such a House would have no more authority than its makers, who would claim authority to make it and remake it again and again, 'until in the end we shall come to that which the vast majority of Hon Members do not want to see – single chamber government'. Hence no system of nominees could at once give the government a majority and provide checks and delays on the part of the Upper House.

Powell then played a leading role in turning the committee stage into a constitutional conference. This generated filibusters (notably Sheldon's long but cogent speech) and wrecking amendments: as Michael Foot artfully put, 'Even though I hate this bill, I am prepared to see whether it is possible to amend or improve it, making a silk purse out of a sow's ear.' Such an approach devoured the Government's time for other business: exemplifying one of the major checks that back-benchers can apply to legislation, unless the government is able and willing to apply the guillotine, which itself can be opposed with considerable unpleasantness for the government.

The bill provided a preview of legislative procedure to come, which Foot identified and attacked: the use of the preamble to assert a principle which the Government was not willing to define in detail and which went beyond the clauses in the bill. Powell applauded Foot's stand, even though it included the admonition that his long-term objective was to remove a weighting in the constitution 'on the side of reaction, the elderly, the establishment, and similar forces in our society'.

Powell, in his speeches, concentrated on the absurdity of a House of Peers that would be a house of unequals, some having the right to vote and speak, others only to speak; an affront to the whole principle of parliamentary responsibility in either house: 'that our vote must follow our voice is a tremendous discipline'. Such an arrangement would either produce a house that would be a creature of the executive, or a rockbound, indefensible opposition to the popularly elected house. 'We want a house with an independent life which springs from a different principle of existence, expresses a different need . . . with all its . . . imperfections we at present have a second chamber that does fulfil that specification. . . .'[11]

The readiness of the hereditary peers to accept the sweetener of life membership to barter away the principle of the Upper House was, to Powell as to other members, a foretaste of the corruption to come: a further sign of the overweening powers of the executive to manipulate Parliament, to take every opportunity to speed the process of undermining its power and independence. These themes, stated in 1969, were to be restated in the years ahead. Powell argued that British institutions were corporate bodies with corporate attributes, belonging to past, present and future.

> The British constitution is not the personal property of any particular generation of members of either House . . . We who sit here are not in possession of the fee simple cf the House of Commons, so that if sufficient inducements were offered to us, we might agree to barter it away. . . . Similarly . . . the prescriptive chamber is not the possession of any group of noble lords now living. Good or bad, it is the possession of the nation . . . It is something they did not create and do not own.[12]

Rather daringly, Powell, in attacking the mercenary-minded aristocrats – the leisured class that irritated his Black Country instincts – invoked the plebs: 'it has been the common people, the people represented in this House, who have shown the truest appreciation of the prescriptive parts of our constitution'. In other words, as the back-benchers represented the common people, so their revolt was the people's revolt. This pleased the back-benchers, whether or not they had use for Powell's proposition that the constitution belonged to the nation through time. Powell had invoked the wisdom of the people, indeed the wisdom of the simple, before this (for example in his retorts to the press over his Morecambe speech) and his faith was destined to be put to the test in the referendum on membership of the Common Market. But he opposed enlisting the wisdom of the people's instincts in such a manner until that time. It was for sovereign Parliament to know and voice it.

Powell had always argued that there were loyalties beyond party. His position after 1965 in particular was based on two interlocking premises. One was that party was the price of democracy, and that therefore parties must be sharply differentiated in principle and policy. As Disraeli said when Peel repealed the Corn Laws (and Dingle Foot quoted in the Lords debate) 'above all maintain the line of demarcation between parties, because it is only by preserving the distinction between parties that you will preserve the integrity of public men and the power . . . of Parliament itself'. The other premise was that ultimately, on issues of supreme importance to the nation's life or survival, the MP was answerable to his conscience alone. There was prescience in his remarks to the committee, busily engaged in wrecking the bill, on the compact between right and left wings of either party against the compact of the centres:

> All members know that in the last resort our individual influence, indeed the whole structure of politics in this country, depends on the ultimate right of an MP to detach himself, perhaps finally and irrevocably, from the party under whose banner he has entered the House. I do not believe that any of us would submit to coming into this House upon the condition that we were here only as supporters of a particular party. We get into a similar difficulty when we attempt to put members of another place into that situation.[13]

But the mass of MPs belied his words as they tramped through the lobbies sullenly negativing the rebels' amendments. Powell set up such echoes as he could: of his own rebellions on points of principle (see pp. 25, 53) and of Labour's own honourable revolts, from which they had drawn inspiration subsequently.

The bill was lost because the Government did not, in the end, dare to propose the guillotine to end the committee discussions; they risked defeat. In April an embarrassed Wilson in a gabbled statement withdrew it, which caused Powell to call out, 'eat it slowly'; this sounded vindictive, but he was underlining an important moral to both front benches: not to ride roughshod over the House of Commons. The success of the back-bench revolt encouraged him to think that the true nature of Parliament lived on from its roots, so that the encroachments of the executive could still be resisted. It accounts for his optimism that the Common Market legislation could be similarly defeated in 1971, for then the balance of public opinion was opposed, and Labour back-benchers even more strongly critical than over the Parliament No. 2 Bill. He told an audience in the 1970 election:

> Let no one say members are mere lobby fodder, and that the government will get its way, no matter. It is only a year or so since, on a subject where public opinion was much less deeply exercised – the future of the second chamber – a major government measure, to which the official opposition was at worst benevolently neutral, was destroyed by the determined action of private members on both sides of the House.[14]

In 1977 the domination of the Labour Party National Executive Committee led to the adoption of the abolition of the House of Lords as an election pledge. This generated fresh demands for reform on the other side. But in none of the discussions does one prime purpose of the Lords seem to get properly aired: to reject an attempt by a House of Commons usurped by left wing extremists to prolong its own life and postpone, perhaps indefinitely, elections; for under single chamber government in Britain the sole check, as Marxists know, is the monarch's veto. This issue was too remote, apparently, to discuss in 1968; and it might have divided the rebels. Thus the issue of 1968 is not now academic. It will be fought over again, and perhaps more fiercely.

3   The 1970 Election

Soon after the abandonment of the Parliament No. 2 Bill the shadow of the next election fell across politics. Powell's separation from what would be called mainstream politics occurred against a background of Labour failures, and Tory anticipations. Until early 1970 it looked as if Heath was coasting to victory, a victory in which Powell's activities would be virtually irrelevant, except insofar as they induced Heath to adopt a tougher policy on immigration controls. Speculations that Powell was animated by ambition to displace Heath made no sense in this context.

But in 1970 Labour's fortunes revived, and as the prospect arose of Heath leading the Tories to a second electoral defeat, the commentators became more excited about Powell's hypothetical tactics to get the leadership when later that year the Party found itself still in opposition. It was Heath rather than Powell who was making or unmaking the Party's fortunes at this stage; he gave so much publicity to his own proposals for giving the country a new lease of life and enterprise (some of them adapted from Powell) that Wilson seized the opportunity to attack the Tories as if they were in office, a more congenial role for his genius than defending such Labour failures as Barbara Castle's abortive industrial relations initiative, 'In Place of Strife'. Heath had held a conference on freeing private enterprise (under direction) at Selsdon Park; Wilson immediately coined the phrase 'Selsdon Man', an image of a top-hatted capitalist devoid of social conscience which rested in some degree on Powell's vigorous defence of the profit motive and capitalism. (Powell of course was not present, and the Wilson caricature was wildly at variance with Heath's real intent.)

All this was misrepresentation under the rules of the party game, but Wilson was sustained by a revival in world trade, and an improvement in the balance of payments to which Chancellor Jenkins's orthodox, not to say powellian, budgets contributed – admittedly under duress from the World Bank and Britain's creditors. The public, to Labour's surprise, was impressed; in the *Sunday Express* in April Powell acclaimed Roy Jenkins as the real architect of Labour's recovery – in contrast to the Macmillanite expansionism that ended in the Conservatives' defeat. Powell's praise in public for Jenkins's partial conversion to monetarism deepened the Conservative leaders' suspicions that he wanted and would work for the Party's defeat.

Wilson called the election in June after Labour's good showing in the borough elections as well as in the opinion polls. He planned a low-key summer election, and all the experts anticipated that he would win. Powell's 'disruptive' tactics were the more fiercely resented in the Conservative camp, though nobody supposed that his criticisms of Heath's centrist policies and promises of indicative planning had any effect on the masses. It was simply assumed that his 'racism' had hurt the Tory image: indeed, that his very existence, as a prominent and vocal but dismissed and disgraced member of the Party, merely *looking* dissident, was a grave electoral liability: 'the difficult situation with Enoch' as Sir Michael Fraser, deputy party chairman, put it. The *Financial Times* called it 'an ominous challenge'. This view made sense only on the assumption that those sympathetic to Powell would abstain, thus ensuring Labour's survival in the marginal seats Heath needed to win.

What occurred was exactly the opposite. But so convinced was the Conservative leadership that amongst the odds they battled against was Powell's disloyalty that they hailed their final victory by thirty seats as the result of Heath's unwavering faith and charismatic leadership (particularly helped, in R. A. Butler's view, by Heath's emphasis on a coming economic crisis, borne out by bad trade returns). Heath therefore emerged with a unique authority. It confirmed the very tendencies to resent criticism and surround himself with men who deferred to his views – 'Heathmen' – which had led to his rejection of Powell.

It is widely believed that Powell tipped the balance in favour of Heath, whether he was aware of his pulling power or not. The polls showed Labour ahead until the last day. The significant development in the last week of a dull campaign was five speeches by Powell, which got through to the masses because the newspaper strike temporarily muffled other news. Even without those speeches there is evidence that the rank and file party workers were galvanised by Powell's presence. Feeble as the Conservative manifesto had been, his personality seemed a guarantee that a Heath government would be a change for the better. The late swing is consistent with some days of rumination by ordinary folk that he was right and that he, along with his ideas, should be voted in. The 6,000 letters that he received at the time were analysed by Diana Spearman of the Conservative Research Department,[15] and showed that his speeches during and before the campaign had mobilised the large, but volatile, working-class Conservative vote, the vote on which he held Wolverhampton so firmly. But every region, every social class was responsive. The theme of the letters was stated in many ways, but one was typical: 'But for your final speech, I would not have bothered to vote.' Others were going to abstain in protest at Heath's treatment of Powell – but for his plea to them to ignore it. The letters, and the movement of the poll findings examined in retrospect convinced Powell's supporters that he carried the vital twenty marginals for Heath.

The psephologists, refining the statistics provided by the polls, have subsequently agreed with this view. The number of 'Powellites', defined by the pollsters as people who in the course of an interview selected Powell as the politician who most closely represented their political views, increased greatly in numbers between 1968 and 1970, and, whatever party they normally supported, in 1970 switched to the Tories by a seventy-seven to twenty-three margin. Anti-Powellites moved evenly between the parties. Thus the 'Powell effect', at first disputed (for example by David Butler in his study of the election), has subsequently been shown, on the evidence of the opinion polls, to have been decisive. Heath needed a swing of 3·6 per cent to break even with Wilson. Not until the morning of the election did a single poll give him more than this. In the event he swung 4·7 per cent: after Powell's speeches had worked up to their dramatic climax.

The 'Powell effect', however, was disparaged as only a personalised protest vote against the immigration which all parties had allowed to happen; Powell's solitary position, attacked on all sides, gave his final appeal great authority – but only with 'racialist' voters. This is no doubt part of the explanation. The situation was conveniently dramatised by Anthony Wedgwood Benn who early in the campaign imputed to Powell Nazi racialist attitudes which found their expression in Belsen. Powell routed him with the retort that at the outbreak of war he had volunteered and served against the Nazis for the duration – 'I am the same man to-day'. This incident further intensified the interest in Powell's statements. Questioned in his regular press conference about this exchange, Heath attacked Benn for smearing the entire Conservative Party, abstaining from any direct defence of Powell and so leaving his hearers open to the impression that in this, as in other matters, Powell was not of the Party and had brought Benn's obloquy on himself.

Yet of Powell's five speeches only one dealt in detail with immigration. The five taken as a whole distilled the essence of all that Powell had been saying on national issues between 1968 and 1970, and indeed since 1963. They reiterate the précis of powellism offered by 'A Conservative' in *The Times* in 1966. They embody Powell's 'alternative Conservatism': 'the great traditional themes of conservatism' in the words of the *Guardian* at the time; and that no doubt explains why he was accused by the Heathmen of running a parallel campaign of his own which was not loyally aimed at putting over and installing in office the Heath party line.

In the first of these speeches[16] he refuted all Wilson's and Jenkins's claims to skilled management of the economy as proved by the surplus on the balance of payments: Wilson was effectively ribbing Heath with such jibes as 'When will the Conservative leader get it into his head that the £550 million balance of payments figure is a surplus, not a deficit; a plus, positive, above the line, black, not red!' Powell showed that the trade deficit before 1967 was the result of an overvalued pound; the surplus that ensued was the result of the overdone Wilsonian devaluation which undervalued it – and that sensible public finance required neither surplus nor deficit, but a balance to be readily achieved by a floating pound, which found its natural level in the market. He then reminded his audience that in 1965 he had predicted that soaring socialist public expenditure would mean inflation because it would mean money-creation, and added 'if trade unions had never been invented and the population had consisted of Benedictine monks, the consequence would still have been . . . the rise in prices (including wages) which we have experienced.' Presumably because Powell did not blame trade unions, this speech, like the others was regarded by his own side as anti-Conservative.

In his second speech, also in Wolverhampton, on 11 June, he turned to the issue of immigration which he said 'exceeds all others in its importance for the future not only of this town and other areas directly affected, but of the entire nation.' Heath was compelled to answer questions on it next day to the exclusion of the points he wished to make himself. Yet this speech said nothing new. What it did was to insist that his previous warnings on the magnitude of the immigration and growth of the non-indigenous population had been proved correct: 'I was right and my traducers were wrong.' But he added that the country had been deliberately misled about the numbers involved 'till one begins to wonder if the Foreign Office was the only department of state into which enemies of this country were infiltrated.' Powell had shown the figures were wrong, but it was, of course, brutal to hint that they were fudged by the Home

Office with unpatriotic motives; uproar ensued. Powell also repeated his Birmingham statement that continued immigration would generate violence, but that a remedy existed:

> I declare then that in my judgement, based upon what knowledge I have of human nature and upon what observation I have made of events in the world, the prospective growth in this country of the Commonwealth immigrant and immigrant-descended population will result in civil strife of appalling dimensions. . . . On the other hand it is not in my judgement too late to prevent or greatly reduce these consequences – namely by a great reduction of the prospective number.

This was to be achieved by the Conservative commitment to assist repatriation, a boost for the Party's pledge which could only give his colleagues offence if they had no intention of fulfilling it so sincerely. Powell insisted he had no animus against the immigrants, holding no man inferior because of a different origin; it was in their, as in the natives' interest to prevent strife. This speech was reported to have so upset Heath that he discussed with his advisers whether to repudiate Powell publicly. They recoiled; but a friendly reference to Powell in a speech to be made by Sir Alec Douglas-Home was excised.

Two days later Powell made a speech[17] which was attacked by *The Times* as paranoid, and by others as animated by the conspiracy theory of politics, but which is understandable against his earlier warnings about the upsurge of violence for its own sake, the new techniques of protest, terrorism and media misrepresentation which were not only undermining national security but impairing clear thought about current issues. It was illustrated by pickets shouting 'Powell out!' as he made the speech. This new enemy, as serious as any we had faced before, was – Powell specifically stated – hard to identify. It was unlike an enemy in war. He designated it as 'forces which aim at the actual destruction of our nation and society as we know them or can imagine them'. Such forces worked against America and other free countries. These forces used any combustibles to hand – the students' restlessness, the divisions in Ireland, racial tensions, industrial grievances, ever-rising costs of living.

He did not signal out any group – the Communists, the New Left parties, the Tribunities, the anarchists. (He made, subsequently, a reference to Maoism, and, later still, to 'the new nihilism'.) Whether any reference to these would have in 1970 strengthened the accusation of paranoia is a question. Basically he saw the New Left political organisations and sects as all emanations of what he thought of as 'The Thing' – the formless mindless, sloganising, debased verbal aggro, interlarded with calculated abuse, which was beyond the reach of reason and logic – eluding pursuit and attack, in Marcuse's description – a sort of mental pus produced by the disintegration of society and civilised standards. The burden of his warning in this speech was that the slack-mindedness of the liberal establishment was the essential, active ingredient of the destructive forces at work: the revolutionary minority would get nowhere but for the perverse reversal of moral judgements, the warped sense of guilt, the sloppy submission to 'anarchist brainwashing' by the opinion-makers, so that they repeated 'manifest absurdities as though they were self-evident truths'.

> The public are literally made to say that black is white. Newspapers like the *Sunday Times* denounce it as 'spouting the fantasies of racial purity' to say that a child born of English parents in Peking is not Chinese but English, or a child born of Indian parents in Birmingham is not English but Indian . . . In the universities we are told that the education and the discipline ought to be determined by the students . . . this is nonsense, manifest arrant nonsense which it is already obligatory for academics to accept and mouth . . . We are told that the economic achievement of Western countries has been at the expense of the rest of the world and has impoverished them, so that what are called the 'developed' countries owe a duty to hand over tax-produced aid to the governments of the undeveloped countries. It is nonsense, arrant nonsense, but it is nonsense with which the people of the Western countries . . . have been so . . . saturated that in the end they feel ashamed of what the brains and energy of Western mankind have done, and sink on their knees to apologise for being civilised and ask to be insulted and humiliated. Then there is the 'civil rights' nonsense. In Ulster we are told that the deliberate destruction . . . of ordinary property is due to dissatisfaction over the allocation of council houses and opportunities for employment. It is nonsense, manifest, arrant nonsense . . . Most cynically of all, we are told . . . and by bishops forsooth, that communist countries are the upholders of human rights . . . but that large numbers of people in this country would be outraged by the spectacle of cricket matches being played here against South Africans. It is nonsense – manifest arrant nonsense, but that did not prevent a British Prime Minister and a British Home Secretary from adopting it as acknowledged fact. . . .

It was hardly standardised election tub-thumping; it did not obviously call the hearer to vote Heath; but it provoked ordinary people against the received and superior wisdom – whetted the appetite for the powellian summing-up.

Powell had stated in his election manifesto that he would oppose entry into the Common Market. In his fourth speech, at Tamworth on 15 June, he repeated this and called on every candidate to 'come clean' with the electorate where he stood on the issue. This was unpopular, because both parties were playing down the Common Market as well as race. Powell emphasised that 'Mr Heath never spoke truer words than when he said "that the greatest mistake would be for the British people to go into this without themselves realising the full implications."' He summarised the arguments against, relying on the freedom Heath had given to Conservatives to put their individual points of view because the Party was only committed to negotiation if elected. But, as everyone who knew Heath knew, he was totally committed to British membership, which seemed to him the core of a 'dash for freedom' economic policy, this likewise was seen as a wrecking intervention.

Yet, having won an extraordinarily large audience by his speeches, Powell came down decisively for voting Conservative in his final appeal at Wolverhampton the following evening. The effect was the greater for any mystery that had attached to his stand previously – though he had already told questioners at meetings that his loyalty was to the leader of the Party, Mr Heath. Still, like a good dramatist, he kept the dénoument for the right moment. Party, he said, offered the only available choice, and we 'must regain, before the die is cast, the view of those great simplicities in the light of which the nation's decisions are taken.' The best chance was with a Conservative government. His own demotion was not to be a factor in anybody's choice.

I have no personal gain to expect from the outcome, other than that of any other citizen. I am not among those candidates at this election who can look forward with assurance . . . to achieving political offce . . . Whatever might have been obscure or undefined about the policies of the Conservative party, this at least has been made crystal clear . . . that if there is a Conservative government after Thursday, I shall not be a member of it . . . Nor have I received in the recent past from men who will form a conservative cabinet even the ordinary loyalties and courtesies that prevail generally between colleagues in the same cause. Not for them to repudiate attacks on me which were unfounded and which they knew to be unfounded . . . No wonder that electors have been writing to me . . . that they would not be voting Conservative because Enoch Powell would not be in the Conservative Government . . . It is precisely because of this that I claim the right to say . . . 'This election is not about Enoch Powell . . . This election is about you and your future and your children's future and your country's future' . . . If a Socialist majority is returned on Thursday, then before another three or four years are over, the ownership and control of the state will have been extended . . . over the greater part of British industry and business . . . The point is eventually reached when the remaining elements of free enterprise . . . give up the unequal struggle. This is what socialism is about. This is the capture of the commanding heights . . . In the last four years socialism has been forming up to withdraw the fundamental freedoms of personal and family decision . . . In another four years who dare be sure that parents will be allowed to choose and buy the education for their children that they think best? to choose and buy the care in health and sickness that they think best? to make provision and save in the manner they think best for their retirement? Listen, then, for there comes a time when it is too late to listen . . . On Thursday your vote is about a Britain that, with all its faults and failings, is still free, and great because it is free. On Thursday your vote decides whether that freedom shall survive or not. You dare not entrust it to any government but a Conservative government.

In the next two days there occurred the late swing which falsified the apparent predictions of the polls, and it is legitimate to presume that this speech had its effect in adding impetus to, if not actually initiating, that swing. But, though the last few sentences were unexceptionable, the speech at the time was reckoned by the Conservative leaders unhelpful and counter-productive in intent.

Powell could hardly have urged voters, and particularly his own supporters, to vote Conservative without explaining his own relationship with the Party. After Heath's failure to defend Powell personally over Benn's attack on him, the Conservative leaders could hardly expect anything else. But the speech showed that Powell knew, or at least thought, that he was a power in his own right within the Conservative Party, deriving from his support in the country. This could only incense and chagrin a man of Heath's temperament. The suggestion that Powell won the election for him must have been even more embittering. For it was easy to conclude from the course of the campaign that many voters backed Heath only because they felt that Powell would be a powerful voice in Parliament to keep the Conservatives on the right lines; indeed many may have read Powell's message the other way round: 'I can vote Tory because Powell will be available, and what Heath says about him to-day is not the last word – he'll come into his own if we give him a chance, and that requires a Conservative government.' The public attitude to Powell and Heath is perhaps reflected in a National Opinion poll in October 1969 which showed that, while those asked rated Heath ahead of Powell as a leader and the man most likely to solve the country's problems, they rated Powell above Heath in his sincerity and strength of beliefs.

The speech, however, also bound Powell. Its forebodings of trouble to come are unmistakable. Meanwhile Heath had the centre of the stage, and Powell rather naturally stayed in the wings. When he did not appear at the triumphal party conference in October 1970, it was put about that he expected and would have preferred Heath's defeat. The answer to that *canard* is to be found in the speech: those who had not extended to him the ordinary courtesies that prevail between colleagues were now ministers on the platform; commonsense excused him from clapping after putting them there. A number of people turned up wearing Powell masks, symbolic if hardly to his taste.

Chapter 9

Powell *v*. Heath IV:
The Common Market.
1965–1974; 1975

1   From Free Trade Area to Superstate

The foreboding of trouble to come centred on his election pledge to fight entry into the Common Market. It was fulfilled in his struggle against Heath's European Communities Bill in 1971–2; and in 1972 he first had a presentiment that he might not be able to remain in the party. Indeed, he confided it to James Molyneaux, speculating that perhaps the only cause which would keep him in public life would be Ulster's.[1]

Though he reiterated that he was only availing himself of Heath's concession of liberty of conscience to all party members, he was once again accused of changing his position only after his break with Heath.[2] He first came unreservedly out against entry under the terms of the Treaty of Rome in March 1969. This stand against the Market, it was alleged, followed the discovery that the majority of the public, as the polls indicated, was opposed to entry – just as his immigration speeches followed the discovery that the public was seething with racial resentment. Yet at the 1969 Party Conference so much opposition to entry was voiced that Sir Alec Douglas-Home had to give assurances that it was too soon for the Party to make a final decision; only on this condition did the platform get its majority. This occurred when everyone knew Heath was committed to entry and Sandys had said 'the decision is taken'.

Powell never denied that he had changed his thinking about the EEC; and just as he blamed himself for not realising the gravity of immigration sooner (see p. 115), so he apologised for misunderstanding the implications of membership of the Community when, as one of Macmillan's ministers, he supported the bid for entry. In the introduction to his collected anti-Market speeches, published as an opening bombardment in 1971, he wrote:

> I was not an opponent of British membership of the EEC in 1961–2. I was prepared to accept it, on the grounds of trade, as the lesser evil compared with being excluded. But we *were* excluded; and the events of the years that followed convinced me that this judgement had been mistaken. Meanwhile it

became clear that the Community, if it survived at all, would be something quite different from a free trade area, and something to which Britain could not belong.[3]

In 1971, in an interview with the *Guardian*, he explained the Shadow Cabinet's decision to back Harold Wilson's renewed application for entry – that is, for negotiations – in 1967.

Very little thinking or rethinking had taken place on this subject between going out of office in '64 and the splash of a Labour government into EEC water at the end of '66. I think probably most of us thought that, to use Alec Douglas-Home's famous words, this was a dead duck and one doesn't give much thought to dead ducks. However . . . it seemed to all of us, including myself, that for the Conservative Party, having come out of office after its own failure to get into the Community . . . and certainly having done no fundamental thinking or talking on the subject in the intervening two years, suddenly to say 'No' just because the Labour party had said 'Yes' did not make sense either politically or intellectually . . . Now . . . for the past three years I have been able to apply my mind to these matters as an individual. Of course as a member of a party, but as one with no collective responsibilities – and in the meantime many things have been changing. The economic aspects of the Community as compared with the political had been receding . . . Quite openly . . . the political grounds were now given priority by the British government, while inside the Common Market . . . negotiations and studies had placed increasing emphasis on the Community as an embryonic political unit. Viewed in this light, the Community seemed to me to be something which Britain cannot join with full intent. . . .[4]

Speaking to a French audience in an attempt to extend his front by warning the European public of the hostility of British opinion to membership as a factor to be taken into account in their own attitude to British entry, he explained his change of front in more detail:

Eight years ago, when your President pronounced the funeral oration upon Britain's previous negotiation with the Community, the issue was seen and presented on our side of the Channel as, I do not say economic, I say merely commercial: the substitution of one system of preferences and trading arrangements for another. It was viewed in the context of a progressive expansion of trading opportunities which had been taking place: the liberalisation measures in OECD; the negotiation for a free trade area with the Rome Treaty countries; the proposal of a European free trade area . . . Some pedants insisted on actually reading the Treaty of Rome and talking about political unification; but this received scant attention, on the ground that such ideas were typical Continental theorising, remote from practical possibility and in any case destined to be held in check by British pragmatism once Britain should be 'inside'. All the greater was our astonishment when the

President's veto seemed to be concerned with Skybolt and Polaris, Americans and Anglo-Saxons. What on earth had that to do with being inside or outside a customs union or with what had seemed to us the only burning issue – Commonwealth preference? As for myself I had entered Mr Macmillan's cabinet only six months before the veto fell; but I am prepared to confess that in those days I used to argue the case, and counter the objections, on purely commercial grounds. . . .[5]

Like so many other Conservatives who gave general support to joining Europe on 'purely commercial grounds,' Powell did not read the Treaty with care; had he done so, he might have realised earlier that it was unlikely Britain could avoid surrendering sovereignty if negotiations were to succeed. For the Treaty gave rise to a 'governed organisation', like the Schuman Coal and Steel community which he had opposed because it was a cartel, legislating its own behaviour, not a general tariff (and it became one of the communities within the Brussels system). But he had this excuse: the conditions of accession were never before him, and he never participated in the decision even to negotiate. The failure by Macmillan's cabinet to realise the implications of the Treaty was nonetheless fatal.

Perhaps in 1960–1 the Treaty was interpretable in terms more commercial than political, since De Gaulle was himself antipathetic to unification, and talked of *l'Europe des patries*; hardly a federalist expression. But the chance to mould the association into a free trade area ('a fresh start' in Powell's own words) was probably lost by Britain back in 1955–7, when the Treaty was being negotiated; instead EFTA was set up as the preferred arrangement. If Britain had joined the Community before the Common Agricultural Policy had hardened, history might have been different. But Churchill had said Britain was in the European Movement but not of it; he and Eden believed in the mystic intersecting circles of the Empire, Europe and the 'special relationship' with the United States. The very tendencies that showed what the Treaty might become put British feelings off. There was scepticism whether it could succeed even when it took shape; EFTA was seen as a means of discouraging it. De Gaulle's advent was expected to be fatal to it. It was forgotten that, while Churchill had advocated an Anglo-French union in Britain's peril in 1940, when in 1945 De Gaulle had asked for fresh consideration for an Anglo-French association to help France in her travail, Churchill turned him down, and so settled his conviction that Britain was not European, if not perfidious. The Gaullist veto of 1963 was shaped in those years.

For all his genuine Europeanism, as demonstrated in his defence policy and his campaign against the Commonwealth mythology, Powell seems to have ignored these developments, nor realised that from 1961 Macmillan could only initiate negotiations about transitional arrangements. And as Britain was progressively weakened by Macmillan's and Wilson's economic failures, the possibility of negotiating substantial changes for a new Europe of the Ten became remote. The departure of De Gaulle impelled the Six even faster along continental lines and away from British traditions – and from Powell's concepts of a modern version of *laissez-faire*. Until 1969 he did not include the Common Market issue in his Tory alternative.

He then gave his full attention to the implication of the texts, and sensed 'one of those spontaneous movements of popular opinion' which had turned British sentiment away from the Common Market. He knew that Heath was for entry, yet as determined to keep the EEC issue, as he was the racial issue, out of politics. He determined to bring the arguments into the open.

The first of the pro-Marketeers' propositions was a generalised assertion, unsupported by figures, that as the empire and Commonwealth could no longer be the basis of Britain's world trading, or political, position, the only alternative was Europe. Many who had previously rejected the Market were, like the *Economist*, converted to EEC membership, on almost any terms, by this presumption. But the whole thrust of powellian economics – a free market producing a naturally efficient and competitive industry, especially if made flexible by a floating exchange rate – implied that Britain could as easily go it alone as Japan or Switzerland. The argument that there was no alternative to the Market was a concealed socialist argument for perpetuating a state-controlled, ailing economy whose adhesions it should be Conservative policy to break.

His first major statement[6] in 1969 was followed with a series of speeches which examined every argument advanced in favour of the Market. He rested his campaign on Heath's two statements that Parliament would need the 'full-hearted consent' of the country to take Britain into Europe and that Europe would have to be similarly convinced that it wanted Britain – an acknowledgement that Britain was very different from the Six. He added that on the morrow of De Gaulle's second veto it was opportune to think anew. Even when Wilson renewed Macmillan's negotiations 'I was far less sure of the wisdom or the prospects'; the slate was clean when these had failed: 'we have carte blanche'.

The Powell alternative was to use, outside the Market, the full advantages of a world trading nation to buy in the cheapest market and sell in the most profitable: 'We do not need to be tied up with anybody. The UK is not self-sufficient, but then neither is almost any other country, not even Russia.' Britain's resources of brains and hard work provided 'a very comfortable situation to be in – much better than sitting on oilfields'. Those who denied this were denying that Britain had brains or could work: the defeatist assumption that the nation could live only by dependence on others or on oil. Insofar as Britain had performed poorly in comparison with the EEC countries he ascribed it to 'the hair-raising tomfoolery with which we play with exchange rates' and not to inherent national ineptitude in business or even to trade union sabotage – all of which he had disproved back in 1963: 'so let's have none of the "eleventh hour" stuff, please; no jumping to conclusions and saying "if it isn't this, it has to be that. If it isn't Europe it has to be America or the Commonwealth or something or other".[7] This was a take-off of the Macmillan attitude inherited by Heath.

In June he turned to the argument that joining the Community would strengthen defence. In terms of the nuclear deterrent this would only be true if the Community was already one nation, with a single authority wielding it. But the Community was still a committee in defence. Even in 1940 Britain would have been hard put to prefer extermination to defeat, and therefore only a nation and not a committee could make such a decision with such a weapon.

> Suicide by unanimous vote in committee is one of those scenes at which we have never assisted. Thus to contemplate an Anglo-French nuclear deterrent, or a European nuclear deterrent, is to assume that there already exists not merely an alliance or a confederation of nations, but a single nation so conscious of itself and of its unity that it would not hesitate . . . to sacrifice any of its parts for its whole, or its present for its future.[8]

Defence set a problem for powellian logic, nontheless. On the one hand if, as Powell argued, the Community to which Heath was surrendering British sovereignty was a superstate it would be able to make the centralised decisions that would give credibility to its nuclear deterrent. If, however, it was a committee which could not credibly deploy the nuclear deterrent of its members, then it was no superstate, and any surrender of sovereignty to it was not as total as Powell made out. Powell's reply was that to obtain the advantages of defence claimed for going into Europe, the surrender of sovereignty in defence (as in economics) would have to be so absolute that the British nation-state ceased to exist; but if it was only partial, then maximum damage was done to Britain's freedom to buy cheap and sell profitably in the world with no gain whatever in security. So far as conventional warfare was concerned, he noted that if the superstate had the necessary authority, it could impose conscription on its members – including Britain.

Powell envisaged the superstate emerging gradually, as part of a political dynamic to which British entry would give another push; but for this reason the British public would not notice how their independence was lost in irrevocable instalments. At first it would be a matter of a few law cases. Later when the whole range of economic decisions had been transferred from Westminster, and military decisions followed, it would prove too late to secede from the superstate whatever theoretical vestiges of sovereignty Westminster might retain. The veto, which the Marketeers soothingly said would remain in Westminster, would become as unusable as the nuclear deterrent.

One reason for this prognosis was that he did not believe that the superstate would be fully parliamentary in the British sense: 'an elected parliament cannot exist unless those who do the electing see themselves as a single whole.' An elected European assembly would be heterogeneous. If administrative unity were achieved, for the sake of defence, Britain had to become a mere province, which would be incapable of secession or vetos on anything.

In his fourth speech, made, despite scenes of violence, in Kingston in January 1970, he took as his text a remark by Jean Rey, President of the EEC Commission, that by 1980 the Community would in fact have a common currency and just such a parliament, elected by universal suffrage. Powell in reply developed the constitutional objections to British membership which thereafter were to be his main theme through to the Referendum of 1975. He pointed out that a common currency implies a common economic policy, because modern currencies are not gold but fiat money – managed paper promissory notes – which requires budgetary and fiscal policies to control its supply (volume and velocity) in such a way as to keep it in step with production, to maintain employment or to cause or halt inflation.

> Imagine that all this time we had, not a currency of our own but one common (let us suppose) to six other countries. There would have to be common policies from hire purchase to the size and scope of public expenditure; there would have to be a common freeze and a common squeeze, a common prices and incomes policy, a common inflation and a common policy on unemployment. It would not be the Bank of England and the Treasury which controlled the banking system. . . . There would have to be a common government.[9]

He sought to bring home to his hearers what such a quasi-federal transformation of their lives would mean: 'No use to go to the polls at the next election and turn out the little local show at Whitehall. "You can't blame us", they would say, and rightly say, "we have nothing to do with the currency nowadays." ' Their only recourse would be to vote against a continental government in which their representatives, even if all were sent packing, would be in a minority. Rey, he said approvingly, had brought the centre of the debate from the economic to the political, 'because the economic presupposes the political'. Talks about the benefits of European unity meant that Westminster would be subordinate to a federal parliament, court and laws. To a bishop who said he would accept such a loss if it meant Europe would be spared more wars, Powell replied that civil wars had often proved crueller than international conflicts.

He found an additional defence for his changed attitude to the Market between 1960 and 1970. In 1957–60, while the Market was in process of formation, it could not be known how its exclusive institutions and common external tariff would affect British trade. But in 1969 he could show that the disasters the pro-Marketeers predicted had not eventuated: the very market from which it was vital Britain be not excluded had grown by 40 per cent in two years. Therefore there was no reason to suppose 'the pattern of trade which would result from being inside the Market would be more beneficial than the pattern it would displace.' The growth in trade showed that Britain's misfortunes could not be ascribed to our exclusion from the Market.[10] (The British motor trade then believed that, inside the Market they would dominate the production and marketing of European cars!)

If the Market were, against Rey's prognostication, to become a free trade area, it was best to wait for this outcome since waiting involved no loss. But in the meantime Britain's unique nationhood was incompatible with a Brussels bureaucracy which was shaping a superstate neither truly federal nor parliamentary. On this latter point he quoted Professor Hallstein, the former President of the Commission, who predicted that 'no major field of economic or social importance has been excluded from the Commission in a way that prevents the Community from taking action on it.'[11] He gave an early warning that one implication of such a statement meant inroads upon Britain's efficient low-cost agriculture and on its fishing resources.

In the election he tried, but in vain, to make other candidates tell their constituents where they stood on such issues; but above all to pledge themselves that they would honour Heath's promise that nothing would be finalised without 'full-hearted consent', so that there must be an appeal, in another election, to the people to pass verdict on the terms negotiated. Otherwise, in the 'next election but one,' he predicted,

> my fellow candidates and I, even if we are candidates for the European and not the British parliament, will have a very different tale to tell you. Prices, let us imagine, will have been going up five or six per cent a year and you the electors . . . want to turn out of office those responsible, much as you are going to turn out the Labour government later this week. But we will say to you 'Sorry, these are the results of the policy followed by the European government which controls the European currency. We have done and we shall do our best, but this is how the majority in the Community insist on having it.'[12]

The prediction reads ironically in late 1978. In due course it was the two succeeding British governments which allowed prices to rise far more than 6 per cent, and the European national currencies which looked so much more wisely managed by comparison. But this does not, of course, invalidate Powell's argument on Britain's minority status in running the currency policy of a Europe politically unified, as he feared it might be, by 1980 or soon after.

2   The Battle Against the Bill

Immediately after the election Heath and Geoffrey Rippon began negotiations on terms of entry. Periodic, but non-committal reports were made to Parliament, but by the end of the year Powell criticised them as 'about less than nothing'. He complained that the major issues were being smothered in minutiae: 'the prior questions, transition to what?' were ignored and had 'not properly been asked, let alone answered. It is as if there were a conspiracy to be silent about them in the hope that no one would notice that they exist.' Heath was treating this issue of principle as settled.

> It is all very neat, very clever: the old dodge of suggesting that the principle of anything can be left over until the details are worked out, and then, when the details have been worked out, exclaiming with simulated surprise and even indignation 'But surely we wouldn't have been to all this trouble if we were not really agreed on the principle to begin with?' The trouble is . . . the dodge is too clever by half.[13]

He protested that the people had still to be heard on the principle, which did not turn on the period of transition or the quota in the budget, but on where the transition was to be made to. Even in material terms this was not made clear – for example that Britain was to become part of a high cost food area based on low-efficiency farming, and that Britain's market for expensive foodstuffs, not anglophilia, was the incentive to the Six to let us in. The loss of control over trade and food prices was being concealed from the people under cover of material blandishments. For example, Prior, Minister for Agriculture, assured the House that if one asked 'the average British person' whether he wanted a couple of bob in his pocket with sovereignty or four shillings without it, 'I have no doubt what answer he would give'. Powell struggled to keep the principle in view against such talk, and asked rather of the electorate 'can they, will they, so merge themselves with others that in the face of the external world there is no longer "we" and "they" but only "we"?' His answer was that it was inconceivable that they would identify themselves politically with Germans and French and Italians as 'One Nation'; a nation in whose assembly they would have (he added, without realising the full irony of it) no more power than the seventy-odd Scots constituents could exercise over the policy of the United Kingdom. Imperial episode be what it might, he also insisted, for whole periods of history crucial to our (constitutional) development Britain 'had stood with her face to the oceans, her back to Europe'.

Roy Jenkins spoke for the Europeanists – and for others not of his mind on Europe – when he angrily retorted that the pharisaical suggestion that Britain was not as other nations are 'is the most dangerous and unacceptable of all arguments against entry'. He did not deign to argue against Powell's particularism; had he done so he would have found Powell's arguments were founded not on superiority of nature or pride of race, but on institutions. In no other European state was there any relationship such as that subsisting between the British and their Parliament; the assemblies of the Six were all the creation of recent political acts, but, uniquely,

> the House of Commons is the personification of the people of Britain: its independence is synonymous with their independence; its supremacy is synonymous with their self-government and freedom. Through the centuries Britain has created the House of Commons and the House of Commons has

moulded Britain, until the history of the one and the life of the one cannot be separated from the history and life of the other.[14]

If Jenkins did not agree, he did not say so: the whiff of racism was potent.

In April 1971, Powell declared that the nation had been misled, the Conservative manifesto torn up. He called the Government line, publicly, a trick which implied Heath was the trickster.[15] He suggested that the trick was to present them all with a *fait accompli* and say, 'Well, it's too bad; you have to support it now. But cheer up, you'll find you'll get used to it.' He agreed that any government was entitled to report that it had promised one thing, but that circumstances forced it to do another thing (cf. Neville Chamberlain in 1939). That could not be claimed of entry into the Community, because neither the case nor the circumstances had altered between the Party Conference of October 1969 and possession of power in 1971. If Heath persisted, he 'would go down to history bearing with him the indelible brand of broken faith and trust betrayed'. As yet, Powell's accusations were conditional; a nuance not conveyed by press headlines.

He had to meet the objection, from Roy Jenkins or from the foreign audiences he sought in Europe to impress with the idea that Britain was unassimilable, that even if British sovereignty was reduced by entry into the community this was no less true of the sovereignty of the other Six; and were they not as proud of their nationhood as we of ours? In effect, Powell said No, they are not – or at least not in the British way. Typically, he coolly faced French, Italian and German audiences with this distinction, speaking in French, Italian and German.[16] He offered several reasons. The first was that the sacrifices made of their sovereignty by the Six had come from genuine political necessity: to prevent German hegemony and a new German nationalist revival. Acknowledging the force of this need, he replied that Britain's adhesion would not strengthen the chances of success, but might well injure them. His second point was that the democratic institutions of the Six were more recent than the slow-growing British variety; they were more alike on the Continent, springing from Napoleonic and subsequent shared historical experiences, and partly from a common social base in peasant agriculture. The consequent homogeneity in administration, law, institutions and outlook, notwithstanding language differences, gave the Continental federal idea a flying start. Finally he put to Continental audiences the same argument he put to the House of Commons: that subordinating British institutions to an external authority was not simply to modify them, but to kill them.

To British audiences he put the argument that if the decision to enter was right on political grounds, the economic consequences must be accepted; but even if it was economically right to go in, it did not follow that the political consequences must be accepted.[17] He asseverated his belief that the political issue would be decisive with the people once they grasped it; then they would not be deflected by arguments about prices or economic growth; they would put first things first. He believed in the autumn of 1971 that this process was happening; speaking on the Government's White Paper on entry he said that the expectations of those who predicted from June onwards that opposition would decline had been falsified; after June majority opinion had reverted to opposition, in spite of an official propaganda campaign of great magnitude. (The questions asked by the pollsters, providing such evidence, were based more on economic benefits than on political principles.) 'The straw votes show it and the politicians know it. The foreign correspondents said so. This is the situation of which we in the Conservative Party have to take stock.' In September, Powell predicted that 'it won't happen', because, though the debate would run its course, the full-hearted consent could not be had or demonstrated.

In October, however, Heath put the general question of the principle of joining before Parliament on a free vote, as indeed he had promised. He obtained what Marketeers ever after contended was an expression of 'full-hearted consent' for joining on the basis of any bill, containing any terms subsequently put into it. Powell regarded this move as part of the 'trick', and hotly dissented. 'The House of Commons does not know . . . the idea that if a principle is first debated, and after a division if necessary, decide that principle is then accepted by those that disagree, and treated as binding them to limit debate and division thereafter to the means of applying that principle.'[18]

He hoped, nonetheless, to persuade the House to produce as massive a vote against the principle of entry as the known opposition within both major parties would imply. To his party colleagues he said,

> We have been helped by the fact that the Prime Minister no longer intends to make the principle of entry a matter of confidence . . . The majority can vote against the market and still continue to enjoy the benefit of a Conservative government undiminished in strength and reputation . . .[19]

And he asked that the principle of keeping the survival of the government separate from the market question be extended to the debate on the bill itself. The occasion enabled him once again to state the basic relationship between an MP, his party, and his constituents.

> I hope I have personally given evidence enough that I believe it often to be a Member's right and duty to take a line, whether with his party or not, which he knows does not at the time command the assent of a majority of electors. Without this there could be no consistency of policy or stability of administration.[20]

This Burkean rule of representation, however, was sustained and made possible only by its exceptions:

> From time to time there arise issues where this principle does not hold good, but where on the contrary it is both impossible and wrong to attempt to proceed without the support of the mass of the people. In his now famous

words about the 'full-hearted consent of Parliament and people' Mr Heath showed that he recognised that the joining or not joining of the EEC was one of those great exceptions.[21]

Another example, of course, was immigration, though Powell did not rub that in. What he now defined as the essence of such issues was their *irreversibility*, the irreversibility of entry was implicit in the nature of the Community as expressed in a Treaty concluded for an unlimited period. Any government which persisted in making an irrevocable commitment against a majority of the voters' wishes, 'would destroy itself'.

But Powell was up against two powerful influences. One was that in the Conservative Party everyone knew that Heath was so committed personally that if a free vote went against him he would probably regard himself as repudiated by his party, whereupon the government would crumble. On the Labour side, on the other hand, there was an analogous fear of a massive split in the party, which Wilson and Callaghan were manoeuvring to prevent. Powell again, as over the Lords, had to place his hopes in so-called extremes:

> There is a kind of organic law of Parliament, whereby often, though not always, if the prevalent instinct of the country is not voiced by the governing majority, it finds expression, willy-nilly, by means of the opposition . . . which has assumed the role that was otherwise vacant: the role that the preponderant voice of the people is heard . . .[22]

He sounded a note he was to repeat: 'the Conservative party cannot for long cease to speak for Britain without ceasing to be the Conservative Party we knew.' The vote went for the market 356–244; Powell commented that a majority of seven to five could not be repeated. He was compelled, however, to explain it away to his foreign audiences. At Vaduz in January 1972 he correctly predicted that the figure

> was a freak which owed its occurrence to the internal politics of the Labour Party . . . we shall not again witness a mass of sixty-nine Labour Members who by not merely abstaining but by voting with the Government converted into victory what would otherwise have been a substantial government defeat . . . In the long march from division to division through the weeks the great majority of the opposition troops will find their way back to the colours.[23]

Those who were lighting bonfires on the continent would be dismayed to find the majority for British entry would be halved and halved again 'until the legislation walks on a knife edge where a single slip could be fatal.' He had to try to deal with the continental presumption, derived from their own institutions, that the matter was now settled.

However different British and continental democracy, that instinct proved right under Heathian management. Heath now insisted that he had full-hearted consent, and the majorities for the bill were party finagling of no historic significance. Provided he got them, that was enough; and there continental and American observers agreed with Heath, however amused they might be by Powell's portrayal of him as Napoleon in 1813 after the battle of Leipzig, giving orders to an army that no longer existed.

But Powell could not believe, even now, that the Commons could swallow a bill so unprecedented in form, so insulting to parliamentary convention. It was unconditional: not a jot or tittle of the far-reaching changes in the law which the bill made and entailed could be altered or amended in Committee; the bill as it stood could only be accepted or rejected holus-bolus. It was to be pushed and guillotined through to honour Heath's signature on the Treaty in January 1972, simply because the Government, if it lost any part of the bill, could not go back to Brussels to renegotiate that part. Moreover, even if the House amended the bill, the Government would still ratify the Treaty; and when it was in force, the amendment would be *ultra vires* Community law and so void, as the essence of the bill was to give Community law precedence over British law. This was what made the House of Commons, from the date of signature, a subordinate assembly, which could and would be told, for the first time in centuries, 'you must do this, you cannot do that'.[24]

Powell pinned his hopes to the fact that not until the House had specific proposals before it could the debate become real; and this was the point at which to vindicate the nation's liberties: 'it does not help us from the necessity of taking a decision now to refer to a white paper of last year . . .' He tried to show how those liberties were threatened inasmuch as the House of Commons was shown in the bill to lose its supremacy:

> . . . this House loses its exclusive control – upon which its power and authority have been built up over the centuries – over taxation and expenditure . . . moneys received in taxation from citizens of this country will be spent otherwise than upon a vote from this House and . . . without the opportunity to debate grievance or call for an account of the way in which those moneys are to be spent . . . in clause three . . . the judicial independence of this country has to be given up . . . the citizens of this country will not only be subject to law made elsewhere . . . the applicability . . . to them will be adjudicated elsewhere . . . There is a fourth consequence which, though not manifest is inherent . . . the progressive strengthening of the Executive as compared with this House. . . .[25]

Powell scorned Heath's paliatives – that the matters transferred to EEC jurisdiction were not very important, that Britain would participate in decisions made about them, that tariff and agricultural policies were small items compared to the whole sweep of the legislation. He retorted that the initial small areas alienated were intended to lead to full union, and what began as a minimum would under the bill be allowed to spread to a maximum. Heath was developing his argument that 'sovereignty' was not something to be 'hoarded up' but 'shared' with Europe; Powell stuck to the constitutional fact that sovereignty was one and indivisible; it could not be shared – only, in British conditions, given up.

On the plea that the House could regulate the process he replied that its only recourse would be to scrap the Treaty, and asked 'Is that the dishonour the House intends – to enter it with the *arrière pensée* that if we do not like anything we break the Treaty?'

He reminded them (a favourite point) that the power of Parliament is in the last resort the power to reverse or correct previous decisions, to admit and rectify mistakes or injustices; what use was the right of the electorate to send representatives to Westminster unless they could undo what the electors felt had been wrongly done in their name? But this reversing gear was jammed when one joined a superstate – wholly given up in a unitary state, largely given up within a federation. The Lords debate was echoed in his words:

I am very far from saying that there are no circumstances in which it would be right, wise and beneficial for a country with its eyes open to surrender its sovereignty . . . But there is a condition attached to such a course being embraced. What is given up, what is paid, is not the personal property of Hon Members of this House or any one Parliament, but comes from, and is held as a trust for the entire people of this country . . . That condition does not exist.[26]

It did not and could not exist because it had not been put to the people at all:

I ask Hon Members to address themselves to the question, 'did I tell the electorate in June 1970 whether or not I was in favour of entry?' [shouts of 'Yes!'] I will complete the sentence. Did Hon Members tell their electorate whether or not they were in favour? ['Yes!'] – I will start again. The syntactical construction was perhaps a little difficult. Whether or not Hon Members were, or expressed themselves, in favour of joining the Community, did they say to their electors plainly that they were in favour of this House giving up its legislative supremacy and surrendering its control over taxation and expenditure and of an overriding superimposition of other courts of law over the courts of law of this country? If they said that, and only if they said that this would be done without further reference to the electorate, they would have some excuse for neglecting the evidence that the people have not given them full-hearted consent.[27]

The immediate answer to this question was cries that Powell had supported the original application to join, which gave him the easy rejoinder that the price of surrendering sovereignty was never proposed at that time – only negotiations. He added crushingly that none of the written constitutions of the Six permitted a proportion of seven to five in their assemblies to carry such a constitutional change. 'All have safeguards which require a larger margin.' The Marketeers had thenceforth to amend history by declaring that the public was fully informed in June 1970 that a Tory government would do what it duly did; Heath varied this excuse later on by quoting Churchill's maxim that 'one was enough' in any vote in Parliament, implying that one vote (let alone the eight which passed the bill at second reading) constituted 'full-hearted consent of Parliament and people'.

But even one vote was not then certain: and Heath intimated that a government defeat on this central issue implied resignation. Powell regarded such a resignation in the middle of a coal strike as inconceivable – so anticipating future events.[28] But the warning took effect, the whips were able to get the eight-vote majority. Four Labour MPs voted with the Government. Thirty abstained and thirty-eight Tories voted against; the Liberal vote of six went to the bill. The pro-Market press accused Powell of using the question of good faith as a trans-parent excuse to bring Heath down.

'Once a Chief Whip,' Powell said of Heath, 'always a Chief Whip.' Powell noted the pressures put on members then, and subsequently, when speaking in the Referendum campaign, alleged that 'those who could still not bring them-selves to vote against their beliefs were sent for individually by the Prime Minister so that he could personally threaten them with the consequences if they followed their conscience'; some thirty-nine being so hectored.[29] Heath denied the charge. The antis kept up the fight in Committee through the spring and summer, but the wafer-thin majorities held, including the motion for the guillotine.

All amendments were voted down. The most notable of these was on Clause 2, sub-section 1, which was shown to limit Parliament's sovereignty not only immediately but indefinitely, in the wording, 'all such rights, powers, liabilities, obligations and restrictions from time to time created or arising by or under the Treaties . . . are without further enactment to be given legal effect or used in the United Kingdom . . . and be enforced, allowed or followed accordingly.' This mechanism made legal in the United Kingdom not only the forty-two volumes of Community laws and secondary legislation in existence, but all that were enacted in Brussels in the future, as the Treaty stated 'binding in its entirety and directly applicable.' A commentator in *The Times* agreed with Powell's assessment: 'there has been nothing like it since the Pope's privileges and jurisdiction within England were repudiated in the sixteenth century'.[30]

Attempts by Powell and others to interpose some parliamentary scrutiny of future EEC legislation was voted down. (Though this idea lived on and germinated when in 1977 the bill to provide direct elections to the European Assembly was debated – cf. p. 245.) Powell argued that the words 'directly applicable' in the Treaty was not a synonym for 'without further enactment' in the clause: the Treaty left the procedure whereby applicability was secured in law to each country to prescribe for itself, and he therefore proposed that Parliament should legislate in each case. Rippon insisted that such 're-enactment' by national assemblies was excluded by the rules: which was indeed to imply a full-blown federal sovereignty rather than Treaty relationship. The clause stood. As Powell put it, they were 'legislating in anticipation and complete ignorance of what we are enabling to be written into the law'. Sir Robin Turton offered to resign and fight a by-election solely on whether the voters endorsed such a bill; but he was deflected from this interesting experiment.

In defeat Powell was portrayed by some members as Becket to Heath's Henry II: not an inapt appraisal as events turned out. Powell had to make as much as he could of the wafer thinness of the majorities, achieved by bullying members, and so morally invalid; the House was being so overridden not by a Tudor despot 'but by the men of Brussels, the fixers who have it fixed, and the self-styled Europeans who seek their country's greatness on a politically unified Continent.'[31] The man who had willed it would 'go down to history bearing with him the indelible brand of broken faith and trust betrayed.' This attack on Heath was well within Commons conventions, but the press played it up hard. For good measure Powell added that Roy Jenkins had ambitions to take decisions for Britain not at home, but for all Europe, in Paris, Luxembourg 'or wherever else the imperial pavilions are pitched'. Jenkins sent him a letter to expostulate; Powell said all the evidence of Jenkins's speeches justified the deduction;[32] and time has vindicated the presage if not the venom.

Powell insisted that Parliament could still undo what Heath's 'fixings' had done, but his own future was put in question by his conclusion: 'what we have to ask ourselves, is whether any British party and government, least of all a Conservative Government, can do this and survive'.

It was now only logical for Powell to take the issue to the people, and argue, up and down the country in 1973, and thereafter, that the British public was in a position to reverse Heath's deal if it chose: in other words to vote for any party that promised before a general election to make the repeal of the Communities Act a major plank of its policy. But he warned that the next election (which he then assumed would be autumn 1974 at the earliest) would be their last chance. He returned to the disadvantages which the consumer would suffer – in the prices of butter, cheese and lamb – as though he feared that materialism would weigh with them more, after all, than the high issue of national independence. He began to foresee political upheavals which would put the choice in a new context for voters;

> . . . in a democracy opposing parties tend to move closer together because their outer wings have no alternative refuge . . . and can therefore be taken for granted, while the supposed floating vote lies in the middle, and each party aims at detaching from its opponent that portion of their political spectrum which lies nearest itself . . . the political earthquakes which alter the physical geography of politics for a long period afterwards can only occur when this rule is suspended . . . when the outer wing of one party finds that some single object, which for the time being seems to it more important than all the rest, is procurable not from its allies . . . but from its enemies.

The historic and endlessly instructive case in point is the great split in the Liberal party in 1886. Joseph Chamberlain and his followers were . . . the

radical wing of the Liberal Party; they were constantly pulling Gladstone and
his colleagues towards what we should call the left. Then, all of a sudden, an
issue arose which appeared to them to overshadow all other political issues
and to place country in the opposite pan of the balance to party.[33]

3 Labour to the Rescue of Sovereignty

Powell was startled to see how soon his predictions of Heath's high-handedness
were fulfilled. Hardly was the ink dry on the royal signature than the Prime
Minister went to Paris and, in concert with the other leaders,[34] proceeded to
commit Britain to the objective of complete economic and monetary union by
1980. The intention to do so, as soon as the bill was law, he had withheld from the
House.[35] Powell renewed his accusations of bad faith, but was heartened: he
could not believe that the Government could get away with it. Whichever side his
friends had voted on, he told an audience in Yarmouth,[36] they were concerned
that the Government keep faith. Heath and Rippon had continually reassured
the House that there would be no rapid changes; to encourage those who thought
Powell's warnings about the loss of sovereignty were too fanciful, an election
would intervene before that occurred.

> Now suddenly the rug is pulled beneath their feet. There is what is to be called
> 'European Union' in the next eight years . . . To this the Government has
> committed itself in the precise terms of a timetable without a vestige of
> authority from the electorate or even from Parliament . . . Little did the House
> know that within forty-eight hours 'economic and monetary union' which
> throughout the long debates . . . had been treated as a remote and theoretical
> eventuality, would have been accepted for 1980 without parliamentary, let
> alone public, debate by a government which was quick to assure the world
> that 'Britain does not go back on her word.'
>
> Before the guillotine was imposed on one of the most momentous bills ever
> laid before Parliament, Members on both sides . . . were pointing out that it
> would enable future governments in effect to legislate without coming to
> parliament, simply by using the prerogative power to conclude agreements [in
> Brussels]. I wonder what they would have said if they had known that HMG
> would barely wait for the Royal Assent to the Act, not to mention actual entry
> into force of the Brussels Treaty, before agreeing to a sweeping extension of
> the Treaty of Rome within the present decade. . . .[36]

The implication was that as Gladstone's Home Rule for Ireland drove the
Chamberlainites into the Conservatives' arms because they opposed
dismemberment of the United Kingdom, so the Powellites were being driven
towards Labour because Labour rejected the European Communities Act (or
seemed to). Indeed Powell thought the risk to Conservatism was greater than to
Liberalism in the respective cases, since the Conservatives were the party of
patriotism, and Heath's action offended the country's patriotic sentiments, while

Labour was offering to recover national independence. Powell was warning the Party against a split, and the implication was that only a change in leadership could prevent it. But the premise was that Powell had followers with the same convictions as himself, who were ready to put them before party if necessary.

But this was in question, though in 1973 it may not have seemed so. Furthermore, Powell's thesis would fall down if the electorate in fact proved not to care about their independence. Powell's faith in the commonsense of the people as opposed to the cleverness of the élite led him to think, or at least to assume, that the electorate would see through the cant and verbiage in which membership of the Community was rather often clothed. At Stockport he told them that power had already passed from the House of Commons:

> The range of subjects on which Community law comes forward is extensive and rapidly extending. On banking, insurance, patents, as on driving standards and the size of vehicles; on trade (all trade) as on agriculture (all agriculture) on companies as on unions – on all these, as on a host of other subjects, the Community is legislating, legislating, legislating – for the Community is the new state.[37]

The appetite of the new state for power, he told an audience in Barrow-in-Furness soon afterwards, would have no limit:

> One superstate, one code of law. Sir Christopher Soames last month told the assembly that 'the enlarged community is something qualitatively different from the nation-states of which it is composed; it is not simply a new Roman Empire . . . but something unprecedented. . . .'[38]

and added 'Not in its extreme bureaucratic arterio-sclerosis did the Roman Empire attempt to fix the grade of beer and milk in Britain.' He told the farmers how they would fare in prices when the 'Intervention Board at Reading' did just what it was told by Brussels. Farmers or otherwise, he told his audience that in effect they were now increasingly under an autocratic government. 'Europe in history has only been unified by despots. A Europe of free men is a Europe of nation-states, and that is the only Europe of which a free Britain can be part, because a free Britain is the Britain of the British Parliament.'[39] This thought perhaps reflected the argument of the Marketeers that Britain had to join because otherwise our power to influence the Community would diminish while its power to affect our future would proportionately grow.

Powell denied any such necessity, provided Britain's relationship with the Community, as with any big trading state, was 'equilibrated through the exchange of currencies' on the basis of a floating pound. On the other hand, the government of the Community would be bureaucratic 'on a Parkinsonian scale', wholly interventionist by necessity. Because economic relations between the units (former states) would be equilibrated by the free movement of people and resources, regional problems, exacerbated by national affections, would be a political irritant. In the end, it would be found necessary to harmonise all relationships by means of a single tax system, a single system of social welfare and insurance in consequence, and a uniform system of law: and this harmonisation by decree would always occur 'in an upward direction'. 'It is 100 per cent politics and nil per cent economics', he told his American public; that already, after 1 January 1973, Britain had ceased to have a trade policy of its own.[39]

When the principle of entry passed Parliament, Wilson said that if Britain was a member of the Community when Labour returned to power, they would reject the terms negotiated by Heath and Rippon, and offer to renegotiate them; if this was refused 'we would sit down and amicably discuss the situation with them . . . and our posture would be dictated by that determination until we had secured our terms.' This was the flexible formula whereby Wilson kept the Marketeers and anti-Marketeers of his party together. The Labour Party conference in 1972 then came out for a referendum on the renegotiated terms. The unions, in their opposition to the CAP, borrowed the arguments, even the language, that Powell had used in 1969. Powell himself now put the responsibility on the electorate for what happened if that referendum gave them the decision whether the Act was to stand or be repealed, and they did not choose rightly:

> Do not blame the whips; do not blame the members; do not blame the patronage machine; do not blame the pressures, the promises; the bribes. It is the nation that will have judged itself. When it should have spoken, it will have remained dumb; when it should have voted, it will have remained idle.[40]

4   The Referendum: Provisional Verdict

The election of February 1974 kept the issue open – until Labour redeemed its promise to hold a referendum. It is convenient to follow the EEC story to this decision, leaving for the next chapter the circumstances, closely related to Powell's ideas and reactions, which stultified and then doomed, Heath's administration of 1970 to 1974.

Powell was back in the House as an Ulster Unionist, Heath had been replaced by Margaret Thatcher as Conservative Leader of the Opposition, when James Callaghan, as Foreign Secretary, conducted the final stages of the 'renegotiation' which was to be put to the electorate in a referendum in 1975. Powell had withdrawn his objections in principle to the referendum as a means of obtaining an electoral mandate on one issue; those objections, stilled rather than overcome, derived from his opposition to anything that derogated from the supremacy of Parliament. But the election in 1974 had not turned upon British membership of the Community, much as he tried to bring it, and the issue of broken pledges, into his speeches. Even in October 1974, the polls intimated that voters were more concerned about prices, inflation and the country's financial crisis than the promised referendum.

Callaghan's renegotiation, as some had forecast, produced a minimal result.

The Treaty, the loss of sovereignty, was unaffected; the transitional terms were eased. But it gave Wilson the formula whereby Labour could have it both ways: the Cabinet, like the party, could – amazing precedent – take different sides in the campaign: 'for the duration'. The Referendum institutionalised, for a few weeks, the split; and the verdict of the people would rebind them again into a single party. Wilson felt able to give the assurances that the market was changing, that the renegotiation was itself a catalyst of change, and on that basis the Government was justified in recommending a vote to stay in. In the debate on this decision, Powell was scathing:

> When we joined in 1972, the outcome of the negotiations . . . was embodied in a long series of articles and protocols in the Treaty of Brussels. But of every one of the changes and alterations which the Government, rightly or not, claim they have achieved, not one is embodied in the same permanent form . . . In every case the Government have said either, 'Well, we think the circumstances have changed' or 'We do not think this as important as it appeared to be two years ago,' or else they say that 'this is the part of a continuing negotiation'.[41]

It was Douglas Jay who pointed out that of the 3,936 legislative acts adopted by the EEC which claimed legal force in Britain in 1974, over 3,000 were adopted by the 'unelected commissioners' and of these 2,980 were regulations, 'legislation in secret', by officials but binding on the British courts. One way and another, the anti-Marketeers who spoke in the debate took Powell's line on the loss of sovereignty, and repeated, or brought fresh evidence for, the arguments he had deployed in 1971–3. Powell himself hit on an underlying motive which was to be effective in the Marketeers' own campaign in the weeks ahead. As he listened to their speeches, he said,

> I found that a paradox which had puzzled and worried me all through these years began to find its explanation. I never understood why it should be the Conservative Party, devoted to the protection of British institutions, the party devoted to nationhood and national independence, which in these last twenty years has been the pacesetter in this matter . . . But . . . there has been a note struck more and more insistently and that note has been the word 'power'. The debate has revealed how for many people membership of the European Economic Community is a surrogate for Empire. It supplies the same sensation . . . of belonging to a great and powerful show.[42]

But this was both a fallacy and a hallucination. He restated his abiding principle of British national being:

> I believe a nation has certain genius or national character of its own and that its institutions conform themselves to that character or genius. . . . They cannot be renounced without danger to that nation and . . . cannot . . . merely be transferred to others whose genius is different. I believe that the

government of this country under a parliament which has the sole right to legislate and to tax, with an unwritten constitution which leaves the whole defence of the subject as well as the welfare of the country in the hands of this House, corresponds uniquely to the genius of its people.

To this, Heath made his increasingly standard reply:

To me sovereignty is not something to be hoarded, sterile and barren, carefully protected in a greatcoat with its collar turned up by the Rt Hon Member for Down South . . . [it] is something for us as custodians to use in the interests of our country . . . I answer without hesitation that the sacrifice of sovereignty . . . or the sharing of sovereignty, the transfer of sovereignty . . . is fully justified.[43]

The Government's policy – to recommend acceptance of the results of the renegotiations – was affirmed 398 to 172; and this was taken to be a flying start for the pro-Marketeers (the Britain in Europe Movement) in the Referendum. On 24 January 1975, the Gallup Poll had found that 33 per cent of those who were interviewed want to stay in, as compared with 41 per cent wishing to leave; but if the Government recommended staying in, the percentages were 53 per cent to 22 per cent. Thus the outlook for Powell and the Get Britain Out Movement was dubious; and by April the polls found 57 per cent were for staying in, and 28 per cent for leaving.

Powell's speeches in the campaign, which were commended for their calm reasoning and intellectual clarity, stressed the loss of national independence and parliamentary supremacy; as did Michael Foot's. The other anti-Marketeers, like Douglas Jay and Barbara Castle, focused on food prices, which the polls showed had more appeal. On the economics of staying out, there was a palpable division in the Get Britain Out ranks: Powell repeated his view that Britain could go it alone, like Japan, on the basis of a market, *laissez-faire*, free-enterprise economy; Peter Shore and others seemed to advocate a siege economy.

But the dominant figure in the GBO campaign was not Powell, but Wedgwood Benn. He had taken a prominent part in pressing for the Referendum, and his parliamentary star was rising. He attracted something of the publicity in 1975 that Powell had done in 1968 – but it was wholly counter-productive. His speeches enabled the pro-Marketeers to argue that he headed a left-wing, indeed marxist movement, to whose chariot wheels Powell had eccentrically and perversely chained himself; Benn would not sit on a platform with him. *The Times* called GBO the voice of the marxist left, and the *Daily Express* turned against Powell, temporarily, for associating himself with it. The raggedness of the GBO leadership – such as it was – contrasted with the chumminess of the Labour and Conservative leaders sitting together on their platforms. In vain Powell inveighed against the argument that membership was being urged as 'a talisman against political hobgoblins' and insisted that Britain could as easily fall prey to socialism or communism within the Community. He returned to his 1969 attack on an attitude which said to the British people 'You can no longer rely on yourselves, on the British electorate, to reject the policies you abhor.'

The atmosphere of 1975 was different from 1972. The electorate had been frightened by the crisis of 1974, the collapse of the stock market, the inflation that accompanied the 1974 wage explosion, rising unemployment, the sense that the nation had barely escaped an unimaginable disaster and was not out of the wood. Paul Johnson drew a pertinent comparison with the demand for 'a doctor's mandate' in the election of 1931. The BIE's message was neatly summed up by Christopher Soames in the emotive phrase 'it's damned cold outside'; Carrington made sophisticated fun of Britain as a rundown offshore island 'with our sovereignty safely locked up in a deed box in Barclays Bank, as irrelevant as gumboots in the Sahara'. The BIE movement had a consensus of leadership, and the overwhelming support of the rich and the businessmen, as well as the full weight of the Conservative political machine. The nation was told, in a dozen ways, to keep tight hold of nurse in Brussels, for fear of something worse.

Powell knew early in the campaign that the cause was lost. He made only six speeches, and played a small part in the ramshackle GBO organisation. He could above all see that the MPs of both parties were rallying to their leaderships irrespective of their deeper convictions; Edward Du Cann, Chairman of the 1922 Committee, produced a small uproar when he echoed Powell's accusations of 1972 that party loyalties and pressures were overcoming inner convictions: 'but for this,' he said, 'I have no doubt that at least as many Conservative members would be seen publicly to be against our remaining members of the EEC as are in favour.'

Powell's main hope, as the campaign proceeded, was not for the victory he had thought so likely in 1974, but for a relatively inconclusive result. There was little 'Powell effect' to ensure any such thing or to swing the results against the Heath and Wilson bandwagon. The polls suggested, in the event, that he did not take his former immigration-derived following with him in his fight against the EEC. He influenced rather more voters to vote No than Yes, but this amounted to only 700,000 to 800,000 votes. The Referendum had been made possible only by his advice to electors to vote Labour in 1974, but that same advice, David Butler concluded, ensured that when it came the majority would vote Yes.[44] Philip Goodhart thought that Powell had dealt a body blow to anti-Market sentiment among Conservatives by his defection. Had he somehow avoided it, Goodhart thought, and remained MP for Wolverhampton SW, the volume of Tory opposition would have been two or three times greater. He claimed a collapse of morale and influence of party workers in his own constituency who had previously supported Powell, and believed it was true of others. The Britain in Europe movement had fearfully set up an 'Enoch-watching department' – but 'they need not have bothered.'[45]

The Marketeers' victory also owed much to the skill with which Wilson and Callaghan manoeuvred to get a Yes vote without splitting the Labour Party. The mass of moderate Labour voters could vote as their own leadership recommended. In the end, the vote went two to one for membership; but of the total number of registered voters less than half – 43 per cent – had voted Yes. Not one in a hundred voters, Powell thought, had the remotest idea that they were voting to substitute the Treaty of Rome for the Crown in Parliament; and this was the measure of his, and the anti-Marketeers' failure, 'though many of the advocates of British membership, who have been as explicit as any opponent, cannot be blamed.'

The result fulfilled his own warnings about the result of consensus politics, the separation of the country's leadership for so long from the real feelings of the people. They had not been offered a genuine alternative: 'a large number of our people', he said during the campaign, 'have become so alienated from our institutions as not merely to have lost faith in them but to feel nothing strange or shameful in the idea of invoking external authority to . . . supplant them.' The 1975 Referendum thus bore out his predictions that a sense of helplessness would produce cynicism and anomie.

> Never again, by the necessity of an axiom, will an Englishman live for his country or die for his country: the country for which people live or die was obsolete and we have abolished it. Or not quite yet. No, not yet. The referendum is not a verdict after which the prisoner is hanged forthwith. It is no more than provisional . . . and that will be so as long as one Parliament can undo what that or any other Parliament has done. Hence those golden words in the Government's referendum pamphlet, 'Our continued membership will depend on the continuing assent of Parliament.'[46]

The political commentators saw no comfort for Powell in that; the Referendum had, they thought, meant that his battles throughout the 1970–74 Parliament were in vain; and his sacrifice of his power base in the Conservative Party wasted. But Powell had not fought his last battle and his struggle from 1971–74 was not only, even if centrally, about the Common Market. It was about the soul of the Conservative Party, and about parliamentary and constitutional principle. That struggle went on after 1974 and 1975; it was still engaging Powell's parliamentary powers all through 1978.

Chapter 10

Powell *v.* Heath V:
The Conservative Government,
1970–1974

1   The Divisions in the Party

Powell's record in the 1970–74 Parliament was dramatised by the press and
media as a personal struggle with Heath for the leadership. Alternatively it was
presented as a play of revenge for inability to wrest the crown from Heath. Even
the reasoned argument and passionate debate over the entry into the Common
Market was interpreted in terms of personal rivalry, as if the principle on which
Powell's opposition was based was that Heath had staked his political life on the
outcome. Powell's prospects of the succession as the result of some débâcle was
reviewed regularly as part of the state of play. Few noticed that if Powell was
aiming at the leadership at any cost, he played his hand with strange ineptitude.

A realistic bid for power required the careful choice of points of opposition
which would consolidate a body of Powellites as a disciplined group exercising
leverage on the leadership and the whips, and converting the Party progressively
to the need for a new policy under new management. There were opportunities
for doing this in a parliament in which rebellions were endemic and both parties
were divided by issues other than the Common Market. At least forty-five Tories
withheld their support on half of eight important issues on which Powell opposed
the Government; about thirty voted even more nearly as he did.[1] He did nothing
to organise this body of dissidence. T. E. Utley, his first biographer, did not think
he had it in him to do any such thing: 'he talks only briefly and precisely to his
colleagues, he does not form or even join dining clubs; his interest in and capacity
for intrigues – the most important qualities for a prospective Tory leader – are
negligible.'[2] So there never arose a 'right-wing' faction with a concerted policy;
just as the left of the Party, when disturbed by Heath's racial compromises,
merely fractioned off as individuals. Those who shared Powell's views on
immigration and Rhodesia, if often on cruder grounds, did not agree with his
exoneration of the trade unions from responsibility for inflation. Those who were
at times with him on the Common Market demurred at his demand that Rolls-
Royce should be put into receivership and auctioned off. Many, glad to enlist his

eloquence for particular causes of their own, nevertheless objected to his range of criticism and believed that he had mismanaged his prospects of office to the detriment of conservatism in general.

The conflict, on the surface one of power politics, was fundamentally one of ideas. The drama arose from the contrast in personalities; but Heath and Powell by 1970 embodied different concepts of conservatism. Heath set the tone of his approach to power and administration with his words 'we were returned to office to change the course of history of this nation, nothing less'; and induced growth at 5 per cent a year was to be the first measure of that change. Powell on his side never attacked Heath for being a Marketeer as such. In June 1973 he said in a bitter attack on Heath's method of achieving membership, 'I have repeatedly and publicly affirmed that, if he believes it, an Englishman may honourably contend that this country ought to become a province of a larger state, and a Member of Parliament may honourably vote to reduce the Parliament of the United Kingdom to the status of a subordinate assembly.'[3]

It was for the Prime Minister to propose and set events moving; for Powell to react on the basis of his publicly-stated beliefs. This posture gave rise to an impression of undeviating, indiscriminate opposition. Powell tried to correct this impression in interviews, when he could point to occasions on which he could support the Government, for example over parts of the Industrial Relations Act. But faced with a Government often making changes even when change was unnecessary (for example, the disastrous Local Government Act) a propensity Powell had condemned as inappropriate to conservatism in 1964, he had difficulty in finding many examples. As Powell saw his position in 1971: 'I am in the heights of politics in the sense that on most of the subjects on which I speak, what I say is as well reported as what most politicians, including those in office, say.'[4] This was a mild way of putting it. Heath could not see that he forced the role of critic – indeed of Cassandra – on Powell. He saw only disloyalty. In February 1970 when he declared that Powell would hold no office in an administration of his, he explained that this was simply because Powell was opposed to almost every article of party policy.

This was not so; for Powell accepted the party manifesto in 1970. Indeed he most inconveniently stood upon it in much of his criticism: the issue between himself and Heath was the breaking of the pledges in the manifesto over the Common Market, then over immigration (at least on repatriation) and incomes policy – the abandonment of the Selsdon Park concept thought to be a commitment to market forces. It was not just Powell, but a powellian nemesis at work.

He had no choice but to accept that he had no hope of office under Heath. Undertaking a last-minute engagement to speak to the Purchasing and Supply Institute in October 1970, which had printed on its programme that the address would be by a senior member of the Government, he quipped 'instead you have been presented with the one person who has had a public and official guarantee that he shall never be a senior member of HM Government!' A few days later he told Chris Montcrieff of the Press Association that he had probably left behind him the stage of holding office. 'In the last five or six years my life in politics has been concerned with the shaping of ideas and with the demand to express a certain view on the future of this country. I cannot turn my back on all that in order to return to an earlier stage of the political animal; the more time goes on, the more office has a significance only in relation to the purposes and causes which have come to be one's own.'[5] He was prepared only to do a vital job, such as Minister of Repatriation, for which, if the work were properly financed, he had offered himself; or to be Number One himself. The press, undaunted, kept on asking the question.

In the ensuing years the truths of powellism were to be tested against the received wisdom of Macmillanite progressive conservatism; it was the latter that actually brought the government down, the former which provided the best explanations of why the policies boomeranged. (Powell always insisted that his was no sterile theorising; he advocated no remedies he could not carry through in practice 'subject to the inevitable exigencies of power'.) Both Heath and Powell were convinced that their policies were both right and practical; both thought patriotism was involved, a patriotism both expressed in irreconcilable terms. For both thought the nation's whole future was at stake; both were on record that a Conservative administration, after the years of Wilsonian mismanagement and creeping socialism, might be the last chance to break out. But for Heath it was the 'dash for growth' and the expansiveness of the European link, while for Powell it was the revolutionary return to first principles – another holocaust of controls, and reliance on the restoration of initiative and responsibility to the people. Neither could believe himself mistaken (nor does he to this day). The drama, the tragedy, lay here. Powell's analysis was vindicated, but both men fell victims to the proof.

Powell's refusal to form a dissident group was matched by Heath's refusal to compromise with his party. At the end of his premiership, Powell referred to 'one-man government' and this was nearly as true as at the beginning, certainly after death removed Iain Macleod's influence. Heath appeared an arrogant and insensitive leader, impatient of criticism in the House, intolerant of it in Cabinet. The high-mindedness that inhibited him from using the honours system to lubricate, at a difficult time, the party machinery did him credit (he was less niggardly, however, than some back-benchers thought). He ruled by fear and fiat – especially fear of a general election. His confidences with an inner circle of ministers, his personal reserve, the impression he sometimes gave that government was a thing apart from Parliament – at times reminiscent of Anthony Eden – his limited preferments to minor office, caused estrangement. He proved almost incapable of the kindly word in the smoking-room, the magnanimous praise for an effective critical speech, the deft touch of social condescension which had solved problems for Macmillan.

Heath had chosen, as Powell would have chosen, a hard path and pace for his party.[6] Powell's criticisms were of government policies or methods, but both

were rendered more vulnerable to Powell's gunfire by Heath's style. When
Powell said in a press interview that Heath was afraid of him, he was alluding to
the force and range of intellectual argument; but also to the factors, not
intellectual, which had made him a focus of national sentiment, deep but
inarticulate (he once said that over immigration he had served as a lightning-
conductor). 'We fear things we don't fully understand, and forces that we
apprehend may perhaps be bigger than ourselves.'[7] Subsequently he added, in
1973, 'I represent something in politics which is foreign to his comprehension,'
and identified this as 'imagination' – though Heath had an imaginative quality
too. But Heath had defensively turned away from this interpreter of the national
genius, removed an independent judgement rather than grapple honestly with the
phenomenon of nationwide support for Powell's line on immigration. It was a
step away from reality as Powell saw it. Thus an emotional and an intellectual
obstinacy locked horns.

2   Rhodesia, Rolls-Royce and Money Supply

Powell found the appointment of John Davies to be Secretary of State for Trade
and Industry, a Cabinet appointment, after only a few weeks in Parliament,
significant of the new style of Conservative government. He saw it as an attempt
to de-politicise government – to insulate government decisions from the political
environment. It offended his sense of the uniqueness of British parliamentary
government,

> not in the literal and untenable sense that parliament governs, but in the sense
> that men come to govern by way of parliament, by way of the political arts
> which bring them to parliament and keep them there . . . which enable them to
> survive in that assembly and, in one style or another, to predominate in it.
> These are arts that are not communicable . . . learnt they must be, and time
> and the hard school of experience are the only tutors. . . .[8]

He pointed out that 'instant ministers' – men brought in from the non-
parliamentary world like trade unionists and administrators or businessmen –
were usually failures, though in war-time it happened as part of an executive
approach to accepted priorities. But Heath had indicated that in his view
experience in the House was not requisite for high office: 'for him government is
not what Parliament is about; for him government is about administration . . .
and not about politics or persuasion; for him in the last analysis government is
about means and not ends.'

The executive approach was manifested early on in the manoeuvres by which
Leila Khaled, the terrorist, was whisked out of the country and embarrassments
of British jurisdiction: Powell found them both cowardly and unconstitutional,
as interference with the course of justice. In November he voted against the
renewal of sanctions against Rhodesia, and opposed Sir Alec Douglas-Home's
'last attempt' to find a peaceful settlement (it led to the negotiation of a new

constitution which was accepted by Smith, denounced by British liberals and black sympathisers, and finally rejected by the Rhodesian blacks testifying to Lord Pearce's commission. Powell still found British interference nonsense:

> My Rt Hon Friend is not saying 'I am going to initiate if I can a new round of negotiations with the Smith regime. But make no mistake I shall be back with this order next year and the year after and the year after that until . . . I get a settlement on the five principles' . . . the reality is that if the Government claim these powers in order to make 'one more try' . . . when that try is over they will not again ask for sanctions. He will in effect be going to Mr Smith and saying 'this is your last chance. This time you had better settle or we shall have to consider removing sanctions.' What an arm-breaking clinch. . . !⁹

Twenty-three Conservatives voted against the Government.

It was generally believed that under Heath there would be a return to 'market forces' in some degree – if not as far as Powell advocated at any rate as far as Sir Keith Joseph did. Powell praised Barber's autumn budget with reserve as neutral on inflation, but opposed his plan to help the very poor with the Family Income Supplement of up to £3 a week instead of the increased family allowance promised at the election. In this he feared a recrudescence of the Speenhamland system. An eighteenth-century device to help those whose earnings barely provided subsistence, it ended by keeping wages in many areas below subsistence level because employers treated the subsidy as part of wages, and deducted it from what they would otherwise have paid. Certainly in the past eight or nine years, the dependence of the low income groups upon social security of all kinds has notoriously increased.

The Government's decision to save Rolls-Royce from bankruptcy over the RB211 engine provided an early example of the irreconcilability of Powell's economic thinking and the Government's. He said first it should be allowed to go bankrupt, because the readiness of the state to finance failure was a commitment to inflation and an abandonment of reliance on market forces; second that it was wrong for them to accept that state ownership is the proper instrument for restoring unprofitable assets to profitability: 'they have cast doubt and discredit on the belief in capitalism and private enterprise for which this party stands.'¹⁰ He was perfectly ready to 'Dutch auction' parts of the company producing for defence; much of defence production was in private hands, and bankruptcy implied only a change to more efficient ownership. Yet a Tory government was nationalising a loss-making private firm to make it a profit-maker.

Inflation, after two orthodox Jenkins budgets, and even after Barber's expenditure cuts in September, was still rapid; rising prices were seen to be followed by demands for high wage settlements. Powell saw in Rolls-Royce a key sector in anti-inflation strategy which ought to be defended at all costs – the suggestion that a vital defence interest had to be preserved for the nation he regarded as a plausible excuse (for the company, if sold off at asset value, would continue to produce what was ordered from it). The Government was insisting that it would not give way to demands for a wage freeze or an incomes policy, which was, Mr Maurice Macmillan remarked in impeccably powellist terms, a demand for compulsion. But Powell was concerned with underlying tendencies which might wash away the Government's resolution. 'I must confess', he told an audience in Renfrew in November, 'that I view with dismay the manner in which the political and public debate about rising prices and rising wages is being carried on.'[10] Once again he stated the monetarist view, a view he was to reiterate for the ensuing three years with all the persuasiveness that he could deploy, using every turn and twist of events to bring home the central moral contained in the story of 1958 and after. 'Wage claims, wage awards, strikes, do not cause rising prices, for one simple but sufficient reason: they cannot. There was never a strike yet that caused inflation, and there never will be. The most powerful union, or group of unions, which was ever invented, is powerless to cause prices to rise . . . inflation is a matter of money . . . it is the Government which finances inflation, actively or passively . . .'[11] As he rose to speak, they knew what to expect.

The City was said to welcome the Powellite economic policy to which Heath seemed originally to have committed himself in rejecting a wage freeze.[12] Powell, however, vented his fears that the Conservatives would, when the pressure grew, succumb as Labour had done (and Macmillan before them) to the temptation to seek the answer to rising prices in controls. The £42 million given to Rolls-Royce was a step further down the slippery slope of money-creation.

Direct subsidy by the Government to industry is no doubt not the major way in which government expenditure finances inflation: but it is the most obvious and the most dramatic. When Rolls-Royce and Mersey Docks were told last week that the all-providing public purse would bail them out, it was as good as saying the buck would, for the time being, go on. Oh, I know that there are exceptions; every case is an exception. Unless sin were pleasant there would be no sinners. But virtue still resides in that monosyllabic word No. It is only the government that can say it, and it has to be said until the money flows in no faster than there are extra things to buy with it.[13]

But when inflation continued despite expenditure cuts and orthodox budgets, nerves began to fray. Powell had to warn that this was explained by the time-lag from Labour expenditure and borrowing of two years previously: one must persevere. The other cause was the apparently healthly balance of payments surplus. To prevent sterling rising the Treasury borrowed fictitiously from the banking system to buy up the foreign money, which increased the credit base and permitted an addition to money supply which had no counterpart in buyable production. This discrepancy, inevitably, swelled the pressure on prices. The correct course Powell identified as neutralising the inflow, either by repaying debt or by allowing sterling to rise against other currencies, or both. This advice looked just deflationary to the Bank of England, Lord Balogh and the anti-monetarist school generally. But the battle was beginning, and Powell kept it up. In the new year he recalled the resignations of 1958, and declared that in 1971 the country faced precisely the issue that was disastrously decided in the opposite way in that year. 'Thirteen years ago the Chancellor was derided for daring to mention money supply; today money supply is at the centre of political and economic debate both sides of the Atlantic; the relevance of government expenditure to inflation has been acknowledged in theory and practice.[14] The 'Keynesian view' still prevailed, however. The Government's policies were self-contradictory and a crisis was in the making.

Against the background of rising prices, strikes and wage demands, the government introduced the Industrial Relations Bill promised in the election manifesto. Powell supported its principles insofar as he had long proclaimed that the privileges of trade unions had got completely out of hand; even if these did not include the power to cause inflation. During the debate on the bill he offered to go before the Wilberforce tribunal on the miners' claims to contest the Treasury view that labour costs were inflationary. He wanted the bill to be wholly dissociated from suggestions that it was designed to prevent wage increases. 'The case for reform is wholly independent of inflation; it would be just as strong if inflation had never been invented.'

Though Conservative Central Office deployed Powell's backing for the law — no doubt because it would weigh with the skilled working class — he regretted that the Act was divided into three parts which 'are different in character, depend on different reasoning and are not of equal cogency'. He accepted the plan to make trade union privileges and immunities dependent on registration, which would discourage sympathetic strikes and lockouts, enforcement of a closed shop, and other restrictive practices, because this part of the bill restored to the civil and criminal law actions other than by registered trade unions. The provision for the legal enforcement of collective agreements between employers and unions he liked less, because it seemed to give undue power to unions to pressure their members, and he called it a matter for 'experiment and experience'. He opposed the proposals which enabled the Government to intervene where an industrial dispute would 'seriously endanger the national interest'. He considered that while it was the Government's duty to protect the public from injury by interruptions of services – like gas or sewage – this duty was fully met by existing emergency powers. He had long denied that definitions of 'national interest' could cover, as the new law intended, economic problems or risks to the balance of payments.

For the Government to intervene in one trade dispute out of many by reason of the supposed economic consequences of that particular dispute implies a view of the economy, and the government's role in the economy, which is essentially socialist and not Conservative . . . it would be a poor bargain if, by insistence on this element, we were to blur the clear image of a reform of the law designed to bring the legal framework within which citizens regulate their

mutual dealings into accord with public opinion and the general sense of what
is right and fair.[15]

Powell foresaw that a government pursuing what he would think a misguided
policy on, for example, exchange rates, would invoke that political decision as
the public interest and intervene in disputes in a way public opinion would not
support. And he was to be proved right.

But the Government was already fearful of the effects of industrial disputes,
especially in the public sector, on foreign confidence in the pound, on exports and
on the balance of payments, which by 1971 began again to look shaky. It placed
hope in the provisions for tribunals of enquiry and cooling-off periods, which
imitated American practices suited to American conditions. It was worried too
by the rise in unemployment even when the balance of payments was favourable,
after several orthodox budgets, and in a period of rising prices. The economy was
not responding to stimulus. As Powell put it: anyone predicting a state of affairs
in which they had 750,000 unemployed with 10 per cent inflation a few years
previously would have been called an economic ignoramus. The stagnation was,
in fact, the negation of the 'Keynesianism' the Treasury stood for; to Heath it
represented, in some unexplained way, the vicious circle from which the country
must heroically break free.

In the budget debate in April 1971 Powell urged the House to accept that
industrial relations and inflation were not causally related: 'it is not the asking,
but the supplying' of money for more wages that mattered. He noted that the tax
reductions were not balanced by lower expenditure, and offered the conclusion to
the House that the government was still feeding the inflation that it had inherited
from the Labour period at a rate he calculated to be about 12 per cent a year; and
predicted that this injection of money would produce additional inflation
sometime in 1972.

Once again he told the House that reducing inflation, which everyone
demanded, meant additional transitional unemployment; 'the penalty to be paid
for past mismanagement and the reinstatement of "honest money" until a new
pattern is established'.[16] Entranced by his exposition, the consensus of the House
was still against his conclusions. Grimond voiced a general view in saying that
the logic of not manufacturing the money to enable Fords to pay higher wages
was 'crude: theoretically possible, practically impossible.' The refrain was that
the transitional unemployment entailed by powellian honest money was
'intolerable', and nobody was prepared to discuss whether the ultimate effects of
inflation in producing unemployment might be worse – that was some way off –
far less to accept that the existing total of 750,000 out of work was the responsibility of previous Labour and Tory Chancellors. The tenor of the debate was that
there must be some way of stopping inflation without hurting anybody if only
someone could come up with it . . .

3   The Immigration Act

In the debate on the Expiring Laws Act in November 1970,[17] Powell had cited a paper by Mr Clifford Thomas of the Institute of Biological Sciences that, on a projection of a coloured population of 4,000,000 by 2000, Birmingham's population would then be not a third, but more nearly one-half coloured. In February he again[18] accused the Home Office of producing inaccurate immigration figures 'so that when the true situation could no longer be concealed, it was irreversible'. The Home Office had at length to admit errors in statistics which Powell declared increased the existing coloured population by 500,000. The Registrar-General put the coloured population at 1,400,000. Unknown to Powell, but later revealed in the Crossman diaries, there had been a bitter argument within the Labour Government over numbers, because projections about the future immigrant and immigrant-descended population were enormously affected by assumptions about its birthrate. Labour ministers preferred to think that this would fall to the native level, itself about to fall further; the Registrar-General had shown a larger eventual coloured population on the basis that the immigrant birthrate would remain higher than the native one.

When the Heath Government introduced its Immigration Bill in June 1971, Labour Members hastened to describe it as payment of the squalid debt owed to Powell for getting it elected. The bill carried out the official Conservative pledge to equalise conditions for entry as between Commonwealth citizens and aliens, apart from East African passport-holders. The effect of the bill was to make the control of work permits an administrative matter; those accepted were subject to a five-year qualification for permanent entry without an unqualified right to bring in dependants. In appearance it promised to restrict future entry, but Powell found it unsatisfactory.[19] He objected to the new concept of patriality, which was designed to keep out as many non-whites as possible while letting in people (including male fiancés) from Australia, Canada, etc., with British-born forbears; the so-called 'grandfather clause'. Powell had wanted legislation to define British citizenship and sweep away the 1948 and amending legislation; instead he found still more 'legislation by exception'. The new clause would allow in some Australians but not others, exclude Americans with patrial qualifications, and qualify for entry a growing number of Asians of future generations. He pointed out that the only correct description of those who could 'freely enter, leave and reside in Britain' was now 'a British subject, citizen of the UK and Colonies, to whom the provisions of the Commonwealth Immigration Act 1962, as amended in 1968, do not apply. I'd on the whole rather be an Englishman.'[20]

So he tabled twenty-nine amendments to strengthen the bill. To opprobium from the Labour benches he welcomed the removal of the statutory right of dependants of immigrants arriving after 1973 to enter. He frankly regretted that in 1964 he had propounded an inescapable obligation to admit wives and young children instead of proposing instead a status of visitor, returning to his home and family, in place of that of settler preparing a home for them. This recantation was prompted by the unceasing and apparently unending flow of dependants, swelled of course by the East African passport-holders' rights. (In 1969 it was officially stated that there were only 190,000 dependants to come; in 1975 there were still 180,000 anticipated officially.) Once again Powell pressed for the treatment of Eire nationals as aliens in accordance with their real status of citizens of a foreign country.

But he found that the main inadequacy in the bill lay in Clause 29, framed to meet past Conservative pledges on repatriation. Heath and Maudling now talked only in terms of helping misfits to go home. Powell had come to his conclusion that a big programme of well financed, voluntary repatriation would be the only real hope the bill could offer to reduce the future immigrant-descended population, since natural increase rather than immigration was building up the numbers unacceptably. But instead of a plan for 'massive, albeit voluntary, repatriation', entrusted to a Government department, responsibility was given to an outside body, International Social Services, with very limited resources; and a House of Lords amendment, at the Government's instance, confined payments specifically to those who had failed to make a success of settlement. Powell sent to Maudling a list of 300 applicants for finance for repatriation, and Maudling claimed that this showed how small a provision was needed. Powell called the Government's behaviour over repatriation 'as nice a little job of sabotage as you could wish to meet.'[21]

Powell's references to the Asian settlements in Lord Radcliffe's term of 'an alien wedge' was too much for some Young Conservatives. At one meeting, he rounded on them: 'How foolish can you get? How far can people go on deceiving themselves that a large and growing population of Indians and Pakistanis in the towns and cities of the Midlands and the North is not in every real sense of the terms alien?'[22] and so, he added, would be comparable concentrations of a white nationality speaking another language. Powell drew attention to the changing composition of immigrant settlement. In 1969–70 the published figures showed that there were 18,000 births to Asian families as compared with 12,000 to West Indian domiciled families; the West Indian influx had tailed off as anticipated in the early sixties – indeed some re-emigration, even without assistance, was about to justify Powell's views on reuniting families in the place of origin rather than in Britain; but therefore, he concluded 'It is more truly when he looks into the eyes of Asia that the Englishman comes face to face with those who will dispute with him the possession of his native land.'[23] He warned 'this generation of politicians' that they would fail in their endeavour to push the problem into the future for others to solve: this generation of political leaders would be called to account, 'not by posterity, but in their own lifetime, perhaps while they still hold office or have the prospect of it.'[24]

In September the Home Office was reported to be bitterly resentful of his suggestion that it ran a 'propaganda machine' to conceal the fact that immigration was rising not falling by taking only the figures of those admitted for settlement and not the figures for net immigration as used by the Registrar-General, which showed more were staying on. In November the Home Office had to admit that the number of students and others admitted as visitors, but finally settling permanently, raised their figures by fully 10 per cent, but explained that they had not disclosed these figures because they were thought 'misleading.' Powell insisted that the net figure was the only reliable index of demographic change because it took into account the emigration of the indigenous white population. He criticised Margaret Thatcher, Secretary of State for Education, for confessing that she could not produce true figures of the numbers of immigrant (and immigrant-descended) schoolchildren, on the ground that such a disclosure 'did not command the support of local education authorities and teachers'. Subsequently she discontinued the collection of any statistics. Dr Prem Chand, chairman of the conference of Asian Organisations, joined Peter Hain and others in asking Heath to somehow silence Powell, particularly on the implications of his demand for repatriation. Heath replied simply that Powell's views were his own, not the Government's.[25] Powell retorted that coloured people had stopped him in the street in Wolverhampton, to say 'Mr Powell we respect you, we do understand what you say.'

Powell's sense of betrayal was sharpened when the Government passed special legislation to allow Pakistanis settled in Britain to become United Kingdom citizens when Pakistan, in leaving the Commonwealth after the war with India, had legally rendered them aliens, depriving them of their right to bring in dependants and making them liable to repatriation like other aliens. Heath carefully waited until Pakistan had passed a law permitting dual citizenship before so legislating; and then passed a second act to give the citizens of Bangla Desh, the new state which had emerged from the war, the same rights for its citizens merely because it decided to join the Commonwealth. Powell had seen in the stance of these two states, one renouncing the Commonwealth, the other having to solicit membership, a God-given 'second chance' for Britain to reduce the immigrant population by perhaps 300,000 almost at a stroke and correspondingly to eliminate the future claims for dependants to be allowed in. A perfect legal right, unaffected by anything that had been done since the baneful 1948 Nationality Act, existed for Britain to take this step; Powell thought that Pakistan's resignation might even lead India and other states to end the Commonwealth 'bubble of pretence' and so abolish the legal basis on which immigration flourished. Instead Heath, who had toughly upheld Britain's sovereign rights at the Commonwealth Prime Ministers' conference in Singapore, took steps to reinforce the rights and claims of immigrants and would-be immigrants. The acts implied that provided one had once been in the Empire, one's citizens inherited all the nationality rights (subject to the Acts of 1962, 1968 and 1971) which had facilitated the massive inflow of coloured people. Powell warned that the Conservative Party would not be forgiven or deserve to be forgiven.

4 'Death of Keynes': The Pound Floated At Last

Thus, within a year, Powell was finding that the Government was backsliding on its election manifesto at almost every point: on the halt to large-scale immigration, on rolling back government interference, on reversing nationalisation, on Selsdon, on trade unions, even. He feared its impatience over unemployment was driving it, behind the scenes, towards a fatal abandonment of control over money supply in favour of a disastrous new attempt to control prices and wages which would bedevil industrial relations. All these U-turns were overshadowed and compounded by the issue of the EEC, to which, from the middle of 1971, Powell was devoting most of his energies. But his range of criticism as the Government began lurching into expediences prompted demands for his resignation from the Party, to which ministers replied soothingly that he was a spent force ('Poor old Mr Powell,' said Geoffrey Rippon, 'His tragedy is to have a brilliant mind'). The Party Chairman (Peter Thomas) tried another tack: the public, he averred, had all along twigged that the pledge only to negotiate really meant 'negotiate to get in' and then get in, so no pledges were being broken.

But ministers were worried. The polls showed Labour in the lead, despite Heathite dynamism; and worse, that after Heath and Wilson, Powell was the most respected politician in the land. He was seen as a power, back-bencher though he might be. The argument that he had helped Heath to victory, that he was influencing policies and that he had long-standing and reputable ideas for meeting the nation's discontent had sunk into the public mind. Besides the speeches in Parliament that stirred up controversy in the press, he was writing articles, speaking to public audiences, getting reported almost daily; his paperback editions were selling well. An organisation, 'Powellight', was circulating full texts of his speeches, noting his engagements, and quoting comments on his activities; it was not set up by Powell, whose speeches were circulated by Central Office – though later, when it refused to circulate those that became too critical of the party line, Powell circulated them from his home. He took care that the public should know that his work and thinking ranged over the whole field of politics. A film was made for ATV about his life and work; in March a series of interviews appeared in the *Sun* on what he would do if ever he became Prime Minister. The substance of his remarks was a simplified version for popular consumption, of all his economic and social prescriptions, including those he made in his 1968 'budget' – the alternative Toryism. This 'response to insistent public demand' caused the highbrow commentators to raise their eyebrows, even to suggest that adulation was turning his head. Yet the House filled to hear his cogent speeches. Antony Howard in the *Observer* opined that he was being torn between his reputation for well-informed speeches to his peers in the Commons and that of an 'unblushing merchant of the vernacular'. Most politicians envied his power to shift key: what he said was exactly the same.[26]

The normal relationship between any government's popularity and the state of the economy had reasserted itself. Inflation, rising prices, unemployment had not succumbed to Selsdon or Powellite treatment – or not within fifteen months. Heath's maldroit phrase 'cut prices at a stroke' was carefully misquoted against him by Labour speakers (never by Powell) at every opportunity. Powell's persistent and consistent statement of the remedies that he believed would work, though far from painlessly, won him audiences ready to follow his economic reasoning. In June, in an article in the *Director*, he discussed the wholly unexpected change in the economic environment which had falsified the Treasury's assumptions, when Heath came in, that inflation would be moderate, the balance of payments would shift from surplus to balance, and unemployment would stabilise. Powell made the important point that needless inflation was being imported from the United States which had 'continued to pump out more dollars of diminishing value and the rest of the world . . . has continued to import the American inflation by taking the dollars across the exchanges with fixed parity and converting them into a flood of additional domestic money.'[27] This phenomenon is now generally accepted as a major cause of post-war inflation since the sixties, the other being, of course, the financing of internal budgetary deficits. The answer Powell had said in March, was to let the pound price itself freely against other currencies so that 'a balance of payments (no surplus, no deficit) is always and automatically maintained.' Failing this the 'accursed surplus' persisted. Powell told the businessmen:

> If anyone had been told that this was going to happen in the first year of a new Conservative government, he would have said 'they must be going to halt inflation and deflate too quickly . . .' What nobody thought to see was high and continuing inflation and rising unemployment . . . at the same time. Reared for a generation on the doctrine, or at least the distorted tradition, of Keynes, politicians have found themselves stranded with a vocabulary which didn't fit the situation . . . so we have the Government denounced in classic fashion for deflationary policies and exhorted to 'reflate' – and all in the middle of a roaring inflation, for which the Government themselves have promised to maintain the necessary growth of money supply unless and until the inflation somehow stops of its own accord; for that is what the Chancellor of the Exchequer in his bewilderingly contradictory assertions on monetary policy is evidently trying to tell us.[28]

Powell well knew that Chancellor Barber was simply the agent of Heath himself; it was Heath who dictated, far more than Macmillan ever did, financial policy.

In August, however, the pound was floated and as Powell anticipated, no disaster supervened; but this did not mean that the rate of exchange was freed from intervention completely. But in November Powell risked the pronouncement that 'Keynes is dead.' The era which had started with the White Paper of 1943 on full employment was over, the unemployment lobby had lost its case. Unemployment would now be reduced only when a new pattern of supply and demand had been established 'in accordance with technological change and new processes.' He was hailing non-intervention; but he was to be disappointed.

5   Ulster: Deterioration in Public Life

Powell developed a close relation with the Ulster Unionists during 1971, and became increasingly critical of Heath's handling of the worsening terrorist attacks as the Provisional IRA tightened its grip on the Catholic population. Most British politicians shunned any involvement with the province, leaving policy to their leaders and voting when they had to exactly as the whips required. They correctly diagnosed that there was no mileage with their constituents in a concern about Ulster, and certainly not in any quixotic attempts to educate them on the subject. The growing murder and mayhem on television merely deepened a feeling that the Irish were a race and a place apart; from the first the commitment of the Army was unpopular. Powell's determination to row against the political tide was put down either to his unpredictability, or to mischief-making – even the Irish stick was good enough to beat the Heath administration with.

In reality, he had no choice. The Ulster people were part of the British nation by their majority choice; they were under attack; therefore the United Kingdom as a whole was under attack. The fact that the killing had not spread (or not as yet) to the mainland did not alter the principle. British indifference to Ulster's ordeal was part and parcel of the trial of British nationhood, of which the attempt to enter the EEC was also part and parcel. He could not deal with one without being committed to taking a position on the other. He told a Londonderry audience in January 1971:

> The violent events in Ulster in the last eighteen months have been watched from the other side of the water . . . with an alarming detachment . . . The commitment of the British Army . . . has not been seen by the people of Britain generally as an alarm signal directed to themselves. Instead it has been widely regarded as anything from an infernal nuisance to an embarrassingly distressing commitment . . .[29]

On the other side of the water he seized any occasion to shake that detachment. 'When one part of a nation is under attack', he told Conservatives in Buckinghamshire 'the whole of it is under attack.'

> It is incredible, if it had not actually happened, that for a year and a half there should be areas in the United Kingdom where the Queen's writ does not run . . . If these areas were described as what they are – namely, pockets of territory occupied by the enemy as surely as if they had been captured and held by enemy troops – then perhaps it would be realised how preposterous is the situation.[30]

He attacked as nonsense any attempt in Britain to treat Irishness as a special problem, and singled out homilies directed by ministers in Westminster to Ulster on the need to live together as 'dangerous incomprehension'. It was not an arcane subject for specialists on Ireland; human nature was for political purposes the same everywhere, and politicians who assessed political situations in terms of special kinds of nationalist traits were showing themselves on the wrong track. He denounced the United Kingdom government's posture of neutrality as between its attacked citizens and their attackers: 'the public in Britain are being invited to regard Ulster, as, in a famous phrase "a faraway country of which we know nothing" and the presence of British soldiers under attack there as similar to their presence in Malaysia . . .' This was a kind of paraphrase of Mr Maudling's private comments on Ulster when he returned from his first visit. Powell struck a note he was to repeat with growing vehemence:

> The truest, deepest responsibility for the deeds of violence in Ulster does not lie in the backstreets of Belfast or Dublin . . . It lies at Westminister, it lies with Her Majesty's government in the United Kingdom and with the Parliament of the United Kingdom. Only when their policies and actions, as well as their professions, bring conviction to friend and foe alike that the realities of this province are understood and that the unity of the realm will be maintained, will the guilt of innocent blood depart from Westminster.[31]

This accusation, while it pleased the Ulster Unionists, upset the Government and the Conservatives, and indeed even Labour members; it is unpleasant to be told they had responsibility for the shedding of innocent blood. Yet this assertion that Westminster could not escape responsibility stemmed from arguments similar to those which animated his much-applauded speech on the Hola killings in 1959. But Powell showed his independence of both Unionists and Government when Stormont was suspended in 1972, welcoming any move which assimilated the Province to the rest of the kingdom, and rejecting devolution, imposed as Home Rule in 1920, which had become the mechanism of the Protestant ascendancy. This was unpalatable to the Unionists; but the Government disliked his diagnosis that the abolition of Stormont was in reality a surrender to the terrorists, that it substituted weak and compromising government for one which was not inflexible but did realise that it was engaged in a life and death struggle. Eight Conservatives, including Powell, voted with ten Unionists – and with Bernadette Devlin whose opposition was idosyncratic and marxist.

The breach between the Ulster Unionists and the Conservatives began at this point, eventually ending in Unionist rejection of the Tory whip, and separation which made it possible, in the fullness of time, for Powell to join them. It also coincided with a period in which Heath and the whips were exercising pressures on Members over the Communities bill which Powell found debasing to public life itself – going, that is, far beyond what was normal in getting a difficult piece of legislation through. He was particularly disgusted at the pressures brought on the Unionists, after the suspension of Stormont, to help the Government to get the EEC bill passed. Seven of the Unionists accepted Powell's arguments why the EEC bill, wrong for Britain, carried special perils for Ulster, and voted steadily against it. But Powell's attacks on the whips, from February, for their 'unparalleled exertions' were intensely resented, and they carried the warfare into Wolverhampton South-West. Powell set the limits of legitimate pressure:

> Who would complain if the political rewards for good behaviour were seductively applied to wobblers and waverers? That is what promises and threats are for, and as hope and credulity spring eternal, there will always be a supply of the gullible who mistake a kindly word for a firm undertaking, a frown for a sentence of political death.[32]

But to go out and twist arms in constituencies was beyond permissible limits: 'when the system of bribes and threats is exported to the country to constrain MPs to vote against what they know to be the wishes and interests of the electors.'

Powell, wrestling with this new development of party discipline, abhorrent to his concepts of a Member's obligations to his constituents (which are indeed enshrined in single Member representation), gave the Press Gallery a bowdlerised but mordant picture of Francis Pym's operations in ensuring that votes did *not* follow voices:

> Here is a man who would stand for a principle and demand to be satisfied before he would go into the lobby; his colleagues cheered him, but the minister gave him nothing that he asked; yet he voted all the same, and his colleagues' cheers ring mockingly in his memory. . . . Here is another who spoke and voted for his conscience and his native land; and the next week, behold, he was a minister in the government he had condemned. What do you think it is like to be that man? Over there an honourable Member, who has stood by his cause for years, is explaining to his friends that his heart is with them still and he wishes them success, but he has no means of support apart from his parliamentary salary, and his family must come first. With him goes, to vote for what he detests, a man who has declared from a score of platforms to applauding audiences that he for one would be no party to it; but lately, it appears, he discovered that he had 'difficulties in his constituency' and the mighty voice is hushed. . . . There goes another, a second and a third, who know the sorrowful secret written into their election address, but who also know there is a big redistribution of parliamentary boundaries and the main thing (is it not?) is to be sure of a seat in the next House, even if that House is never more to be the House of Falkland and Fox, Burke and Pitt, Disraeli and Churchill. . . .[33]

The urbanity of relations between ministers and members like Powell was naturally abraded by such blunt and caustic language; Powell intimated that Heath and Pym (though not they alone) were corrupting, or increasing the corruption of political life. Later on he publicly described the process as comparable with the eighteenth century: 'It is not seats and offices that are bought with money, but men that are bought with seats and offices; and when I say "men are bought" I mean they are bribed in this currency to default on their obligations to the electorate.'[34] If he did not put it quite so strongly in 1971–72, his condemnation was no less pointed, and it could not but rankle with Heath and his colleagues that it was Powell's guerrilla warfare that was inducing them to fall below parliamentary standards which they believed had been lowered deplorably in the Wilson era that they so despised.

6   Dealing with Amin and the IRA

The irreconcilability of Powell's moral position with that of the Government was demonstrated again in the summer of 1972 over Amin's expulsion of the Asians from Uganda and Whitelaw's secret dealings with the IRA leaders. Heath considered that it was a matter of honour that when diplomacy had been exhausted and the Asians either had to be brought to Britain or face persecution and possibly massacre, their British passports must be accepted as giving them the right to take up residence in the United Kingdom. Whitelaw considered it no less his duty to talk privily with the men of blood in Ireland for the sake of his search for 'a sensible policy of reconciliation.'

Powell invariably objected to actions taken on grounds of high principle at other people's expense – in these two cases, at the expense of the poor English folk who would have to live with the additional Asian pressure, and at the expense of the people of Ulster who would suffer even more from a policy of appeasement that would only whet the ambitions of those waging what they thought was a holy war of terrorism against the British people and state.

Over the Uganda Asians the Government advanced two quite different arguments. Sir Peter Rawlinson, the Attorney-General, advised Parliament that Britain was bound in law, and Robert Carr, the Home Secretary, insisted that the Asians' passports carried the right of entry, ignoring an answer in Parliament that no specific undertakings were made about the rights of entry, and stating flatly that 'the grant of a United Kingdom passport does not in itself confer a citizenship or other status on the holder. It recognizes the status he already has and is accepted internationally for travel purposes.' Powell accused Rawlinson, therefore, of prostituting his office. Heath's insistence on the moral obligation not to allow British passport holders to become stateless refugees seems to concede the weakness of Rawlinson's case on status; and Powell readily granted they were refugees with a claim on British humanitarian feelings. But he concluded that this condition was irrespective of the passports they held (some were issued by the High Commission, some were colonial, some were non-British) so the obligation was shared by all civilised states to parcel them out; Britain had only to take its share as a humanitarian act, not as a legal one; and that the humanitarian obligation would be satisfied by taking far fewer than the number of those who held, or could claim, the type of passport over which controversy had raged in 1968, to limit the rights of which Callaghan had passed the 1968 Immigration Act. He was overborne.[35] Though other countries took a few British passport holders, 28,000 were brought to Britain virtually stripped of their property (and Amin received kudos from this exercise of dictatorial power which was to inspire him to fresh exploits). In spite of elaborate preparations to disperse them they settled in the areas where they could expect family and cultural support, exemplifying in a few months Powell's warning that the implanting of almost self-sufficient alien colonies would stultify the process of assimilation which the pundits had promised; and it also turned out that many were quite recent arrivals in East Africa from India, and not the 'waifs of Empire' or grandchildren of the East African railway coolies for which the tear ducts were being milked. But Powell's analysis was howled down. Peter Hain, for example, called such an interpretation of natural urbanisation in Leicester scaremongering; Shirley Williams dismissed it as tripe. Powell received 5,000 letters from those due to be squeezed, a larger mailbag than the Prime Minister's. The next opinion poll showed that more of the sample questioned wanted him as Prime Minister than Heath. And a year later the Home Secretary, Robert Carr, demolished both the moral and political plea by admitting that the operation would never be repeated.

When William Whitelaw became Secretary of State for Northern Ireland he said he did not expect help from Powell in his task. Powell urged him, incessantly, to grasp the meaning of the conflict and to treat it accordingly. His criticism had not carried many Tories (who rejected guilt for what they preferred to think of as Irish thuggery on both sides) but when Whitelaw had it dragged out of him inch by inch that he had been parleying with the IRA leaders flown to London under safe-conduct, with the understanding that their terms for a cease-fire would be passed to the Prime Minister, they finally jibbed. It did not make Powell popular, but it reversed Whitelaw within a week into a short burst of Powellite policy – he had the no-go areas reoccupied – and it deepened the breach between Conservatives and Unionists. Powell took this opportunity to effect a measure of reconciliation between the factions among the Unionists, appearing on the same platform with Brian Faulkner (who leaned to power-sharing) and William Craig (who then opposed it). This episode deepened Powell's feeling that the battle for Britain's future was on two fronts – against the EEC and against the IRA and all that the IRA symbolised in the Anglo-Irish imbroglio.

7   The Betrayal of 'Selsdon Man'

While the controversy over the Ugandan Asians continued, and Whitelaw's dalliance with the IRA ended in the reoccupation of the no-go areas, Heath was retreating from Selsdon Park, and discussing a voluntary wage policy with the TUC. In return for limits on wage settlements he offered controls upon prices and dividends. The fruit of the Barber policy of pumping money into the economy only to achieve minor increases in production was thus ripening. In February the government had been defeated by the miners, who went on strike when the Coal Board did not meet their demands; violence accompanied their successful blockading of the flow of coal to the power stations. The government had to call a state of emergency; and the Wilberforce enquiry which followed, according to the provisions of the new Industrial Relations Act, recommended in great haste that the Coal Board should go beyond its offer. The miners' leaders finally settled with the Government direct. Powell commented that this development only showed that the doctrine that the public sector must set the pattern was untrue; what it proved was that national ownership and control was 'an intolerable form of management in a free society.' The unions mostly refused to register under the Act, and tried to expel those that did. It was seen (as Powell feared) as an unfair way to enforce political policies under the guise of law.[36]

Powell had been preparing a speech for the Shoreham Young Conservatives urging, in this débâcle, reliance on market forces to decide wage settlements, now that the pound was partly floating ('dirty floating') and would move to correct any changes in the balance of payments caused by temporarily excessive wage settlements. On the night he was to deliver the address, he was warned that if the TUC rejected voluntary control (a 'social compact' as it was later called), so far from adopting the Powellite solution Heath would bring in compulsory controls, a freeze; and he seized the moment to expose, with sad foreboding, the fallacies the Government were espousing:

> The desire to have the cure without the cost is the cause for the recurrent search for an incomes policy – or an incomes-and-prices-policy, or (we shall hear it again) an-incomes-and-prices-and-profits policy. The theory is simple: if everyone would stop raising their prices, and everyone would stop raising their incomes faster than total production, inflation would end of its own accord . . . this is a pure fairy tale. A world in which everybody deliberately varies his own prices upwards and downwards, and increases his own income or diminishes it, in such a way that prices *in general* remain stable and *total* income matches *total* production is not a real world. It can neither happen by compulsion nor by direction for the simple reason that no human being has the means of knowing in advance what the magic numbers are . . . All the efforts to do the trick that have ever been made, end in failure . . . not for want of trying, nor because of the un-co-operativeness of the trade unions, nor because of the greed of industrialists . . . it is because the thing itself is inherently impossible . . . it is positively harmful. When men come together in a venture foredoomed to failure, they seldom part at last without mutual recrimination.[37]

He was quickly proved right. The TUC wanted a degree of price control that was inherently impossible in a period of world inflation, and the talks broke down in November. Though Heath tried to part on a friendly note, recrimination followed. The Government proceeded immediately to the ninety-day freeze of prices and wages while a new compulsory policy (Stages Two and Three) was formulated; in a one-sentence supplementary in Questions in the House Powell asked if the Prime Minister had 'taken leave of his senses' in imposing controls 'in contravention of the deepest commitments of the Party'. On 11 November, the Government announced its plans for subsidies of £1,000 million to the mining industry in the hope of buying peace in that quarter. The £3,000 million steel programme followed at Christmas, and Powell predicted that it would prove 'grotesquely inappropriate' to future conditions (it did by 1978).

Speaking against the Temporary Provisions Bill, Powell declared it futile and also divisive, because anomalies (over differentials) would grow and class would be set against class; he again implored the government to take his arguments seriously.[38] He noted the change in the Prime Minister, who wanted consensus and cooperation, yet had ended the dialogue with the trade unions: the confrontation which was unnecessary had begun. Prior replied that if Powell's remedies were so simple, why had they not been tried? and Arthur Lewis from the other side denounced his policy as 'an arid, dismal cut-back, a deflation, a fierce restriction of the money supply.' Others evaluated his remedies as 2,500,000 unemployed. Thus his arguments fell again on deaf ears, even as Tories and Labour members quarrelled over the measure itself. Tory uneasiness at the implications of the new bill, however, was reflected soon afterwards in the heavy defeat that Heath sustained when he proposed new regulations for immigration, under which nationals from Common Market countries would have preference before nationals from the old (not to mention the new) Commonwealth.

The Government was launched not just on *dirigisme* but on a Conservative version of socialism – control of every sector of the economy, which would involve compulsion, pressure, departmental fiats. In December Powell reviewed the record:

> The greatest weariness of politics is the necessity of arguing and demonstrating all over again what has already been proved ad nauseam by experience ... All through the years from 1966 to 1970, from the first phase to the last of the Labour government's statutory prices and incomes policy it was necessary, point by point, example by example, to show that such a policy is irreconcilable with the rule of law ... when the Labour government's policy collapsed under the weight of its own impracticability ... it was pardonable to hope that the lessons had been learned ... at least by the Labour government's political opponents. Alas it was not to be. The dreary cycle has begun once more ... the instances multiply again which prove that the attempt to control prices and wages by law is accompanied by the ... disregard of law itself.[39]

For some time Powell had argued that crime and violence in Britain had been encouraged by the tendencies of successive governments to act administratively beyond the powers given them by statute. He was thought egregious, irresponsible, when he urged businessmen to oppose such encroachments by George Brown's regime. Now he found himself saying the same harsh things about a Conservative government displaying the same cloven hoof.

Powell objected first to a request from the Department of Agriculture to retailers to sign a monthly declaration that they were keeping to the terms of the price freeze as 'a usurpation and a tyranny', since it had no legal justification. Within a month of the Counter-Inflation Act becoming law, he noted, the Government was exceeding the powers it vouchsafed them to make it work. Negotiations between the General and Municipal Workers Union and the Gas Council had hardly begun when both parties received letters from Mr Heath stating that 'until such time as the Government is able to announce guide-lines, negotiations, whether in the public or private sector, should not be carried to the point of offers of improved remuneration.' Powell reacted with the comment: 'the effrontery of it is breathtaking,' and emphasised that the letter did not say 'until such time as further provision is made by Parliament,' but 'until such time as the Government is able to announce.' Powell asked Heath whether he was under the impression that the government could make laws and orders by simple 'announcement.'

> Until dictatorship has been formally inaugurated in this country, a letter from the Prime Minister, [he told his audience] has no more force, unless backed by law, than a letter by me or a letter from any one of you, and moreover, even if it were backed by law, it is no part of a prime minister's function either to interpret the law or to enforce it.[40]

Such a statement was merely reported by political journalists as evidence that Powell was indiscriminately attacking anything Heath did or said.

On 4 January 1973, Phase Two was announced; it included a Pay Board and Prices Commission which was hailed by Labour members with ironic gratitude for providing a socialist infrastructure for them to use (and they did) later. Powell described all parties to the fated confrontation as prisoners: the unions locked in by their rules for bargaining for maximum pay; the Labour opposition locked in by reason of its own essays in the policy in 1967–8; the Government tied to a projectile 'like Mazeppa on the back of the wild horse'. He noted the cost of subsidising coal, railways, steel, even mortgages, in terms of fuelling money supply and inflation.

In the summer of 1973 he reviewed in Parliament the record during a debate on the Incomes and Prices Commission. They had had eight months of the policy – five of freeze and three of Stage Two. The unions and employers had obeyed the law punctiliously. The policy was being carried through as planned. Yet inflation was still running at the same rate as before. The government had therefore had to stop blaming the unions for inflation. They had looked round and found a new culprit – world prices: 'The behaviour of anchovies off Chile, the appetites of Argentines, and the most regrettable shortages in the USSR and

China.' He then showed by quotation after quotation that Chancellor Barber knew quite well that what was really wrong was excessive money supply and that wage control was irrelevant.

> The fact is there is no stage three. There cannot be a stage three. No rules can be laid down in advance, or administered by any body of men or government, so as to decide, prescribe and order, without the most evident and unacceptable injustices . . . how all prices and wages are to start to move in relation to each other as well as all moving up together at whatever rate of inflation it is decided to accept for the time being.[41]

Powell showed up Barber's dilemma: a voluntary pay policy that would be unenforceable because events would overwhelm it; or a continuing flat rate under coercion which would collapse as the contradictions between it and reality became 'screamingly intolerable'. The only way was to turn the tap off in the Treasury: to stop expenditure soaring above revenue, perhaps by an autumn budget. The House was not impressed. Powell persisted, adding that the facts were known to many who were keeping quiet for fear of risking their political skins as advocates of higher taxation. As there was no disposition to put on the brakes, he predicted events would take charge. They did.

8   Labour Offers a Referendum

In June 1973 Powell startled his own followers by saying in a broadcast (on Radio 4) that he would be ready to accept Labour rule for his lifetime if that meant that Parliament would regain the power to decide under what principle Britain was to be governed. Such sovereignty left it open to Parliament in the end to reject socialism as heartily as did Powell. This statement has to be set against his fear that a point could be reached when socialism would be irreversible (see pp. 61, 71, 143). Throughout 1973 he was recording in speeches from which he did not keep his agony of mind, that within a few months the House of Commons had learned that power had passed from it. Decisions made in Brussels could not be debated; as Community decisions they became British law automatically.

> Already those who may be affected by such decisions know better than to come to Members of Parliament . . . They go where actual power resides – not even to Whitehall, but to the Community. Men soon discover who their real masters are . . . those who make the law wield the power. There may be some who imagine that while all this may be, indeed is, true, it touches only the fringe of life and government. They are pathetically misguided. Even now, when the wood is green, the range of subjects on which Community law comes forward is extensive . . . on banking, insurance, patents, as on driving standards and size of vehicles; on trade . . . as on agriculture . . . and a host of other subjects, the Community is legislating, legislating, for the Community is the new state.[42]

But Parliament still had the power to withdraw. A general election still stood in the way of any final sealing of membership. The Labour Party, split on the Market like the Conservatives, was considering the possibility of a referendum after a 'renegotiation'. Consequently Powell's ability to remain in the Conservative Party formed a frequent topic of speculation. Powell himself hinted at party upheavals under the strains being placed on simple loyalties; at Stockport in June he told an audience that there arose sometimes overriding aims which the outer wing of one party found procurable not from its political allies but from its enemies only. The press at once wanted to know if this was a call not to support Heath's government in the next election. Powell retorted that 'a Powell speech is worth reading many, many times'; when pressed on his 'Delphic utterance' he told reporters not to be silly, but 'very, very careful.'[43]

They could see, if they cared, that the speeches were phrased in conditional terms; that they were addressed to his own party which had the power to ensure that the situation under which Joseph Chamberlain abandoned the Liberals over the overriding aim of union as opposed to home rule should not find a modern parallel, with the Tory Party 'marching into battle under the banner of higher food prices with the House of Commons a provincial council'. In declaring that it was a perilous moment for any party 'when the appeal of party conflicts with the appeal of country, and to the Conservative Party it is a conflict that could be mortal', the words he used were still the words of a loyal Tory trying to save the Party from within its own ranks and by means of public pressures which he predicted would be such as to obviate all need for the referendum.[44]

Conservative leaders scoffed at such pretensions, for they noted that whereas Chamberlain in 1886 had a body of Liberal-Radicals behind him, Powell had refrained from organising behind himself any comparable body of patriots against the Market. Yet he was surely entitled to envisage that, if the warnings were spurned, there might occur a sudden fusion or coalition of anti-Heath or anti-Market forces and splits in both parties – history does not exactly repeat itself. He was putting together a book of his speeches opposing the Market and urging renegotiation. He was fortified by the findings of the opinion polls, so far as they meant anything: 41 per cent of one sample thought him 'an asset' to his party compared with 34 per cent who thought Heath an asset; while another sample of the electorate in another poll showed the public was opposed to membership of EEC by a sizeable margin.

Powell did not sweeten his overtures to the anti-Marketeers in Labour's ranks by playing down immigration as a matter of tactics; so making it easy for Wilson to announce that 'in no circumstances' would he ever cooperate with Powell. This intervention served as a reminder to his own rebels that their most effective ally on the other side was a political untouchable. But Powell was impenitently hitting back at those who accused him of a conspiratorial attitude to politics by again attacking the secrecy with which immigration was treated by the Home Office. It was increasingly hard to understand or interpret the figures given. In a debate with Crossman in April 1973, he said 'I believe that right from the middle fifties [the Home Office] behaved on this subject in a way in which Government departments don't behave on other subjects where it is vital for ministers to be presented with information.' Crossman demurred, but Powell alleged that the Home Office took care that the vital factor in population increase, the number of births, was not investigated. He examined such figures as he could get of coloured children in schools as a profile of the future; in some areas prefiguring a population one-third coloured after the lapse of another generation. It was, he said, intentional:

> 'Why should we not be silent?' they ask. 'For what can we do? Anyhow in a few years we ourselves will have departed and then, what matter?' Of what other national peril would those in authority keep silence? Their first concern would be to estimate its magnitude and to place that before the public; for there is no . . . hope . . . of solving the problem when the only concern of government is to deny or minimise its existence. The first step, the indispensable step, is for those who govern us to tell us the truth.[45]

Nevertheless, at the end of the year he was able to say 'slowly, however painfully slowly, the materials accumulate which will eventually make it impossible to withhold from the British people the full picture not only of the present in which they live, but of the future which they face'.

From the 1971 Census results he deduced that immigrant-descended children were under-enumerated by one-quarter, on top of figures that revealed that the proportion of Birmingham's population under twenty-five years old that was coloured was 13 per cent; but 15 per cent for those under fifteen, and nearly 19 per cent for those under five: the city 'one-third coloured', for which he had been reviled was coming into existence inexorably. He called on Robert Carr, who admitted that the cities would have a substantial coloured population 'as they have children who will grow', to use his office to quantify his statements. Then the future would be known, tolerable or intolerable; if intolerable it could be decided how it could be prevented from coming true.

Such demands for facts, such deployment of the few facts known, hardly amounted to a powellian intrigue to replace Heath by Wilson, for Powell's demands for facts upset Labour more than they did Conservatives. Bidwell and Foot attacked Powell's statistics with the retort that the nation had always been eugenically crossbred with outsiders; presumably the process could advantageously continue.

Furthermore Powell lost no opportunity to strike at Labour for its socialism. He found Harold Wilson as unsound, indeed as hypocritical, on inflation as the Conservative front bench. Wilson knew, he remarked, what the cause of inflation was – deficit financing – but 'he has not the slightest intention of denouncing "the true causes of inflation" because they are embedded in socialism itself . . . a future Labour government, like past Labour governments, would be a government which expands public expenditure regardless, unless and until it strikes some exterior obstacle' (the need for IMF support in 1976, as it happened).[46]

But Wilson's call for subsidies on food and for stabilisation of council rents, and such other irrelevant nostrums for ending inflation were, however wickedly insincere, less obnoxious to Powell than the march of Heath's 'managed capitalist state' in the teeth of everything Tories stood for. He found himself almost at a loss to explain it, until he bethought him that what Heath was after was a corporate, paternalistic state emulating the Japanese system. Anything, in fact, that seemed to promise growth. In March 1973 he commented sardonically,

> From the nationalisation of Rolls-Royce at the beginning of 1971, right through to this week's announcement of £5 million of public money to be invested in a new motor cycle manufacturing enterprise, the conventional quip has been that the Conservative government had turned socialist. In fact, when it was announced last week that a Labour member would move a motion on the 'implementation of a socialist programme,' a Tory MP was heard to enquire 'what's *he* got to worry about?'[47]

A managed capitalist state was as remote from a powellian free society as a socialist state.

Powell's contumely got under the Cabinet's skin at this stage. The war of the Day of Atonement flared when the Conservatives prepared for their annual conference. Heath arranged for Chancellor Barber to put Powell down, and the press was briefed to report his annihilation. Calling him a 'frustrated fanatic', Barber proceeded magisterially, 'I am truly saddened that an old friend should have such moral conceit and intellectual arrogance'. British inflation, he told his uneasy audience, was no worse than German inflation; there now was a huge trade deficit but it was rapidly declining; there was no budget deficit whatever. The Government was borrowing like any wise business for growth, and public expenditure would rise by £6,000 million in that laudable endeavour. 'I utterly disagree with those who suggest that the restriction of the money supply would solve inflation.' And that was supposed to be the end of powellism. But the cheers for Powell sounded louder than those for Barber.

9   Standing Alone

He stood alone, and the political commentators concluded that his popular appeal was waning that autumn. But standing alone did not mean standing for nothing in particular. He met the criticism.

> You ask how I can justify being the one man in step when the regiment is out of step. [That] depends on what you think a political party is about. If you think the purpose of party is, having put before the electorate one set of choices in clear terms, to govern on quite different principles . . . then I am guilty, I am a nuisance. But if you think there should be some connexion

between the function of a party and government and what the electors thought
they were voting for when they put them in, then I am at least doing a job of
work.[48]

That job was trying to make the party change course and persuade its leaders to
think themselves mistaken. In October 1973 there still seemed nearly two years
in which to do this. Before Barber spoke out, Powell had pleaded, 'Let no one
mistake for faction or disloyalty the debate within the party [which is] the
essence of parliamentary politics.' In a party purporting to be saving the country,
contradictions must be aired. Events had, however, indeed taken charge, and
were now to show Powell's reasoning on inflation and industrial unrest to be
correct, though in a way neither Powell nor Heath could have foreseen.

For all Barber's protestations, the balance of trade was disastrously in deficit
and not improving. The floating pound was therefore floating downward, but the
authorities were wasting the reserves in trying to cushion the inevitable
correction of its value in terms of other currencies. Though the retail price index
rose from 170 to 188, production had almost ceased to rise. Notwithstanding the
Counter-Inflation Act, money earnings rose inexorably by over ten per cent.
Heath was unable to persuade the TUC to accept the Pay and Prices
Commission, charged with slowing down such adjustments to rising prices. The
settlement of 1972 having run its course, the miners put in a new claim far
beyond the limits (7 per cent plus extras) set by Stage Three. After unsuccessful
negotiations Heath declared that the Board and the Government must stand up
to them (and to the power engineers) this time round.

The confrontation was thus in train when the Arabs cut the production of oil
as a means of exerting pressure on the West to modify its support of Israel after
their defeat in the Day of Atonement war. A rise in oil prices was overdue in a
world inflationary boom, but they were forcefully jacked up – eventually
fourfold – and Barber's budget deficit and the trade gap opened like an old
wound. Powell noted that the final effect of the oil price increase would be
neutral in the world economy after a redistribution of income between the oil
producers and the rest took place. But all energy producers were affected: at a
stroke the miners were put in an almost impregnable position. Coal had become
vital, and stocks were low. On 12 November the miners ceased to work overtime. Heath had next day to declare an emergency to reduce use of energy. The
NUM rejected the Coal Board's offer a week later; and the familiar deadlock
between the miners in the nationalised industry, and the Government as the real
employer asserted itself. The Board became almost irrelevant. This was precisely
what Powell had diagnosed as intolerable about nationalised industry,
aggravated by the third part of the Industrial Relations Act. Heath said there
could be no surrender, but Gormley, the miners' leader, urged him to hold an
election rather than expect a miners' ballot. Others, like McGahey, were
reported to be saying they now had the power to bring the Government down.

The rising tide of disputes and emergency measures, the intimations of a tremendous crisis in the making, rallied the Conservatives behind Heath, but it was on a class against class basis. Powell had warned against just such a development, and in November 1973 he analysed the growing tragedy in terms which produced more editorial comment that he had 'finally destroyed himself'.

> Just over a year ago, when the statutory prices and incomes policy was announced, I ventured to enquire of the Prime Minister in the House of Commons 'whether he had taken leave of his senses'. . . . The government had embarked upon a course on which their predecessors had shipwrecked; which in opposition they had consistently . . . denounced; on which at the general election they had promised not to embark. . . . It has failed, of course – as the Conservative party's own manifesto explained that it must. . . . The greater evil still of all statutory counter-inflation policies is the antagonism, at once futile and dangerous, which they inevitably set up between the state on one side and the various classes and interests of the community. . . . The danger of this was frighteningly illustrated by the Prime Minister's outburst last week against the miners, who, whether or not they are wisely led by their trade union, have neither done nor threatened to do anything which is against the law. Yet the accusation was brought against them that because the House of Commons had approved a Government white paper and a code which . . . is binding only on the Price Commission and Pay Board, therefore the miners are defying Parliament. . . . To say this is to blur, even to deny, the very distinction on which constitutional liberty rests, the distinction between law and not-law. If possible still more breathtaking was the Prime Minister's assertion that . . . the responsibility of the Government expressed in the pay and prices code 'is not the responsibility we sought; it is the responsibility which Parliament gave us because there is no other way of containing inflation. . . .' One cannot but entertain fears for the mental and emotional stability of a head of government to whom such language can appear rational.[49]

This fierce criticism of his nominal leader followed his earlier warnings that Heath was acting beyond the law, in a managerial not a parliamentary spirit. A fortnight later he put his reasons frankly to his own worried constituency association: 'a party is not the private property of its leader.' Powell explained to them the fact that Heath was in complete control of the Government, that he had sought and obtained and defined the anti-inflationary powers, and that his misrepresentation of the true constitutional position was inexplicable.[50]

Heath was no doubt under enormous strain, yet in a sense filled with the euphoria of directing great decisions in the face of gathering dangers – which he did not see were in any way of his own making. They were brought on by the settled hostility of the unions; inflation was caused by world prices and the oil crisis; just when the dash for freedom was succeeding, fate had cruelly struck. In Parliament Heath announced the three-day week, reiterating his warning to the miners and others that they must settle within the pay policy.

But the policy for growth was in ruins and the Government were headed for yet another U-turn – this time on financial policy. Barber had been resisting City advice for some time that Powell and the monetarists were indeed right, but his doubts were gnawing. As far back as the party conference he had begun to express them to Heath; the vehemence of his attack on Powell was perhaps resistance to the breaking-in of the truth about money supply. The Arabs gave him the heaven-sent excuse. The Government was not adopting the Powell line, perish the thought – they were merely surrendering to foreign pressure. By December all the pundits were in full retreat from growth. On the 11th Sir Michael Clapham publicly besought Heath to drop the growth-at-all-costs policy and recognise that a policy for sheer survival was the only one left; the press began calling for expenditure cuts, which Barber conceded to them, to the tune of £1,200 million, on 17 December; but as such cuts seemed ludicrously disproportionate to the need, the first rumours of an early general election were started. Adequate or not, Powell immediately welcomed Barber's recantation, suggesting that the Chancellor had laid the foundations of a reconciliation; he promised them 'understanding and support' now they were travelling in the direction he had so long been indicating.[51] And as the first move had been taken to end inflation – even if it had to get worse before it got better as the past expansion of money supply worked through the system – there was no need for an election, certainly not one about overtime bans and working-to-rule by trade unionists which, however inconvenient, were perfectly within the law.

He thought, as many others did, that the Government had the obligation and responsibility to lead the nation through the crisis, come what might (he had scouted the idea of an election during the 1972 miners' strike). The Labour party was clearly reluctant to face the voters, even if Mr Gormley was not. But over Christmas Heath was being urged by his 'kitchen cabinet' that 'Who rules the country?' must be a winning slogan for a Conservative government in a crisis. The latest opinion polls showed the Party ahead of Labour – by 40 per cent to 35 per cent. This appreciation left out many variables in the equation – public sympathy for the miners, for example, and a natural shrinking from a showdown with organised Labour; and the rise of the Liberal protest vote which complicated all constituency calculations in the marginals. It is evidence of Heath's disbelief that he owed anything to Powell, or to the Powell vote, in 1970 that he finally accepted the case for an early election: he saw himself winning another personal vote of confidence. Indeed he did win a plurality of votes. He would have done better to have accepted Powell's urgent advice not to precipitate an election. But to have taken that advice would have involved a second, and far greater, surrender to the miners – and that would have finally destroyed (as Powell could see) his personal ascendancy. He hesitated; but given his personality, the decision was not in much doubt – as the miners' leaders, who had seen a good deal of him at No. 10, perhaps knew better than most. So the trap closed on Powell as well as on Heath. What might also be called the 'endlessly instructive' crisis of 1974 had begun.

Chapter 11

Ulster and South Down, 1968–1978

1 Nationalism and Loyalism

Powell's remark to one of his inquisitors that the immigration issue had found him, not he it, might have been applied to the Northern Ireland issue. It envenomed his conflict with Heath: because most politicians kept away from Ulster affairs, it was alleged that Powell's interest in it was perverse and excited only by the opportunities it presented to embarrass Heath further. But on the contrary, Powell would have opened himself to charges of inconsistency and opportunism if he had drawn back the hem of his garment like the rest. Given Powell's principles and passion, his intervention could not be lukewarm.

For the issue went down to the roots of his position on nationhood, on British national identity, on the uniqueness of parliamentary government. It proved to be interwoven with the issue of British membership of the Community, with the long-term implications of immigration, and with devolution for Scotland and Wales. At first he did not appreciate that an old problem woven into British history had reemerged. Eventually it involved him in his reappraisal of the 'endlessly instructive' episode of Joseph Chamberlain's split with Gladstone over Home Rule in 1886, from which he drew the moral in speeches on the Common Market, and which led him to put Chamberlain's career into a new perspective.

He was a departmental minister when the IRA campaign of 1959–62 petered out ignominiously for lack of support either side of the border, thanks to the vigilance of the B-Specials and the Ulster CID. This occurrence lulled the authorities into complacency. In Ulster it was followed by the inauguration of some reforms by Stormont; in Britain it encouraged a complacent belief that the irrational and atavistic Irish conflict was yielding to the treatment provided by post-war economic growth, spreading affluence, and the impact of the welfare state. Insofar as this treatment was boosted by regional subsidies Powell's prescription for leaving the location of industry to market forces was somewhat at odds with settled policy for Northern Ireland; but he never mentioned the province or its peculiar needs. In his identification of the British Nationality Act 1948 as the fatal legislation which opened the Pandora's Box of coloured immigration, he did not until the late sixties couple with it the subsequent Act of 1949, which was entailed by that of 1948 if Irish nationals were to be confirmed in the possession of the full privileges of British subjects that they had enjoyed before the Free State declared itself a fully independent Republic.

This disinterest in Ulster affairs was in contrast with his not infrequent references to Welsh and Scots nationalism. He caused surprise by joining in Welsh debates and insisting on the importance of English Members doing so. His ancestry, his Welsh cultural studies, his knowledge of the language, and the insights he gained in writing the Conservative Charter for Wales in 1948 nonetheless sharpened his sensitivity to the dormant nationalisms in the United Kingdom. They contributed to his concept of United Kingdom nationhood as well as 'Englishness', and forced him to a characteristically radical analysis: that if ever the residents of the principality or Scotland preponderantly decided that they were separate nations their demand for independence must be conceded, provided they accepted the full attributes of nationhood, of being a nation-state going it alone: 'it means being approximately as the Republic of Ireland is today'.[1]

Nationhood, he told an audience in Prestatyn in September 1968, when nobody realised that the civil disorder in Ulster presaged civil war, was an absolute. No such thing as semi-nationhood or semi-nationalism existed. He adduced the decentralisation and disintegration of the British Empire during the twentieth century under pressure of nationalist self-assertion as proof that 'nationalism, if it is real, cannot be bought off with less than the real article. To propose what are called concessions is either to repudiate the claim of nationhood itself if the concessions are regarded as satisfactory "solutions" or else to concede the claim of nationhood if the concessions are regarded as . . . something on account.'[2] Heath was, as it happened, about to propose initial concessions to Scottish nationalism and put them in the Tory platform. Powell, presciently, based his argument on Irish home rule, when the Irish members under Charles Parnell's leadership used their position as a balancing party, strengthened by the electoral reform of 1885, to work for the repeal of the 1801 union, and separation of the two kingdoms. The growing nationalism of other Dominions cracked the thin shell of imperial unity based on British sovereignty under the Crown until eventually nothing remained (and now, in some of these successor states, sub-units assert separate nationhood).

But Powell drew at once a sharp distinction between Ulster and the workings of nationalism elsewhere. He rejected

a prevalent but dangerous opinion which is supposed to be founded on the case of Ulster. 'But look,' says the opinion, 'it can be done: Ulster has had local autonomy for fifty years and no demand for more.' It is the neatest example of the exception which proves the rule; for Ulster, self-government was the outcome not of nationalism but of the very opposite, Ulster Unionism. Ulster not only was not (in 1922) demanding autonomy of any kind but was repudiating and resisting it, was protesting against being separated from the rest of the United Kingdom and accepted only with reluctance the unique form of autonomy which emerged by a sidewind during the tangled process of the separation of the Republic. Ever since then the motivation of Ulster has remained not nationalist, not separatist, but the opposite.[3]

The essence of a nation, Powell went on, was that the parts instinctively view their good as subordinate to the good of the whole, and hence a single parliament can represent the mosaic of parts, each and every one in a minority *vis-à-vis* the rest; but when a single part no longer accepted that position, the question of a separate nation arose.

2 Studying IRA Tactics

From this position Powell first related the growth of violence in Ulster to the spread of anti-authority agitation generally in the sixties. When foreign students were arrested in the Londonderry rioting in August 1969 he said 'We shall do well to ponder that news item deeply, for as Douglas Reed used to say in the 1930s "This means you".'[4] He added, 'The thing which has happened in Ulster in the last two or three weeks has little kinship with the Irish troubles of the 1920s and before. It has great kinship with what has been happening in the universities of the United States, with what happened in Paris last year, and with what happened in Berlin the year before.'

He underestimated the readiness of the IRA to seize the opportunity to ride on the back of the general wave of demonstrations and 'unnegotiable demands' in favour of civil or human rights to renew its assault on both Dublin and Stormont in the historic cause of Irish unity. The SDLP gathered strength from the readiness of a succession of Ulster premiers – O'Neill, Chichester-Clarke, Faulkner – to make concessions to the demands of the minority, and to recognise that Ulster's institutions needed modernisation and reform; this record was presented to the British public as the concessions of a semi-fascist (or at least very undemocratic) sectarian regime to pressure – too little and too late.

By 1970 Powell was fully briefed on the looming catastrophe and its nature. In the debate in the House of Commons in April he offered a radical treatment after a radical diagnosis. He still saw the cult of international violence – violence designed 'not to replace one order or one set of institutions with another, but to tear down without replacing' – as a factor. But he then distinguished from it 'violence in support of the aspiration that the six counties of Northern Ireland might become part of the Republic' in direct refutation of Mr Gerry Fitt's excuses for the violence as the inevitable exasperation produced by Stormont's refusal of overdue reforms and by the level of regional unemployment, so much higher in Ulster than England – he did not compare Eire. Powell retorted that discrimination had nothing to do with the matter: Britain was dealing with an act of war, which could be answered only one way:

The nature of violence is that it lives on hope of success. Even if success were probably available by peaceful means, there is still a premium on violence to

seize it sooner and to seize it in circumstances in which the violent will have the
upper hand over the peaceable. Contrariwise insofar as the prospects of
success recede . . . the premium on violence is replaced by a penalty. Violence
will not continue indefinitely where the object which it proposes to itself
appears to be unattainable . . . I believe we have to apply the anatomy of
violence to Ireland . . . Anarchist violence lives by grievance . . . as a means
of division and as a weapon for self-justification and further advance . . .
grievance . . . exaggerated or artificially manufactured [so that] violence itself
may be held to be proof that grievance exists and that when reforms are made
they are credited to the violence.[5]

It followed that violence would cease only if the prospects of absorbing Ulster
into the Republic were 'removed to a remote future'. His preconditions for this
were threefold. First, 'every word or act that holds out the prospect that
[Ulster's] unity with the United Kingdom might be negotiable is a contributory
cause of violence' and must be repudiated by British politicians. Second, to show
the IRA that their assault was reinforcing rather than weakening that unity, there
must be 'a greater amalgamation and uniformity of administration, government
policy and economy.' These two points formed the tactical case for integration,
about which he had already talked bluntly to Ulster people; but the third
precondition was for Britain to act upon: a reciprocal counter-offensive to
emphasise the differences between the two nations either side of the border by a
withdrawal of the anomalous privileges of Irish citizens in the UK. This, he
had already observed, accorded fully with the Conservative pledges to treat
aliens and Commonwealth citizens alike for purposes of immigration control.[6]
He had indeed complimented Quintin Hogg for his work on this policy. Dublin
reacted bitterly, on the grounds that dual nationality (under which Irishmen in
England get privileges which Englishmen in Ireland do not) was an immemorial
tradition; and Hogg repudiated Powell's deductions hastily: 'he is convinced of
the ruthless efficiency of his own intellect and this compels him . . . when he has
not got the feel of a subject, to apply purely intellectual criteria . . . the result is he
sometimes gets himself in a muddle. . . .' Nevertheless Powell's speech to
Parliament in April 1970 was the keynote of all that he argued subsequently –
and saw reluctantly adopted.

Powell fitted Ulster into his election speech in which he attacked the years of
false thinking which had conditioned the British public to accept nonsense as
reason, assertion as fact, which so dangerously encouraged the undermining of
authority and the structure of society – more so 'than the frontal assaults of
orthodox socialism.' In the Northfield speech, condemned (notably by *The
Times*) as the conspiratorial theory of politics, he said,

A considerable proportion of the British Army is at this moment on active
service in a province of the United Kingdom. But it is not in Northern Ireland
to put down a rebellion, nor is it there to repel invasion, though both these
things may be woven into the future pattern of events. It is there because

disorder, deliberately fomented for its own sake as an instrument of power, had come within an ace of destroying the authority of civil government . . . That the enemy has utilised the materials of religious division is almost as fortuitous as that a mob should use missiles from a nearby building site.[7]

He compared the religious conflict in Ireland with the accumulating racial tension in Britain and also dismissed as 'nonsense, manifest arrant nonsense' the argument that denial of 'civil rights' in housing or jobs inspired people to kill and bomb each other − 'but that has not prevented the Government of the United Kingdom from undermining the morale of civil government in Northern Ireland by imputing to it the blame for anarchy.'

He did not specifically put the blame on the marxists of the New Left or the growing Terrorist International.[8] Four months later, however, he had some wry fun when Heath, standing before the United Nations as Prime Minister of Britain with the bloodshed in Belfast to explain, remarked that 'we must recognise a new threat to the peace of nations . . . the growth of a cult of political violence, preached and practised not so much between states as within them . . . the use of violence has become not the last resort of the desperate but the first resort of those whose simple unconstructive aim is anarchy . . . it may be that in the 1970s civil war will be the main danger we will face.' Which was precisely what Powell had been attacked for saying in June. Soon after, *The Times* printed a sober, uncontradicted report by its Belfast correspondent that 'details have emerged that a preconceived plan has been put into effect. . . . Nothing that has happened in the last week seems to bear the remotest relation to the province's social problems.' General Freeland confirmed that attacks on British troops were organised and controlled.[9]

3 Fighting Appeasement

When his own party came to power, Powell was determined that it should see the Ulster challenge in terms of British nationhood. Early in 1971 he put the question in basic English in a speech in Londonderry:

Are the people who inhabit the six counties part, or not part, of the nation which inhabits the rest of the United Kingdom, and is this territory they inhabit part or not part of the United Kingdom?[10]

The Irish Republic's constitution said No; a minority of the residents of Ulster said No; the great majority said Yes. Powell said, 'it is not an issue on which both views can be satisfied: one or the other must prevail.' This was not the view of Wilson or Whitelaw, and Powell quickly found that the Tory attitudes which had imbued the Chamberlain era in the thirties now resurfaced in the IRA confrontation.

Powell, on the contrary, found his thinking about the imperial entanglement and immigration highly relevant to Ulster, now that it was in flames. The accident of empire had produced the absurdity that hundreds of millions of people with nothing in common with the inhabitants of the United Kingdom had become in law indistinguishable from them; the compromise of the Irish Free State, which came into existence in 1922 with a kind of honorary Commonwealth status, had sown the dragon's teeth of a new Anglo-Irish problem for the 1970s. The treatment of Eire citizens as British citizens in the 1920s could be regarded as a 'statesmanlike use of a legal fiction', but became a disaster when the empire fell away and 'what happened to the Burmese in 1946 did not happen to the Pakistanis, Indians or southern Irish'. He hoped that the 1971 Immigration Act might 'clear away the debris of 1920 and the humbug of 1949', and told an audience in Londonderry,

> The moment is an apposite one for all the people of the United Kingdom. This is where the issue of identity for all the inhabitants of Northern Ireland merges into the issue of identity for all the people of Britain. We are about to make another legislative attempt to cope with the absurdities . . . which we have suffered from having no status of our own.[11]

His hopes were dashed; his amendments to the bill to secure these objectives voted down. He began to warn Ulster people of the enhanced danger in which they would stand if the United Kingdom entered the Community, for then it would be impossible ever after to close the frontier against southern Irish labour (eligible for voting qualifications in due time) under the free migration clauses of the treaty.

Having provided an anatomy of terrorism, Powell now had to produce an anatomy of appeasement. The IRA demanded the status of combatants on the grounds they were conducting a war with Britain, a formal invasion. There was a muddled disposition in Britain to treat terrorists as different from ordinary murderers, because they proclaimed their political cause; distinctions were made in their treatment in prison, as though in some sense they were prisoners of war to whom the Geneva rules applied even though they did not apply these to their own hapless captives. Powell was prepared to consider some recognition of a difference, provided the logical deductions were drawn from such a recognition of a state of war; this was not so popular with the IRA or Mr Fitt:

> There is a world of difference between a citzen who commits a crime, however mistaken, in the belief that he is thereby helping to preserve the integrity of his country and his right to remain a subject of his sovereign, and a person, be he citizen or alien, who commits a crime with the intention of destroying that integrity and rendering impossible that allegiance. The former breaches the peace; the latter is executing an act of war . . . the one is a lawbreaker, the other is an enemy.[12]

If the IRA demanded and received combatants' rights, Powell insisted, they should be pursued with the same ruthlessness as any other enemy in all-out war.[13] He dismissed the preposterous assumption that the troops were there to keep two lots of thugs apart, or that they were acting as policemen: they were there to defeat Britain's ruthless enemies, a role that had nothing to do with impartiality. The no-go areas proved it was war, not civil war. He denied to British audiences the existence in Ulster of 'a large and growing (which it is not), oppressed (which it is not), disloyal (which it is not), religious minority in Northern Ireland whose existence is evidenced by the campaign of violence, and thus brings down deserved retribution on the majority.'

He had not objected to the Hunt Report on the Royal Ulster Constabulary when it was first published, nor protested at disbandment in 1969 of the B-Specials, the frontier force of the past; but he came to think of the report as 'the most foolish of all the foolish acts of the British Government for the past three years'; and finally stigmatised its recommendations as the greatest disaster to befall Northern Ireland for fifty years.[14] In November 1971 he said 'when events indicated that the police needed to be reinforced in strength in reserves and in equipment, the opposite deduction was drawn: to weaken the police and replace them with soldiers'. This view perhaps underestimated the problem of strengthening the RUC, which lacked trained men as well as numbers; and many of its senior officers themselves mistook the challenge of 1969, and welcomed the Hunt proposals that they should be remodelled on the lines of an English county force. The results of the miscalculation were, however, undeniable:

> Troops are being used for what they are not, namely, policemen – to control the public and apprehend malefactors. Hence the nightly spectacle on television of soldiers in situations where no soldier ought to be. Hence the progressive conversion of the arms and armament of the British army into the equipment of the Tokyo police. Soldiers firing rubber bullets are a sardonic caricature which illuminates the underlying truth. There is no remedy but to retrace our steps . . . Northern Ireland must have a police force larger in size, larger in reserves, stronger in arms and equipment and higher in morale than before . . . Only when there is again such a police force . . . will the army be able to do what the army can alone do: defend the realm . . . and . . . support the civil power in emergency with firearms.[15]

That rebuilding had begun in 1971; but was to take five years, and even then the force would be reliant on the army's firearms as well as its own.

Until 1972 Powell's speeches on Ulster had not brought him into direct conflict with Heath over policy. He had been seeking to educate both Britain and Ulster on misunderstandings of the underlying situation. In Ulster his efforts were better received; he was saying with force, wit and authority things that the Ulster Unionists themselves, in any case a small band, put over much less effectively: they were no match for Mr Fitt in the absence of a firm commitment by British MPs. Relations with their new ally developed; a particular one sprang up between Powell and Captain Orr, Unionist leader and Member for South Down. Powell's visits to Ulster and frequent discussions with Orr and his colleagues familiarised him with the embattled but increasingly fissiparous Ulster unionism.

He criticised the visit of Heath and Whitelaw to Lynch, the Fianna Fail Prime Minister dedicated to Irish unity. 'The impression is conveyed to friend and foe alike that HM Government does not really regard Ulster as the front line of defence of the United Kingdom, does not really regard the war as their war, our war, at all.'[16]

> When the British government is seen as taking counsel about peace and security in a part of the United Kingdom with the prime minister of the very country which is dedicated to the annexation of that part . . . what must people think? They think, 'Oho, so the British are wobbling and preparing to get out, or else why would they be parleying with the residual beneficiary of their embarrassments?'[17]

Only when the policies and actions of the British government convinced friends and foes alike that the unity of the realm would be maintained 'will the guilt of innocent blood depart from Westminster.'

This chilling sentiment Powell repeated in the debate in Parliament on the visit, and much affronted his front bench thereby. But the Cabinet was probably more impressed by a Gallup poll which suggested that nearly a third of the British electorate wanted the province abandoned to Lynch. Powell had grimly said, 'the nation which turns away from those who insist on identifying with it will not for long insist on its own identity.'[18] Heath and Whitelaw put pressure on Faulkner, the Northern Ireland Premier, to accept power-sharing – Catholic and Republican representation in government, to meet the SDLP demand. But the SDLP realised that if Faulkner agreed, they would thereby become part of the Stormont system, which the IRA, then virtually their masters, were set to destroy, and they backed out on various pretexts. The IRA were right, as Powell predicted; after the 'Bloody Sunday' affair, Heath and Whitelaw ordered Faulkner to go further – to surrender security to London and to accept, in addition to power-sharing, a 'Council of Ireland' elected on proportional representation to secure larger minority participation. Faulkner resigned, Stormont was suspended; and Powell could only denounce the act as the concession of the IRA's first major objective. Terrorism had achieved its first reward. He told the House,

> The people of Great Britain should understand . . . with what explosive they are playing – or rather what explosive is being played with in their name. . . . Hitherto the war in Northern Ireland against the United Kingdom, against law and order and security itself has been sustained by doubts as to the seriousness of purpose of the UK Government. . . . Now the outcome which the UK is apparently prepared to envisage . . . is known to be no other than that of the terrorist himself – the differences are those of method and timing.[19]

Powell complained that the only tolerable accompaniment to the abolition of

Stormont, a real integration of the six counties with the rest of Britain, was carefully avoided. Indeed, the incoming colonial regime rather emphasised the division. But the abolition of devolved government (including local government) opened the way for a justified demand for additional representation of Ulster in Parliament. The representation of only twelve had been originally accepted in recognition that the Stormont legislature handled Ulster's internal affairs (often by simple re-enactment of Westminster measures), but now 'an extinguisher is placed over the affairs of Northern Ireland in Westminster'. He hoped, however, that the right to greater voting strength in London and the effects of colonial rule in Stormont would turn the minds of more and more Unionists away from the demand for restoration of the old Stormont system. More seats in Westminster in proportion to the representation of other similar parts of the United Kingdom (supposedly nineteen to twenty) would seal the union and prove a decisive blow to the IRA. He continuously urged more representation at Westminster, and abandonment of a form of devolution inherited from an irretrievable past.[20]

He also pointed out to the Ulster Unionists the relevance to their struggle of the Government's campaign to enter Europe. The Unionists resisted Heath's threats to withdraw support from Stormont, which he duly made good. But they accepted the logic of the argument that if the EEC bill went through, one certain consequence would be the merging of Eire and the United Kingdom into what would become a single state which would eventually make the border totally permeable from the south. He drew the lessons of the Republic's referendum on joining the Community:

> This is what the Prime Minister of the Republic said: 'for the Republic to join the EEC means that we begin a process that will gradually make the border less significant: we cannot afford to draw the boundary of the EEC through our country by our decision.' Events cast their shadows before: a fortnight ago the Council of Europe, whose Northern Ireland subcommittee has prepared a report on this country, decided to request an early meeting with Mr Whitelaw to discuss 'the causes and possible solution of the Northern Ireland problem.' That illustrates perfectly the sort of thing the Republican government had in mind when it told its electors 'Ireland has no control over British decisions, no say in them. Joining the EEC will put a stop to that right away. As equal EEC members we shall have a vote and a voice in all decisions taken.'[21]

He told his audience that it would accordingly be naïve to think that Ulster would long survive in its attachment to Britain when Ireland and Britain alike were European provinces. 'We have learnt by now that every nationalism is tolerated before British nationalism.' Ulster loyalism would find no friends in the Community, in the United States, or in world opinion: but he offered the solution – to uphold and participate in the undiluted sovereignty of the Westminster parliament. A vote for Europe was, in fact, a vote against Ulster.

In language that must have recalled the Bible, or Bunyan, he constantly exhorted his audiences not to be moved from the rock of a sovereign parliament in which Ulster was a part:

> All kinds of snares and temptations will be displayed in front of you, in the endeavour to make you abandon or compromise your purpose. There will be dozens of diversions: provincial autonomy; Ulster nationalism; fancy constitutions; special franchises; artificial links between irreconcilable opponents; plans, all sorts of plans, community plans, development plans, administrative plans, social plans . . . They are manufacturing them now in Londonderry and Belfast as they manufacture bombs and booby traps. They are manufacturing them at Stormont Castle and in Whitehall.[22]

He went on to attack Whitelaw's particular plans with a picture of Heath saying to the Secretary of State

> 'for God's sake go and put a stop to that squalid nuisance in Northern Ireland, at least for the time being; we can't have it interfering with our glorious enterprise in Europe, upsetting the Americans and even annoying my old friend Mr Lynch. Just tidy it away. . . .'

4   The Myth of Power-Sharing

The Unionists could appreciate the force of Powell's satire when in September the full truth of Whitelaw's dealings with the IRA came out, despite efforts to suppress it. Powell excoriated Whitelaw at Ballymena in September, in a speech not circulated by Central Office.

> On the afternoon of 22 June the Secretary of State, Mr Whitelaw, made a remarkably brief statement to the House of Commons. It consisted of two paragraphs. He first quoted the statement put out on behalf of the Republican movement, to the effect that the IRA will suspend offensive operations from midnight provided that a public reciprocal response is forthcoming from the armed forces of the British Crown. The second stated that 'If offensive operations by the IRA in NI cease on Monday night HM forces will obviously reciprocate'. . . . A perfect avalanche of cheering burst upon the minister and the government.[23]

Then Powell pulled to bits Whitelaw's denials that he had made a pact with rebels personally; how within two weeks the ceasefire had ended and Whitelaw had to admit that the IRA leaders were flown to Britain with the status of combatants and did confer with him, and how he had to admit to the House that he had signed a note with the IRA – all behind Parliament's back; even when the humiliating admissions were forced from him, Whitelaw refused to disclose the note he had signed. Powell ominously noted that while he had no word of approval for those who broke the law on the Protestant side, 'yet, in all candour, if their policy cannot be excused, it can be comprehended'.[24] They were asking whose side the British government was on. He rounded on Heath for calling on Ulster people to assert themselves against the men of violence when he had failed to defend those very people himself.

The EEC bill had passed before the events of 1972 could complete the estrangement between the Tories and 'the Unionist platoon', as Powell called it. But Whitelaw's reputation as a negotiating genius was actually enhanced. He had the no-go areas reoccupied to blunt the Protestant reaction and soon afterwards started, exactly as Powell predicted, a new initiative for power-sharing with an 'Irish dimension', calling all the parties to a conference in Darlington to shake up the political situation.

He was successful: partly because the Northern Irish politicians, out of office, out of power and out of funds, hungered for jobs. In March 1973 came the proposals for the power-sharing executive, combined with a Council for Ireland and the abolition of the office of Governor – an office that hardly fitted Powell's preference for integration, but which had been a symbol of loyalty and of control of their own destiny to the Protestants; and, reciprocally, objectionable to the Catholics. Faulkner led the campaign to make the new constitution work. In the ensuing elections the anti-power-sharers won twenty-eight seats to Faulkner's twenty-two, the SDLP's nineteen; the Alliance Party, a non-sectarian coalition, and the white hope of Whitehall, got eight. The SDLP made no concessions, as Powell predicted; it refused to call off the current strike until it was installed in the executive and it pressed for prompt implementation of the all-Ireland Council pledge. The assembly dissolved in fisticuffs in July. In September Heath visited Dublin to solicit Lynch's successor, Liam Cosgrave, to put pressure on the SDLP to be reasonable. On his return he told pressmen that the only visible alternative to power-sharing was full integration.

Asked what would happen if the executive failed, Heath said on 18 September

> Under the Constitutional Act if it is not formed then we go back to the responsibility at Westminster, which is direct rule. I think this time people would feel we cannot have continuing uncertainty, and it is much better the whole thing should be arranged on an integrated United Kingdom basis.[25]

That very evening Powell was reviewing the situation in a speech at Portrush, of which the press already had advance copies. Reviewing the failure of every successive British policy he said: 'I can at least look back without regrets. As each successive expedient was propounded, trumpeted in prospect and ignominious in retrospect, I have been one of that tiny band of Ulster Unionists and a few others who prophesied the outcome, gave reasons for their conviction and followed their lone voice with their lone vote.'[26] Powell also at this stage rounded on those who had in 1970 attacked his intervention on the ground that he did not understand Ireland and its peculiarity: 'Far more disasters are perpetrated by politicians through determination not to see simplicities than through unwillingness to grasp complexities; and nowhere more so than in Northern Ireland.'

They say the real trouble is all about economics and unemployment and development and housing. It is not. Then they say it is all about civil rights and non-discrimination and community relations. It is not. Then they say it is about tolerance and learning to live together and the habit of co-operation. It is not. It is about one thing and one thing only: whether this province is to be a province of the Irish Republic which claims it, or whether it is not. . . . Of course, of course, in public everyone on either side professes to believe that violence cannot annex Ulster to the Republic. Why should Republican politicians, why should any but those actually organising violence profess otherwise? Their work is being done for them. It is not professions that matter but facts, and the facts are that violence has made more progress in the last four years since the British Government and Parliament were drawn into direct involvement than in forty years when they were not.[27]

The folly and perfidy of the Westminster record was such, Powell feared, that Ulster, so far from seeing its safety in closer union with Britain – the form of union he had of course been urging – would see it in isolationism; talk, in fact, of an independent Ulster state. 'Unionism is the authentic expression of the self-consciousness of the Ulsterman and of his determination that he and his children and his land shall not be absorbed into a foreign state. Only incomprehension, ambivalence or (worse) rejection could succeed in turning unionism into that denial of itself, isolationism'.[28] Once again he blamed the Conservative Party's European policy for this outcome – particularly as it influenced the manoeuvrings over the Darlington talks: 'For those whose eyes are set on European union the central life-and-death issue in Ulster is obsolete, and even meaningless, and Dublin gains all . . . of the relevance which Belfast loses.' He asked why Heath had shown irritation with the ingratitude of Ulster people for Whitelaw's executive 'which would be unworkable anywhere and which Parliament would never have dreamed of introducing in any other part of the United Kingdom?' It was simple:

> The British Government does not intend that in Northern Ireland such political power as is devolved shall be exercised by an elected majority: the whole contraption is devised for no other purpose than to prevent that. . . . In the sole central, crucial, question of Northern Ireland . . . to belong or not to belong, it says that HM Government and the Westminster parliament are not on the side of the belongers, the majority. They wish if possible to be on both sides; but since in the long run that is not possible, they will wobble and fumble and drift and blunder towards the other side – towards the 'non-belongers', towards the 'Irish dimension', towards Dublin. If it were not so, why all this huffing and puffing and the white papers and the fancy constitution mongering?[29]

He pleaded with the Ulster people that in such a situation the only answer to the British government's mood of appeasement was not isolationism, which was incipient, but integration:

The mould of Stormont is broken and, like it or not, cannot be put together again. There is only one way in which the determination of the majority not to form part of any other state can be expressed . . . full representation, and exclusive representation, in the Parliament of the United Kingdom . . . If the people of this province will make this demand, they cannot be refused. The one boon that Westminster cannot deny is to grant the principle of its own existence . . . equal representation . . . one nation, one Parliament.[30]

And so, for a brief moment, Heath and Powell were agreed on the remedy.

Heath had said the one thing that frightened the Ulster politicians into cooperation. But he also frightened Whitelaw. He withdrew his statement. Even so, it was enough to enable Faulkner to bring the SDLP into his executive. At the new Sunningdale talks, the Unionists there accepted the Council of Ireland, and got the new formula that Britain would not prevent a United Ireland if the Ulster people freely voted for it, while Dublin recognised that such unity could only come about by peaceful means.

The reaction was not long in coming. Faulkner was deserted by the majority of his party, which as the 'Official Unionists' joined Paisley's Democratic Unionist Party and Craig's Vanguard as the UUU Coalition to fight the February 1974 election. They won eleven seats; the pro-Sunningdale, power-sharing candidates were defeated; even Fitt's majority was slashed. Heath and Whitelaw had created an Ulster front bitterly against the Conservative party and its manoeuvres, so bitingly dissected by its foremost rebel; when Heath found himself in a minority, he knew he could not ask the UUUC eleven to support him, and so his appeal to the Liberals, to join him in an anti-Socialist combination to reflect the electorate's actual voting preferences, merely humiliated him further. But the UUUs, and particularly Ian Paisley, had not accepted Powell's argument for integration. Their objective was to reassemble the mould of Stormont again.

5   Fighting in South Down

A politician represented as trying to retrieve the lack of a seat in England by acquiring one in Ulster might logically be expected to soft-pedal his commitment to a solution of Ulster's problems which every Ulster party rejected. Powell was popular among Protestants because he proclaimed the Unionist cause regardless of the effect on his English following, which was far more worried about immigration or socialism or the Common Market. There seemed little overlap between any of these causes, except the latter (as the result of his own efforts), in Unionist top political circles, and Ulster's cause. Powell saw them as a whole: as yet, few others did. But he had felt that Ulster was right, and he had thrown himself into Ulster's fight.

A prospective member of the Unionist party, even a distinguished. Privy Councillor with a Midlands-Australian accent, should at least reflect the attitudes of a party which had governed for fifty years through the Stormont constitution. After all, they had only twelve seats to dispose of, and one was anti-Unionist anyway. But, just as Enoch Powell had never compromised in England, so he never compromised in Northern Ireland. He continued to say the mould of Stormont was broken and that full integration was the only real safeguard against the betrayals of Westminster governments, of which Mr Harold Wilson, fully committed to the 'Irish Dimension' (adopted in his great 'mission' to Ireland in 1971) was the latest representative.

Powell addressed the Unionists in Belfast in April 1974, and said many things which struck home to them:

> Whatever else the recent general election did, it transformed the outlook of the loyal majority . . . they now have a visible hope . . . of making good their proud but simple claim to live at peace in their own part of the country, the United Kingdom. As one who all along asserted that this claim was binding on the Government, parliament and people of Great Britain, I hope I may be allowed to rejoice with you . . .[31]

Declaring that it was always by 'the few' that nations in extremity were saved, he reminded them that he had gone into the lobby with the little band of Unionists 'under ridicule, contempt and hostility, to go on record against one device after another for depriving the people of this province of their rights.' He widened his breach with the Conservative leadership by congratulating the Ulster Unionists on their breakaway, remarking, to cheers, that Heath's government had done more damage to Ulster in three years than any British government on record, and did it with impunity only because they were Conservative. As for the power-sharing executive bequeathed by them, it was 'a waterlogged hulk'. (The Ulster Workers' strike a month or so later was to sink it finally.)

But then, to fewer cheers, he told them that the proper next step was to demand full representation at Westminster. Wilson had a narrow majority destined to shrink; fate had given them the key, he implied, and the only reason to refuse them was Whitelaw's white paper dictum that integration was unacceptable to Dublin. Anything unacceptable to Dublin simply must be right for Unionism. Overriding that myth, the Conservatives could not indefinitely deny to one part of the kingdom equality of treatment with the rest, while the Labour party was in principle also heirs to the radical programme of 'equal constituencies and voting power.' Powell was saying that the leverage of a small party in a nicely balanced situation could work upon the consciences of the rank-and-file of both parties to overcome the compromises of their leaderships. But he added, at various times, that a campaign to get the extra seats would take five years . . . delivery hardly before 1979.

The immediate response of the Labour Government to the Ulster Workers' strike and the end of the power-sharing executive was, however, direct ('colonial') rule; and the loyalist reaction was to demand Stormont back. Indeed, the rise of Scots and Welsh nationalist representation gave the Unionists arguments for calling for a devolved Ulster in a devolved, even federal, United Kingdom: a line of thought repugnant to Powell's principle of parliamentary sovereignty – as events were to bear out.

Nevertheless, the news that in April Powell had attended the UUU Coalition conference generated press speculation that at the next election he would be offered an Ulster seat; and from there the commentators filled their columns with scenarios of how he would use his Ulster 'base', perhaps leadership of the UUUs, to get back into the Tory Party and challenge Heath for the leadership once more.[32]

But parties do not usually find room for candidates who plan to hijack them. Discussions had been proceeding since the outcome of the February election, when West and other Unionist leaders approached Powell and asked him how he could continue to help them. Of their own accord they decided that the only sure way was for him to join them and in May, West, Craig and Paisley came to Powell's London home and put before him the text of the UUUC agreed policy to be propounded at Portrush in April. Powell told them that he could support it as it stood, and they then urged him to stand as a UUU candidate if a seat could be found; Powell stipulated that nobody must be asked to stand down to make room for him. Only on the eve of the adoption of candidates in July, however, did the possibility of a vacancy in South Down emerge.

In the intervening months between Portrush and adoption he spoke in Ulster to increasingly enthusiastic audiences; he said little that was new, however, except possibly that if more secure border control involved residents and visitors to Ulster carrying identification cards, they willingly would. But the expedients in 1974 of a minority Wilson government educated the UUU members in the idea that an independent party in Westminster of perhaps fifteen (some of Powell's planned extra seats would go to the SDLP after redistricting) would be better able to defend the Province's interests. Their cry was still for 'the institutions of 1922'. Powell sought a compromise, and used the plans for Scots devolution, now humming after the Scottish Nationalist Party's successes, to find it:

> No one has the impertinence to suggest to the Welsh or the Scots that because they are Welsh or Scots they ought to be under-represented at Westminister . . . they would be indignant to be informed that by being fully represented, they were being 'integrated'. The full representation of this Province in Parliament no more prejudices or prejudges future arrangements which may be thought best for its administration than it does those of Wales or Scotland.

For historical reasons Scotland was over-represented, and it was open to the Ulstermen to ask for a similar weighting in the bargaining process to come. Powell was bridging the apparent gap between his stated positions and the UUU one; and in August he made the relationship between devolution and Westminster representation clearer:

When the unique form of local autonomy which was originally imposed upon a reluctant Ulster fifty years ago, but which has been loyally and successfully operated, was suddenly and brutally destroyed by the Conservative Government, this electorate put forward the simple and indefeasible claim to be as fully represented in Parliament as their fellow citizens in any other part of the kingdom, and to share on the same terms and basis in whatever form of devolution might in future be introduced in Great Britain.[33]

This statement left Powell free, if he became a UUUC MP, to oppose devolution throughout the United Kingdom, and to urge Ulster to avoid support for Scots and Welsh schemes in favour of full reliance on Westminster. It met the UUUC requirement, committing him to demand for Ulster anything the Scots got – he would hardly have been likely to want Ulster to be an exception or 'special case'. But these issues were in 1974 seen as far in the future compared with a justified demand for more MPs now that Ulster had neither assembly nor proper elective local government.

In August Captain Orr, the Ulster Unionist leader at Westminster, decided for personal reasons not to contest South Down again, and from abroad sent a message to his constituency association 'in my opinion not only Ulster, but the United Kingdom as a whole, would be well served if my old friend Enoch Powell were selected'. Powell made it a condition of his acceptance that the invitation should be unanimous and uncontested; it was. He did not wish, as an Englishman, to seem to be pressing himself, though the UUUC leader, Mr West, was reported to set store by his offering himself. In touring the constituency Powell said 'I have become entirely one of yourselves' and his audiences, the press reporters agreed, were enchanted.

Campaigning in South Down was a new experience for Mr and Mrs Powell – it was unusual in Ulster for a candidate's wife to carry so much of the load. Like other candidates he had to hold meetings under police protection, but he stuck to his rules of intense door-to-door canvassing; unlike some local politicians he went about unarmed. Though the IRA were reported to have put him on their 'list', they left him alone. Local people who went doubting to his meetings came away satisfied that he understood their bread-and-butter problems as well as the major issues. They found he had a fresh new way of stating these, ridiculing their opponents and providing entertainment as well as rallying the faithful in the approved manner. He had little time to make a personal impact over so large a constituency, but his reputation in England drew the election throughout Ulster to English attention in a way that would otherwise have been unlikely. He appeared on platforms with West and Dr Paisley, the most powerful advocate of devolution and a return to Protestant – possibly Paisleyite – ascendancy: even before the poll speculation was rife that the new Carson would lead the UUUC in Westminster.

He was expected to increase Orr's majority. He did not, and this may have cost him the leadership. But the loss by West to the Republican candidate in

Fermanagh was a reminder of the narrowness of the Unionist vote in some areas. South Down itself was becoming more and more marginal; in 1974 it was reckoned 50–50 denominationally. Newry was strongly republican; to enter it involved an operation into enemy territory in that year. The constituency's Faulknerites (and Faulkner lived there) had to swallow Powell's past criticisms of his advocacy of power-sharing. There was prejudice against his mainland origins; ironic because Powell had always argued that the strength of the union of all the parts of the kingdom was attested by the way Scots and Welsh (and Ulstermen) stood for English constituencies; it did not happen quite so much the other way round, and in Ulster, with only twelve seats, very rarely.

In the outcome, though the Unionist vote increased by 2,000 ($2\frac{1}{2}$ per cent) on a much larger turnout than in February, his majority, at 51·8 per cent, was smaller than Orr's had been (and he had latterly been chronically absent from the constituency). For all that Powell was back in the House – the fates, as he had predicted, had found a way.

Powell did not put himself forward as Parliamentary leader in West's place, though James Molyneaux, who became the compromise selection, hoped he would. Molyneaux had known Powell well; knew his disgust with Parliament in 1972 and his feelings that if it surrendered its sovereignty to the EEC he contemplated leaving politics, unless, perchance, he found in Ulster a cause he could fight for; they henceforth worked very closely together, and in view of the inherent stresses inside the coalition, it was probably the best arrangement to maintain unity.

Powell now divided his time between Ulster and London. As in 1950, he set himself to turn an (unexpectedly) marginal constituency into a safe one. He gave his constituents a service such as they had never known. He made no distinction between Protestant and Catholic although he was assured that he was wasting his time on the latter. But as an Englishman, he could approach them as no Orangeman could; and Powell never joined the Orange order, finding its objects incompatible with his religious position, as well as with English origins; indeed he sometimes doubted if they were fully compatible with full-hearted unionism such as he himself professed. It was hard work in the huge constituency devoid of any natural centre, and he had to take up in London or with the colonial bureaucracy in Belfast many matters which, but for direct rule, would have been handled by county councils or the like. He bought a cottage at Loughbrickland, as strategically placed as possible on the 'enemy'-ward side of South Down, to dwell among his adopted people as much as possible, and he became adept in the constituency's history and archaeology as well as its social and denominational structure.

A certain dualism in his new avatar was unavoidable. He was a national figure. To serve the Ulster cause he had to remain one. He was expected in England to pursue the causes he had made his own from Wolverhampton – the coming referendum above all, but also finance and inflation, the march of socialism and the public sector, and immigration. Nor was he finished with the soul of the Conservative Party, as his relations with it since March had shown;

the question of the circumstances in which he could rejoin it remained, perpetually intriguing the political experts. For, as a Tory, he was bound to work for the regeneration of his old party, and, as an Ulster Unionist, to make it possible to resume the former alliance between like-minded people.

The cause for which he had been elected comprehended all he had fought for against Heath: sovereignty, nationhood, the uniqueness of the British Parliament as the personification of its people who made and unmade it. Only such a parliament could give Ulster what she needed and atone for the years of betrayal, as he saw it. And the new parliament, where the minor parties held an influential position, and seemed destined to hold the balance of power, was rich in possibilities for Ulster. The reverse of that position was that Ulster in its steadfastness under fire was s shining example of what English nationalism and patriotism should mean on the mainland. He told interviewers of the satisfaction he felt at being in the fight, in the target areas, and how in the past he had sometimes felt ashamed when speaking for Ulster in the House of Commons to know that his colleagues in that cause, unlike himself, would spend the next weekend in a theatre of war.

6   Devolution and Integration

Though the Ulster and the British cause after October 1974 were entwined, there was a geographical separation and indeed a second political dimension for Powell in Ireland; it is logical to treat his two major concerns in two channels, like two arteries carrying the same blood stream. In Ulster, his prime care was henceforth to defeat any renewed attempt by Whitehall to impose power-sharing; an instrument existed for this in the Constitutional Convention set up by the Wilson government when the Faulkner-led executive disintegrated in May and was put in legislative cold storage. Powell was called on to secure, by using his parliamentary expertise, an undertaking from the government to provide the extra members – seven or eight – at Westminster, presumably through the constitution of a 'Speaker's conference'. He pressed for a return of elective local government and for stronger police and security organisations.

In December 1974, he hailed the passage of the Prevention of Terrorism Act as the turning point in the war with the IRA. It came about, not because of the sufferings in Ulster, but because the IRA carried the war into Britain and killed some English people. Merlyn Rees had visited Belfast in the autumn when the massive bombing of the city centre had almost stopped traffic. The anger of the Ulster people even penetrated to the touring Secretary of State who, seeing their faces, heard that they were saying that such an outrage would never be permitted in an English city without something being done. They were exactly right.

The bombing of Birmingham a little later produced like lightning the results Powell had dreamed in vain for years – the recognition of the frontiers between the Republic and the United Kingdom. He suggested that this piece of realism might be followed by the extension to Irish nationals of the rules applying to other EEC citizens, so that when the electorate voted Britain out of the Community in the coming Referendum, as he hoped they would, the rules applied under the 1971 Immigration Act to 'persons who are not patrial' would apply to them – for once turning EEC rules to Ulster's advantage.[34]

He was not to succeed. The conviction of British ministers and officials that the Republic would not, even under Cosgrave, cooperate against terrorists unless it was given a one-way special relationship was one reason; but there was another, cogent, one. It had been established that far more immigrant Irish, like New Commonwealth immigrants, voted Labour than voted Conservative. Nevertheless, at the outset of 1975 he told his constituents that 'the sky ahead is lightening'.[35] Whatever mayhem lay ahead, the first requirement for peace was being fulfilled: the IRA was being at long last deprived of political hope. The only future was terrorism for the sake of terrorism: but there was plenty of life in that motive. Moreover the infiltration of criminals into the gangs was providing a dangerous economic incentive to keep terrorism and intimidation going.

But the continued violence, the spread of inhuman sectarian murder, the acquiescence of Mr Wilson's government in a cease-fire that was a sham prolonged mainly to give the IRA the advantage of semi-recognition through the cooperation of police and troops with it in the so-called 'incident centres', put a breaking strain upon the divisions in the UUUC. The need to get security under local (Protestant) control seemed increasingly urgent to Paisley and West, however impracticable Powell told them it was. He attacked the 'colonial' civil servants in Stormont in strong language for their 'diligent communication' with 'thugs and murderers' and he called in question the honour of 'men who, with their knighthoods and decorations, will submit to be employed in this fashion, let alone mis-advise their political chiefs to be responsible for this mischief'. As with the Home Office over immigration, and the Foreign Office with the EEC, 'they ought to risk their places and pensions rather than engage in near-treasonable activities.'

In these conditions of near treasonable activities by the Whitehall officials, the bait of devolution in some form, held out by the negotiations within the Constitutional Convention, was tempting, notwithstanding the strings of power-sharing attached to it. Powell wanted to trample it underfoot with the unanswerable retort:

> We will be governed as you are governed, we will be represented as you are represented; we will have the same privileges as you, our fellow citizens . . . in short, we are British, so we will have British rights, British standards, British liberties. . . .[36]

He told an audience in Antrim in October that the proposition that Ulster should draw up plans unilaterally for its own self-government were actually anti-Unionist; they risked becoming not devolutionists, but nationalists, such as were the Scottish Nationalist Party; and if so they had to ask themselves in what did they differ from the Nationalist Republicans with whom they were at war. If they took such a line they would play into the hands of those in Britain who were sick of the Ulster entanglement: 'if Ulster nibbled at the bait of self-determination, down comes the chopper,' severing the Province from Britain.

In September Craig resigned from the deputy UUU leadership in the Convention and took those who followed him out of the coalition; the rest of the members decided to refuse to discuss with the SDLP a constitutional settlement embodying the new formula of 'voluntary power-sharing'. Powell's influence in this was descried by Whitehall. In October he defined his position again, to meet what he called the press misrepresentation of him as a 'total integrationist':

> I repeat what I have said over and over again – that I am as deeply committed as any man to devolved government for Ulster . . . within the framework of the United Kingdom exactly as was set out in the Portrush declaration and the UUU manifestos. . . . But what would be a cruel and dangerous deception of those for whom we are responsible would be to pretend to the people of Ulster that a devolved government would be a kind of talisman for destroying the IRA, and that therefore whatever concession or compromise would purchase an Ulster government entrusted with security would be a cheap price to pay.[37]

Powell denied that full control of security was in any case negotiable, simply because the control of the army would not be transferred to any devolved government, and the army remained indispensable. He went further and warned that the type of men eager to take office in a devolved assembly 'would be the very generation of politicians who, long before 1969, let Ulster's guard slip . . . [and] allowed itself to be deceived by one false promise after another [and] which up to this moment is shilly-shallying away the safety of its fellow-citizens.' Faulkner and his tribe were no substitute for Cragavon and Brookborough . . .

Powell was seeking to educate his party, indeed even Craig and the Vanguard, on the realities of devolution; he never went back upon, and indeed constantly reinforced, his statement that the mould of Stormont was broken. In February 1976, for example, he demonstrated that 'the prospect of getting back an Ulster assembly and executive is not on offer at all except on terms which have been solemnly forsworn not only by the UUUC, but by Vanguard and William Craig himself.' The moment the presence of SDLP members within a devolved executive was accepted, that type of power-sharing would be riveted on Ulster for good. 'Let them first set about telling Scotland that there will be no devolution until the Scottish politicians agree to share power between those who wish to take Scotland outside the United Kingdom and those who want to preserve the union.'[38] Contrariwise, if Scotland could get devolution in which the majority ruled, Ulster could insist on the same.

Powell sought two complementary things: the progressive integration of the Ulster Members in all Westminster decisions to make a reality of integration, and the reform of direct rule both by an improvement in the administration of Ulster in Westminster and an elective local government: 'when the present district councils were established under the Macrory report it was never imagined that there would be no elected representatives between the district representatives and the MPs, and that the gap would be filled by faceless bureaucratic bodies.'[39]

But his ill-wishers represented his programme, which included his efforts to improve the Ulster MPs' power to criticise the Orders in Council flowing from the Northern Ireland Office, as inconsistent. The general frustration – which Powell felt only elected representatives at every level could siphon off – was growing. There was unremitting pressure in 1975 and 1976 from local Protestant para-military associations to compel, by violence of their own, some stronger action by Government; action which duly came when the nominal cease-fire collapsed. Throughout this period Powell insisted in speeches, 'that about nothing is the Unionist more absolute than the duty to obey the law. His loyalty being to the Crown in Parliament, he accepts as the hallmark of union that all parts of the kingdom and all citizens are bound equally by the law which their Parliament makes.' This jarred the inherently anti-government and conspiratorial instincts of Paisley and the Democratic Unionists as well as some of the official Unionists; but Powell was unrelenting on a number of occasions in setting his face against any sort of illegal action: 'it is blasphemy to attach words like loyal and loyalist to anyone who does not accept the law of the land.'[40]

When the Convention was finally dissolved, and power-sharing shelved once again by Whitehall, Powell conceded to direct rule, 'for all who uphold the union there can be nothing distasteful in being governed as part of it'. The immediate problem was to secure that Ulster was genuinely 'governed as part of it', and in the same way, he said in May 1976 'the aims of Unionism can only be attained under and through Parliament'. As an example of what, even then, could be done Powell instanced the amendment of the Fair Employment bill to meet Ulster's special needs. But above all, he was in sight of delivering his promise: '. . . the Government has at last seen the necessity of abandoning its attitude of total refusal to consider . . . fair and equal representation of this province' at Westminster.[41] This achievement followed not so much from a recognition of justice, but from the progressive weakening of the Government's position in the House of Commons. As Callaghan lost his wafer-thin majority, the importance of the Ulster Unionists grew; and so did the participation of Ulster MPs in the whole working of the House, much to Powell's delight: 'the representatives of Northern Ireland,' he said, 'have become an integral part of the House of Commons . . . they are no longer a contingent of half-strangers who come from outside to complain or acquiesce.'[42]

7 Towards a New Deal

The breakthrough was achieved in spite of the disintegration of the coalition in the spring. When the Convention Report came before Parliament in the early months of 1976, the divisions that had developed in the Convention forced Craig to separate himself from the UUUC. Paisley and Ernest Baird, both inclined to direct action of some kind were resentful of the dominance of Powell's logic, which began to be reflected even in statements by the Orange Order. They criticised him for 'supporting integration with Great Britain instead of fighting for a properly devolved Government', whatever Paisley meant by that phrase.[43] Conservative feelers soon afterwards went out to see if the talk about the decline of Powell's popularity would make possible the renegotiation of the Tory-Unionist alliance, and there were talks with Colonel Brush, Powell's President, but whatever the discontent over Powell's tough legality, Mr Airey Neave and others found that, for the time being, his position was unshakeable.

In September he was readopted unopposed as official Unionist candidate for South Down; the tattle about his individualistic, not to say idiosyncratic, performances died down. If not as spectacular as Carson in his achievements he was recognised as the architect of the UUUC successes at Westminster. Powell was careful not to seem to use Ulster as a 'base' for his broader national interests; he regularly made speeches to his constituents about the relevance to their affairs and destiny of the EEC, inflation and immigration, for example. Anything that was weakening British morale, 'hollowing out' the nation, weakened Ulster. He reminded Ulster above all that the men of Brussels had arrogantly grouped Northern and Southern Ireland together for treatment.

In particular he discussed the relevance to Ulster of the Scottish and Welsh devolution bill, which Paisley was ready to support for what he supposed were sound tactical reasons. In January 1977, in Molyneaux's constituency, he recalled that at Portrush the party had grasped the dangers of devolution, and explained how the *type* of devolution on offer to Scotland would undermine Ulster, pointing out that the SDLP, so bitterly anti-Stormont, accepted it as a stage nearer their goal of a united Ireland. Hence there could be no question of voting for legislation that would weaken the Union itself and that disregarded cynically Ulster's claims to equal consideration; as the UU amendment put it, 'this House declines to give the bill a second reading so long as Northern Ireland, an integral part of the United Kingdom, is denied fair and just representation in this Parliament and remains deprived of any devolved or local administration above the level of the district councils'.

Paisley tired of the slow haul and in April repudiated Westminster as dramatically as he could (blasphemy to Powell) and whipped up feeling in his own constituency for a second workers' strike like that of May 1974. Powell denounced it as unconstitutional and predicted it would flop. He repudiated, besides Paisley, Ernest Baird's Council against Direct Rule, which called for civil resistance. The Official Unionists agreed with him; Powell declared that 'I could not and would not contemplate seeking election to Parliament in any circumstances which linked me with persons who repudiate the lawful authority of the parliament of the UK, or who approve . . . any courses of action except such as are strictly within the law.'[44] He was understood to reject anyone within the Unionist ranks with contacts with the Protestant paras.

The strike of May 1974, in Powell's view, had kept within the law, was disciplined, had avoided violence, and had an attainable objective; moreover it was not directed against Parliament since the implementation of the 1973 Act dealing with the Executive was conditional; therefore Powell saw no parallel with 'an act of criminal irresponsibility perpetrated against the province by a small knot of men . . . as reckless of the lives and safety of what they dare to call "their own people" as they are contemptuous of the opinions and will of the majority'.[42] Within a fortnight the strike collapsed, and he was largely responsible for its ignominious end.

In the local elections which followed, on proportional representation, Molyneaux and Powell urged their supporters not to vote for any candidates on the ballot paper involved in the strike – in effect the Paisleyites – but to leave the space blank, even though it was realised that such advice would provoke retaliation. Paisley had been nursing a local candidate in South Down *in terrorem* over Powell, and in June he approached the official Unionists to drop 'the Englishman' in favour of a joint – i.e. his own – candidate to unite the Protestant forces against the SDLP challenge. Mr O'Loan, Powell's constituency chairman, retorted that no such candidate would be acceptable to his party: Paisley could incur the odium of losing the seat to the SDLP by splitting the loyalist vote – he could not get it for himself. Subsequently the SDLP chose a powerful challenger in Mr Eddie McGrady as their candidate.

In March 1977 Powell and Molyneaux persuaded Callaghan to convene an all-party Speaker's conference on increased Ulster representation. Agreed just before the Government was given a new lease of life before the Lib-Lab pact, Powell stated that it was not the result of bargaining for Unionist support but an unconditional promise, which included a pledge also to consider Ulster's claim to the elective upper tier of provincial (or regional) local government and a review of the functions of the existing weak district councils. Such an arrangement would hardly have been feasible had not Powell, with his record of discriminating support for the Labour Party, been such an influential member of the official Unionists, who indeed stifled their instincts and refrained from embarrassing the Government until May 1978. The Speaker's conference had by then produced in February 1978 recomendations for an increase in Ulster's representation from twelve seats to seventeen or eighteen, by the reduction of constituencies' sizes to the Welsh average, about one member to 57,000 electors, according to a redrawing of boundaries by the usual commission.

It would, of course, have best suited Powell's interests if that commission could have reported in time for the additional members to be elected in the next parliament, but, as he explained to a meeting in Dromore, this was an impracticable timetable even if Parliament lasted its full term to October 1979. Powell would have to fight his marginal seat on the same terms as in October 1974, and therefore it would be some time before the Unionists could exert more leverage in the event of a 'hung' parliament. However, the Conservatives renewed their efforts to make sure that in such an event they could rely on a UU-Tory pact rather than deal with the Liberals.

Thus Powell's prediction that Ulster's claim would prove irresistible in Westminster was justified. Paisley and other irreconciliables looked the gift horse in the mouth, fearing that the extra MPs in Westminster prejudiced their demand for autonomy under Stormont. They were, however, forced to be circumspect as the Scottish and Welsh bills were worked over by the House; for if these failed to pass, or if the voters rejected them in the referendums, the chances of Westminster making an early exception for Northern Ireland became remote. On the other hand, if the bills did form the charters for limited devolution in those countries, Ulster was unlikely to get anything better, for many years at least. Craig hailed devolution as 'a fast-moving revolutionary process leading to a federal UK'. But it was not the cause of Stormont that had won through, it was powellian political logic.

But Powell's struggle to maintain integration depended on elective local government, with or without a provincial council. Speaking on the Welsh bill he argued that 'administrative devolution' was a misnomer; whatever the façade, its officials remained ultimately subordinate to Parliament, so that even local government electors could insist on taking their grievances, one way or another, to their MP in Westminster. Meanwhile, the Government, dependent both on Liberal and Irish republican votes, felt it had to insist on proportional representation for elections to the European Assembly. Powell denounced it again as a device to give the secessionist minority 'a contrived position of power' with which to continue loosening the links between Britain and Ulster.

On 8 May he used the opposition amendment to the Finance Bill to reduce income tax to protest on behalf of all the official Unionists at this refusal to provide Ulster with precisely the kind of local government for which British electors everywhere else voted on 4 May. Powell's preference for income tax, the nearly ideal tax as he called it, was well known; but the circumstances made the debate a political, not an economic one. The Unionist defection ensured Callaghan's defeat, but his refusal to treat it as a vote of confidence (to everyone's private satisfaction) left Powell with more time to prepare his role in the coming election, both in Ulster and in Britain.

In debates on Ulster government and administration during the summer he developed his arguments that direct (and increasingly bureaucratic) rule from Westminster was unable to take into account the geographical and agricultural differences between the Ulster region and the other British regions, which demanded the 'bringing back of government to the understanding, control, sympathy and support of the people themselves.' It was the social and organisational singularities which required devolution, not any constitutional difference. Ulster, he said on 30 June, had a 'claim of right' to enjoy this proper democratic rule over *local* administration; on the other hand 'devolution in the sense in which devolution is being sought to be applied to Scotland and Wales' was a claim not of right: 'Should it prove possible without damage to the integrity and structure of the United Kingdom for devolution to be brought [i.e. by affirmative referendums] into being and made to work in Scotland and Wales the people of Northern Ireland would have an equal claim to the application of the same principles on the same basis.' He did not expatiate on the conditions in which one could agree that the Scottish and Welsh Acts were not splitting the kingdom as powellian logic had predicted they must eventually do; and therefore he left open the timing of a similar devolution for Ulster. On this position about Stormont's future, and his unequivocal demand for elective local government, he got ready to face his constituents.

Callaghan's decision not to hold an election in autumn enabled the Ulster Unionists to bring enlarged representation nearer. The Queen's Speech in November promised a bill, and in the last day of the debate Powell intervened to say that, obedient to the remit their electors had given them to get justice for Ulster, they would not vote against the Government. Callaghan survived and the bill was introduced. Powell prepared for the election of 1979 on the basis of political union between Ulster and the United Kingdom: the rest was a matter of method, not of principle.

Chapter 12

Devolution, Direct Elections and Westminster, 1974–1978

1 A Tory of No Party

Powell's friends were glad to see him back in Westminster in October 1974, blooming in health from the air of South Down and ready, when he encountered Edward Heath, to say 'Well, Ted, how's it going?' But many feared Ulster was a dead end, a *faute de mieux*, for considerable efforts had been made to save him for the Conservatives between March and August when he was finally adopted for South Down. It seemed clear to many Tories, as to outside observers, that the only hope of winning the election which Wilson was expected to hold in the autumn was to achieve a reconciliation between Powell and the party leaders. If this were done, a seat could be found; if not, any local association trying to rope in Powell would be blocked by Party headquarters. Powell, as it happened, had ceased to be a paid-up member of the party at the dissolution in February, for he was then only a party member by virtue of being a Conservative MP. But recalling him to the colours was always a forlorn hope. Heath knew that if he lost the next election his leadership would be at risk; yet if he won it with Powell's aid he would have opened the gates to the Trojan horse. It was Hobson's choice for Heath, even leaving aside the aversion he (and his huscarls) felt for what they stigmatised as treachery.

Powell was in contact with the Ulster Unionists, but he was prevailed upon to make a gesture of reconciliation; if there was to be one it had to come from him. He evidently felt he owed it to his old party; and if anything had come of it, no doubt a seat in England would have had to be weighed against one in the Ulster outback. The insuperable objection, which alone enabled him to go to Ulster, was the Conservative commitment to the EEC, and Powell's commitment to getting out. But after March, this commitment had changed, if only a little. Powell had broken with his party for reneging on their pledges on EEC; but he shared his opposition to EEC membership with many other Conservatives (as du Cann was later to claim, more than half). The pledge issue as such was dissolved by the election. The death of Pompidou and the retirement of Brandt appeared, just at this juncture, to change the outlook for the EEC, which the new German Chancellor, Helmut Schmidt, had denounced as 'incompetent' and which everyone else admitted was in disarray, with the goal of 'economic and monetary union by 1980', Powell's particular target, postponed *sine die*. Indeed, Powell had already said the situation could change under Heath.[1]

On 18 May he chose a meeting of a Tory discussion club, the Trident Group, to restate his position in the light of these events. He let it be known in advance that he was going to raise the question of reconciliation. Publicity was thus secured – the media had, after February, been keeping him from the public eye and ear and after the furore continued to do so until he became an MP once more. The press generally first reacted to the speech that he was suing for entry, offering an olive branch; then after reflection it was decided that he had made an impudent take-over bid, stating his terms for the Tories to rejoin Powell.[2] Re-read, it seems to have been rather the sort of exploration of possible common ground which is frequent in diplomatic tentatives. Its keynote was that neither side had to recant or abandon principle; a new situation had to be assessed. Powell made a genuine gesture without being inconsistent with his record. But he also made it for the record. It shows no sign that he expected the auditor who mattered in the immediate future – Edward Heath – to respond. In a sense, the speech has a parallel with Powell's candidature for the Party leadership in 1965. It was something he had to do, as part of his political logic. Most notable in the speech, in the longer run, is his assessment of the significance of the party divisions in the 1970–4 parliament. He stated the reasons for starting a new leaf; he examined exactly where the Powellite argument stood in May 1974, and he left open how far it could be accommodated in the party line of the period; but made clear that he thought it could be. The moment when that line was about to be restated for the coming election was the right moment for reconsideration of Powell's and the Party's positions.

> When most of the rest has been forgotten, the parliament of 1970 to 1974 will be remembered as that in which MPs debated and voted on the question to end all questions: whether it was right for the UK to have a future at all as an independent nation and parliamentary democracy. The issue was posed in that starkly absolute form not merely by the content of the legislation itself, which explicitly surrendered overriding legislative, fiscal and judicial power to external authorities, but by the official commitment to economic and monetary union by 1980.
>
> What a far cry it seems already from those days, though by the calendar they are less than two years ago! . . . it is the EEC in its present form which is now the object of unsuppressed scepticism among those who were the . . . most persistent advocates of British entry. Surely there is no need for the Conservative Party to tear itself apart over what we all know is not going to happen – indeed over what we all know does not exist as a political reality.[3]

He repeated that he had never impugned the patriotism of those who wanted a united Europe, but 'the cooperation of Britain and Europe will be built of different materials and to a different pattern', an optimistic reference to the prospective Callaghan renegotiation. 'What was surrendered can therefore be recalled, with neither triumph on the one side, not discredit upon the other, and friends who fought can make common cause once more.'

He also examined past differences between himself and the leadership on inflation and immigration: here too he found that cirumstances had changed the equation. Now that the reversal of policy had proved, and been seen to be, disastrous, surely there was hope for a Conservative fiscal and monetary policy which learned from experience; while on immigration the party could gather the full facts which faced 'the next generation' of British people, put them to the people, and frame policy accordingly.

The speech was treated as a systematic attempt to use back-bench dissatisfaction with Heath to insinuate Powell into the Party again; the interpretation put on it was that in the guise of jettisoning recantations by either side it amounted to requiring Heath to admit his errors, which he would implicitly do by grasping the 'prickly olive branch' thus held out. Heath was reminded that six weeks previously Powell had categorised his administration as one 'in which the U-turn became the norm', throwing up yet again the charge that he had broken all the pledges of the 1970 Party manifesto.[4] It was to this charge, rather than the olive branch, that Heath replied the following day, without mentioning Powell: 'The Party will not go back on policies which we worked out in opposition and pursued in government just because we are in opposition again.'[5] In short there had been no U-turns, no broken pledges, above all no broken pledge about 'full-hearted consent'; he had done exactly what he had planned and told his people he had planned – if anyone was out of step, it could therefore only be Powell. Heath was making no compromises, perceived no change in the situation – nor did he subsequently – and Powell's approaches had therefore no basis. Powell had his answer, he got no other; he was out.

Talk of a Tory constituency for Powell proved to be idle; the conditions did not exist. Powell's supporters, like Peter Tapsell and Joan Quennell, miscalculated; Powell could hardly have done. What he had done was to plant more seeds of doubt in the Conservative ranks about Heath's political judgement. Powell had been made into an even more dangerous enemy, the Party nailed to a preposterous set of policies – indeed to one man's obstinacy. For Powell, the way to Ulster unionism was open, his position on Conservatism on record in fair and conciliatory language. On 29 May he hailed the collapse of the Faulkner executive with the reminder that he had always predicted this end for it, and had warned of the prolongation of bloodshed it would entail. In July he dropped the hint that he might again have to advise the electorate to vote against Heath-type Conservatism.

Whether the future of the EEC was a matter for scepticism or not, there were no big differences between the major parties on the worsening economic crisis – and the current rises in prices were the results of Conservative rather than Labour inflationary finance because Barber's expansion of the money supply was still working through, and the 'explosion' of wage settlements was a response to it, not the cause of the inflation. So the main issue was the EEC still: the electorate had installed the party which promised to submit membership to them by referendum after a fundamental renegotiation of the terms; they would soon have to choose between reaffirming that decision or reversing it in favour of a party pledged to regard membership as settled for good.

Accordingly, when he was adopted for South Down he was asked if this was the final and irrevocable break with the Conservative Party, to which he gave the standard powellian reply that final and irrevocable events were rarer in politics than in journalism. But the way the wind was blowing was indicated a few days later when Sir Keith Joseph broke the Heath line with a speech on Tory economic mistakes which Powell described as 'an admirable anthology from my speeches on the subject in recent years.' Sir Keith made no acknowledgements; powellism without Powell suddenly offered big political rewards, and Sir Keith set up, soon afterwards, an institute to depowellise the alternative Conservatism with which he proposed to transform the Party, and perhaps his own position in it.[6] Describing the speech as a post-mortem repentance, for it could only be construed as a lack of confidence in Heath's policies for electoral victory, Powell said: 'I have seen nothing said or done in the last six months which has altered circumstances as I saw them in February . . . still, if we are to have post-mortem repentances daily from the Conservative Party, who knows but that they may chuck over the Common Market as well?'[7]

They did not; and in the ensuing election campaign Powell, besides travelling 3,000 miles in South Down, travelled a good deal in England to insist that the difference between the two parties on Europe left him with no alternative but to give the same advice on voting that he had done in February.

He used the platform of the Get Britain Out movement in Bristol and Manchester to do so. 'If the party which stood for the surrender of political independence were also the party which offered to restore the honesty of our money and thereby our national self-respect, then the dilemma would be hard for many to resolve,'[8] he agreed, but Heath offered no more rational prospect than Wilson of any such thing. As for Heath's proposals for a coalition, it was 'another leap into an abstract future denuded of circumstances': a 'union of all the talents with no indication on what principle the nation was to unite or all the talents were to govern'.[9] He predicted that the 'increasingly neurotic emphasis' placed by Heath on a government of national unity to do unspecified things would harm the Conservatives (and not prove the winner it apparently was in 1931). So it proved.

Though he himself did not return to Westminster as leader of a party, Labour's majority of only four over all others gave him a favourable terrain for his influence and justified the UUUC's recruitment of him – had Wilson done better Powell might have been just another frustrated Unionist vote. He predicted, when few others did, that Labour would stay in office for little short of its full term (autumn 1979); and as a normal government's erosion turned it into a minority administration, it would be slowly delivered into the hands of the minority parties.

It was, however, a complex pattern, because on almost all the issues that arose, Powell was obliged to criticise, if not always vote against, the Government. Moreover he had to restrain the inclinations of some Ulster Members which were to put Labour out as soon as Mrs Thatcher presented an alternative. It seemed odd to them that they should find themselves on occasion allied with Messrs Fitt and McGuire, anti-Unionist, pro-Dublin opponents, in keeping Wilson, and then Callaghan in power. Most of them still wanted devolution. Powell did not, but he did want, and knew it would not be easy to get, a commitment from a Labour government for additional members for Ulster (not that a Conservative government would be any more eager to strengthen a minority party). He could show how Ulster was ignored when devolution bills for Scotland and Wales were brought in. The big majority that seemed assured for the Conservative Party if Labour fell promised Ulster's cause nothing at this stage. Powell had to keep his colleagues' eyes pinned to the politics of Ulster's interest. For some unexplained reason his critics found this unprincipled.[10]

2   Mrs Thatcher and Powellism

Soon after the election, Sir Keith Joseph put on heavier sackcloth for the Conservative reversal of its economic policies between 1970 and 1974. It recalled to Powell 1968: 'it is great fun to see someone else get into hot water over a speech. I almost wondered if the River Tiber was beginning to roll again.' But Sir Keith was risking nothing; he knew Heath was for the tumbril now the Party had lost the election. Powell 'found something distasteful about men who followed him through briar and thicket turning on him now as if it never happened.'[11]

But he also thought Heath might survive for some time yet. Among the unsatisfactory alternatives to Heath, he told interviewers, there was no front runner, and that was 'the beauty of it' from Heath's point of view. The longer Heath hung on, of course, the longer the leadership issue was kept open, and this was the consideration that interested the journalists. If Heath fell, would Powell be able to serve under a more agreeable successor. Powell had once more to suggest that 'it wasn't on a matter of personalities that I departed from the Conservative Party . . . the journalistic observers of politics don't seem to believe that politicians are sometimes interested in issues . . . in principles.'[12] He pursued the theme that in politics what often happened was the unexpected. He thought a new leader would be 'the most surprising person, probably.' Of his own future he took the same attitude: 'It's barely a year since there was all that Tory hierarchy up on the platform at Blackpool applauding the attack made on me by an individual almost forgotten now. He was Chancellor of the Exchequer then, and I was supposed to be ground into dust; yet all of them are now playing different parts. Well, what will another twelve months bring forth?'[13]

If he had been interested in mending relations with his former colleagues (with whom he was soon on pleasant parliamentary terms) and keeping any sort of possibility of cooperation in the future alive, he would hardly have reacted to the final downfall of Heath as he did. He stigmatised them as sycophants while Heath had the power and jobs to offer, but after the election saying 'Ted must go' for their own sakes. Yet, in a sense, how else can politicians change their leaders? It is usually a gory business for Conservatives. Powell could not have been a foxhunter unless he was satisfied the fox was killed without pain; and when Sir Alec was the quarry in 1965 Powell stood by him though the end was sure enough. What disgusted him in 1974–5 was the contrast between the slavishness with which the bulk of the party as well as the ministers followed Heath in his reversals and the way they impugned his judgements after the election; the circumstances of Alec Home's loss of the leadership, if not pleasant, were of a different order. As Powell noted, they were saying of a defeated man what Powell alone had said to his face when he was in power.

A thread of underlying distaste for certain features of Conservative Party life had run through all of Powell's career; notably in October–November 1963 over the succession. In the end Margaret Thatcher was indeed the surprise choice. But in January Powell had told the Selsdon Group that 'if the Conservative Party is seeking a successor to Mr Heath who will re-establish the principles which were trampled on in office'[14] they should not look among his ex-ministers.

> 'Oh,' they say 'but she – sorry, he – used to murmur and grumble a lot in private'. Maybe; but it is not among private murmurers and grumblers, disloyal colleagues, willing to wound but afraid to strike, holding one opinion outside the Cabinet Room but inside acquiescing in the opposite, that the new leadership needed is to be found. All very well to recant when recantation carries no penalty. It was then that those ladies and gentlemen were found lacking . . . then that they failed the party far worse than Edward Heath . . .[15]

Such a comment invited Mrs Thatcher's announcement two weeks later, that she had no place in her cabinet for Powell – at the time he was involved in the usual multi-racial outcry over his fresh discoveries in the 'numbers game' which Mrs Thatcher did not, or did not then, play. Powell retorted that Mrs Thatcher was right enough as he was not a member of her party, 'and until the Conservative Party has worked its passage a very long way it will not be rejoining me. I stand . . . where it stood in 1970 on all the major issues. It has got to get back there, and when it gets back there, bless my soul, there will be our old friend Enoch on the shore to welcome them.' 'It must return to the rock from whence it was hewn',[16] he said to another audience. He took every opportunity to tell Conservatives to their faces how their principles had been 'desecrated'. The party of One Nation had produced class conflict more bitter than the thirties by blaming the unionised workers for inflation. It had promised Scotland an elected legislature incompatible with the parliamentary union (of 1707) with England, and had treated Ulster with contempt. On immigration, they should have been the first to voice the fears of those (Cyril Osborne?) who saw the population of British cities being transformed. 'Instead, they drove into exile anyone who dared to speak of the future of their own people' and made it clear that 'only the language of wishy-washy liberalism and the policies of the race relations industry were to be tolerated by the Conservative Party'.[17]

Yet Mrs Thatcher had apparently taken to heart Powell's words about the need for conservatism to be identified with the national institutions. She privately accepted much of Powell's critique of the Heath interventionist policy; she extolled private initiative; she was soon being stigmatised by the left as a reactionary like unto Powell. She was firm on law and order. She was never a convinced Marketeer, though she accepted, a condition of leadership, the European commitment; she left the referendum campaign largely and probably thankfully to Heath (when it began there was no certainty that Heath would have a triumph). Powell commended this particular stance. 'There is no point in the new Conservative leadership spiking itself on the commitments of the former discredited leadership' he noted during the campaign.

In a sense, Margaret Thatcher was elected leader as a substitute Powell. Her general position seemed to bring them politically nearer than at any time since the 'olive branch' speech of May.[18] Nevertheless there was no rapport, indeed the reverse; a magnetic repulsion. Mrs Thatcher wanted the inventor of powellism at arms' length. His unrepentant, unremitting campaign on immigration, regardless of the establishment, was one excuse; but his disloyal record was a better one: he was disruptive, difficult, above all 'rigid'; this was the line on Powell. Powell's supporters were disappointed, and those outside the inner circle were sufficiently misled to speculate that a reconciliation was still possible. Powell himself said time was the healer; the Tories would someday return to form. The question was when.

He certainly did not encourage hopes that the healing process could be quick. On the contrary, 'time and suffering are needed for forgiveness which follows repentance.'[19] He excluded nobody from self-criticism. When, after the October election, he reflected upon the corruption of the Party under Heath, he included even those who had rebelled with him:

> There were some who tried to salvage their position by self-contradiction. They spoke out against wages and prices controls at elections at which the Conservative Party was fighting to secure endorsement of them. They spoke out against the EEC at elections where a Conservative victory would have . . . ensured Britain's continued membership on existing terms. They told the electorate their firmly held and widely publicised belief regarding what was right in the nation's interest, and at the same time by their very candidature [in February] they did all in their power to prevent it. Why? Because without the party label . . . they would not have been elected. They wanted a seat in Parliament so badly that the price of acting against their own most cherished opinions appeared not too high to pay for it.[20]

However effective the point, they could not relish being told that they had not drunk of the cup Powell had drunk of. Indeed, he slightly softened these asperities in a speech in September the following year: they had acted as they did because 'the only alternative to the self-contradiction which they accepted, and of which the more sensitive will carry the scars as long as they live, was the end of their political life – something which can be contemplated with more equanimity at sixty-one than at fifty-one or forty-one or thirty-one. For that reason among others I point no finger and imply no judgement.'[21] He readily conceded that he had been lucky to survive politically, and they might not have been. It showed that the more crucial an issue is to the life not just of a government but of the nation, 'the more cruelly is the possibility of public dissent from those inside a political party eliminated.' But Powell was determined to diagnose the sickness of the party and could not spare the Biffens and Frasers. Further, he was continually being badgered to explain his action in February 1974 as if he had never set out his reasons for sacrifices in a cause 'for which better men than I am would not have hesitated to leave behind them much more than a parliamentary seat,' as he put it to an audience in the course of the Referendum campaign. A year later, on further reflection, he reminded a Conservative audience that the entire press had reported prominently his statement in 1973 that he had identified the EEC as one of those supreme questions over which, like Joseph Chamberlain over Home Rule for Ireland, politicians not merely quit, but actually destroy the parties they were reared in.[22]

3   Educating Callaghan and Healey

As Callaghan encourged the impression in 1974–5 that he was negotiating toughly, Powell hopefully referred to the Labour Party as superseding the Conservatives in patriotism and in defence of British institutions and liberty. The referendum seemed to promise to overthrow Heath's handiwork, and Labour, who Powell said had 'an understanding of the genesis of inflation', might yet be educated in economics: which meant in the futility of the much-prized and electorally-invaluable 'social contract'. But however favourable might be his references to Labour on these points, his continued playing of the immigration numbers game kept him in the moral leper category (the Chamber always filled up when he rose to speak, as he provided such wonderful cues for deliciously self-righteous indignation by Members on both sides).

He had not been back in the House four months before he was challenging everybody's statistics once more by the calculation that in 1975 there must be a population of at least 1,100,000 actual immigrants and 750,000 children, or first generation immigrants, increasing at 50,000 a year; the total of 1,850,000 made no allowance for the second generation of children 'born to the children of immigrants and which could no longer be identified in the school population because Mrs Thatcher, when Minister of Education, had discontinued the counting; thus the all-black school with not a single immigrant on the school roll was becoming technically possible. Having again stated that these statistics confirmed all his earlier forecasts of cities one-third coloured, he asked again remorselessly what sort of England that inevitable future implied: 'it will be an England rent by strife, by violence and by division on a scale for which we have no parallel here.'[23] He based this prophecy simply on the observed way in which 'men react, always have reacted, and I believe always will react to the stresses when sharply differentiated populations share the occupation of a limited territory.' This was hotly denied; and examples like Cyprus were dismissed as totally irrelevant to Britain, particularly under the much stiffer laws against racialism which the Government proposed to introduce as a prophylactic measure. Powell advised them not to:

> The attempt to reduce these stresses by creating new rights and obligations hitherto unknown has the opposite effect, because these are seen by one section as signs that it is feared by the other section, and so become weapons in the struggle for supremacy. There follows an inevitable escalation, as the failure of these methods to pacify is taken to demonstrate not that they are futile but that they must be redoubled. The outside world also makes its contribution to the tension by taking sides . . . The balance of numbers is in effect neutralised by the majority being thrown psychologically and emotionally on to the defensive . . .[24]

He asked again for a true count, a real census, and suggested that if the Race Relations Board could fine a publican for discriminating against the 'lightly coloured' it must be a practicability. He was told that no such census was needed; his facts were wrong, so his deductions were wrong, all that was needed was more race relations legislation. (But the 1981 Census may take his advice.)

In April 1975 he reviewed Healey's contribution to the inflation so expertly fuelled by Barber (who had retired from politics to run a bank). His diagnosis was that public expenditure was being underpinned by borrowings from the oil-producing countries far in excess of British earnings. Borrowing enabled the Treasury to sustain an overvalued pound sterling with less local manufacture of money. This would reduce inflation in time, producing transitional unemployment – which he predicted would rise and prove hard to bring down until the ultimate structural readjustments of the economy had taken place. He saw no future in propping up mismanaged industries in the Heathian way: to finance Leyland by putting public money where private money would not go because it would be lost was simply to propound that no profitable use existed for a million men released from unprofitable undertakings. If so, he asked, how did people imagine that the rest of the workforce obtained employment doing things 'not even imagined ten or twenty years ago?' Leyland was, and would remain, bankrupt.[25]

Powell saw no rescue from North Sea oil, for all that it is a national asset (though only in economically favourable conditions). He saw it as a natural reaction to the multiplication of the cost of oil by the OPEC cartel: that is, more production – an example of his dictum that the world is an oil-filled sponge, extractable in terms of price. But it was high-priced oil, just as cartelised Arab oil was; its use pushed up the price of substitutes, and of everything into which energy entered, so that costlier oil meant less of other things. Its control gave Britain a vested interest in keeping up the cartel price – and limiting competitive expansion that would bring prices down again. Hence North Sea oil would not reduce British costs generally; the position was the same as if it had been imported at the same price; worse, if imported oil became available more cheaply. Powell at one stage (when lower oil prices were much discussed) thought Scotland might be cursed by the oil that the SNP wished to hog for themselves. The dreams of oil bonanzas Powell reduced to a picture of Britain like 'a tramp wrapped in a newspaper snoozing happily in a maudlin dream of the fortune he will wake up to find he has inherited from a distant relation'.[26]

What mattered, he considered, was the effect it had on the flow of payments. In 1975 Britain was using the surplus money of the oil producers lent at high interest rates to sustain a standard of living not earned by ordinary trading; meanwhile accumulating debts had to be repaid. Should the tap be turned off, Healey would have to print money to pay the state's bills, with renewed inflationary results. Thus the pound was held at a higher exchange rate than Britain's real economic performance justified; Powell would have preferred it to stand at its true level. When the oil revenues came in, they ought to be used to pay back the huge debts incurred – not to reduce taxation or otherwise purchase for Britain a higher standard of living than its sales and services to foreigners warranted. In oil, whatever its advantages, there was no implication that Britain was substantially richer, and needed to earn less in other ways to pay for imports.

4   Digging In After the Yes Vote

By spring 1975, Powell had to digest the unwelcome reality that Callaghan had carried through no 'fundamental' renegotiation; he suggested that the Foreign Secretary had somehow succumbed to the 'mephitic' influence of a pro-Europe Foreign Office. The opinion polls began to record that under pressure of unemployment, stagnation, inflation, gloom and a sense of crisis and failure ('the sheer disenchantment of being British' as he told an Ulster audience) the public were moving from No to Yes in the approaching referendum – the rubber life raft that Callaghan had prepared to save Labour from disintegrating as a party. The Party was enabled to campaign against the Government, only to be silenced by the electorate's Yes, with faces saved all round.

It was hardly for such operations – a Cabinet calmly and publicly divided, with the doctrine of collective responsibility put on ice for four weeks – that Powell had urged the country to vote Labour; nor did it in any way add to the Community disarray on which he had been able to make his 'olive branch' speech. The two-to-one vote was duly proclaimed as the missing 'full-hearted consent'. Powell could only fall back on the sovereignty of Parliament that could undo even referendums (see p. 166).

Still, it was hardly invigorating. Labour ministers like Castle and Shore resumed cabinet solidarity; Mr Benn resumed radical stances in departmental harness. The commentators saw Powell as the greatest loser – even Ulster had recorded a majority for Europe. It was reduction of the issue to a personal power game that was typical of national cynicism. He could only assume the role of that Varro who refused to despair of the republic after losing an entire army. It was, he said, September '38, not September '39; there was still time to defeat the machinations of the Foreign Office, working like a spider to tie up the nation in the Brussels web; he called the FO officials 'near-treasonable' too.[27]

But in the autumn of 1975 his energies had to be partly deflected to the demolition of the Ulster Constitutional Convention (see p. 212). There was a move to make the Convention, in which Faulkner and others were falling for the snare of a devolved but power-sharing executive, into a negotiating body. He warned that this was contrary to its mandate, denounced the Chairman (Sir Robert Lowry) for countenancing the change, and carried the day by explaining that to participate in the Convention as a negotiating body would saddle the loyalists with the guilt for IRA terrorism. Fitt grimly admitted that his logic won. The Convention dissolved.

By the end of the year he was back fighting on the EEC front. A new threat to the nation-state, which he insisted was still the underlying reality, had developed in place of 'economic and monetary union by 1980'. Callaghan promised his EEC colleagues to bring in legislation to send British representatives along with those of the other eight, to an elected European assembly by 1978. This seemed to Europeanists the logical retort to those who complained that the Community was run by a monumentally complex, insensitive, overprivileged and unsupervised bureaucracy; it would convert the centralised superstate into a federal democracy 'accountable' to the public.

Powell found such reasoning disingenuous. Such a 'parliament' would provide no better brake on officialdom than the French assembly did. Its real object was to give recognition and potential for growth to the superstate by adding to it the authority of a European electorate. The consequences would be disastrous for the sovereignty that still resided, a two-handed engine at the door, in Westminster.

> It will no longer be possible to pretend that Britain has not ceased to be a nation and Parliament to be a sovereign assembly. The debate about a federal Europe or political union has descended suddenly from the clouds . . . if there are direct elections debate about a federal Europe is over before it has begun; for in a federation at least the component states possess some entrenched rights and powers, whereas the Treaty of Rome knows nothing of all that. Once its parliament is directly elected, the Treaty is the foundation charter of a unitary state.[28]

He wished to dispose in advance of airy assumptions that the national vetoes and controls which existed while the new state was in the making would persist in a federal form as states' rights (in the American phrase). The sixty-seven British deputies to Strasbourg (it was later set at eighty-one)

> will derive their authority from the same electorate and by the same process as Members of Parliament derive theirs. It will soon be perceived that whatever they decide or approve along with the directly elected members representing the rest of the inhabitants of the Community can no more be reviewed or overturned by the British House of Commons than the Worcestershire County Council can reject an Act of Parliament. There will be an end to the fiction that British ministers in the council of ministers will have to take their orders from the House of Commons or accept its censure. They will say to the House of Commons thereafter 'What we have done has already been approved under the constitution of the Community (which Britain has accepted) by the representatives of the British people, directly elected and sent precisely for that purpose, being duly authorised thereto by the electorate from the very fact of their being elected. Who are you, and what is your authority to interfere, you minnows of Westminster? Did you not yourselves authorise, back in 1972, the supremacy of the Community and its laws over your own assembly and its laws? Be off with you and mind what little business we are good enough to leave for you to do . . . We take no orders from you . . . we take them from the representatives of the whole people of the Community.'[29]

An opposite but not less intimidating peril to the nation-state emerged at the same time in the plans for devolution which took shape in 1976. After its losses to the Scottish National Party in February 1974, the Labour Party put a vague commitment to some form of devolution of government to the Scots and the Welsh in its October manifesto; and once the EEC issue was out of the way, the Party managers decided, despite divergencies among Scots Labour MPs, that this pledge had to be redeemed lest separatism grew and the Labour Party was destroyed in Scotland. Entered into for such party reasons without thought of the constitutional difficulties, the commitment presented Wilson with embarrassing problems when it came to producing a coherent scheme. Powell at once staked out the arguments with which he (and others) were to attack it when it became specific.

Basically these were the same arguments that he had deployed against an elective House of Lords in 1968 and that he was currently using against direct election to a European parliament: it was not possible for the same electorate to be represented directly and in the same way in two representative bodies politic, without there resulting a conflict between them for supremacy. Either one would defeat and subordinate the other – even if after a long struggle – or else their respective sovereignties had to be delimited in a constitutional instrument or treaty. In the latter case the once-unitary state became federal, and the terms of the allocation of sovereign functions to the respective assemblies were adjudicated when they seemed to clash by a supreme court (as in the United States or Canada).

But such arrangements would end the unique British institution of the Crown-in-Parliament as the 'essential unifying element in the realm'. British history could only be understood in relation to this principle. He told the House of Commons in January[30] that it was incredible that a course of constitutional action should be set in train 'which must lead either to the conversion of the country to something totally different . . . or the destruction . . . of this realm . . .'. He served notice that he would fight it, whether the invading sovereignty were to be seen from the inside (devolved assemblies) or from the outside (an elective Community assembly). He declared that his opposition was based on the constitutional 'conviction in which I have lived, . . . for the sake of which I tore and destroyed the links of my whole political life. It is a conviction from which I will not depart.'[31] He told his Ulster audiences that the debate about devolution was about the existence of the United Kingdom, the sovereignty to which they wished to belong. Powell's effort to educate them to oppose for Scotland what they, or most of them, hankered after for Ulster, began.

A note of pessimism, however, began to sound in some of Powell's speeches in 1976. It perhaps sprang from the Yes vote; the failure of the people to understand the key issue, their readiness to be led astray by promises of material gain, or warnings of the economic loss which they would draw down on themselves if they did not follow the advice of the 'responsible' people. After 1975 he rarely if ever spoke of the innate commonsense and clarity of vision of simple people. In explaining the significance of direct elections in February he ended his speech with the words 'I do not know whether Britain is still a nation. That is something which a people can only prove by the way they act.'

> So far the omens have been unhopeful. The people of Britain, not just passively but with apparent relish, have relaxed and enjoyed the rape of their national and parliamentary independence to a point where already they are told they cannot recall it. Perhaps they did not know what was being done to them . . . but before many months are out there will no longer be any room for . . . misunderstanding. If the British people . . . consent to take away the exclusive representation of themselves from Parliament and confer it upon a British contingent in the assembly of a European state . . . this generation will . . . have foresworn the independence and nationhood of Britain.[32]

In March he returned to the inner loss of conviction in self and institutions: 'whether such a loss is temporary or permanent, an episode or an irreversible event, we from inside history can neither predict nor determine. We can only, as I am endeavouring tonight, perceive and warn.'[33]

He asked particularly why Parliament, rather than the electorate, had lost its grip on reality. He found reasons in the administrative role that Heath as well as Wilson and the Socialists gave to it, so that to be an MP was more and more to be a careerist official rather than a 'unique distinction to be purchased if necessary with personal sacrifice.'

> There is the enormous growth of committees of all kinds, to a point where they not only conflict with one another's demands but are more and more normally expected to take priority over the chamber, where the diminution of true debate proceeds apace with such changes as the officially acknowledged obsolescence of the prohibition against reading speeches.[34]

He attacked the periodical increase of the MPs salaries. He opposed the award of such increases by MPs to themselves to be taken in the same parliament without reference to their constituents to query if they desired. (He never accepted such increases himself until an election intervened.) In July 1978 he debated this principle singlehanded against the entire House when it moved for large increases of salaries and expenses on the plea of rising living and professional costs and of comparability with foreign parliamentarians, especially with the proposed £20,000 a year for Euro-members. Powell demonstrated that the current salary of £4,782 had kept up with the rise in prices – which was Parliament's own doing – that had occurred since he himself became a Member in 1950 on £1,000 a year, a sum he had found adequate. Nor did he think that MPs needed full-time secretaries to meet an increased constituency correspondence since he had not found he needed one even after taking on a far larger constituency with more onerous responsibilities than he had in Wolverhampton; he objected to research facilities when the House of Commons library met all their needs; and he spurned comparisons with other parliaments or with the 'rate for the job' in any other profession. The other speakers insisted that they were harder worked and even in 1950 had not made ends meet, and some said that if Powell held them responsible for the inflation they could claim responsibility for the rise in standards since 1950, in which they were entitled to an equal share.[35] (They got the £6 a week under the pay guidelines.)

In June 1975 Powell refused to participate in the register of outside interests which had been instituted to meet the criticism that MPs were being financed by lobbies of all kinds, from trade unions to foreign governments, to eke out their resources. He considered that such a provision, affecting the legal qualifications of an MP, required an Act of Parliament to make it obligatory, and he objected that in principle it reflected on Members' honour, suggesting that they could be improperly influenced. Such a generalised accusation should not be possible: a Member was either clean or he was properly arraigned and expelled as happened to Stonehouse or induced to resign as in the case of Cordle. A register would reduce MPs' repute to the level of dubiety and corruptibility, lamentably to be seen spreading elsewhere through British men, institutions and standards.

The gloom and apprehension which hung over the country in the mid-seventies was generally thought by businessmen to be a matter of economic poor performance (though by philosophers to be spiritual); Powell was pragmatic: the trouble was political. 'It is the nation that is dying, it is dying politically – or

rather, perhaps, is committing suicide.' For a moment Nietzsche peeped out: 'it
has lost the will to live.' He told a Chamber of Commerce audience in July 1975:

> Wherever one looks, near or far, in small or great, one sees the same
> morphology: the nation is abdicating. Two-thirds of the nation confirmed at a
> referendum the embodiment of this country in the EEC . . . on the ground that
> it was no longer capable of being a nation-state . . . It is too easy to pretend
> that the electorate 'knew not what they did'. The fact remains that to be a
> nation self-governed and self-taxed, living under its own laws and accepting
> no external authority, meant nothing to the majority of them. What their
> fathers and their remote ancestors had lived and died for they waved aside
> with less than a perfunctory sigh . . . The mirror-image of external abdication
> is internal abdication. As we no longer believe in the independence of the
> nation we no longer believe in the unity of the nation. Parliament is to abdicate
> − 'devolve' is the in-word − its exclusive law-making authority to anti-
> parliaments established not for . . . efficiency but to satisfy the assertions of
> Wales and particularly of Scotland that they are nations. The centripetal
> power and attraction of a united nation, which once gave pride and prestige,
> has been replaced by contempt on the one side and on the other side by supine
> readiness to bargain away bits of national unity to arrive at the lowest
> common denominator . . .[36]

His audience of businessmen had no doubt voted Yes. He contrasted with this
picture of demoralisation Ulster, which had resisted terror and pressure in order
to belong to the nation so described. Finally he etched in the relevance of
immigration to the picture of national disintegration. He asked if in 1966 or 1956
it would have been possible to envisage the dismemberment of the country; or
even more, that

> we would set about replacing millions of the population . . . with a population
> obtained from Asia, Africa and the West Indies and that all politicians and
> parties would laud and magnify the achievement by describing the result as 'a
> multi-racial society'.[37]

These three self-destructive activities were aspects of the death of the nation.
Self-assertion had been drained away. France notwithstanding its membership of
the EEC remained a nation because it preserved self-assertion as its national
characteristic: 'France did what nobody else did, and nobody wished her to
do . . . *vive le Québec libre!*' He put the same thought in more powellian terms in
an article written for *The Times* on his return from Russia in June 1977: 'I have
seen a nation which in its past honours itself and its future. I wish I thought I had
returned to one.'

His despondency over the nation's zombie-like, sedated, condition did not
quite amount to despair. Through 1976 he nourished the hope that as the
majority within the Labour Party was still antipathetic to the EEC, forces were in
being that would yet pull Britain out; hence he surprised − even embarrassed −

Labour MPs by calling them patriotic. He hoped that the capture by the EEC of Britain's fishing resources, the spectacle of ministers failing to obtain what British interests required when they went to Brussels, would produce the public animus on which the Labour malcontents might take a stand. In June he organised an abstention of all UUUC Members in a vote of confidence which saved Callaghan from defeat. The Conservatives were baulked of their prey and raged: Powell told them that it was a unanimous decision of the party because Ulster had no interest in an early election and the overwhelming Tory victory indicated at that juncture by the opinion polls. He set Callaghan on the path that led, through the Lib-Lab pact, to a more stable period of government; and he did so at a time when on almost every other issue than the ember of revolt against the EEC he was at odds with the Labour benches.

5 From Powellism and Racism to Thatcherism

In 1976 Powell's regular statements about the rise in the immigrant and immigrant-descended population became such a scandal to the Labour benches that action was taken to silence him. When the inaccuracies and evasions of the Home Office finally elicited that in 1973 immigration was 86,000 net. Powell added it to estimates for natural increase and produced a corrected and cautionary figure for the growth of the coloured population of 140,000 in that particular year, and 'rapidly rising'.[38] Nobody could prove that year on year it was much less than 100,000, though year after year official spokesmen announced it was due to decline any year now.

In January 1976, he challenged the race relations organisations by declaring his impenitence for the Birmingham speech of 1968; and as the figures then given in outline were filled in, and as racial tension did boil over into sporadic if minor violence, he quoted that speech with assurance: 'what never occurred to me, even in my gloomiest forebodings, was that eight years later we should be heaping that funeral pyre not just at the same rate, but twice as fast.'[39] He continued to criticise the supersession of figures which showed the difference between arrivals and departures in any one year by the figures for permissions to settle issued in any year as a method of underestimation. Such a figure omitted illegal entry and over-extended stays, and he announced that the immigration officials had been privately advising him that large numbers granted temporary permits did in fact never leave again. Their superiors in the Home Office discouraged them from taking action. Powell commented:

> if a good conviction record is an asset for promotion in the police, a good refusal record is a black mark in the immigration service; for above them, somewhere above them, are the people whom the Home Secretary called 'those closely concerned' and whom the Prime Minister's famous phrase [in 1966 about Marxist shop-stewards] about a tightly knit group of politically motivated men would fit very nicely.[40]

He thought this group – speaking as one who had run a department – was large enough to keep information from their Minister and Under-Secretary.

Lyon, the minister of state concerned, however, wanted to relax the rules (and he could since the 1971 Act gave administrative discretion over admissions); he believed that all the dependants of people legally resident should be brought in, draining the small pool that remained, in the interests of good race relations. But Callaghan, when he formed his government, dropped Lyon; and it gradually became known that the administration of the Act was becoming considerably less relaxed. The police were reporting the muggings of elderly white residents in areas of West Indian settlement, and Powell himself underlined these disturbing signals, but Peter Hain and other liberals declared that such developments were caused by a materialist society inflicting 'multiple deprivation' on immigrants and their offspring, and called for tougher measures to ensure racial equality, whatever that was. The Government began preparing the necessary legislation by summer.[41]

With a new race relations bill in Parliament, on 24 May the House of Commons debated the changing demography of the country. Powell focused attention upon the debate by quoting in the House and releasing to the press the unpublished internal report made recently by a Home Office official, Mr Charles Hawley, after he had been sent to India to assess the waiting lists of dependants applying for entry. Lyon and his successors in the Home Office assessed this reservoir in 1975 at about 180,000,[42] which could be drained in two years. Hawley, on the contrary, reported that as fast as entry certificates were given, new applicants with apparently valid claims joined the queue, which at 50,000 to 70,000 showed no sign of diminishing. It was, he reported, common knowledge that suitable documents could be purchased in the areas whence the immigrants mainly came. The Indian joint family system and customs of arranged marriage combined with the British definition of dependant to give the greatest scope to keep up the flow: second and third wives were entitled, with their dependants; husbands, fiancées, teenage children, bogus children ferried over by 'wives' on identical sets of documents were well known: while the Labour government's decision to give women with British nationality the right to bring in fiancés, with full eligibility for British services, produced a situation in which 'marrying out but staying here could continue indefinitely' – and immigration became a consequence rather than a prime cause of the proliferation of the non-white minority.

The House was shocked at Powell for letting this cat out of the bag. Hawley was disowned and another official went out to make a different report; Whitelaw said of Powell 'he feels he has to shock this House, once he has shocked us we shall have to deal with the fear by inspiring confidence,' which in a typical speech he then tried to do. Jenkins had to disavow Lyon's reckoning that all obligations could be discharged in the lifetime of that parliament (i.e. by 1979 at latest): there were 66,000 passport-holders to come, and 250,000 dependants. (In

1978, demographers reckoned 300,000 still to come).[43] Such was the confusion over contradictory figures that MPs on both sides asked for a register of claims. Powell's comment that so far from emptying a finite pool we were trying to bail out the ocean was considered peculiarly un-called for, and he left the Chamber to screams of 'fascist'.

Asian leaders, surveying the headlines, urged upon Callaghan that to cite even official figures ought to be construed as deleterious to race relations under the new Act: Bonham Carter urged that Powell be pressed to denounce violence (which carried the implication that he advocated it); Mr Praful Patel said that if there were to be any change of policy (i.e. in immigration rules and procedure) Labour would lose the next election; Mr Dhani Prem said but for immigrant support in the last one 'Mr Callaghan would not be Prime Minister', thus neatly confirming Powell's analysis (p. 239) of the way in which immigrants' voting pressures would be used, as numbers built up, to squeeze fresh concessions and strengthen immigrants' privileges.[44] Powell was accused of being the cause of the Asian riot in Southall (following the murder of an Asian youth) at which the police were forced to use their discretion to release two men they had arrested for obstruction. There followed the riots which accompanied the Notting Hill West Indian carnival in which the police were again worsted.

The new Race Relations Bill, introduced in February 1976, came into force in April 1977. The major change that it made in the law, in Clause 70, was that the crime of fomenting racial hatred became no longer a question of motive and intention but of 'likely results'. This was the clause that it was widely hoped would silence Powell or bring him into court. Early in the new year he examined the effects of the new Act.[45]

He described the stages through which official attempts to suppress all discussion of immigration had gone, and asserted that this suppression was greater than the efforts made to silence those who in the 1930s warned of the dangers of Hitlerism – Churchill himself being denounced as a warmonger. The motive was identical: the eternal hope that if danger is not mentioned, it will go away. By making the danger unmentionable the resentment of politicians and public at being forced to face a prospect with 'no readily procurable happy ending' was assuaged. He again brought together the forces of a 'new nihilism' and the catastrophe in preparation for Britain: 'all round the world the same formula for rending societies apart is being prepared and applied, and there are those who are determined to see to it that Britain shall no longer be able to escape'.

But until the Act, there had been a bulwark against suppressing open debate upon immigration as a public danger: 'the necessity for those who aimed at suppression to prove evil intent on the part of their prospective victims'. In debating great public issues, strong feelings and fears would necessarily be touched in open debate. If, then, it became criminal to activate such fears, debate was rendered impossible – and not just on immigration.

It ought to be understood that, in the intention of the legal advisers of the Crown, this bulwark is now to be swept away. That was made clear by a recent exchange of published letters between the Attorney-General and myself regarding the effect of section 70 of the Race Relations Act, 1976. For a criminal offence under that section to be committed, two conditions must both be fulfilled. Speech or writing must be 'threatening, abusive or insulting'; and it must also be speech or writing by which, 'having regard to all the circumstances, hatred is likely to be stirred up against any racial group in Great Britain'.

Powell denied he had ever used threatening, abusive or insulting language, but Mr Sam Silkin had asserted that it was insulting to quote Lord Radcliffe's expression 'alien wedge', or to express the opinion that 'in the foreseeable numbers and circumstances, the New Commonwealth immigrant and immigrant-descended population in our cities is not likely to be able to live and work in harmony with the rest of the population'. (Powell had indeed put it rather more strongly.)

The Attorney-General has further asserted that in his view race hatred against coloured members of the community was likely to be stirred up by what I said. He added that he did not believe a court would find this was my intention. However, when Section 70 of the new Act comes into force, intention will become irrelevant. Thus it is clear that the Attorney-General believes the uttering or publishing of such speech or writing will thereafter be criminal, and that as Attorney-General he would expect to give his consent to prosecution of the speaker and the media which report the speech.[46]

Powell then restated precisely this view, and therefore presumably under the terms of the Act for the last time, of the strife that would occur unless 'heroic measures' were adopted 'operating with human nature as it is, not measures which purport to alter human nature' (as the Act purported to do); such measures would never be adopted 'if a prohibition is placed on rational and temperate free speech'.

In this restatement he used only two statistics, revised from his earlier ones and extending 'far into the twenty-first century': that in 1977, taken as the base the coloured population was over 2,000,000 (contrary to official estimates) and that it was increasing at 'nearly' (or 'over') 100,000 a year – i.e. would be 4,300,000 in 2000 and still growing. In such circumstances an unavoidable mechanism of violence would come into play. The indigenous population was diminishing relatively, so the proportion of coloured to white was growing faster – and therefore very much faster in the key areas where coloured settlement was concentrated. To this phenomenon had to be added a big enhancement of the potential influence of such numbers by an atmosphere and legal context which promoted the idea that the coloured population had rights which the indigenous people were guilty of withholding – and that Britain had become part of a world conflict in which whites oppressed blacks. In the narrowly balanced party politics of Britain, leaders – ever more extreme – would arise to exploit the balancing position; and 'those commanding a position of political leverage would be superhuman if they could refrain from pointing to the acts of terrorism and, while condemning them, declaring that further and faster concessions are the only means to prevent such acts being repeated on a wider scale'.[47] He applied once again the tactics of the IRA to a future coloured leadership in Britain: but the results would be deadlier than in Belfast because the 'uniform of colour' would polarise the communities more than differences of religion in Ireland: it would reinforce differentiation and segregation, and this in turn would prevent the assimilation which smaller numbers would make possible in an absorptive culture.

This was a considered restatement of 'the prospect of eventual conflict upon a scale which cannot adequately be described by any lesser term than civil war', as he had put it while the new Act was under discussion; he had then dealt with the argument that such predictions might be wrong: 'what nobody can seriously pretend is that on the basis of human history and contemporary experience such an outcome is improbable'. If it were even possible, then it was unarguably the duty of responsible leadership to discuss how to avoid the catastrophe. Silkin was urged to act on such statements as that

> Those who catch faint glimpses, in Birmingham or Notting Hill, of what others have dreaded for years, those who find themselves strangers and aliens in one familiar area after another . . . those who hear from others' lips with diminishing incredulity the circumstances in which less fortunate fellow-citizens live, should repeat to themselves over and over again one single sentence, sad, simple and true: 'You have seen nothing yet'.[48]

Action against Powell by Mr Silkin would have had to be under the old Act, and the Attorney-General held back: wisely in view of the failure of a subsequent prosecution under it.

But the challenge to the Act was not to come from Powell – but from Mrs Thatcher, who in January 1978[49] started a tremendous outcry by saying, in reply to a television question during a meet-the-people tour, that people were feeling 'rather swamped' by immigrants and that it was Conservative policy to halt it, partly by instituting a register of dependants which newcomers intended to bring in. The opinion polls recorded an immediate gain in Conservative support. Labour ministers protested vehemently that this was irresponsible politicking because the inlet tap was already screwed down as tight as possible without breaking pledges to dependants and fiancés; Mrs Thatcher's ideas would hardly affect the already falling inflow and were racist to boot. Some of Mrs Thatcher's aides, studying what was increasingly called 'the ethnic vote' in the marginal constituencies, agreed; and so did Edward Heath.

Above all Powell himself agreed – on the practicalities, while applauding the belated concern for people feeling 'rather swamped'. He again tried to move the discussion from the conditions of 1968 to the facts of 1978. He described the talk of going back on pledges as humbug – every immigration Act had withdrawn previously existing nationality 'rights'. Powell agreed with Heath that 'when a person has been given permanent residence . . . it is impossible to refuse him the right to be joined there by his wife and dependent children or indeed by other genuine close dependants'. It was the process of staying here but marrying out, the established natural increase in the alien settlement, which guaranteed the size of the coloured population at Mrs Thatcher's estimate of four million by the end of the century. Even the withdrawal of the new right to bring in male fiancés, which Powell dismissed as absurd under law and natural usage from time immemorial – a sop to sex egalitarianism which he had already disposed of as a nonsensical concept – would still leave immigration 'open-ended'. He claimed that even under the new category of 'accepted for settlement' immigration had averaged 42,000 between 1973 and 1977 and was 50,000 in 1977, the same as in 1968, ten years and several Acts of Parliament later. (Subsequently the Census Office, worrying how to get people to provide reliable information of their race or origin in the next census, estimated the immigration in 1977 as only 33,000 and the natural increase at only 42,000, projecting a coloured population of only 3,400,000 at end-century.)[50] Powell's previous deduction was unchanged:

> So I repeat: it is the cruellest folly or deception to induce the people of this country who are – I quote Mrs Thatcher's words – 'frightened because a minority threatens to become a big one', to imagine that anyone can hold out (I quote again, this time from Mr Whitelaw) 'the clear prospect of an end to immigration', unless it is also the intention to secure that the New Commonwealth population not merely ceases to grow but is actually reduced by positive outflow. Those who flinch from facing that reality had better hold their peace.[51]

And they all flinched, except Powell. He returned consistently to it – 'call it repatriation, call it resettlement, call it assistance for returning home, call it what you please' – but always as voluntary and taxpayer-financed, and, he came to add, 'claiming the consent and cooperation of the New Commonwealth population itself and of countries to which they belong by origin, by sentiment and still preponderantly by legal citizenship'.[52] In April 1978 he had suggested that the payment of accrued National Insurance benefit should be offered as part of an inducement to emigrate, while firms employing much immigrant or immigrant-descended labour should set up factories in their homelands to employ them there, even competitively with the British firm. There was no response from politicians or from the leaders of the coloured communities who, after all, could on Powell's analysis see a very good time coming for them.

And indeed when in July Whitelaw engineered the Tory retreat from the dependants' registers after his visit to India, Powell could see the proof of his prediction that the minorities would be able to exert pressure, using the 'cynical opportunism' of vote-seekers like Whitelaw, upon the narrowly balanced major parties to improve their peoples' position, prospects and even privileges. The President of the Confederation of Indian Organisations not only rejected the register as racist and discriminatory, but also opposed any restriction on male fiancés as breaching the Hindu system of caste and arranged marriages, which was a matter of religious toleration.

6 Scotland and Wales

In November 1976 Powell, in a speech he was barred from making to a meeting of Young Conservatives, declared that there was nothing in the interests of the United Kingdom, or of those of Ulster within it, his special concern, to require the replacement of the Labour by a Conservative administration, notwithstanding the Government's heavy losses in by-elections. To the reproach that he, a Tory, was keeping Socialists in office, he replied, in words very different from those of the sixties, 'the great issue of our time is not in my opinion another instalment of the secular debate between Socialism and Capitalism'.[53] In the country's dismal economic and financial servitude he found on balance Healey's (unconfessed) monetarist methods the more hopeful.

The issue was 'the matter of Britain,' as it might be called – the servitude to the EEC, the hollowing out of the cities by coloured settlement, the threat to the kingdom's unity by the Scotland and Wales devolution bills. Callaghan was delaying the direct elections legislation in deference to the misgivings of his own rank and file; on immigration he was at least ensuring that the 1971 Act was tightly administered (otherwise there was nothing to choose between the acceptance by both parties of multi-racialism); while on devolution he saw a good prospect of defeating the government without denying it 'the means and authority to govern.'[54]

The Scotland and Wales Bill passed its second reading in November, but Powell could see that the House was as unhappy about it as it had been over the Parliament No. 2 Bill in 1968, and it might well be destroyed in committee. In his speech on the second reading he prepared for that stage by bringing out the inconsistencies in the measure: first pointing out that the basic idea of bringing government closer to the people was not exemplified in the bill, since that requisite was a matter of administration, and neither Wales nor Scotland were administrative areas. The bill was about nationalism, as the Prime Minister had said, and Powell attacked the verbal recognition of Scotland and Wales as nations in a measure that did no such thing, since it gave to the two assemblies the power to legislate but not to tax – a power even Edinburgh district council had.[55] Power devolved was power retained, he had always said, and the abolition of Stormont showed it. 'That retention [of power]' he told a Glamorgan audience in May 1974, 'is the very reason that makes devolution acceptable . . . There is nothing intermediate between belonging to a particular political unit, and not belonging.'[56] As time went on, Government spokesmen talked less about Scots nationalism and more about 'bringing government close to the people'.

In the service of destroying the bill, Powell found his status as an Ulster Member, and his knowledge of Irish parliamentary and constitutional history, invaluable. As he was to sum it up in a speech in Committee: 'the case of Northern Ireland proves to be a dialectical means whereby we can clarify the nature and inherent contradictions of what is attempted in the bill.' He had just completed his biography of Joseph Chamberlain, which clarified the events that led in 1922 to the peculiar Ulster type of devolution: the history of Ireland and Britain from the 1860s established 'by constant experiment' that one cannot give the power to legislate to a component part of a unitary state. Proved 'to destruction' in debates from the mid-nineteenth century, such a plan broke down invariably on the permutations of the 'in-and-out' arguments now applicable to the bill – 'how a Scotland which has power of legislation in its own Parliament or Assembly would be represented in this House.' If the Scottish UK members had the vote on all subjects they would decide issues in England which English members were debarred from discussing for Scotland; if they absented themselves on English questions, they could find themselves supporting a government in the United Kingdom which had lost its majority to carry purely English measures in the largest part of the unitary state. In practice, the whips would inevitably try to bring the Scots votes into English measures to get Government policy through: it was an impossible situation.

> The hour of ten o'clock comes and the Government needs to get the Suspension. Do we take it that the Scottish Members will not vote on the Suspension? Will they not vote on Closures? Will they not vote on anything that is necessary to enable any Government to get any of their business, to remain in control of the affairs of this House?

Northern Ireland was, as Powell and Molyneaux demonstrated, the exception that proved the rule. No such 'in-and-out rule' applied to the Ulster Members, who voted Conservative and between 1951 and 1955 sustained a narrow Conservative majority; but Ulster's contribution to that majority was never more than six or seven net.

> It was a *de minimis*, and there was indeed a kind of unspoken compact. This House, disastrously for Northern Ireland, I believe . . . made a compact to ignore the affairs of Northern Ireland . . . It seemed worthwhile having six Members added to the Conservative strength in the House in return for not having to bother about Northern Ireland for those fifty years. We should not take any comfort from this minimal exception to the rule, which was tolerated for reasons well understood; whether it would be tolerated again, even at that low intensity, I am not sure.[57]

In short: an anomaly however small could not be deliberately reinstated.

The difficulty was met by a federal system. Put forward in 1893 for the whole empire, it could not be resuscitated simply because 'we do not want it. The House and the vast majority of people behind members are not prepared to consider the notion of resolving ourselves into a federal state.'[58] That was that (see p. 232).

Powell's own solution – the federal one dismissed without discussion – was disarmingly simple: do nothing. The existing single Parliament made different laws for the different regions perfectly well. Of the demands of the SNP and Plaid Cymru he said 'Apply the Irish precedent':

> A nation is a people who have made good the right to be a nation – not necessarily by force but, according to our institutions, by proving overwhelmingly that they are not content to remain part of another state, in our case the kingdom as it is at present constituted. That was how the Irish proved over and over again in the nineteenth century . . . that they were a nation. They sent 70, 80 or 90 men to parliament who came here and said 'we are sent here to say we do not belong'.[59]

When the Scots did as much they must go their own way – but the bill perverted the processes by which they could come to a true decision. In Committee the support for the bill began to seep away as it had for the Lords bill. Powell made five major interventions to expedite the parliamentary educational process. He exposed the absurdity of having a legislative assembly for the Scots nation, a consultative one for the Welsh (had Ulster been treated like Wales, he said, he would have made a covenant with himself).

> The people of Wales have been told that they are a nation and that because they are a nation they are going to have devolved government . . . Would they not happen to notice the difference between what was proposed for them and what was proposed for the other nation? . . . There cannot be grades of nations: primary-legislation nations and secondary-legislation nations. What sort of Welshman is it who, going abroad, would be prepared to say 'I belong to a secondary-legislation nation'?[60]

The amendment to designate the Scottish assembly as a 'parliament' stumbled over the difference between a body with, or without, a degree of sovereignty: an assembly could be a local government body with delegated powers from Westminster, but a parliament implied that the sovereign was involved – as the Crown had been part of the Ulster Parliament (as it is of the New South Wales Parliament). Once the Crown is involved the 'sovereignties have to be separated – or else they imply independent states, a return to the status of the Scottish Parliament before 1707 when the sole link between two kingdoms was the Crown.' This dilemma was further exposed when Powell dealt with the nature of the executive or 'cabinet'. Local authorities had a fixed life, but if a Scottish executive lost its majority, how did it get a dissolution? If not from the Crown, but from Westminster it emerged as subordinate to Westminster. He showed the impossibilities of any arrangement for the seventy-one Scottish members at Westminster to vote only on Scottish matters ('in') and abstain on English matters ('out'), notably because finance involved inextricably English and

Scottish issues and interests. He objected to the referendum designed to pass the final decision to the Scots people to take or leave the hotch-potch offered them – for it was a constitutional change for the whole kingdom, and the issue should be put before the whole electorate.

The sheer impossibilities of the bill seeped through and by 22 February 1977 the Government failed to win the motion for the guillotine. For, as Powell said,

> The result of a guillotine will be that we shall pass into law legislation of which we cannot explain the working, legislation which, as far as anyoner in this House can foresee . . . must be a constitutional shambles, legislation which, so far as anything goes which has yet been said in Committee, will result in setting the different parts of the kingdom not into greater unity but at each other's throats.[61]

The bill was withdrawn, and Powell had seen the arguments that had been steam-rollered in the Communities Bill of 1972 triumph over the devolution bill. But it was a short-lived triumph. After the Lib-Lab pact came into operation, the effort to achieve almost exactly the same forms of devolution was resumed in the new separate bills for Wales and Scotland, little changed in substance for all the demonstration of unworkability.

But now the Labour members who had fought the previous single bill had become convinced that Labour, after all, could win the election if Callaghan could hold on long enough; he must not be defeated by his own side on the 1974 pledges. Accordingly the majorities not only for Welsh and Scottish devolution but also for direct elections to the European Assembly proved forthcoming. Some face-saving concessions were indeed forced upon the Government with the help of Labour doubters, notably the 'Cunningham Clause' that the advisory referendums must produce a minimum of a 40 per cent affirmative vote of the registered electorate, which effectively meant that to get a 51 per cent majority, something like 60–65 per cent of those normally voting would have to vote yes. The odds against a majority were thus increased – unless the turnout was quite exceptionally high. In the Direct Elections Bill some safeguards to prevent the concession of wider legislative powers to the Assembly were inserted as the result of Powell's warnings; those who scoffed in 1972 began to fear for Westminster's power and a few recanted their vote for membership.

Powell resisted every inch of the way. Both on the devolution bills and on direct elections he appealed to Michael Foot, the leader of the House, to be guided by the precedent of the Lords Bill of 1968, and

> to allow the House of Commons to use its procedure in committee unconstrained, at least at first, so as to see if we can resolve the contradictions with which all Hon Members know that these bills, and therefore they themselves, are beset, and therefore avoid saddling those whom we represent with consequences for which otherwise they will curse us.[62]

This appeal, described by other Members as moving, was in vain; and so was a speech, acclaimed for its power, which appealed to Foot not to force through the direct elections bill by the same guillotine method:

> a [guillotine] motion which with almost indecent haste will ensure that that measure which he detests is fastened upon the statute book, and that that change in our constitution, the danger of which we have learnt from him as much as from anybody, is fastened upon this country.[63]

Foot closed his ears to Powell's eloquence and to their shared past a second time. Powell asked if the third reading of the bill for direct elections to the European Assembly was 'a requiem to the proud, sovereign, independent House of Commons.' He doubted it could enforce the limits set in the bill to the Community's dynamism, which provided a way out for other Members' consciences, and in words that echoed so many of his forebodings, pronounced that

> the very nature of direct elections is that it gives . . . an authority. . . . Those who in future propose these advances will be able to turn round to this House . . . and say 'what then did you think you were doing when you passed a bill to institute direct elections? You, of all people, ought to have known what an elected Assembly is about and what its claims are. When you set up another one, you must have intended the natural consequences of your actions . . .'. The assertion was made that the Assembly could gain only such powers as were ceded to it by the Council of Ministers. I am sure that that is so, technically. Likewise this House of Commons has no powers except such as have been ceded to it by the Crown, but they are our powers now . . . we have taken them because we spoke for the people. . . . We took them by convention, by encroachment, by usage, by practices that could not be gainsaid as they grew up.[64]

Against this process the checks and controls they had devised on either the European legislature or executive would, he added, prove weak. 'When the electorate of this country has chosen its own representatives in a European Economic Community context to serve on their behalf in the Assembly of the Community it will become more and more unrealistic for this chamber to claim to control the legislation which the EEC makes or the policy it adopts.' But the House professed to find his forebodings and historical parallels as exaggerated as it had his predictions of the size of the coloured population, and the implications thereof.

7 Powellism in 1978

As the interval before another general election shortened Powell saw the Callaghan government, with Liberal help and approval, completing the work of the Heath administration. The direct elections and devolution bills conformed to Heath's view that the nation-state, and with it powellism, were obsolete; and the body of Labour Members on the left on whom he had relied to defeat them left him in the lurch for the prospect of continued office and power to press on with the socialist programme of the party executive committee. Powell's efforts and sacrifices since 1970 seemed to have availed little to stem the tide, except in Ulster.

Yet Powell's ideas were gaining some ground, and some of his predictions were seen to be coming true. Even his view of budgetary policy seemed to be sinking in as Healey put the control of inflation as his first objective and duly presided over the increase of unemployment which Powell had said had to be borne in consequence; what was howled down in 1973 proved tolerable, with suitable hand-wringing, in 1977–8. The promise of a national bonanza from North Sea oil helped Healey to sugar the pill, no doubt; but the limits to the benefits of the oil revenues became clearer in 1978, while statistics and reports accumulated to quantify the decline in the country's industrial performance under ever-increasing bureaucratic interference, supervision of prices, quality, conditions and business policy, and under sanctions of penal 'non-law' of the powellian kind (the government's black list of uncooperative firms bore out all his warnings of the sixties). The debilitation of capitalism, innovative enterprise and risk-taking beyond the power to recover, to which he had referred at the 1970 election, seemed very near by 1978. Powell never said this point had been reached, but significantly admitted that trade union Luddism might necessitate, *faute de mieux*, the adoption of protection, which would be more honest than begging the Japanese not to send cars: '. . . it will be better for our ego, though devoid of economic advantage, to slap a protective tariff on this or that class of beastly foreign articles so that we can enjoy our own dearer and inferior products.' This was the price of rejecting powellian economics – or at least the lessons of the German 'miracle'.

By 1978 the nation was beginning, Powell thought, to repent the referendum of 1975. Though the pledges to send elected representatives to the European Assembly (duly restyled Parliament) went through, the remit they would take seemed to be to limit rather than extend its powers. Jenkins and Heath in 1977 deplored British back-pedalling, in policy and in national mood. But that mood was generated by disappointments that the Marketeers found hard to explain away. The loss of British fishing resources to other EEC fishermen, the failure to expand into the EEC's market of 250,000,000 consumers, the growth of a deficit of £2 billion in trade with Europe, the losses to British farmers while food prices were ratcheted up – all fell out as Powell had feared in 1972. The hope was canvassed publicly that Britain might be rescued from its miscalculation by the expansion of the community to include Spain, Portugal and Greece, the accommodation of whose interests, almost as opposed to those of the orginal Six as were Britain's, might at least destroy the CAP and possibly reduce the organisation to little more than the free trade area which Powell originally found acceptable.

The possibility that Labour's performance might lead him to make peace with the Conservatives was periodically raised in the press, but the idea found no echo in his speeches. He did public rhetorical penance for advising voters to support the Conservatives in 1970: 'I can only . . . deserve to be forgiven . . . on one condition, namely that I do my utmost to ensure that the people of this country are never again deceived by the Conservative Party, or anybody else, as they were in 1970.' In 1977, in a 'clinical' speech to the Swansea East Conservative Association, he dissected the Party's self-betrayal, first indicated in his own rejection by its leadership in 1968:

> to represent a people is not only to speak for them in their sense of being a nation . . . It is also to speak for them in their fears as well as their hopes for the future . . . the tragedy of the Conservative Party is to have made itself incapable of voicing that great fear for the future which hangs ever more darkly over an ever-growing proportion of the nation, to the point where apprehension has passed for many into despair . . . Before their eyes their land is becoming a land of strangers, and no end to the process is in sight . . . a nation which could be unmoved before such a prospect would be giving the strongest evidence that it is a nation no longer . . . In its fear, as in its other great emotions, it must have voice, expression, representation . . . This representation the Conservative Party has calculatedly and systematically renounced during the last ten or fifteen years.[65]

It had done so by crushing those in the Party that might have spoken for England, 'for Britain's right to be a nation, . . . and for an industrial harmony not contrived by compulsion.'

In January 1978 he seemed to be giving the Party another chance. Speaking in the direct elections debate he asked,

> What sort of an opposition are they? They are involved in one of the greatest issues for not merely this House but for the country, yet they remain deliberately dumb, deliberately self-contradictory, and give no advice – but perhaps I am wrong – to their supporters behind them. Perhaps I am wrong: for it is rumoured that the word has been passed round 'You watch which way who goes'. What a splendid fashion to conduct opposition! If that is not sufficient guidance for Hon Members, they have been told, 'Well, of course, but you see, if there is an election in October and if' – this becomes decreasingly probable – 'a Conservative administration should be formed following that election' – [Hon Members 'Heaven forbid'] – Labour Members say Heaven forbid, but I hear that it is said, 'we should have to pass the bill if the Government do not do so . . . we might have to have the whole thing over again . . . Let them do the dirty work for us and then they will take the blame. In that way the bill will be on the Statute Book when we come into office.' I say to Her Majesty's Opposition, 'In God's name, give a lead. Whatever it is, give a lead. For only if you do so, will you earn the possibility of being asked by your fellow countrymen to lead them . . .'[66]

There was no such lead, on Europe or on immigration, but the EEC emerged as the leading issue for Powell as the year advanced. In May he told the House of Lords Committee on cooperation between United Kingdom parliamentarians and British members of the European Parliament that there could be no such cooperation, and that only conflict was to be anticipated, a duel in which only one parliament could survive; in the struggle Westminster's weapon was the ultimate right to legislate Britain out, but the European Parliament wielded growing authority by reason of its European mandate after direct elections. He told the Committee 'Any views I have to offer . . . have to be understood in the context of my unrelenting opposition to that repudiation of the nation as the supreme unit of political organisation which is implicit in UK membership of the EEC. To help to destroy, or radically modify, that membership is my principal object in the remainder of my political life.'[67]

Powell resolved his position and unveiled his tactics for the election on 3 June. He announced that he would advise the electorate to vote neither Conservative nor Labour as both parties had failed the nation: they were conspiring together against the majority of the nation which was opposed to membership. Powell thus renounced a cardinal principle of his political beliefs – that the party system would always provide a choice on decisive issues, and that voters had to vote a party into power as a government. Instead, and for the first time, he called on voters opposed to membership to vote against any candidate not committed to bring Britain out – and when there was no anti-EEC candidate, to abstain wholly from voting.

> The party system has broken in our hands. We will appeal above its head to the electoral system itself, the elector's right to vote for the candidate who offers what he, the elector, wants and to vote for no other. Those candidates, and only those candidates ought to receive our vote at the next general election who are individually committed . . . to do what we would do in their place, namely, to vote on all occasions and on all subjects in such a way as to terminate Britain's present membership of the Community. Whatever his other services and merits, no member who voted to drive that measure through under guillotine need come before us in the expectation that we will demean ourselves . . . by helping to return him: he will need recantation . . . If we believe that a man should put country before party when the two conflict . . . we shall use our vote and let it be seen and known that we shall use our vote, for that superior purpose and that alone . . .[68]

Powell reckoned that the committed anti-Marketeers constituted a voting pressure group that could have a decisive effect if it consistently acted in this sense. Such a group, of course, did not coincide with the powellite vote of 1970 or 1974, which was based largely on anti-immigration sentiments, though it certainly overlapped with the anti-Marketeers. The question was, however, whether this anti-Market feeling in 1978 or 1979 was as decisive – especially in marginal seats – as Powell thought; or, to put it more precisely, whether such an organisation as the Safeguard Britain Campaign, to whom he delivered his manifesto, could organise that group to put its anti-Market feelings above other deep-seated party or personal loyalties in the privacy of the polling booth, and to make clear in every constituency which candidates were to be voted against after forcing them to commit themselves. For, like Alice through the Looking-Glass, Powell had only said 'if'.

Chapter 13

The Powell Contribution

If Enoch Powell holds South Down in the 1979 elections he will have achieved an ambition in Great Britain as in Ulster. He will have demonstrated, against the tide of defeatism running through the country, that his campaign to keep Northern Ireland an integral part of the United Kingdom had the backing of a critically important electorate, divided almost half and half between Protestant and Catholic and stretching from the border to within ten miles of Belfast. He will have shown that a major and sustained contribution to supreme constitutional issues can be made from the Ulster bench at Westminster by an English-born representative with the approval and broad understanding of Ulster people. This will be a triumph for a cardinal principle of Powell's rationale of British nationhood, the more instructive perhaps because it will have been won from a frontier territory. Fortified by it he could carry on his rearguard fight against the disintegration of the British nation state under the encroachments of the European parliament, Scottish nationalism, the pressures of non-British and anti-British minorities in the English homeland, and the other developments which in his analysis destroy identity – the sense of 'being ourselves'.

If he is rejected, another count will be added to the superior verdict that he is a 'failed politician', a leader of lost causes who has lost his last cause. If becoming the leader of one's party is the criterion, most of the most eminent politicians fail. Some of the handful who get to the top of the pole face embarrassing verdicts from contemporary events even before history pronounces on their performances. Powell has studied more carefully than his critics the meaning of success and failure in politics. In his biography of Joseph Chamberlain he concluded 'all political lives, unless they are cut off in midstream at a happy juncture, end in failure, because that is the nature of politics and of human affairs.' He wrote of course of those who aspire to make or to change the nation's history; those who, for example, dedicate themselves to 'a revolution so quiet and yet so total that it will go far beyond the programmme for a parliament' in Mr Heath's words. Men with such plans for the nation always fail. Enoch Powell has 'legislated' in this wider sense also with policies – whether amounting to a revolution or a counter-revolution may be debated – to preserve the nation, to reform its abuses and restore its fortunes. In such an endeavour Cicero and Demosthenes also were failures; but history records the names of few of those who shouted them down from the back benches.

It may be said that having clear-cut, logically presented ('simplistic' to his critics) policies, in which he believes with the conviction of a John Bright, Powell has failed to manoeuvre himself into the one position from which he could apply and test them in action, rather than justify them against the progressive failure of his opponents' alternatives. Such a criticism resolves itself into one of tactical errors. In terms of political chronology it amounts to asserting that he ought to have served under Sir Alec Douglas-Home in 1963–4 so as not to leave the field so completely to Heath; that he should not thereafter have given Heath a golden excuse to eject him from the Shadow Cabinet in 1968; that having clung to the Heath bandwagon, he should then have got the thing ready and chosen the right moment to strike Heath down, possibly by splitting his party like Chamberlain or by waiting until the contradictions of Heath's 'revolution' boomeranged and delivered the leadership to Powell. By the same token, it would be delivery to a pseudo-Powell of a modified, homogenised, bowdlerised version of the Powell alternative. It would not have been Powell or powellism; it would fill neither halls nor books, a contradiction in terms. Such rewriting of history 'if it had happened otherwise' is a parlour game. There could not be a Powell like a Joseph or a Thatcher; nor would such a person have given the Conservatives their four years of power to use or misuse, and, when in his judgement they misused it, have taken it away again.

The principles and passion that made Powell a force in politics unmade his career as a man of office and power. That is exactly why he made his unique contribution to British political experience. 'Powellites', a group not easy to define but usually defined in derogatory terms, may have been disappointed, as people who make simple assessments of politics are. What is instructive is the esteem in which Powell continues to be widely held for his stand on principle (journalists have recorded how that reputation, still very high in the polls' popularity charts, is played down); from Ulster he remains a great figure in the national scene. And for a good reason. He is perceived to be not fully and completely a politician. As the years pass, and events increase the cynicism with which (to Powell's anxiety) British politicians are viewed by the public, his record stands out in sharper contrast. In some respects he might be described as an anti-politician: a politician inside-out, to politics what anti-matter is to physics. While conforming to the mathematics of politics, he showed up what politics is and is not; he posed the question whether a politician in modern democracies – 'the policy-administrative continuum' – can have principles beyond 'guidelines'. It was not politics to 'say it like it is' on immigration, the IRA, trade unionism, or patriotism; it was not politics to round on his own leadership when promises made at the polls were treated, once it was safely elected, as very loose approximations. It *was* politics that those who were convinced by him could not vote him the slightest personal power to take action. But this was his service.

Nobody else could have done it. It needed doing. His unpopularity in the circles where he is most waspishly derided speak to that.

It is most convenient to call him an enigma, unexplainable in ordinary political terms; and certainly nobody would call him transparent. Yet he has done all he can to make his political life and motives an open book to be read by the man on the Clapham omnibus. True, he expects every word to be read for its meaning because he thinks words are supremely important. He is factual and logical, not capricious or unpredictable. His reaction to political events can often be anticipated from his known principles. Thus nobody who had followed his consistent defence – and understood the reasons for that defence – of prescriptive British constitutional forms evolved through centuries, need have been surprised or put off when in December 1978 he had valid occasion (not out of caprice) to voice his view that for the Bill of Rights to be amended to permit the Sovereign to be married to a Catholic would endanger throne and nation. That view follows from his interpretation of the unity of secular and spiritual authority in Britain and of the unique parliamentary institution which brooks no sharing of power with any external authority whatever (and is already endangered by subscription to the Treaty of Rome). In a period of sloppy thinking, false emotionalism and 'permissiveness', when he considered Britain had lost its way, his demolition of humbug and assertion of fundamentals cleared a new path; he tried to set Britain's steps thereon. Is his success as a parliamentarian to be judged by the proof over time that he was right – over money supply, inflation, prices and incomes controls, for example – or merely by the mental and political resistance to his exposition?

Powell entered Parliament in 1950, and the changed estate of the nation in the past thirty years ought to be some yardstick whereby the ordinary voter and taxpayer is entitled to measure success or failure among Powell's contemporaries who have enjoyed so much more 'success'. How many of those who held office for long periods (or who, not favoured with office, trod the party line to the whips' admonitions) can be proud of the work to which they set their hands? How many, as they move up to the Lords or out to the Boards, murmur with Pitt, 'my country, how I leave my country'?

Their retort is that it is the country's fault. They take refuge in the historians' finding that Britain is 'ungrateful', rejecting men of vision like Chatham, Chamberlain, Cripps or Henderson – or Wilson or Heath – and discarding Churchill himself in 1945. 'She remains a free spirit, drifting, seemingly aimlessly' was one comment; a country that expected nothing from its leaders but survived them somehow. Certainly she used to survive them – but through no mystical spirit. Britain survived because the damage her leaders could do was limited, because decision-making was decentralised. When Burke despaired 'the cement is gone, the cohesion is loosened, and everything hastens to decay and dissolution', Britain was about to recover from the loss of her American colonies and her international position – but not because of William Pitt: because of James Watt and Adam Smith. Britain survived the incompetence of Victorian politicians, generals and officials because 20,000 businessmen were minding the nation's real business; progress outpaced the myopia of Oxford and Cambridge because hundreds of scientists and inventors were making the breakthroughs on their own premises.

It is different now, and Powell warned of the consequences and pinned the responsibility. 'We are at the beginning of a period in which a massive transfer of decisions from the citizens to the state is projected . . . a vast accretion of power and powers to central government', he said in 1965; as Powell satirised him, George Brown was the prototype of the British Inca setting dates for seedtime and harvest. It becomes ever harder to survive the concentration of decisions in 'a little group of fallible men working on projections drawn from the past by staffs of economists', 'a group of gentlemen variously described as the state, the Government or a public authority', 'the higher wisdom of a little group of men somewhere in the centre.' Over and over Powell insisted Britain's problems are 'politician-made'. Naturally he annoys the establishment and they do what they can to gang up on him. He has pointed out that North Sea oil, found, and then under a high-price regime made profitable, by private enterprise, never came into planning forecasts in 1963 or so; now the establishment homes in on this success story, which temporarily offsets the other massive economic failures in Britain that are, Powell incessantly says, 'politician-made'. The rise of Britain in the past was not 'politician-made'; its decline is. Powell has offered his remedy; but 'politician-made' inflation continues.

Patriotism, Powell said in 1967, could not coexist with the theories and attitude of socialism; he was referring to the reciprocal relation between free enterprise and a society shaped by consumer preference on the one hand and individual liberty confirmed by parliamentary institutions on the other. This combination was the secret of Britain's greatness, and its still unexhausted potentiality. Then he found that the attitude and theory of his own party had become equally inimical to it, and denounced this betrayal. In a small party fighting to belong to the disintegrating kingdom he found a patriotism that he could serve. This line is called romantic with the implication that it is unreal; yet Powell has defined patriotism in grassroots anthropological terms: having a *patria* to live for and die for, a motivation rooted in the territorial instinct, slow to outgrow (except perhaps by intellectuals) and plainly not outgrown by a scientific socialist society, the USSR.

Even now he denies that Britain is incapable of an effort of national will that could overthrow the fates. However, in the powellian prognosis the time for recovery is getting short, the 'conquest' of the nation marching on. There is for a patriot like Powell at this time something to take to heart in the icy words of Francesco Guicciardini, applied to the Italian states in the fifteenth century: 'all states, all kingdoms are mortal: everything comes to an end by accident or the course of nature. A citizen who witnesses the end of his country cannot feel so distressed at her misfortune with so much reason as he would lament his own ruin: his country has met the fate which in every way she was bound to meet: the misfortune was wholly for him whose ill-luck caused him to be born at a time when such a disaster had to occur.'

So long as he is in Parliament he can work against the fates, and those who supposed that translation to Ulster would make him an 'exhausted volcano' have had reason to revise that judgement between 1974 and 1979. He once told an interviewer 'one of the personal characteristics that makes political life tolerable or intolerable to a man is whether he lives happily or not in a state of utter insecurity or utter unforeseeability.' Powell possesses himself in that still centre of his mind; the end, like parliamentary sovereignty, is 'not quite yet'; the record and the verdict had better be left open. His political alternative remains relevant. This may be said by anyone who studies it: if it ever becomes in all respects manifestly academic and impracticable, those of Powell's countrymen who notice that disappearance from our political and moral options will bitterly rue the circumstances that make it so.

Notes

Chapter 1 The Crisis, 1974

1 Interview with Ludovic Kennedy on BBC Radio 4, 28 December 1975.
2 R. W. Johnson and Douglas E. Schoen, 'The Powell Effect', *New Society*, 22 July 1976; D. E. Schoen, *Enoch Powell and the Powellites*, Macmillan, 1977; *The Times*, 23 November 1973; Dudley Studlar, 'Powellism', *Am. Pol. Sci. Rev.*, November 1973.
3 *Daily Telegraph*, 8 February 1974.
4 Speech at Birmingham, 23 February 1974.
5 MPs have permanent facilities for a postal vote in case they are unable to be present in their constituencies at local elections; these facilities can be exercised in general elections though normally they would not be.
6 D. Butler and D. Kavanagh, *The British General Election of February 1974*, Macmillan, 1974.
7 *The Times*, 9 February 1974.
8 *Ibid.*, 18 February 1974.
9 *Ibid.*, 16 February 1974.
10 *Ibid.*
11 *Ibid.*, 30 November 1973.
12 Speech to the AGM of Wolverhampton S-W Conservative Association, 14 December 1973.
13 Interview with Robin Day on BBC Radio 4, 15 January 1973; *Newsweek*, 10 January 1973. The reference was to the discovery of academic evidence in the Bodleian Library which exposed a scholar's deceptions.
14 Speech at Bloomsbury Central Baptist Church Restaurant, 23 January 1974.
15 Speech to Aberystwyth University College Conservative Association, 1 February 1974.
16 *The Times*, 25 February 1974.
17 *Ibid.*, 8 January 1975.
18 Speech to South Kensington Young Conservatives, Kensington Town Hall, 30 September 1976.
19 Speech to Get Britain Out Movement, Shipley, 25 February 1974.
20 *Ibid.*; *The Times*, 21 and 26 February 1974.
21 *The Times*, 11 April 1974.
22 *Guardian*, 9 March 1974.
23 Speech to Hillingdon Young Conservatives, 22 November 1974; *The Times*, 11 March 1974.
24 *The Times*, 22 July 1974.
25 *Spectator*, 20 October 1970.

Chapter 2 The Making of a Tory Intellectual, 1912–1963

1 A. Roth, *Enoch Powell, Tory Tribune*, Macdonald, 1970; T. E. Utley, *Enoch Powell, The Man and His Thinking*, Kimber, 1968; *Sunday Express*, 3 and 10 April 1970; *The Times*, 26 April 1968; *Sun*, 15 April 1968, 2 March and 28 December 1973; *Sunday Telegraph*, 15 April and 13 October 1968, 30 April 1969; *Guardian*, 24 September 1970; personal communications.
2 *The Listener*, 8 June 1972.
3 Address in St Lawrence Jewry, 18 January 1977.
4 J. Enoch Powell, *Greek in the University*, OUP, 1938.
5 R. A. Butler, *The Art of the Possible*, Hamish Hamilton, 1971, p. 140; the Earl of Woolton, *Memoirs*, Cassell, 1959, pp. 331–48.

6 Angus Maude and Iain Macleod (eds.), *One Nation, A Tory Approach to Social Problems*, Conservative Political Centre, October 1950.

7 Address to Barnsley and District Chamber of Commerce, 21 February 1971; J. Enoch Powell, *Still to Decide*, Elliott Rightway, 1972, p. 92.

8 J. Enoch Powell, *Medicine and Politics: 1975 and After*, Pitman Medical, 1975, pp. 5ff.

9 *Spectator*, 17 January 1974.

10 *Ibid.*, 24 April 1971, 13 October 1973, 9 October 1976.

11 Harold Macmillan, *Pointing the Way*, Macmillan, 1970.

12 Nigel Fisher, *Iain Macleod*, André Deutsch, 1973, pp. 243ff. Powell on Macleod, *The Times*, 10 May 1973.

13 Speech at Bridgnorth, 25 May 1974; J. Enoch Powell, *A Nation Not Afraid*, Batsford, 1965, p. 25.

14 Personal communication.

Chapter 3   **A Rationale of Welfare. 1950–1963; 1975**

1 Iain Macleod and J. Enoch Powell, *Social Services, Needs and Means*, Conservative Political Centre, 1950.

2 J. Enoch Powell, 'Conservatism and Social Problems', *Swinton Journal*, Autumn 1968, p. 8.

3 *Ibid.*, p. 11.

4 Address to South Kensington Young Conservatives, Kensington Town Hall, 30 November 1970.

5 Macleod and Powell, *Social Services, op. cit.*

6 Speech at the Annual Conference of the Conservative National Advisory Committee on Education, 22 June 1968; cf. J. Enoch Powell, *Income Tax at 4/3 in the £*, Tom Stacey, 1969.

7 Powell, 'Conservatism and Social Problems', *op. cit.*

8 Interview with Anthony Shrimpsley, *Sun*, 5 March 1971.

9 Powell, *Income Tax at 4/3 in the £*, *op. cit.*, p. 127.

10 Speech at Wolverhampton, 6 March 1964.

11 Cf. *Swinton Journal*, October 1969.

12 Speech at Wolverhampton, 6 March 1964; J. Enoch Powell, *Freedom and Reality*, Elliott Rightway, 1972, pp. 93ff.

13 *Sunday Times*, 14 March 1969.

14 Speech in East Lothian, 1 October 1970.

15 Hansard, 21 November 1956, cols 1759–77.

16 *Sunday Times*, 14 March 1965; address to Chartered Surveyors, Sheffield, 2 April 1970.

17 *Ibid.*

18 *Ibid.*

19 Speech to Harborough Division, Conservative Association, Leicester, 27 September 1968.

20 Speech at Aldridge, Staffordshire, 2 October 1964.

21 Powell, *Medicine and Politics, op. cit.*, p. 68.

22 Speech at Romford, 5 October 1964.

23 Powell, *Medicine and Politics, op. cit.*, p. 67.

24 Maude and Macleod, *One Nation, op. cit.*

25 Speech at Crewkerne, 20 September 1963.

26 J. Enoch Powell, *The Welfare State*, Conservative Political Centre, October 1968.

27 *Ibid.*

28 Powell, *Medicine and Politics, op. cit.*, p. 26.

29 *Ibid.*, p. 14.

30 *Ibid.*, p. 40.

31 *Ibid.*, p. 41.

32 Speech at Crewkerne, 20 September 1963.

33 Speech to Executive Councils Association, Llandudno, 28 October 1960.

34 Hansard, 27 March 1973, cols 1124–6.

35 Powell, *Medicine and Politics, op. cit.*, pp. 67ff.

Chapter 4   **The Cause and Cure of Inflation, 1950–1968**

1 Powell, 'Conservatism and Social Problems', *op. cit.*

2 Speech at Bromsgrove, 6 July 1963; Powell, *A Nation Not Afraid, op. cit.*, p. 24.

3 Macleod and Powell, *Social Services, op. cit.*

4 Powell, 'Conservatism and Social Problems', *op. cit.*

5 *Ibid.*

6 Angus Maude and J. Enoch Powell (eds.), *Change is Our Ally: A Tory Approach to Industrial Problems*, Conservative Political Centre, May 1954.

7 Speech at Newcastle, 29 November 1957.

8 *Ibid.*

9 Speech at Westbury-on-Trim, 26 February 1965; 'Resignation and Recovery', *Spectator*, 24 April 1971.

10 J. Enoch Powell, 'What Did the Government Do?', *Financial Times*, 6 January 1960.

11 J. Enoch Powell, 'Inflation for Ever?', *The Director*, July 1965.

12 J. Enoch Powell, *Saving in a Free Society*, 2nd ed, Institute of Economic Affairs, 1966.

13 *Ibid.*, p. 127.

14 Speech at Ormiston, 16 February 1968.

15 Speech at Blackpool, 24 September 1966.

16 Speech at Chippenham, 11 May 1968.

17 Hansard, 15 April 1964, cols 477–81.

18 Hansard, *loc. cit.*; J. Enoch Powell, 'Inflation and the Supply of Money', *The Banker*, January 1973.

19 J. M. Keynes, *A Tract on Monetary Reform*, 1923, *The Collected Works of John Maynard Keynes*, Vol IV, Macmillan, 1971.

20 Speech at Birmingham, 11 January 1967.

21 *Spectator*, 28 August 1971. Cf. *Daily Telegraph*, 14 June 1971.

22 Speech to the Executive Association of Great Britain, London, 30 November 1967.

23 Speech at Gedling, Nottinghamshire, 24 May 1968.

24 *Ibid.*

25 Speech at Blackpool, 24 September 1966.

26 *Ibid.*

27 Speech at Weston-super-Mare, 19 October 1969.

28 Speech at the National Liberal Forum, 28 November 1964.

29 Speech to City of London Young Conservatives, 29 July 1964.

30 *Ibid.*

31 F. A. Hayek, Studies in *Philosophy, Politics and Economics*, Routledge and Kegan Paul, 1963, pp. 282ff.

32 *Daily Telegraph*, 16 November 1969.

33 Speech to Liverpool Economic and Statistical Society, 4 December 1964.

34 Speech at Conservative Party Conference on trade union law, Darwen, 2 March 1968.

35 *Ibid.*

36 Speech at Weston-super-Mare, 19 October 1965.

37 *Ibid.*

38 Speech at St Albans, 28 October 1968.

39 Adoption speech at Wolverhampton, 25 September 1964.

40 Speech at Nuneaton, 1 May 1965.

41 Speech at Bognor Regis, 18 November 1966.

42 Speech at Cardiff, 12 May 1967.

43 *Ibid.*; cf. speeches to Wolverhampton Rotary Club, 6 September 1966 and Northern Young Conservatives, 31 March 1968, and address to Confederation of British Industry, 23 March 1970.

44 Speech at Bowness, Windermere, 17 February 1968.

45 Speech at Maidstone, 23 June 1967.

46 Speech at Bromsgrove, 6 July 1963.

47 Speech at Bromley, 24 October 1963.

48 *Ibid.*

49 *Ibid.*

50 Speech to City of London Young Conservatives, 6 April 1966.

51 Speech at Batley, 11 December 1964.

52 Speech to Road Haulage Association, London, 18 March 1965.

53 Powell, *Income Tax at 4/3 in the £, op. cit.*

54 *Ibid.*, p. 129.

55 Royal Society of Medicine, Lloyd Roberts Lecture, 19 October 1961.

56 *City Press*, 27 February 1969; *The Times*, 12 July 1969; *Sunday Times*, 25 January 1970.

57 Speech to Young Chartered Accountants, 2 October 1975.

Chapter 5   **The Myth of Empire,
             1945–1965**

1 *Spectator*, 6 April 1964.
2 Butler, *The Art of the Possible, op. cit.*, p. 140.
3 Hansard, 16 March 1950, cols 1315–19.
4 *World Perspective*, Conservative Political Centre, 1955.
5 Hansard, 3 March 1953, cols 240–8.
6 *Ibid.*
7 *Ibid.*
8 Angus Maude and J. Enoch Powell, *Biography of a Nation*, Phoenix House, 1955.
9 *Ibid.*, p. 9.
10 Speech at Trinity College, Dublin, 13 November 1964.
11 *Ibid.*
12 *Ibid.*
13 J. Enoch Powell, *Joseph Chamberlain*, Thames and Hudson, 1977.
14 *Spectator*, 7 November 1970.
15 *Ibid.*, 16 February 1974.
16 *The Times*, 11 February 1964.
17 Speech at Camborne, 14 January 1966.
18 *Ibid.*
19 *Illustrated London News*, May 1971.
20 Hansard, 8 March 1971, cols 76–82.
21 Speech at Camborne, 14 January 1966.
22 *Daily Telegraph*, 17 October 1969.
23 Speech to York Conservative Association Supper Club, 23 September 1966.
24 Speech to Chrysler Management Club, Coventry, 28 February 1976.
25 J. Enoch Powell, 'International Charity, a sacred cow', *New Society*, 6 May 1965.
26 Speech to Canada Club, Manchester, 10 December 1965.
27 J. Enoch Powell, *Wrestling With an Angel*, Sheldon Press, 1977, pp. 18, 20ff.
28 *New Society*, 6 May 1965.
29 Speech at Bromley, 25 October 1963.
30 *Ibid.*
31 *Ibid.*
32 *Ibid.*
33 Hansard, 3 March 1953, *loc. cit.*
34 Speech at Trinity College, Dublin, 13 April 1964.
35 *Ibid.*
36 Address to Anglo-American Press Association, Paris, 25 April 1974.

Chapter 6   **Powell v. Heath I: The Party;
             Defence. 1965–1968; 1975–
             1977**

1 *Crossbow*, April–May 1968; speech to Monday Club, 7 December 1967.
2 Margaret Laing, *Edward Heath, Prime Minister*, Sidgwick and Jackson, 1972; A. Roth, *Heath and the Heathmen*, Longmans, 1970; George Hutchinson, *Edward Heath*, Longmans, 1970; M. Evans, *Ted Heath*, Kimber, 1970; A. Alexander, 'The Making of the Prime Minister', *Daily Telegraph*, 21 June 1970; Robert Rhodes James, *Ambitions and Realities, 1964–1970*, OUP, 1975.
3 Speech at Beaconsfield, 19 March 1965.
4 Speech at Maldon, Essex, 23 April 1964.
5 Speech at Bromsgrove, 6 July 1963.
6 *The Banker*, January 1963.
7 Speech at Aylesbury, 25 February 1965.
8 Speech to the Conservative Party Conference, Brighton, October 1965, quoted in Powell, *Freedom and Reality*, *op. cit.*, pp. 229ff.
9 *Ibid.*
10 Speech at Coventry, 28 February 1976; cf. *Spectator*, 6 February 1971.
11 Speech to Monday Club, 7 December 1967.
12 *Ibid.*
13 Speech to Chrysler Management Club, Whitby, 24 June 1967.
14 *Royal United Services Institute Journal*, February 1968.
15 Hansard, 7 May 1975, cols 1486–93.
16 *Crossbow*, April–May 1968.
17 Hansard, 12 January 1977, cols 1463–80.
18 *Ibid.*
19 Speech to Oil Club Dinner, Glasgow, 13 March 1976.

Chapter 7   **Powell v. Heath II: Immigration;
             the Break. 1962–1970**

1 Powell, *Freedom and Reality*, *op. cit.*, pp. 281ff; *Daily Mail*, 9 September 1974.
2 Lord Hailsham, *The Door Wherein I Went*, Collins, 1975, pp. 234ff.
3 Speech to London Rotary Club, Eastbourne, 16 November 1968.

4 Roth, *Enoch Powell, op. cit.*, p. 92.
5 Paul Foot, *The Rise of Enoch Powell*, Cornmarket Press, 1969.
6 *Ibid.*, pp. 51–3.
7 'Facing Up to Britain's Race Problems', *Daily Telegraph*, 16 February 1967; speech at Camborne, 14 January 1966.
8 *Pulse*, 19 July 1975; Hansard, 16 June 1971, col 563, and 11 November 1969, col 320.
9 Speech at Eastborune, 16 November 1968.
10 Speech at Wolverhampton, 25 March 1966.
11 *Ibid.*
12 Speech at Eastbourne, 16 November 1968.
13 Speech to Southall Chamber of Commerce, 4 November 1971.
14 Discussion about immigration with Robin Day on BBC2, 8 April 1978.
15 *Daily Telegraph*, 16 February 1967, *loc. cit.*
16 *Ibid.*
17 Speech at Eastbourne, 16 November 1968.
18 *Daily Telegraph*, 16 February 1967, *loc. cit.*
19 Speech at Eastbourne, 16 November 1968.
20 Speech to Commonwealth Correspondents' Association, 21 January 1969.
21 Speech at Walsall, 9 February 1969.
22 *The Times*, 18 February 1969.
23 Speech at Eastbourne, 16 November 1968.
24 Bill Smithies and Peter Fiddick, *Enoch Powell on Immigration*, Sphere Books, 1969.
25 Quoted in *ibid.*
26 *The Times*, 4 March 1969, 20 January 1970; *Sunday Times*, 13 October 1969; *Frontier*, November 1970.
27 Speech at Eastbourne, 16 November 1968.
28 *Daily Telegraph*, 7 May 1968.
29 *Daily Telegraph*, 11 October 1968.
30 Speech at Eastbourne, 16 November 1968; *Sunday Express*, 10 June 1969; speech at Wolverhampton, 11 June 1970.
31 Speech at Wolverhampton, 10 June 1970; *Guardian*, 10 June 1969.
32 *The Times*, 10 June 1969.
33 Speech at Eastbourne, 16 November 1968.
34 *Ibid.*
35 S. Bonhomme, *Enoch Powell and the West Indian Immigrants*, Afro-American and West Indian Publishers, 1970; *Daily Mail*, 11 June 1969; *Spectator*, 11 June 1969; Dilip Hiro, *Black British, White British*, Penguin, 1973, p. 84.
36 Speech at Bradford, 18 July 1969.
37 Hansard, 11 November 1969, cols 240–57.
38 *Sunday Mirror*, 25 January 1970.
39 Speech to Young Conservatives' Conference, Scarborough, 17 January 1970.
40 *Daily Telegraph*, 5 February 1970; *Evening News*, 21 January 1970.
41 Address to the Institute of Population Statistics, Southport, 1 May 1970.
42 Election speech at Wolverhampton, 11 June 1970.
43 *Financial Times*, 19 January 1970.

Chapter 8　**Powell v. Heath III: The Lords and the Constitution; the 1970 Election. 1969–1970**

1 Speech to Harborough Conservative Association, 27 September 1969.
2 Speech at Bridgnorth, 27 April 1969.
3 Address to the Institute of Journalists, House of Commons, 9 December 1969.
4 Speech at Louth, 8 March 1963.
5 J. Enoch Powell and K. Wallis, *The House of Lords in the Middle Ages*, CUP, 1968.
6 Hansard, 2 February 1958, cols 436–42.
7 *Ibid.*, 19 November 1968, cols 1163–9; Cmnd 3799 of 1968.
8 J. Enoch Powell, *Great Parliamentary Occasions*, BBC Publications, 1966.
9 Hansard, 19 November 1968, *loc. cit.*
10 *Ibid.*
11 *Ibid.*
12 *Ibid.*
13 *Ibid.*, 18 February 1969, cols 304–9.
14 John Wood (ed.), *Powell and the 1970 Election*, Elliott Rightway, 1970, pp. 115ff; speech at Tamworth, 15 June 1970.

15 Wood, *op. cit.*, pp. 19ff; *City Press*, 2
	July 1970; *Time*, 29 June 1970.
16 Speech at Wolverhampton, 6 June 1970.
17 Speech at Northfield, 13 June 1970.

Chapter 9   **Powell v. Heath IV: The**
			Common Market. 1965–1974;
			1975

1 Personal communication.
2 *The Times*, 10 October 1969; *Financial
	Times*, 6 September 1969; *The Times*, 3
	December 1969.
3 J. Enoch Powell, *The Common Market:
	The Case Against*, Elliott Rightway,
	1971, p. 6.
4 *Guardian*, 22 February 1971.
5 Speech to Chefs des Entreprises, Lyons,
	12 February 1971.
6 Speech at Clacton, 21 March 1969.
7 *Ibid.*
8 Speech at Market Drayton, 6 June 1969.
9 Speech at Kingston-upon-Thames, 12
	January 1970; speech at East Ham, 13
	September 1971.
10 Speech at Preston, 5 October 1969.
11 Speech at Smethwick, 5 September 1969.
12 Speech at Tamworth, 15 June 1970.
13 Speech to West Down Unionist
	Association, Banbridge, 16 January
	1971; cf. George Gale in the *Spectator*,
	27 June 1970.
14 Speech at Newtown, Montgomeryshire, 4
	March 1972.
15 Speech at Wolverhampton, 17 April
	1971.
16 Speeches at: Lyons, 12 February 1971;
	Hessischer Kreis, Frankfurt, 29 April
	1971; The Hague, 17 May 1971; Veduz,
	15 January 1972; Paris Press Conference,
	14 February 1971; *The Times*, 15
	February 1971.
17 Powell, *The Common Market: The Case
	Against, op. cit.*, pp. 30, 42, 44, 77ff;
	speech at Doncaster, 19 June 1971.
18 Speech to Nantwich Conservative
	Association, 6 November 1971; cf.
	Hansard, 28 October 1971, cols 2184–9.
19 Speech at Willenhall, 8 April 1971.
20 Speech at Cowes, IOW, 5 June 1971;
	Hansard 28 October 1971, *loc. cit.*

21 *Ibid.*
22 Speech at Newport, 22 October 1971; cf.
	Hansard, 13 July 1972, cols 1924–30.
23 Address to Lichtenstein Press Club, 15
	February 1972.
24 Speech at Newtown, 4 March 1972.
25 Hansard, 17 February 1972, cols
	698–702.
26 *Ibid.*
27 *Ibid.*, 29 February 1972, cols 272–3.
28 *The Times*, 19 February 1972; *Sunday
	Mirror*, 20 February 1972.
29 *Daily Express*, 5 June 1975.
30 *The Times*, 2 May 1972; cf. *Financial
	Times*, 8 June 1970.
31 Speech at Willenhall, 8 April 1972.
32 Speech at Millom, 29 April 1972;
	personal communication.
33 Speech at Stockport, 8 June 1973.
34 *The Times*, 27 October 1973.
35 *Ibid.*
36 Speech to Yarmouth Young Conserva-
	tives, 28 October 1972.
37 Speech at Stockport, 8 June 1973.
38 Speech at Barrow-in-Furness, 13 July
	1973.
39 Speech at Stafford, 24 April 1973.
40 Speech at Chester-le-Street, 29 January
	1972.
41 Hansard, 9 April 1975, cols 1293–1300.
42 *Ibid.* Also speech at Banbridge, 16
	January 1971.
43 Philip Goodhart, *Full-Hearted Consent*,
	Davis-Poynter, 1976, p. 143.
44 David Butler and N. Kitsinger, *The
	Referendum of 1975*, Macmillan, 1976.
45 Philip Goodhart, letter to *The Times*, 23
	August 1976.
46 *Daily Telegraph*, 9 June 1975.

Chapter 10   **Powell v. Heath V: The**
			Conservative Government,
			1970–1974

1 Philip Norton, *Dissension in the House of
	Commons, 1945–1975*, Macmillan,
	1975; *Who Were the Powellites?*,
	University of Sheffield, 1974; *Crossbow*,
	February 1976.
2 *Sunday Telegraph*, 20 April 1969.
3 Speech at Stockport, 8 June 1973.

4 *The Times*, 4 October 1971.
5 *Ibid.*, 4 October 1970.
6 *Economist*, 9 October 1971.
7 *Yorkshire Post*, 16 July 1973.
8 *Spectator*, 24 October 1970.
9 Hansard, 9 November 1970, cols 71–6.
10 *Ibid.*, 8 February 1971, cols 80–3, 103; *Daily Telegraph*, 9 February 1971.
11 Speech to West Renfrewshire Conservative Association, 20 November 1970.
12 Speech at Swindon, 7 February 1971.
13 Speech to West Renfrewshire Conservative Association, 20 November 1970.
14 *Sunday Times*, 29 February 1970; *The Director*, June 1971; *Daily Telegraph*, 1 July 1971.
15 Speech to Bromley Conservative Association, 8 May 1970.
16 Hansard, 28 June 1971, cols 71–7, and 5 April 1971, cols 69–70.
17 *Ibid.*, 28 November 1970, cols 490–9.
18 Speech to Southall Chamber of Commerce, 4 November 1971.
19 Hansard, 8 March 1971, cols 76–85.
20 *Ibid.*, 16 June 1971, cols 448–9, 557–60, 738–43.
21 *The Times*, 18 November 1971.
22 *Ibid.*, 9 September 1971.
23 Speech to Southall Chamber of Commerce, 4 November 1971.
24 Speech to Carshalton Young Conservatives, 15 February 1971.
25 *The Times*, 5 December 1971.
26 *Observer*, 21 March 1971.
27 *The Director*, June 1971.
28 *Ibid.*
29 Speech at Londonderry, 15 January 1971.
30 Speech to South Berkshire Conservative Women's Association, 19 March 1971.
31 Speech to Unionist Rally, Omagh, Co Tyrone, 11 September 1971.
32 Hansard, 8 April 1972, cols 339–49; *The Times*, 14 February and 6 April 1972.
33 Speech to Parliamentary Press Gallery, 13 May 1972.
34 *The Times*, 6 April 1972; speech to Hillingdon Young Conservatives, 5 February 1972; speech to Beaconsfield Young Conservatives, 20 September 1972.
35 Speech to Oxford University Conservative Club, 5 February 1972;

letters to *The Times*, 7 February 1972; *Yorkshire Post*, 7 February 1972; talk on BBC2, 11 August 1972; speech at Merrivale, 17 August 1972.
36 Speech to Moseley Young Conservatives, Birmingham, 20 May 1972.
37 Speech to Shoreham Young Conservatives, 27 September 1972; speech to Young Conservative Conference, Malvern, 28 February 1972.
38 Hansard, 7 November 1972, cols 884–9.
39 Speech in London, 19 December 1972; speech to Institute of Industrial Security, 20 October 1972.
40 Speech in London, 19 December 1972.
41 Hansard, 23 July 1973, cols 1213–20, 1945.
42 Speech at Stockport, 8 June 1973; *Guardian*, 8 June 1973.
43 *The Times*, 11 June 1973.
44 Speech at Rugeley, Staffordshire, 2 December 1972; cf. speech at St George's Hall, 23 February 1973.
45 Speech to South Brent Conservative Association, 7 April 1973.
46 Speech at Walton-on-the-Naze, 14 April 1973.
47 Speech to Motherwell and Hamilton Conservative Association, Lanarkshire, 24 March 1972.
48 Speech at Hilton Hotel Luncheon Club, 29 November 1973.
49 Speech to the AGM of Wolverhampton S-W Conservative Association, 14 December 1973.
50 *The Times*, 24 November 1973.
51 Hansard, 18 December 1973, cols 1197–1204.

Chapter 11 **Ulster and South Down, 1968–1978**

1 Speech to North-West Monday Club, Manchester, 30 October 1971.
2 Speech to North Wales Conservative Advisory Council, Prestatyn, 20 September 1968.
3 *Ibid.*; cf. speech at Northfield, 13 June 1970.
4 Speech at Bridgnorth, 27 August 1969.
5 Hansard, 7 April 1970, cols 288–92.

6 *The Times, Daily Telegraph*, 9 February 1970.
7 Speech at Northfield, 13 June 1970.
8 Speech at Barton Manor, Isle of Wight, 5 June 1971.
9 *The Times*, 6 November 1970.
10 Speech at Apprentice Boys' Memorial Hall, 15 January 1971.
11 *Ibid.*
12 Speech to South Berkshire Conservative Women's Association, 19 March 1971.
13 Speech at Omagh, Co Tyrone, 11 September 1971.
14 *Daily Telegraph*, 14 and 19 August 1972.
15 St Ives Conservative Dinner Address, 13 November 1971.
16 Speech at Omagh, Co Tyrone, 11 September 1971.
17 *Ibid.*
18 Speech at Ormskirk, 8 January 1972.
19 Hansard, 28 March 1972, cols 269–70.
20 Speech at Queen's Hall, Newtownards, 6 May 1972.
21 Speech at Mount Pottinger, Belfast, 2 June 1972.
22 Speech at Banbridge, 10 June 1972.
23 Speech at Ballymena, 30 September 1972; *The Times*, 10 August 1972; *Evening News*, 2 August 1972; *Daily Telegraph*, 21 July 1972.
24 Speech to Armagh Unionist Association, Loughgall, 28 July 1972.
25 *The Times*, 19 September 1972.
26 Speech to Londonderry Unionist Association, 18 September 1973.
27 *Ibid.*
28 *Ibid.*
29 *Ibid.*
30 *Ibid.*
31 Ulster Hall, Belfast, 18 April 1974.
32 *Guardian*, 4 June 1974; *Daily Express*, 20 April 1974; *Financial Times*, 18 April 1974.
33 Speech at Delahoney, 7 December 1974.
34 Speech at Carryduff, 3 April 1974.
35 Speech at the AGM of South Down Unionist Association, 7 June 1975.
36 *The Times*, 1 October 1975.
37 Speech at Orange Hall, Newcastle, 6 December 1974.
38 Speech at Banbridge, 30 December 1974.
39 Speech at Newcastle, 6 February 1975.
40 Speech at Downpatrick, 19 April 1975.
41 Speech to Monday Club of Ulster, Portadown, 28 May 1976.
42 Speech to South Down Unionist Association, 22 April 1976.
43 *Ibid.*
44 *The Times*, 17 September 1976.

Chapter 12   **Devolution, Direct Elections and Westminster, 1974–1978**

1 *Daily Telegraph*, 22 March 1974; speech to South Kensington Young Conservatives, 10 September 1976.
2 *Daily Telegraph*, 18 May 1974.
3 Speech to the Trident Group, 18 May 1974.
4 *The Times*, 9 April 1974.
5 *Sunday Telegraph*, 19 May 1974.
6 Interview with Denis Tuohy on *Midweek*, BBC TV, 3 September 1974.
7 *Sunday Telegraph*, 8 September 1974.
8 *Guardian*, 5 October 1974; *Daily Telegraph*, 14 September 1974.
9 Speech to Get Britain Out Movement, Bristol, 13 October 1974.
10 *The Times*, 9 December 1974.
11 *Newsday*, 22 October 1974.
12 Interview with Robin Day on BBC Radio 4, 21 October 1974.
13 Interview with Lew Gardner on ITV, 23 October 1974.
14 *The Times*, 15 February 1975.
15 Speech to Selsdon Group, the Reform Club, 31 January 1975.
16 *The Times*, 15 February 1975.
17 Speech to Swansea East Conservative Association, 17 June 1977.
18 *Spectator*, 11 January 1975.
19 *The Times*, 9 August 1976.
20 Speech to Hillingdon Young Conservatives Association, 22 November 1974.
21 Speech to South Kensington Young Conservatives, 30 September 1976.
22 *Ibid.*; Powell, *Joseph Chamberlain, op. cit.*
23 Speech to Croydon Monday Club, 27 February 1975.
24 *Ibid.*
25 Speech to Arundel Young Conservatives, 21 June 1975; Annual Dinner, Maidstone Chamber of Commerce, 11 March 1977.

26 *The Times*, 5 August 1976.
27 Speech at Bromley, 16 October 1976.
28 Speech at Rickmansworth, 14 February 1976.
29 Speech to Croydon Monday Club, 27 February 1975.
30 Hansard, 9 January 1976, cols 998–1006.
31 *Ibid.*
32 Speech at Rickmansworth, 14 February 1976.
33 Speech at Renfrew, 12 March 1976; speech at Belfast, 4 February 1976.
34 *Ibid.*
35 Hansard, 28 July 1978, cols 2040–8.
36 Speech to Bromley Chamber of Commerce, 9 July 1975.
37 *Ibid.*
38 Speech to Hampshire Monday Club, Southampton, 9 April 1976; speech to Hackney and Shoreditch Conservative Association, 13 February 1976.
39 Speech to Egham Rotary Club, 5 January 1976; *The Times*, 13 April, 17 April, 25 May, 27 May 1976.
40 Speech to Hackney South Conservative Association, 13 February 1976.
41 *The Times*, 17 April 1976.
42 *Ibid.*, 25 May 1976.
43 Hansard, 24 May 1976, cols 47–55.
44 *The Times*, 27 May 1976.
45 Speech to Stretford Young Conservatives, Manchester, 21 January 1977.
46 *Ibid.*; Ronald Butt in *The Times*, 27 January 1977.

47 *Ibid.*
48 Speech to Surrey Branch of the Monday Club, 4 October 1976; speech to Coventry Management Club, 18 February 1978.
49 *The Times*, 31 January and 1 February 1978.
50 Speech to Coventry Management Club, 18 February 1978.
51 Speech to City of London Young Conservatives, 10 November 1976.
52 Speech to Coventry Management Club, 18 February 1978.
53 *The Times*, 1 October 1976.
54 Hansard, 16 December 1976, cols 1809–20.
55 *Ibid.*
56 Speech to Rhondda College Llwynpia, Glam., 9 May 1974.
57 Hansard, 16 December 1976, *loc. cit.*
58 *Ibid.*
59 *Ibid.*, 18 June 1977, cols 156–62.
60 *Ibid.*, 22 February 1977, cols 1278–85.
61 *Ibid.*, 16 November 1977, cols 1606–11.
62 *Ibid.*, 16 February 1978, col 1648.
63 *Ibid.*, 26 January 1978, cols 1644–50.
64 *Ibid.*, 16 February 1978, cols 828–30.
65 Speech to Swansea East Conservative Association, 17 June 1977.
66 Hansard, 26 January 1978, cols 1646–50.
67 *The Times*, 17 May 1978.
68 Speech to Safeguard Britain Campaign meeting, Westminster, 3 June 1978.

Index